The Future of Religious Freedom

The Future of
Religious Freedom

Global Challenges

EDITED BY ALLEN D. HERTZKE

OXFORD
UNIVERSITY PRESS

OXFORD
UNIVERSITY PRESS

Oxford University Press is a department of the
University of Oxford. It furthers the University's objective
of excellence in research, scholarship, and education
by publishing worldwide.

Oxford   New York

Auckland   Cape Town   Dar es Salaam   Hong Kong   Karachi
Kuala Lumpur   Madrid   Melbourne   Mexico City   Nairobi
New Delhi   Shanghai   Taipei   Toronto

With offices in

Argentina   Austria   Brazil   Chile   Czech Republic   France   Greece
Guatemala   Hungary   Italy   Japan   Poland   Portugal   Singapore
South Korea   Switzerland   Thailand   Turkey   Ukraine   Vietnam

Oxford is a registered trade mark of Oxford University Press
in the UK and certain other countries.

Published in the United States of America by
Oxford University Press
198 Madison Avenue, New York, New York 10016

Library of Congress Cataloging-in-Publication Data

The future of religious freedom : universal right and global prospects / edited by Allen D. Hertzke.
p.   cm.
Based on a symposium held in Istanbul, Turkey.
Includes bibliographical references and index.
ISBN 978-0-19-993091-3 (pbk. : alk. paper)—ISBN 978-0-19-993089-0
(hardcover : alk. paper)   1. Freedom of religion—Congresses.
2. Liberty—Religious aspects—Congresses.
3. Religious pluralism—Congresses.   I. Hertzke, Allen D., 1950-
BL640.F88   2013
323.44′209051—dc23   2012010288

1 3 5 7 9 8 6 4 2

Printed in the United States of America
on acid-free paper

To heroes of conscience across the globe

CONTENTS

PART FIVE   RELIGIOUS FREEDOM, GLOBAL SECURITY,
             AND DIPLOMACY

CONTRIBUTORS

GERARD V. BRADLEY taught law at the University of Illinois for nine years before joining the Notre Dame faculty in 1992. At Notre Dame he teaches courses in constitutional law, religious liberty, and legal ethics. With John Finnis he heads the ND Law School's Natural Law Institute. Professor Bradley is also a senior fellow at the Witherspoon Institute in Princeton, New Jersey, and a visiting fellow at the Hoover Institution at Stanford. His most recent books are *Challenges to Religious Liberty in the Twenty-First Century* (Cambridge University Press, 2012) and *Essays on Law, Religion, and Morality* (University of Scranton Press, 2012). He is presently at work on a book about the legal regulation of obscenity in our digitalized world. Before he began teaching law Professor Bradley served as a trial lawyer in the Manhattan District Attorney's Office.

W. COLE DURHAM JR. is the Susan Young Gates University Professor of Law and Director of the International Center for Law and Religion Studies at Brigham Young University's J. Reuben Clark Law School. An internationally recognized scholar of religious liberty and comparative law, he has authored, contributed to, and edited many books and law review articles dealing with religious liberty, including *Law and Religion: National, International and Comparative Perspective* (Aspen Publishers, 2010) and *Facilitating Freedom of Religion or Belief: A Deskbook* (Martinus Nijhoff, 2004). Durham has advised governments on laws dealing with religious freedom and religious associations in Albania, Azerbaijan, Bulgaria, the Czech Republic, Estonia, Georgia, Hungary, Latvia, Lithuania, Peru, Romania, Russia, Slovakia, and Ukraine. He consulted for the Iraqi government on the development of their current constitution and was present during its signing. He was the 2009 international recipient of the First Freedom Award.

THOMAS F. FARR is Visiting Associate Professor of Religion and International Affairs at the Edmund A. Walsh School of Foreign Service, Georgetown University. He directs the Religious Freedom Project at Georgetown's Berkley Center for Religion, Peace, and World Affairs, where he is a senior fellow. He served in the U.S. Army and the American Foreign Service, and has taught at both the U.S. Military Academy and the U.S. Air Force Academy. Dr. Farr was the first director of the State Department's Office of International Religious freedom, director of the Witherspoon Institute's Task Force on International Religious freedom, and a member of the Chicago World Affairs Council's Task Force on Religion and U.S. Foreign Policy. He is currently a senior fellow at the Witherspoon Institute in Princeton, NJ, and serves on the Secretary of State's Working Group on Religious Freedom, the Boards of Advisors of the John Templeton Foundation and the Alexander Hamilton Society, and the Boards of Directors of the Institute on Religion and Democracy, and Christian Solidarity Worldwide-USA. He is a contributing editor for the *Review of Faith and International Affairs*, has published and spoken widely on religious freedom and its implications, and has appeared on PBS's *America Abroad, Al Jazeera, Alhurra*, and many other media outlets. His book, *World of Faith and Freedom: Why International Religious Liberty is Vital to American National Security*, was published by Oxford University Press.

SILVIO FERRARI is a professor of law and religion, University of Milan and Catholic University of Leuven, and has been a visiting professor at the University of California, the Institute for Advanced Legal Studies in London, and the Ecole Pratique des Hautes Etudes at the Sorbonne. His publications include *Islam and European Legal Systems* (Dartmouth College Press, 2000, edited together with A. Bradney) and *Law and Religion in Post-Communist Europe* (Peeters, 2003, edited together with W. Cole Durham Jr. and E. A. Sewell). He has recently completed, together with Felice Dassetto, a report titled "The Legal Status of Islam in Europe" for the European Parliament (2007). His main fields of interest are law and religion in Europe, comparative law of religions (particularly Jewish law, Canon law, and Islamic law), and Vatican policy in the Middle East. He is president of the International Consortium for Law and Religion Studies and a member of the Advisory Council on Freedom of Religion and Belief of the OSCE-ODIHR and of the Scientific Committee of the Institut européen en sciences des religions.

ANTHONY GILL is a professor of political science at the University of Washington and a nonresident scholar at Baylor University's Institute for the Study of Religion. He is the author of *Rendering unto Caesar: The Catholic Church and the State in Latin American* (Chicago University Press, 1998) and *The Political Origins of Religious Liberty* (Cambridge University Press, 2008), which includes case studies on the United States, Latin America, Russia, and the Baltics. The latter book won the American Sociological Association's Section on Religion's Distinguished Book Award. He teaches courses in political economy, comparative politics, research methodology, and religion and politics and earned the UW's Distinguished Teaching Award in 1999. His research focuses on the reasons for variation in the degree of government regulation of religion, on the importance of pluralist competition, and on the link between religious liberty and human flourishing (economic vitality, property rights, political stability, societal harmony).

BRIAN J. GRIM is a coauthor of *The Price of Freedom Denied: Religious Persecution and Conflict in the 21st Century* (Cambridge University Press, 2011, with Roger Finke) and *World Religions in Figures* (Wiley-Blackwell, forthcoming, with Todd Johnson). Dr. Grim is a senior researcher and director of cross-national data at the Pew Research Center's Forum on Religion & Public Life in Washington, D.C. He is also the coprincipal investigator for the international religious demography project at Boston University's Institute on Culture, Religion and World Affairs, where he coedits the World Religion Database (www.WorldReligion-Database.org). His findings on religious freedom and international religious demography have been covered by all the major news outlets, including the BBC, CNN, Fox, the Associated Press, and Reuters, and he frequently presents to high-level governmental and nongovernmental groups. Dr. Grim has extensive overseas experience. From 1982 to 2002 he lived and worked as an educator, researcher, and development coordinator in China, the former USSR, Central Asia, Europe, Malta, and the Middle East.

ALLEN D. HERTZKE is Presidential Professor, Department of Political Science, and Faculty Fellow in Religious Freedom, Institute for the American Constitutional Heritage, both at the University of Oklahoma. He is the author of *Freeing God's Children: The Unlikely Alliance for Global Human Rights* (Rowman & Littlefield, 2004); *Representing God in Washington* (University of Tennessee Press, 1988), an award-winning analysis of religious lobbies, which has been issued in a Chinese-language translation, and *Echoes of Discontent* (Congressional Quarterly Press, 1993), an account of church-rooted populist movements, and is a coauthor of *Religion and Politics in America* (Westview Press 2010), a comprehensive text now in its fourth edition. A frequent news commentator, Hertzke has been featured in such outlets as the *New York Times, Washington Post, Wall Street Journal, London Times, Time, New Republic, USA Today, Christian Science Monitor, Los Angeles Times, San Francisco Chronicle, Weekly Standard*, BBC World Service, PBS, and National Public Radio. He has held positions in Washington, D.C. as visiting senior fellow at the Pew Forum on Religion & Public Life and visiting scholar at the Brookings Institution. Between 2008 and 2010 he served as lead consultant, first for the Pew Charitable Trusts and then the John Templeton Foundation, to develop strategic recommendations for advancing religious freedom around the globe. In 2012 he was appointed to the Pontifical Academy of Social Sciences. A winner of numerous teaching awards, Dr. Hertzke has lectured at the National Press Club, the U.S. Holocaust Memorial Museum, the Council on

Foreign Relations, the Carnegie Council on Ethics and International Affairs, and before numerous audiences in China.

DENNIS R. HOOVER (D.Phil. Politics, University of Oxford) is vice president for research and publications at the Institute for Global Engagement and editor of the Review of Faith & International Affairs. He is a coeditor (with Pauletta Otis and Chris Seiple) of *The Handbook of Religion and Security* (Routledge, forthcoming), a coeditor (with Douglas Johnston) of *Religion and Foreign Affairs: Essential Readings* (Baylor University Press, 2011), a coauthor (with Thomas F. Farr) of *The Future of U.S. International Religious Freedom Policy* (Berkley Center for Religion, Peace, and World Affairs and Center on Faith & International Affairs, 2009), and a coeditor (with Robert A. Seiple) of *Religion and Security: The New Nexus in International Relations* (Rowman & Littlefield, 2004). He has published in *Religion in the News*, *America*, Books & Culture, and The Nation, and he serves on the editorial board for the book series "Religion, Politics, and Public Life" from Praeger Press.

ANGELA WU HOWARD is International Law Director for the Becket Fund for Religious Liberty. A graduate of Harvard Law School with a Fulbright Fellowship and D.E.S. in European Law at the Université Libre de Bruxelles, she worked for the Civil Rights Appellate Section of the U.S. Justice Department, for Oxfam America, and as a consultant on civil society issues to the Organisation for Economic Co-operation and Development in Paris. She has testified, lectured, and taught on religious freedom issues affecting people of all faiths. She has worked on cases before United Nations tribunals, the U.S. Supreme Court, the European Court of Human Rights, and domestic courts in countries around the world. She served on the governing Bureau of the United Nations NGO Committee on Freedom of Religion or Belief.

TALIP KÜÇÜKCAN is a professor of sociology of religion and the director of the Middle East Studies Institute at Marmara University, Istanbul; research coordinator at the SETA Foundation; and senior advisor to the president of the Higher Education Council of Turkey, Ankara. Dr. Küçükcan received an M.A. from the School of Oriental and African Studies, University of London, and a Ph.D. in ethnic relations from the University of Warwick. He worked as a research fellow at the Centre for Research in Ethnic Relations, University of Warwick, and conducted research as a visiting fellow at the Centre for Research in International Migration and Ethnic Relations, Stockholm University. Before moving to Marmara University he was a senior research fellow at the Center for Islamic Studies in Istanbul. Professor KÜÇÜKCAN works on freedom of religion, comparative secularism, state policies toward religious minorities and Muslim communities in Europe, and the role of higher education in intercultural relations. His publications include *Politics of Ethnicity, Identity and Religion: Turkish-Muslims in Britain* (Ashgate, 1999); *EuroTurks and Turkey-EU Relations: The Dutch Case* (Turkevi Research Centre, 2006, coauthored with V. Gungor); *Turks in Europe: Culture, Identity, Integration* (Turkevi Research Centre, 2009, coedited with V. Gungor); *State-Religion Relations in Europe* (Centre for Islamic Studies, Istanbul, 2008, coedited with Ali Kose, in Turkish).

AHMET T. KURU is associate professor of political science at San Diego State University and formerly postdoctoral scholar at Columbia University. He is the coeditor (with Alfred Stepan) of *Democracy, Islam, and Secularism in Turkey* (Columbia University Press, 2012) and the author of *Secularism and State Policies toward Religion: The United States, France, and Turkey* (Cambridge University Press, 2009), as well as articles published in *World Politics*, *Comparative Politics*, and *Political Science Quarterly*. Kuru is the chair of APSA's Religion and Politics Section.

ROMAN LUNKIN, a sociologist of religion, is a senior researcher at the Institute of Europe Russian Academy of Sciences, Moscow; president of the Guild of Experts on Religion and Law, Moscow; and deputy editor-in-chief of *Contemporary Europe* and editor of *Religion and Law*. He received his Ph.D. from the Institute of Philosophy at the Russian Academy of Sciences. Since 1998 he has been a member of the Russian team of Keston Institute and a field researcher for its *Encyclopedia of Religious Life in Russia Today*. Lunkin specializes on church-state relations, new religious movements, Christian churches in the post-Soviet era, and democracy and freedom of religion and belief in Russia and the former Soviet republics. Selected articles in English are "Russia's Native Peoples: Their Path to Christianity" and (with Sergei Filatov) "Traditions of Lay Orthodoxy in the Russian North," both in *Religion, State & Society*, Keston Institute, 28, no. 1 (2000); "Religion in Russia's Federal Regions: Pragmatism or Witch-Hunt?," *Frontier*, Keston Institute, no. 5 (2004); "The Russian Security Service versus Western Missionaries," *East-West Church & Ministry Report,* Global Center, Samford University, Fall 2004; "The Charismatic Movement in Russia," *East-West Church & Ministry Report* Winter 2005; (with Sergei Filatov) "My Father's House Has Many Mansions: Ethnic Minorities in the Russian Orthodox Church," *Religion, State and Society,* December 2010.

JONATHAN LUXMOORE has been Europe correspondent in Oxford and Warsaw for *Catholic News Service* (Washington/Rome), *Ecumenical News International* (Geneva), and *The Tablet* (London) since 1988 and is a regular writer for other newspapers and news agencies. He is a cofounder of the Polish chapter of Transparency International, and his coverage of religious affairs during the transition to democracy in Eastern Europe won five Catholic Press Association awards and the Silver Award from Worldfest Houston. His books include *The Vatican and the Red Flag* (Cassell, 1999), *Rethinking Christendom: Europe's Struggle for Christianity* (Gracewing, 2005), and *The God of the Gulag: Martyrs in a Secular Age* (forthcoming Gracewing, 2013).

MATTHEW K. RICHARDS is an International Fellow of the International Center for Law and Religion Studies at Brigham Young University and a shareholder of the law firm Kirton McConkie, PC, Salt Lake City, Utah. He has authored or co-authored numerous law review articles dealing with religious liberty, including religious land use, employment practices, and proselytism. He advises religious organizations with regard to religious liberty, and has represented churches in disputes throughout the United States. He received his B.A. from Brigham Young University and his J.D. from J. Reuben Clark Law School.

CHRIS SEIPLE (Ph.D., Fletcher School of Law and Diplomacy, Tufts University) is president of the Institute for Global Engagement. He is the founder of the Review of Faith & International Affairs, a member of the Council on Foreign Relations (New York), a member of the International Institute for Strategic Studies (London), and a senior fellow at the Foreign Policy Research Institute (Philadelphia). He is a coeditor (with Pauletta Otis and Dennis R. Hoover) of the *Handbook of Religion and Security* (Routledge, forthcoming), a coauthor (with H. Knox Thames and Amy Rowe) of International Religious Freedom Advocacy: A Guide to Organizations, Law, and NGOs (Baylor University Press, 2009), and the author of *The U.S. Military/NGO Relationship in Humanitarian Intervention* (U.S. Army War College, 1996). He has appeared on numerous media outlets and is an invited regular contributor to the *National Journal*'s national security blog, the *Washington Post*'s On Faith blog, and the Social Science Research Council's web forum on religious freedom. He is also a frequent speaker at conferences and U.S. military schools and in the intelligence community regarding national security and social-cultural-religious engagement.

RECEP ŞENTÜRK is the Director General and Dean of Graduate Studies at the Alliance of Civilizations Institute at Fatih Sultan Mehmet Vakıf University, Istanbul. He also serves as the head of the Civilization Studies Department. Previously he taught at Fatih University, School of Economic and Administrative Sciences, Department of Political Science (2007-2010). He also has been a research fellow at Center for Islamic Studies (ISAM) since 1998. He holds a Ph.D. from Columbia University, Department of Sociology (1998), and specializes in sociology and Islamic studies with a focus on social networks, human rights, civilization studies, and modernization in the Muslim world. He authored in English *Narrative Social Structure: Hadith Transmission Network* 610-1505 (Stanford University Press, 2005), and in Turkish, *Open Civilization: Towards a*

Multi-Civilizational Society and World (Istanbul: Timaş 2010), *Consumption and Values* (ed.) (Istanbul: ITO 2010), *Ibn Khaldun: Contemporary Readings* (ed.) (Istanbul: İz 2009),*Economic Development and Values* (ed.) (Istanbul: UTESAV 2008), *Sociology of Turkish Thought: From Fiqh to Social Sciences* (Istanbul: Etkileşim 2008), *Islam and Human Rights: Sociological and Legal Perspectives* (Istanbul: Etkileşim 2007) *Malcolm X: Struggle for Human Rights* (Istanbul: İlke 2006), *Social Memory: Hadith Transmission Network 610-1505* (Istanbul: Gelenek 2004), *Modernization and Social Science in the Muslim World: A Comparison between Turkey and Egypt* (Istanbul: İz [1996] 2006).

DONLU D. THAYER is a Managing Editor of Print and Electronic Publications at the International Center for Law and Religion Studies, J. Reuben Clark Law School, Brigham Young University. She received her B.A. and M.A. from Brigham Young University and her J.D. from J. Reuben Clark Law School.

BINNAZ TOPRAK is a member of the Turkish parliament and formerly chair of the Department of Political Science and International Relations at Bahcesehir University in Istanbul. She has published widely on political Islam in Turkey. Among her publications in English is *Islam and Political Development in Turkey* (E. J. Brill, 1981). Her two most recent articles are "Economic Development versus Cultural Transformation: Projects of Modernity in Japan and Turkey," *Turkish Studies* 2005, and "Islam and Democracy in Turkey," *New Perspectives on Turkey* 2006. She has co-conducted two pioneering surveys on religion, society, and politics in Turkey (2000, 2006) with Ali Çarkoğlu and a third on women, politics, and top administration with Ersin Kalaycıoğlu (2004). Her most recent work is based on in-depth interviews in twelve Anatolian cities on the question of identity and social repression. Published as a report in December 2008, the research led to a major discussion in the Turkish media, with over seven hundred articles, columns, and TV debates. The study was subsequently published in a book: Binnaz Toprak, İrfan Bozan, Tan Morgül, Nedim Şener, *Türkiye'de Farklı Olmak: Din ve Muhafazakârlık Ekseninde Ötekileştirilenler* (Metis Yayınları, İstanbul, 2009).

FENGGANG YANG is professor of sociology and director of the Center on Religion and Chinese Society at Purdue University. He received his M.A. from Nankai University (Tianjin, China) in 1987 and Ph.D. from the Catholic University of America in 1997. He is the author of *Religion in China: Survival and Revival under Communist Rule* (Oxford University Press 2012) and *Chinese Christians in America: Conversion, Assimilation, and Adhesive Identities* (Penn State University Press 1999), a coeditor (with Tony Carnes) of *Asian American Religions: The Making and Remaking of Borders and Boundaries* (New York University Press, 2004), and a coeditor (with Joseph B. Tamney) of *State, Market, and Religions in Chinese*

Societies (Brill Academic Publishers, 2005) and *Conversion to Christianity among the Chinese* (a special issue of *Sociology of Religion: A Quarterly Review*, 2006). One of his articles won the 2002 Distinguished Article Award of the Society for the Scientific Study of Religion and another won the 2006 Distinguished Article Award of the American Sociological Association's Section on the Sociology of Religion.

ACKNOWLEDGMENTS

In April 2009 the John Templeton Foundation convened a landmark symposium on religious freedom in Istanbul featuring presentations by leading scholars from around the world. Building on that event, Templeton funded this project to bring together in one volume the most comprehensive research findings on the vital issues of religious liberty, constitutionalism, law, and societal dynamics.

Special credit goes to the Foundation's president, Dr. Jack Templeton, who not only backed this project but took a keen personal interest in it. Under his leadership the Templeton Foundation has become a global pacesetter for ground-breaking research on the foundational nature of religious freedom and its contribution to human flourishing.

In turn, this book could not have happened without the vision and support of Templeton team members. Three former executives were pivotal. Charles Harper inaugurated the project and challenged me to assemble the best scholars in the field for the symposium; Kent Hill shepherded the process of developing the proposal for the edited book; and the final book was brought to fruition under the leadership of Mauro De Lorenzo. Logistics of the Istanbul symposium were managed by the superb cadre of Endel Liias, Judy Marchand, Pamela Thompson, and Linda Kelly, while Rozanne Tarlecky managed the finances for the book. Susan Arellano, editor in chief of Templeton Press, provided vital strategic advice. I am also grateful for a subsequent donation from Templeton, facilitated by Daniel Green, for marketing support.

Credit also is owed to the Pew Forum on Religion and Public Life, which provided institutional support for this initiative as part of a parallel senior fellow-ship on religious advocacy in 2008–2009. Special thanks go to former associates Kimberly McKnight and Michelle Ralston Morris for their astute research work.

I am especially indebted to the University of Oklahoma, my academic home for the past twenty-six years, and to its president, David Boren, who embraced my work on global religious freedom and provided institutional assistance. Support from my department at OU, encouragement by political science colleagues, and a fellowship for OU's Institute for the American Constitutional Heritage greatly buoyed this project. Ashley Edwards, my undergraduate assistant, kept me on track with multiple projects and aided in the final preparation of the manuscript.

Special recognition is due to Michael Bourdeaux, founder of the Keston Institute and a legendary pioneer in documenting the repression of religious communities behind the Iron Curtain. He graciously served as eminent advisor to this project, providing sage advice and pivotal links to potential contributors. It was an honor to collaborate with one whose work I have admired for years from afar.

Hats off to the Oxford University Press team for the splendid work on this book, especially to Senior Editor Theo Calderara for his wise counsel and remarkably energetic management; Assistant Editor Lisbeth Redfield, Production Editor Leslie Johnson, and Project Manager G. Hari Kumar for their adroit supervision of the book's production; and Senior Marketing Manager Brian Hughes for his creative promotion.

Of course, there would be no book without the trenchant scholarship and earnest labor of the contributors to this volume. Readers will learn, as have I, that their collective insights provide pathways to navigate the crucible of the twenty-first century: living with our differences in a shrinking world.

Anyone involved in book endeavors knows the sacrifices of family members, who must contend with angst and disruptions to life routines. Thus I owe a unique debt of gratitude to my loving partner of thirty-four years, Barbara Norton, whose risk-taking spirit took us on a fateful two-year sojourn to Washington, D.C. and plunged me into the global networks of religious freedom scholarship and advocacy.

That immersion linked me to inspiring "heroes of conscience" who—at great risk and personal sacrifice—defend the dignity of vulnerable believers around the world. It is to them that I dedicate this book.

The Future of Religious Freedom

Introduction

Advancing the First Freedom
in the Twenty-First Century

ALLEN D. HERTZKE

What is the status of religious liberty in the world today? How do different governments and societies restrict, promote, or regulate religious life? What patterns do we find in different regions, political systems, and religious traditions? What are the different constitutional models that govern the relationship between religious communities and the state? What are the emerging threats to the freedom of conscience and belief, and how do they shape the frontiers of law? In what ways does a culture of peaceful religious competition contribute to thriving societies? What is the link between religious liberty and other human goods, including international peace and security? What are the challenges and resources in Islam for advancing religious freedom, democracy, and human rights?

Based on a landmark symposium in Istanbul sponsored by the John Templeton Foundation, this book engages these questions by bringing together eminent scholars from around the world to offer some of the best forward thinking and empirical research on religious liberty, constitutionalism, and flourishing societies. The book focuses on ways to constitute a future in which diverse religious communities demonstrate mutual respect and freely contribute to tolerant societies. Multidisciplinary chapters explore the value and challenges of ordered religious liberty, with illustrations from a wide range of historical situations, religions, regions, and constitutional models.

This volume addresses a profound paradox of our age: at the very time that the value of religious freedom is mounting, the international consensus behind it is weakening, assaulted by authoritarian regimes, attacked by theocratic movements, violated by aggressive secular policies, and undermined by growing elite hostility or ignorance. Indeed we see not only widespread violations around the world, but looming threats in the West that jeopardize previous gains.

In spite of UN recognition of religious freedom as a universal human right, only a minority of people today enjoy the kind of liberties of conscience and belief called for in international covenants. According to a massive study by the Pew Forum on Religion and Public Life, directed by Brian Grim, a contributor to this volume, some 70 percent of the world's people live in countries with high or very high restrictions on religion from either government policies or social hostilities. Religious believers and communities routinely find themselves facing serious repercussions from practicing their religion, including fines, arrest, destruction of property, and violence.

As several of the chapters in this volume illustrate, this repression undermines the prospects for greater global freedom, democracy, peace, and prosperity. As documented by Freedom House, after three decades of solid progress freedom and democratic governance in the world reached a high point in 1998. It then stagnated and, ominously, declined for four years in a row up to 2010.[1] Religious repression and strife are pivotal contributors to this trend, in effect acting as a drag on global progress.

In this introduction I synthesize the chapter contributions by placing them into a synoptic global framework. In doing so, I have striven to be faithful to the fundamental arguments of the authors and to the complexities and nuances of their analyses. This introductory essay, however, represents my own interpretation and not necessarily that of the distinguished contributors to this volume. Indeed here and there I note of points of tension with or between the authors. In particular, not all may share my view that the innate right to religious freedom is one of the great discoveries of human history. Or the idea that a brighter global future of peaceful flourishing societies hinges on the protection of what some term *the first freedom*.

The contributors to this volume, however, do belong to a spirited fellowship of truth seekers. Thus not only do their contributions develop the grounds for understanding religious liberty as a universal right, but they illuminate the hard cases, the seeming exceptions, the implementation challenges, and debates over appropriate strategies. The trenchant chapters herein, which speak to each other in profound and fascinating ways, will surely spark fresh questions and new lines of productive inquiry.

The Origins and Grounds of Religious Freedom

In contrast to claims that religious liberty is a Western construct, its threads "weave their way back to ancient Sumeria, Persia, China, and Africa."[2] Some 2,500 years ago, as recorded in both Hebrew Scriptures and Persian documentation, Cyrus the Great established a broad regime of religious tolerance, which included restoring freedom to Jewish exiles and allowing them to return to their homeland.

In diverse sacred texts we learn that homage to the divine cannot be coerced, that, in the words of the Qur'an, "there is no compulsion in religion." Religious freedom is duly recognized as a universal human right and fundamental freedom by the Universal Declaration of Human Rights, adopted by the United Nations in 1948. Article 18 of the Declaration reads as follows: "Everyone has the right to freedom of thought, conscience, and religion. This right includes freedom to change his religion or belief, and freedom, either alone or in community with others and in public or private, to manifest his religion or belief in teaching, practice, worship, and observance." Similar language is found in subsequent international covenants that virtually all nations have signed. The freedom of religious belief and practice is thus explicitly recognized in international law through the UN Charter, the International Covenant on Civil and Political Rights, the Helsinki Accords, the Declaration on the Elimination of All Forms of Intolerance and Discrimination Based on Religion or Belief, and the European Convention for the Protection of Human Rights and Fundamental Freedoms.

The freedom to practice religion is virtually a universal aspiration. In the 2007 Pew Global Attitudes Survey over 90 percent of respondents in every region on earth indicated that it was important to them to live in a country where they can practice religion freely. (Only 2 percent said it wasn't important at all.)[3]

Consequently religious liberty is not merely a desirable thing granted by the state. It is a universal inherent right and aspiration. But why?

At the most basic level all people want to be treated with respect and consideration. Variations of the golden rule—to treat others as we would wish to be treated—are found in virtually every major religion and many philosophical traditions (such as Confucianism). This trait of common humanity—potentially recognizable by people of all faiths or no faith—can provide a justification for religious liberty understood as the freedom to live in accord with one's conscience or belief.[4]

More specifically the Universal Declaration hints at how certain human traits explicitly justify religious freedom as inherent. That landmark declaration anchored universal rights in the "inherent dignity" and "worth of the human person" and in the "equal and inalienable rights of all members of the human family" who are "endowed with reason and conscience." In addition, Article 18 emphasizes the relational aspect of human life, that people must be free "in community with others" to manifest their faith and beliefs.

Dignity, reason, conscience, and community—these provide the clues to the right, and scope, of religious liberty.

In a number of religious traditions the dignity and worth of persons is rooted in their transcendent origins. In Jewish and Christian traditions people are "made in the image and likeness of God" and thus endowed with a surpassing dignity, which mandates respect for their integrity and conscience. This understanding was widely shared by the American founders, who declared that people are "endowed by their creator" with inalienable rights. As Recep Şentürk demonstrates in this volume, a rich Islamic scholarship also grounds universal human rights in the divinely ordained "inviolability" of persons, who are created free and with rights so they can fulfill their duties toward God. In turn, the capacity of human reason propels an innate quest by people everywhere to understand ultimate truths about their purpose, meaning, and destiny. At a fundamental level this suggests that they should be free to explore such timeless questions, whether religious in nature or rooted in some other ultimate concern. This aspiration is one of the most powerful of human motivations.

Recognition of this human aspiration helps to elucidate one of the profound tensions in modern discussions of religion: the question of whether religious freedom can encompass or accommodate the rights of nonbelievers. The chapter by Binnaz Toprak, for example, is explicitly anchored in the Enlightenment fear that unleashing the freedom or autonomy of *dominant* religious communities can produce powerful social pressures against minorities, nonbelievers, nonconformists, or even women in certain societies. As developed by the contributors to this volume (and others), a deeper understanding of the freedom of conscience and belief must embrace the open quest of the skeptic or heretic to explore ultimate questions. A number of religious thinkers, from Roger Williams in the seventeenth century to Abdolkarim Soroush in the twenty-first,[5] make the case that coercion of the nonbeliever is not only sinful but counterproductive because it suggests that the religious message is not persuasive on its own.

This brings us to the next dimension of human endowment: conscience, the human sense of right and wrong. Conscience can be "a demanding mentor," compelling us at times to rise above what may seem as our own self-interest.[6] Respect for "mandates of conscience" vitally animated a number of formative thinkers of religious liberty and continues to motivate its champions today. This insight is too often lost in contemporary debates over religion. Religious freedom is not merely a nice thing tolerated by the state. Rather, as Cardinal Newman put it, conscience "has rights because it has duties."[7] Thus one of the most compelling justifications for religious liberty is the freedom of conscience, the freedom to fulfill obligations—especially sacred duties—that flow from an authority higher than the state.

To be sure, conscience can be malformed or distorted, but people everywhere recognize the essential human trait of—and laud persons for—"good conscience." And when people are denied this freedom they experience it as a powerful violation preventing them from fulfilling their quintessentially human quest for meaning and purpose. A key measure of a free society, therefore, is the extent to which people are not forced to choose between sacred duties and citizenship privileges.

Finally, religion is relational, and true freedom of faith must protect the right of people to gather in communities of belief for mutual expression and succor.

This communal aspiration serves as a powerful motivator, as family life and social networks have deep roots in collective religious experience. In a sense, religious communities are historically and ontologically *prior* to the modern state, and their autonomy deserves protection from overreaching political authorities.[8] Religious freedom cannot be enjoyed without expansive freedom of association. And as democratic theorists note, the freedom of religious communities to operate in civil society serves as a crucial basis for democratic governance.[9]

This discussion suggests that the right to religious liberty lies in human nature itself, *who we are*. But the return of religious freedom to international prominence also flows from the dramatic resurgence of religion and the diffusion of its competing expressions around the globe. Contrary to the predictions of secularization theorists, religion not only thrives in the modern world but increasingly manifests itself in intense public commitments, making this, in a sense, "God's Century."[10] Moreover if modernity does not produce secularization, it does propel and diffuse an enormous religious diversity.[11]

The great crucible of the twenty-first century is learning to live with these intense differences.[12] Unfortunately policymakers often respond to resurgent religion with counterproductive repression that increases religious strife. We see this in theocracies, state-enforced religious monopolies, and authoritarian secular regimes that actively repress peaceful expression of conscience and practice. Such regimes produce abuses of power, repression of minorities, and discord that spills over their borders. But governments of all sorts attempt to control religion with a host of intrusive or paternalistic laws that often produce more, not less, religious dissension and destabilizing strife.

Thomas Jefferson famously asserted that "religious freedom is the most effective anodyne against religious dissension."[13] The accumulating evidence suggests that the way to navigate a world of religious diversity and fervor is to protect the freedom of conscience and belief and to nurture the peaceful competition of religious communities in civil society. How to constitute such societies requires a deep understanding of empirical relationships, political dynamics, sociological patterns, legal norms, and theological insights richly illuminated by the chapters in this volume.

The Status of Religious Freedom in the World Today

What is the contemporary condition of this universal right? A valuable point of departure is the chapter by Cole Durham and his colleagues on the legal status of religious freedom around the world. As an authority in international law on religion, Durham has helped draft constitutional provisions for a number of emerging democracies and routinely consults with governments and officials across the globe on the application of religion laws. His chapter provides a sweeping, up-to-date inventory of international law on religion and a catalogue of its application and status. Durham et al. present two powerful lessons. On the one hand, the right to freedom of religion and belief is now firmly embedded in UN declarations, international treaties, customary law, and national constitutions. This is a profound development in human history. On the other hand, emerging trends threaten to weaken legal norms and protections for religious believers and institutions. So what are the threatening trends so meticulously identified by the authors?

Secularization of elite culture in the West, which runs counter to global trends, is a potent social force chipping away at the norms and legal foundations of religious freedom. Increasing suspicion of faith induces amnesia about how protecting religious liberty helped end centuries of religious conflict. If religion is seen as passé, benighted, or inherently intolerant by judges, policymakers, or public administrators, their defense of religious rights will likely be anemic. Even where such secularization does not produce overt hostility, it can induce indifference. If there is nothing *special* about faith commitments, why be concerned with the autonomy of religious institutions or the conscience rights of believers? Why treat a zoning request by a church any differently from a zoning request by a business? Or see a transcendent duty as distinct from a lifestyle choice? A corollary to secularization is a relativism that questions the validity of exclusivist religious truth claims, even the right to make them. As Durham et al. suggest, relativists who insist on protecting alternative lifestyles demur on religious practice. Thus the fundamental right to peacefully persuade others of one's conception of truth becomes illegitimate proselytizing if it involves religion but not other commitments.

Another trend is the emergence of competing rights and equality norms that often trump religious claims. Laws against discrimination on the basis of gender, sexual orientation, and indigenous status provide grounds to limit the autonomy of religious institutions deemed insufficiently enlightened on these matters. Similarly when the right to privacy is interpreted as the right *not to be bothered* by religious people, it can be deployed as a weapon against religious competition and mission activities.

The rise of identity politics can further undermine the protection of religious practice, particularly when it penalizes expression deemed hurtful to some group. We see this in the push by the Organization of Islamic Countries to sanction defamation of religion. Sold as a defense of faith, it actually represents a grave threat to freedom of speech, inquiry, and belief, as Angela Wu Howard documents. Even in Western Europe individuals have been prosecuted for merely criticizing certain Islamic practices or interpretations, while in a number of Muslim-majority nations vague defamation statutes reinforce authoritarian governance. Just as laws against apostasy invite abuse by the state,[14] laws against defamation empower authorities to repress dissidents or curry favor with dominant groups by harassing competitors. These two trends dovetail, as sanctions against defamation are often leveled in the name of toleration, but are anything but.

A major theme of the chapter by Durham et al. is "erosion by exception." In other words, while constitutional provisions and statutes purportedly protect religious rights, exceptions (intrusions) are frequently granted by courts or agencies for other supposedly compelling state interests. With the burgeoning of state regimes and their regulatory reach, these exceptions mount. Sometimes the rationale is paternalism, protecting people from supposedly dangerous cults or national identity from outside influences. Often the justification is national security. As Roman Lunkin demonstrates in his chapter on Russia, overbroad interpretations of national security serve as a pretext to harass minority sects that threaten the monopoly of dominant religious groups but pose no threat to state security. Authoritarian regimes especially find it convenient to invoke national security to repress independent religious civil society actors. But we see this proclivity in a variety of regimes, suggesting the wisdom of real limitations on abuse of power by authorities.

Howard's chapter demonstrates how the application of law is shaped by the wider cultural and political environment in which it is embedded. As the international law director at the Becket Fund for Religious Liberty, she defends individual religious litigants before national and international tribunals, challenges repressive laws in constitutional courts, and mobilizes testimony before the United Nations Human Rights Commission and the European Union. This experience informs her analysis of the challenges of leveraging legal protection of religious liberty in highly charged cultural and political settings.

One of those challenges is confronting initiatives that seem reasonable on their face, such as laws against defamation of religion and anticonversion statutes, but that actually lead to abuse of state power and invite mob violence against vulnerable communities. Howard's on-the-ground advocacy and reporting in India, Indonesia, and Malaysia provide vivid illustrations of this theme, and they lead to a crucial lesson. If religious freedom is understood merely as another species of tolerance, then it is easily compromised by alternative narratives, state interests, and pragmatic calculations. On the other hand, if religious freedom is rooted in an understanding of the intrinsic worth and dignity of all persons—or, as Şentürk puts it, their God-given "inviolability"—then advocates stand on firmer ground when making their case that violations of religious rights are fundamentally unjust. A proper understanding of the grounds of religious liberty, Howard contends, can also inhibit state authorities from making what she calls "postural errors" that undermine religious freedom protections.

This legal backdrop brings us to the pathbreaking work of Brian Grim, who directed the empirical endeavor of the Pew Forum on Religion and Public Life.

Based on a rigorous and sophisticated coding of restrictions on religion, the Pew Forum produced the landmark report "Global Restrictions on Religion."[15] This report contains a numerical score for every country on two dimensions: government restrictions on religion and societal restrictions (through hostile acts by societal groups against religious persons or communities). Countries are then grouped by degree of restrictions, from very high to low.

The report's key finding is that about 30 percent of the countries (but with 70 percent of the globe's population) have high or very high restrictions on religion, either from government action or social hostilities or both. On the positive side, this suggests that 70 percent of countries have achieved a modicum of religious freedom through protective laws and positive societal norms. But because the restrictive nations include the most populous, the study illustrates the enormous gulf between the promise of the UN Universal Declaration and the reality on the ground for much of the world's population.

While this finding is sobering, Grim's analysis suggests the potential for a huge global impact with improvements in the two most populous nations, China and India. Because China has very high government restrictions but low social hostility, relaxing state restrictions on religion would produce an immediate and measurable gain. India's very high score on social hostility, on the other hand, would be reduced by aggressive government actions that protect religious minorities from mob violence.

What makes this research endeavor so pivotal is that it provides an unprecedented opportunity to empirically test linkages between religious freedom and other human goods. Propositions about such linkages have been advanced for centuries by such great thinkers as John Locke, Roger Williams, Adam Smith, and James Madison. But for the first time in human history we have the capacity to apply rigorous scientific methods to test such propositions.[16] Grim's chapter in this volume provides an elegant summary of that broader investigation. What this research shows is the positive contribution of religious freedom to democracy, civil liberties, press autonomy, women's status, societal peace, economic development, and even health. The theory behind these linkages in turn provides real guidance to policymakers. As Grim shows, government restrictions on religion trigger social hostility among religious groups, which produces more government restrictions and further religious strife. This vicious cycle of religious violence can be broken: when governments relax restrictions on religion and treat all groups equally, greater societal tolerance and civility ensues, leading to positive cycles. This theory is underscored in the book *God's Century* by Monica Toft, Daniel Philpott, and Timothy Shaw.[17] Drawing on international relations scholarship, these authors show that regimes' attempts to repress religion induce the very militancy such efforts purport to prevent.

We see a dramatic illustration of these dynamics in the link between anticonversion laws in India and devastating mob violence against religious and ethnic minorities. As Howard documents in her chapter, the anticonversion law in the state of Orissa served as the pretext for militant Hindu chauvinists to attack vulnerable Christian communities and tribal people with impunity in 2008. Precisely as the religious violence cycle suggests, the state's law, which implied that conversion is an act *imposed* by one person on another, invited violence against Christians falsely accused of such conversions. Then, after hundreds of homes were destroyed and thousands of people were displaced, the government's response was to call for more aggressive anticonversion enforcement, not prosecution of mob leaders or teaching that violence is an unacceptable response to religious competition. This state action sanctions a chilling repression of millions of vulnerable religious minorities, tribal people, and Dalits (untouchables), thus undermining authentic democracy in what will soon become the most populous nation on earth.

Religious Markets, Pluralism, and the State

The constitutions and laws of modern nations play a pivotal role in determining the contours of religious freedom in the world today. Over three-quarters of the world's governments are involved in some way in regulating religion, extending privileges to favored faiths, or establishing a state religion. Such involvement ranges across a wide continuum of possibilities, from banning all faiths to mandating an exclusive state religion, and from intrusive and inequitable regulation to modest requirements applied uniformly.[18]

Given the daunting complexity of these policies, how can we gain scholarly purchase to understand the different constitutional models and provide helpful guidance for policymakers? One of the most influential and helpful theoretical frameworks is the religious economies school, which deploys the analogy of the "religious marketplace" to understand the impact of government laws on religion. Drawing on the work of Adam Smith and others, pioneering scholars of this school take as their point of departure the transition from established state churches in the West, where the state enforced a religious monopoly, to pluralist systems.[19] The model of this transition was the United States, where ideas about freedom combined with conditions of religious diversity to produce a constitutional innovation that ended state establishments and protected the free operation of religious communities. This creation of the first free marketplace of religion produced a booming civil society in which religious entrepreneurs and institutions competed to meet the spiritual and social needs of people.

The religious economies model has proven invaluable in clarifying religion-state relationships and predicting a wide array of outcomes. It suggests that the default condition of religion is plurality,[20] as people from widely different backgrounds and cultures will inevitably find succor in different religious expressions, especially if allowed the freedom to do so. Consequently religious monopolies are artificial, especially in our globalized world, and sustainable only by government policies. Those policies involve heavy subsidies or favors to the dominant faith, which puts religious minorities at a severe disadvantage. Moreover, as Grim shows, maintaining a religious monopoly or cartel requires the state to repress, often harshly, religious competitors. And as predicted by diverse religious dissenters, state-enforced religious monopolies not only produce persecution and strife; they corrupt authentic faith itself as indolent religious authorities rely on state power instead of their own energies and inspiration.

What, then, would lead political leaders to deregulate the religious marketplace? That is the question addressed by Anthony Gill in his exploration of the political origins of religious liberty. As a political scientist Gill brings a hard-headed rational choice analysis to the table. While not discounting the importance of philosophical commitments, he stresses that because political leaders seek to gain and hold power, they must have incentives to break the symbiotic relationship between the dominant faith and the state. In other words, they will end state monopolies and enact policies that promote religious freedom and pluralism if they see such policies as helping them maintain power, which is a penultimate goal necessary to any other aims.

To hold power, rational political elites will strive to enhance economic growth, increase tax revenue, maintain social order, and minimize the cost of rule. As mounting research shows, under the right conditions deregulating the religious economy will contribute to these aims. But political elites will not always see the path so clearly. The frictional drag and social disruptions produced by religious repression must become evident. Gill shows how this can happen by documenting the rise of religious freedom, first in the United States and then in Latin America. Conditions were highly conducive to religious pluralism in the American colonies; pluralism in turn made religious monopolies particularly problematic for the aims of political leaders. The fissiparous nature of Protestantism produced a natural pluralism in the colonies, and the need to attract colonists made it counterproductive to maintain religious restrictions. Thus even if leaders were philosophically inclined to grant religious toleration, they also saw that it would be good for commerce.

While Gill stresses the economic rationale for deregulating the religious marketplace, equally important for political leaders is the need to avoid social conflict. Here we can note the role played by religious dissenters. Quakers, Baptists, and other minorities fought heroically against established churches and asserted their rights of conscience against restrictions, often suffering greatly at the hands of authorities. This made repression costly and embarrassing to political leaders.

Religious freedom came later in Latin America, owing to the powerful integration of Catholic establishments and authoritarian regimes. But as Gill shows, the growth of Protestantism in Latin America helped to propel a pluralism that produced incentives for political leaders to produce a more open religious marketplace. He suggests that this opening of religious competition in Latin America was good for both religion and society. Because they previously enjoyed state privileges, Catholic authorities grew lax in meeting the needs of their flocks. But faced with genuine competition they paid greater attention, especially to the poor, who flooded Pentecostal movements in a number of countries. Thus religious pluralism and competition produced positive externalities and propelled democratization.

To be sure, other factors contributed to this shift. The decisive theological embrace of religious freedom by the Catholic Church at Vatican II moved the Church away from its reliance on state power and placed its imprimatur on the side of democracy. This process, however, was uneven, and Gill's research suggests that Church leaders embraced their new role as defenders of the poor more vigorously where they faced the greatest competition.

This brings us to the important work of Fenggang Yang. An expert on China and a theorist of religious economies, Yang offers an important empirical and theoretical corrective to the dominant frameworks of scholars focused on the dynamics of monopoly and pluralism in the West. Outside of Europe and the Western hemisphere, as he demonstrates, the dominant model is neither monopoly nor pluralism but religious oligopoly, where the state recognizes and allows only select religions to operate legally. Drawing on documentation by Grim and others, Yang suggests that at least half of the countries on earth operate religious oligopolies, including the most populous, China. While multiple religions have operated in China for millennia, authorities suppressed heterodox or sectarian movements. Under communist rule China codified this oligopolistic practice by recognizing only five official religions subject to heavy state regulation. These party-managed "patriotic" associations of Buddhism, Daoism, Islam, Catholicism, and Protestantism are the only religions that can legally operate in the country.

Yang's central theoretical insight is that when a state establishes what he calls a "red market" with a limited number of legal religions, it will also produce a "black market" of banned religions and a "gray market" of ambiguous legality. A black market emerges because the few state religions cannot meet the spiritual needs of people. But because the costs of operating in the black market can be high, people will also seek out avenues of expression not clearly banned: the gray market. In China today the black market includes "house church" Protestants who refuse to belong to the official Three-Self Protestant movement and Catholics who pledge fealty to the Vatican. They often worship in secret and suffer harassment and persecution by authorities. The gray market includes a variety of Chinese folk traditions, healing arts, and Qigong meditating practices that can operate as long as they are not seen as organized religion by the state.

Religious markets are dynamic. For example, when the rapid growth of the Falun Gong sect of Qigong swept China in the 1990s, the regime banned it as a dangerous cult and harshly repressed its followers. Thus a significant gray sector moved into the black market. On the other hand, the explosive growth of unregistered Christianity, especially among professional classes, has made repression of independent Christian churches more problematic. As a result, authorities in a number of places are acquiescing to the operation of nonregistered churches, allowing some to operate aboveground. In other words, parts of the house church sector are moving into the gray market. This has led to incipient, if halting, exploration by scholars and authorities of the possibilities of changing the religion law in China to allow independent churches to gain legal recognition as civil society actors.[21] Such a change could have momentous implications for China's evolution.

Russia illuminates a different dynamic: how growing religious pluralism is undermining attempts by authorities to reintroduce Orthodox monopoly. Authoritarian attempts to repress non-Orthodox faiths are galvanizing defenders of religious pluralism and propelling nascent democratic forces. Our guide here is Roman Lunkin, who uncovers for the first time this paradoxical story of postcommunist Russia. As Lunkin shows, the Russian Federation, flush with the spirit of Gorbachev-era reforms, initially embraced full religious liberty in its sweeping Law on Freedom of Conscience in 1990. Remarkably, by eliminating restrictions on the activities of religious associations, the law created a genuine pluralist religious marketplace. But precisely because of this, the Russian Orthodox Church (ROC), still reeling from the legacies of Soviet repression and imbued with a sense of its unique role in Russian identity, claimed that the law opened Russia to foreign missionaries and alien spiritualities. Orthodox authorities lobbied to change the law, in effect seeking state action to suppress competitors. Intriguingly the result was a 1997 law that employed the oligarchic principle by recognizing four "traditional religions" (Orthodox Christianity, Islam, Buddhism, and Judaism) and subjecting the rest to various restrictions. Of course, such an oligarchy would serve to check the main competitors to Orthodoxy: Catholics and especially Protestants. But vigorous legal challenges actually reversed the most restrictive features of the law, allowing diverse religious communities to blossom.

While the election of Vladimir Putin in 2000 seemed to usher in a new chapter in religion-state relations, again the result was paradoxical. Putin sought to enhance his legitimacy by granting privileges to the ROC and repressing missionary activity. But fierce reaction against harassment of minorities prevented him from successfully stemming the growth of diverse faiths. We see the same pattern during the presidency of Dmitry Medvedev, when Orthodox Patriarch Krill sought to gain state privileges for the ROC in numerous spheres of life. Medvedev's favorable response to Krill's initiatives produced a backlash against the ROC and ultimately reinforced religious freedom as a value. Just as religious minorities propelled democratization in colonial America, evangelical believers have emerged in Russia as among the most vigorous defenders of democratic values.

There are crucial lessons here. One can sympathize with the plight of the ROC, its desire to restore what was lost during the Soviet era, and even its ancient vision of the "harmonious symphony" of church and state.[22] But in the new Russia, Orthodoxy's attempt to deploy the sword of the state to repress competitors only undermined its credibility in society and diverted energies from the task of internal rejuvenation. As Lunkin shows in his striking exploration of religious demographics, the ROC has enormous work to do to gain back its adherents. Moreover, as the religious economies model predicts, not only does the embrace by an authoritarian state ultimately sap the vibrancy of a religion, but it stalls democratization by repressing civil society and its natural religious pluralism.

Church-State Challenges in Democratic Systems

As suggested by several chapters in this volume, religious liberty plays a crucial role in developing and sustaining democratic states. We can also reverse the causal direction of that equation: pluralist democracy provides the greatest protection for religious freedom. We see this linkage most dramatically in the chapter by Jonathan Luxmoore, which chronicles how the greatest expansion of religious freedom in the contemporary era came from the revolutions of Eastern Europe that threw off communist dictatorships and instituted various democratic systems.

But the transition to democracy does not automatically resolve the church-state challenges of sustaining generous protections for religious freedom or vibrant religious life. Indeed the chapters in this section show how dynamic church-state relations are in democratic systems. What seems settled in one generation is challenged in the next by changing demographics, evolving legal doctrines, or new political alignments. Old restrictions on religion may be lifted even as new ones intrude; old threats evaporate, but new ones emerge. We also see great variety in church-state patterns in democratic systems, profoundly shaping the fortunes and interplay of religious communities.

Luxmoore's account is a valuable point of departure because it illustrates both the promise and challenges of modern democratic systems for religious life. In a way, state communism represented a vast twentieth-century laboratory for the systematic effort to stifle the religious impulse and crush its institutional expression. This experiment tested the resistance and adaptability of religious communities in different countries. In Luxmoore's fine-grained account we see the diverse responses of Catholic, Protestant, and Orthodox groups to repression and the variable resources they marshaled in resistance.

The overriding lesson is that churches, to varying degrees, played an active role in the momentous collapse of communist rule and helped drive the democratization process. They were havens for dissent and nurturers of nascent civil society; they shielded isolated human rights actors and mobilized people power; they nursed peaceful transitions at pivotal moments. As embodied in the electrifying presence of Pope John Paul II in Poland, the Church embraced mass protest and inspired solidarity movements. Thus in a fascinating reversal of the French Revolution, religion and liberty marched together in Eastern Europe.

A testament to the human spirit, this story inspires. But the revolutions soon gave way to the practical and exacting task of reconstituting fragile societies and rebuilding shattered religious institutions. Here we see the lingering legacy of communist repression: the decades of expropriated church property, shuttered religious schools, stunted ministries, and psychological burdens. As Luxmoore shows, this legacy produced complicated struggles to determine the place of religion in new systems of law, education, and mass media. We see property disputes, conflicts over religious education in schools, and competition among religious groups seeking government privileges or support. These struggles, which produced myriad church-state variations, revealed strengths and weaknesses of different religious communities and challenged them to adapt to new conditions of open religious markets. Interreligious tensions erupted as historic faiths contended with upstarts.

But equally challenging were secular values that religious leaders confronted during the modernization of Eastern European states and former Soviet republics. In this sense, the postcommunist world represents a laboratory of the kinds of challenges all religious communities face in the modern age. As religious authorities sought to reclaim the central role of faith life in their societies, they found themselves competing with the materialist seductions of free market capitalism. Postmodern values of self-expression and sexual liberation challenge traditional family structures, communal norms, and theologically rooted moral codes, producing, according to Pope Benedict, a "dictatorship of relativism." Thus we see conflicts over sex education, abortion, and gay rights as religious institutions struggle to maintain conscience protections against state policies they find inimical to religious teachings. To varying degrees, religious institutions face hostile politicians and a skeptical media, and they chafe under bureaucratic restrictions or nettlesome regulations.

These collective challenges spark profound questions: Is religious decline the price of freedom and modernization? What inner strengths can be marshaled to protect zones of vibrant religious life? How must religious communities adapt to survive the maelstrom of globalization? Theorists of religious economies argue that religious markets and free competition enhance religious vitality. But some religious leaders in postcommunist states are skeptical of this optimism, and their experience suggests the need for sober reflection on which religion-state relationships best help religious life to flourish.

These questions arise with special urgency in postcommunist states, where religious institutions must recover from decades of assault or neglect. But such questions are beginning to intrude into what had been fairly settled patterns in Western Europe as well. As Silvio Ferrari shows, church-state models are both diverse and evolving in the established democracies of Western Europe. His fascinating picture depicts great variation in the treatment of religious communities and different levels of cooperation between government and religious institutions in education, tax support, media access, and legal registration.

What is striking is how dynamic this picture is. Each of the three church-state models Ferrari presents—Catholic civil religion in Italy, French secularism, and English multiculturalism—faces long-term challenges. In Italy the cross as a symbol of "dignity and tolerance" can protect the rights of Muslim women to wear the headscarf in public schools. But how long will a growing Muslim population accept this kind of civil-religious compact? Even more pressing, how can France maintain a laic state that stifles public expression of religious duty, subsumes religious personalities into a monistic republican identity, and empowers the government to monitor or dissolve sectarian movements? Finally, the limits of the multicultural model are being sorely tested in Britain, as some separatist mosques become havens for radical indoctrination or forms of sharia in tension with English common law. Clearly European nations cannot be complacent but must draw on the best insights of emerging scholarship and fresh thinking about religion and the state. This will involve reexamination of deeply held presuppositions. For example, Ferrari draws a sharp distinction between religious freedom for individuals, which all European states protect, and the status of religious communities and institutions, which are subject to various restrictions or unequal treatment. Ferrari boldly asserts that the Enlightenment tradition in Europe ensures the *absolute* freedom of conscience and that believers and nonbelievers alike are not subject to *any restriction* of their civil and political rights. This assertion can be contested on two grounds. First, if a Muslim woman of cover cannot teach in public schools, or if a Sikh man must violate a religious duty to get a driver's license, in what sense are they not subject to restrictions on their ability to participate fully in civic life? Must people be deracinated of religious particularities to become equal citizens of a modern republic? The sharp distinction between individual rights and communal practice is not one envisioned by the Universal Declaration, which proclaims the right to exercise religious freedom "in community." For some persons corporate worship and fellowship constitute core aspects of religious exercise and duty. Because personhood is embedded in webs of family and communal life informed or enabled by religious bodies, state restrictions on religious institutions cannot be detached from the free exercise of individual persons.

Thus while most Western democracies generally protect religious practice, emerging trends threaten the autonomy of religious institutions and by extension the freedom of religious persons. We see this in anticult laws, discriminatory registration laws, and nettlesome government regulations that burden religious institutions. If unchecked, emerging threats will not only narrow the zone of religious freedom in the West but undermine its ability to model best practices to other nations.

These emerging threats come into sharp relief in Gerald Bradley's account of rapid changes in the legal environment for religious bodies in the United States and related English-speaking nations. Laws and court decisions, as Howard suggests, reflect a worldview or narrative. What Bradley uncovers is how the legal community and elite policymakers increasingly seem to operate with a worldview that sees abortion access and gay rights as more fundamental than the conscience of religious believers or the autonomy of religious institutions. Such a doctrine, as Thomas Farr suggests, could undercut U.S. promotion of religious freedom abroad, especially in traditional religious societies.

As Bradley shows, conscience protection is emerging as a crucial frontier of religious law, as religious institutions and service providers increasingly find themselves subject to legal mandates that conflict with religious duties. This is a new development. In the United States a long-standing and flourishing legal culture provided generous relief to persons and institutions who, because of religious or moral convictions, could not conscientiously undertake certain duties. In the health care arena this meant that faith-based providers were not forced to offer selective abortions. With the expanding federal role in health coverage, however, protection for hospitals, clinics, doctors, and pharmacists is narrowing. In addition, religious colleges, social service providers, and other institutions increasingly face mandates to include contraceptive and abortion services in their employee health plans or face legal penalties.

An equally momentous development, to Bradley, involves the rapid transformation of attitudes and laws against homosexual discrimination throughout the Western world. As this transformation washes through the institution of marriage, traditional and sacramental understandings of matrimony are increasingly equated with racial bigotry and prosecuted accordingly. Thus when government officials refuse to grant conscience exemptions to religious institutions that cannot sanction same-sex marriages, they can force faith-based adoption agencies, service providers, and venders out of business. Bradley sees these powerful forces, if unchecked, converging upon the privatization of religion. Not only would this represent a narrowing of religious freedom; it would undermine the role of mediating institutions so vital to civil society. Moreover because American policy ramifies beyond its borders, this trend produces global fallout.

Howard provides a vivid illustration in her exploration of the reasoning of the Indonesia Constitutional Court in upholding the national blasphemy law in 2010. Despite factual presentations on the widespread abuses of blasphemy accusations, the court operated with a narrative that the statute was necessary to prevent the perceived "secularization of the public square" found in the United States. Though a misreading of current American practice, this interpretation will become more plausible if free exercise constricts as Bradley fears.

As Tom Farr observes, American diplomats often operate as if religion is *already* privatized in the United States, that the separation of church and state prevents positive engagement with religious communities abroad. This debilitating understanding intersects the vital discourse on constitutional law and the Islamic experience.

Constitutional Models, Law, and Islamic Experience

In explaining the institutional requirements of democracy, Alfred Stepan, a professor at Columbia University, developed a pivotal thesis about the relationship between religion and the state he terms the "twin tolerations." Liberal democracy, he argues, depends on a reciprocal bargain between the institutions of religion and the institutions of the state. The state must protect and thus "tolerate" the freedom of religious institutions to operate in civil society; religious communities must agree to "tolerate" each other by not deploying constitutional privileges or state power to squelch their competitors. In return for eschewing state prerogatives, religious institutions gain the right to participate in public policy debates on equal terms with other civil society actors.[23]

This framework provides a valuable context for the spirited discussion, and occasional debate, among contributors to this volume about different constitutional models and their impact. We begin with the important theoretical work of Ahmet T. Kuru, a Turkish scholar now teaching in the United States. In his book-length investigation into different constitutional models of religion-state relationships, Kuru contrasts what he calls the assertive secularism of France and Turkey with the passive secularism of the United States. He shows that very different policies flow from the different types of secularism. In France and Turkey the constitution identifies the nation as secular, and assertive secularism requires the government to take active measures to exclude religion from the public square. Thus the exercise of religious obligations can be constrained in assertive secular states. In the passive secularism of the United States, on the other hand, not only is individual exercise of faith broadly guaranteed, but civic and political engagement by religious communities is also constitutionally protected.

To explore the implications of assertive and passive secular models, Kuru examines the life of Muslims in different societies, with an in-depth look at the

United States. The integration of Muslim immigrants into Western societies touches on profound issues of globalization, pluralism, religious militancy, and the capacity of people from diverse cultures to live together amicably. Thus Kuru's analysis has broad relevance.

Kuru treats the United States as a valuable laboratory of the possibilities for amicable integration of Muslims under conditions of passive secularism. He finds that the strong constitutional protections of religious free exercise in the United States prevented adoption of punitive laws in the wake of cultural back-lash against Muslims after the attacks of September 11. In other words, if *asser-tive* secularism had reigned in the United States instead of state neutrality, legal restrictions on Muslim dress, mosques, and Islamic schools would have been more likely. Kuru also illuminates the evolution of state neutrality in the United States by charting the ongoing processes by which out-groups gain acceptance and protection of their faith practices, albeit grudgingly at times. He sees the potential for Muslims to travel the same path to recognition as such previously discriminated religious minorities as Catholics, Jews, and Mormons. He also charts the enduring struggle between American separationists (who tilt toward a more assertive secularism) and accommodationists (who embrace religious voices in the public square) to define the religion-state relationship. An impor-tant implication of his narrative is that the accommodationist posture tends to provide the greatest leverage for religious groups striving for legal protection and mainstream recognition.

Kuru's analysis of how the twin tolerations can work under passive secular-ism helps tee up the presentation of the debate over the role of religion in Turk-ish democracy. While this debate rages in Turkey, it goes to the heart of broader questions about Islam and democracy and the extent to which Islamic-based political parties can embody and promote liberal democratic reforms. In the light of popular uprisings in the Arab world, this issue burns with special urgency.

The contemporary debate about Islamic parties and democracy was sparked by Samuel Huntington's pessimistic assessment that because law and religion are traditionally fused in Islam, because "God is Caesar," Islam is inherently incompatible with liberal democracy.[24] Huntington and others fear that once Islamist political parties seize power in democratic elections they will enact laws curbing the civil and political rights of women, reformist Muslims, and non-Muslims, thus ultimately undermining liberal democracy itself. Stepan, on the other hand, contends that Islamic-based parties need not take this posture, and he points to the Islamic movements in Indonesia that helped propel and consoli-date pluralist democratic governance in the world's largest Islamic nation.

The debate in Turkey centers on the nature of its ruling Justice and Develop-ment (AK) Party that came to power in 2002—whether it is committed to liberal democratic norms or instead seeks incrementally to Islamicize the nation. In this volume we feature two accomplished Turkish scholars to help frame these issues. Binnaz Toprak operates within a secular-liberal intellectual framework that views the norms of communal religion as an inherent threat to individual liberty and choice. Thus her general concern illustrates the arguments of opponents of the *robust* view of religious freedom articulated in this introduction. Her particular concern echoes Huntington's fears about the repressive nature of Islamic states. To investigate whether the AK Party reflects such a threat, she conducted research on local social pressures that ignited a major controversy in Turkey and received wide global press coverage. Toprak's specific purpose was to explore how the government's Islamic vision affected societal relations at the neighborhood level. This is a crucial question because, as Grim's research shows, social pressures or hostilities can powerfully inhibit the free exercise of faith.

To gauge such pressures, Toprak's team interviewed people who would be considered members of out-groups from interlocking Sunni networks of government officials, businesspersons, and educators—out-groups such as Alevi, Roma, uncovered women, secularist business owners, and nonconformist students. Many of these people reported strong social pressure to conform to Sunni Islamic practice, along with employment discrimination, ostracism, boycotts of businesses, and in some instances physical assaults. One indication of such social hostility was that in town after town women reported that men would offer seats on buses to covered young women even when uncovered older women were standing up. Businesspeople also cited problems operating if they were not part of the government's allies in the Fethullah Gülen movement, which enjoys a certain prominence in the United States for its schools and interfaith outreach. Toprak concludes that social pressure increased with the rise of the AK Party, which controls many government ministries and mayors' offices, empowers Islamic educational and business networks, and emboldens local Islamists. She recommends that an office be created to address complaints of discrimination.

Talip Küçükcan does not discount the existence of neighborhood pressure in Turkey, but he disputes that such pressure necessarily flows from the emergence of the AK Party or that it is moving Turkey toward an Islamist and illiberal future. In contrast to the fear that the AK Party has a secret agenda to Islamicize the country, Küçükcan documents what he sees as its positive push for democratic constitutional reforms and economic liberalization. He also marshals research, presented for the first time in English, that he believes demonstrates broad public acceptance of a pluralist social mosaic in Turkey. The vast majority of Turks, for example, are undisturbed by veiled or unveiled women, reject coercion of religious beliefs and lifestyles, and report that they have not faced discrimination themselves.

Küçükcan also observes that the nationalist ideology of the secular Kemalist regime has historically been a greater source of discrimination against religious and ethnic minorities than Islamic parties. Moreover it has been under AK Party direction that the state has taken initial, if halting, steps toward addressing grievances of Alevi, Kurds, and Orthodox Christians. And in response to critics who see Islamist leanings or emerging anti-Semitism in the party's overtures toward the Iranian regime or the Hamas movement in Gaza, Küçükcan places such initiatives in a broader foreign policy outreach to Turkey's neighbors.

Finally, Küçükcan addresses how the secular Kemalist state massively discriminates against Muslims, especially women. For many pious Muslim women, wearing the veil is a sign of fidelity to the faith and adherence to the mandate of modesty in dress. But in Turkey, the ban on the headscarf in universities, government jobs, and even some businesses forces millions of women to choose between fulfilling mandates of conscience and participation in political and economic life. Yet AK Party–sponsored legislation to lift the ban was overturned by the Constitutional Court as a violation of secularism. Here we see the potentially high cost of sustaining an assertive secular state: preventing a huge cohort of the population from maintaining their identity while entering higher education and public occupations and other employment.

The polarized debate about the public role of religion in Turkey is rooted in the nation's unique constitutional structure. This structure poses serious challenges to achieving the twin tolerations because disputants are locked in an archaic system where the state simultaneously *subsidizes* Islam and *represses* its public expression. This Turkish paradox comes into high relief when we consider this fact: an assertively secular state has created a huge government bureaucracy to subsidize, govern, and run the operations of Sunni Islamic religious life. How can we comprehend such a situation? One explanation is that Kemalists view Turkey's Administration of Religious Affairs (Diyanet) as a means of control. In other words, the secular regime can influence *what* Islam teaches, *how* it is practiced, and *who* leads it. But preventing the autonomous operation of Islamic institutions through this system of subsidy and control comes at a high price, not only for Islam but for religious minorities. Because the Diyanet solely promotes Sunni Islam, the Alevi find it oppressive and want it abolished. Because the state operates Islamic educational institutions and mosques, how can it allow the Orthodox Church to run its seminary and not establish a dangerous precedent? As Küçükcan observes, allowing the opening of the venerable Halki Seminary would be a powerful gesture of goodwill toward Eastern Orthodoxy. Yet this modest step of allowing a religious community the freedom to educate its own ministers—a fundamental tenet of international law—has yet to receive clear backing by either the AK Party or the opposition Republican People's Party.

Underlying the Turkish debate is the nature and fate of Islam in the twenty-first century. Though great variation exists in Muslim-majority countries, the overall picture on religious freedom is sobering. According to the Pew Forum's reports on global restrictions on religion, eight of the top ten countries with high government restrictions are Muslim-majority, as are seven of the top ten in social hostility. Moreover of the fourteen countries where government restrictions increased, ten were Muslim-majority.[25] Thus the Islamic arc is a great crucible in the struggle for freedom of conscience and belief.

Is Islam so antithetical to pluralism and democracy that it must be controlled by a secular state, as Kemalists and others fear? Are militant Islamist movements so plentifully funded and networked that states cannot afford to allow the autonomous operation of domestic Islamic institutions? Or does Islam contain within it theological resources for the defense of religious freedom and pluralist democracy? And if so, how might that theological wisdom inform and inspire Islamic movements and parties? Since theological changes in the Catholic Church helped propel the most recent wave of democratization, developments in Islamic thought on human rights and religious liberty deserve keen scrutiny.

Recep Şentürk represents the vital wave of new voices in Islamic jurisprudence. His meticulous exposition of Islamic theology seeks to recapture and rejuvenate an ages-old tradition in Islam that affirms the universality of human rights, irrespective of religious status, place, and time. He begins by tracing an important division among Islamic schools of jurisprudence. One school emphasized human inviolability—and the innate rights that derive from it—as God-given, universal, and applicable to all societies from the time of Adam. Another emphasized only civil rights arising from and dependent on membership in a political community and thus affording differential rights and duties for Muslims and non-Muslims. Şentürk makes a cogent case that the universalist tradition represents the earliest and richest of Islamic theological principles. He also finds a powerful continuity in the tradition, which can be traced from the eighth century onward, broken only by the rupture of the modern secular era. As he shows, because Muhammad rejected time and place limitations on human inviolability, the universalist school similarly rejected the idea that Islam *discovered* universal human rights. Rather it asserted that God's natural law is accessible through human reason to all people since the time of Adam, so that true Islamic society would recognize and protect the rights of all people, not just members of the ummah.

Şentürk provides fascinating portraits of Islamic scholars through the ages who developed this universal doctrine. Long before Locke, scholars emphasized the universality of life, liberty, and property—and the requisite right to legal personality to protect them. Long before the American Declaration of Independence, these scholars emphasized that since all people are created equal by God, they are afforded with axiomatic equal rights. Moreover, Islamic scholars anticipated the powerful idea that humans must have religious freedom to fulfill their duties toward God. Submission to God must be voluntary and the mind free to give its assent. As Şentürk demonstrates, this idea of divinely ordained inviolability imposed both *obligations* on political authorities and *limits* on state power.

Thus when authority fails to protect the inviolable rights of citizenry, it loses its legitimacy, which is precisely what sparked the remarkable Arab uprisings in 2011.

If the Islamic tradition historically affirmed primordial human rights, why did postcolonial Muslim-majority nations become dependent on Western discourse or resistant to international covenants? Şentürk suggests that with the collapse of the Ottoman Empire and the colonization of Islamic lands, the chain of memory was broken, the tradition forgotten. Thus he calls for the revival and elevation of that rich universalist tradition so that human rights discourse can arise from within the Islamic community, not be imposed from without.

Religious Freedom, Global Security, and Diplomacy

Millions of people around the world are denied the basic dignity of exercising their transcendent aspirations or do so under the threat of legal harassment, arrest, intimidation, and mob violence. This represents a great moral and humanitarian tragedy. But as several of our contributors demonstrate, this denial also represents a threat to global security as it feeds interreligious strife, militancy, terrorism, and instability. Unless this dimension is appreciated, religious freedom advocacy will remain on the periphery of diplomatic attention, easily trumped by powerful economic and strategic calculations.

The scholarship here challenges the assumed trade-offs between security interests and promotion of religious freedom; indeed a compelling case is made for mutuality. To be sure, international diplomacy involves an exquisite balance of competing values and imperfect choices. But new thinking about religion and security can inform and enhance diplomatic statecraft by expanding our understanding of realpolitik. This new thinking is being advanced especially by a cadre of scholar-practitioners who blend academic heft with experience in diplomacy and national security. Herein we have contributions by Tom Farr, former director of the U.S. State Department Office on International Religious Freedom; Chris Seiple, the director of an institute that engages in relational diplomacy around the world in support of responsible religious rights; and Dennis Hoover, the editor of the *Review of Faith and International Affairs*. All stress that the security-religion linkage flows from the enduring salience of religion in human life and its growing public influence on the global stage. Seiple and Hoover suggest that because all people seek answers to ultimate questions, states play with fire when they trample on these natural transcendent impulses. Farr adds that the global resurgence of public religion—the desecularization of the world—makes the attempt to curb faith inherently destabilizing.

These insights help unravel a seeming paradox of twenty-first-century statecraft: that the best way to fight the genuine security threat of religious militancy is not by curbing religion but by protecting its legitimate expression. As Seiple and Hoover note, in the post-9/11 world this proposition is not intuitive. If religious extremism is a big part of the global security problem, then restricting religion—the default position of many authorities—seems the logical remedy. But as these authors show, religious liberty, properly conceived and implemented, is a key tool in containing religion-based violence and thus is foundational to sustainable security.

Seiple and Hoover begin by marshaling a wide array of scholarship to demonstrate the security dimension of religion. They document how state or societal repression drives religious groups underground or into militant diasporas. They chart the processes by which such repression politicizes theology, breeds apocalyptic speculation, and infuses a cult of blood and martyrdom among the persecuted. It is not hard to see how, in an age of global communication and migrations, such religious ideas and movements produce terrorism and instability.

Drawing on the work of Grim and others, Seiple and Hoover also catalogue the positive cycles that are unleashed by greater protections of peaceful religious practice. They note that expansive religious freedom nurtures the spiritual and social capital of diverse religious communities and enables them to contribute to a vibrant civil society. Thus repression and persecution are doubly destructive: they undercut the humanitarian or civic impulses of faith communities while fueling chauvinist or radical movements.

Tom Farr shares this analysis but brings to the discussion a unique vantage point: that of a career diplomat tasked with implementing U.S. foreign policy initiatives on religious freedom. Present at the creation of the State Department Office on International Religious Freedom, Farr was both a high-level participant in the process and a keen observer of what he termed the "religion avoidance syndrome" in American diplomatic circles. He catalogues the bureaucratic resistance to robust implementation of religious freedom policy by the U.S. government and its allies. But more than this, he demonstrates the profound misunderstanding that afflicted U.S. religious freedom policy. Rather than seeing the promotion of global religious freedom as crucial to U.S. security interests, as he believes it is, top foreign policy officials treated it primarily as a humanitarian cause of peripheral concern to the main currents of foreign policy. This often produced rhetorical denunciations of persecution or ad hoc efforts on behalf of particular victims, which allowed foreign governments to manage relations with the United States by releasing a few prisoners from time to time. Thus American diplomats, instead of seeing the Afghan government's "apostasy and blasphemy" prosecutions against journalists, women, and Muslim reformers as a mortal threat to democratic consolidation, congratulate themselves when they gain asylum for a few threatened individuals.

It is important to note that not all observers share Farr's rather bleak assessment of U.S. international religious freedom policy. Perhaps its singular contribution is the increasingly thorough annual report on the status of religion in every country. This report, which has become the gold standard on documentation, is closely read by governments around the world, widely used by NGOs and advocacy organizations, and cited by scholars. What is odd is that the Obama administration, rather than building on this foundation and incorporating the recommendations of scholars and advocates for a more robust and effective policy, seems to be sidelining the policy further. This is troubling because, as Farr shows, Western allies are even more reticent about promoting religious freedom or are actively engaged in watering down protections. Thus American leadership is vital.

Is there a remedy to the "religion avoidance syndrome" in foreign policy circles? Both chapters suggest the need to dramatically expand religious training for diplomats, military leaders, aid officials, and others involved in implementing foreign policy. Also vital is the expansion of curricula in schools of foreign service to incorporate the latest scholarship on the contribution of religious freedom to democratic consolidation, terror prevention, and global security. More broadly, political and diplomatic leaders around the world, often handicapped by secular blinders or religious chauvinism, can get ahead of convulsive religious forces only if they are informed by the best wisdom, insights, and cutting-edge research on religion in the twenty-first century—precisely the kind presented in this volume.

Conclusion

Angela Wu Howard summarizes a conviction animating this project: "a passion for what is just, for what is right, for what is true, irrespective of national, cultural, and geographic boundaries, for the vision of the human person as having an inviolable dignity that should be protected, however unpopular her views." Historic opportunity and unique peril mark our era, and the quest for religious freedom lies at the center of this strategic moment. Religious liberty, though violated by regimes and slighted by rights advocates, serves as a lynchpin of human progress and thriving societies. Protecting the freedom of conscience, belief, and practice is the best—perhaps the only—means of navigating the crucible of the twenty-first century: living with our deepest differences in a shrinking world. In an age of explosive religiosity and pervasive pluralism, where "everyone is everywhere," religious liberty is more vital than ever.[26] The scholarship in this book should help opinion leaders, policymakers, and religious authorities navigate a world of resurgent religious conflict by providing the *big ideas* and charting the *practical steps* to help constitute a more civil, prosperous, and peaceful world.

Notes

1. "Freedom in the World 2010: Erosion of Freedom Intensifies," Freedom House, Washington, D.C., 2010, www.freedomhouse.org.
2. Sandra L. Bunn-Livingstone, "A Historical Analysis: International Religious Freedom 1998–2008," paper presented at the Pew Charitable Trusts Conference, April 30–May 2, 2008.
3. Pew Global Attitudes Project, October 4, 2007, http://pewglobal.org/reports/pdf/258topline.pdf.
4. Kevin Seamus Hassan, *The Right to Be Wrong* (San Francisco: Encounter Books, 2005).
5. Abdolkarim Soroush, *Reason, Freedom, and Democracy in Islam* (New York: Oxford University Press, 2000), especially chapter 9.
6. Hassan, *The Right to be Wrong.*
7. John Henry Newman, "Letter to the Duke of Norfolk," quoted in Charles J. Chaput, *Render unto Caesar* (New York: Doubleday 2008), 148.
8. David Novak, *In Defense of Religious Liberty* (Wilmington, Del.: ISI Books, 2009).
9. Alfred Stepan, "The Twin Tolerations," in *World Religions and Democracy*, ed. Larry Diamond, Marc F. Plattner, and Philip J. Costopoulos (Baltimore: Johns Hopkins University Press, 2005).
10. Monica Duffy Toft, Daniel Philpott, and Timothy Samuel Shah, *God's Century: Resurgent Religion and Global Politics* (New York: Norton, 2011).
11. Peter Berger and Anton Zijderveld, *In Praise of Doubt* (New York: HarperOne, 2010).
12. Os Guinness, *The Case for Civility* (San Francisco: HarperOne 2008).
13. Thomas Jefferson, letter to Rabbi Jacob de la Motta of Georgia, 1821.
14. Abdullah Saeed and Hassan Saeed, *Freedom of Religion, Apostasy and Islam* (Aldershot, England: Ashgate, 2004).
15. The report is available at http://pewforum.org/Government/Global-Restrictions-on-Religion.aspx.
16. Brian Grim and Roger Finke, *The Price of Freedom Denied* (New York: Cambridge University Press, 2010).
17. Toft, Philpott, and Shah, *God's Century.*
18. Jonathan Fox, *A World Survey of Religion and the State* (New York: Cambridge University Press, 2010).
19. Roger Finke and Rodney Stark, *The Churching of America, 1776–2005: Winners and Losers in Our Religious Economy*, revised and expanded edition (Piscataway, N.J.: Rutgers University Press, 2005); Rodney Stark and Roger Finke, *Acts of Faith: Explaining the Human Side of Religion* (Berkeley: University of California Press, 2000).
20. Peter Berger contends that modernity heightens plurality and diffuses it throughout societies, as presented at the Istanbul Symposium, April 2009.
21. Ku Ma, "Rule of Law Best Help to Freedom of Faith," *China Daily*, December 3, 2009. This story is an interview with Liu Peng of the Chinese Academy of Social Sciences.
22. Elena Miroshnikova, The Status and Challenges to Religious Freedom in Russia, paper presented at the Istanbul Symposium, April 2009.
23. Stepan, "The Twin Tolerations."
24. Samuel Huntington, *The Clash of Civilizations and the Remaking of World Order* (New York: Simon and Schuster, 1996).
25. Pew-Templeton Global Religious Futures Project, "Rising Restrictions on Religion: One-Third of the World's Population Experiences an Increase," August 2011, http://pewforum.org/Government/Rising-Restrictions-on-Religion.aspx.
26. This is how Peter Berger described the sociological reality of the twenty-first century in his presentation at the Istanbul Symposium, April 2009.

PART ONE

THE STATUS OF RELIGIOUS FREEDOM

1

The Status of and Threats to International Law on Freedom of Religion or Belief

W. COLE DURHAM JR., MATTHEW K. RICHARDS, AND DONLU D. THAYER

The Evolution of International Law and Freedom of Religion or Belief

The right to religious freedom is the oldest of the rights recognized and protected under international law. It is the "grandparent" of many other human rights, though by comparison to other rights in the modern pantheon, sometimes a neglected grandparent.[1] Already in the Religious Peace of Augsburg (1555) and in the Peace of Westphalia (1648), religious freedom was given rudimentary protections.[2] These early documents focused primarily on the religious rights of rulers, with minimal attention paid to the rights of individual believers. The first of these treaties established the principle *cuius regio, eius religio* ("whose realm, his religion"), which recognized that Lutheran rulers would have equal status with Catholic rulers within the Holy Roman Empire and permitted lay (but not ecclesiastical) rulers to specify the religion of their respective realms.[3] The Peace of Westphalia further refined these principles, accepting the Reformed (Calvinist) Church along with the Lutheran and Catholic confessions, reaffirming the *cuius regio* principle that allowed rulers to determine the religion of their realms, and providing a five-year grace period during which public and private worship was to be "patiently suffered and tolerated, without any hindrance or impediment," but after which time holders of beliefs other than those specified by the ruler could be required to leave the country.[4] This very limited notion of religious freedom, which recognized a right to continued private exercise of religion when territories were ceded by one sovereign to another, persisted in a variety of subsequent treaties.[5]

During succeeding centuries, the international version of religious freedom evolved as constitutional protections of the right took hold in various national legal systems. At first the focus was on the treatment of religious minorities. In this regard Ottoman practice was significant. Ottoman rule allowed a considerable degree of tolerance of Christians. In some cases, Muslim rulers issued "unilateral capitulations (grants), which permitted the Christians to establish communities with considerable autonomy, including the right of free and public worship, over which the foreign powers concerned exercised extensive jurisdiction."[6] As the balance of power shifted toward European nations, a pattern emerged of authorizing European protection of Christian minorities. This ultimately led to a system in which foreign powers could intervene within Ottoman realms to defend religious freedom of Christians. The 1878 Treaty of Berlin contained strong provisions for the protection of religious minorities, and these were ultimately echoed in the various minorities treaties adopted after World War I.[7] Ultimately, however, the minorities approach failed to provide adequate protections, as evidenced most horrendously by their failure to protect Jewish minorities prior to and during World War II.

This led to a shift after World War II from the minorities approach to the affirmation of universal and individual human rights.[8] The fountainhead of further developments in this regard was the Universal Declaration of Human Rights (UDHR), adopted by the United Nations General Assembly in 1948.[9] The key provision on religious freedom is Article 18, which provides, "Everyone has the right to freedom of thought, conscience and religion; this right includes freedom to change his religion or belief, and freedom, either alone or in community with others and in public or private, to manifest his religion or belief in teaching, practice, worship and observance."[10]

The language of the Declaration became the basis of a formally binding multilateral treaty, the International Covenant on Civil and Political Rights (ICCPR).[11] As of August 2012, 167 countries are parties to the ICCPR, and an additional seven countries have signed but not ratified the treaty.[12] The internationally protected right to freedom of religion or belief has been further solidified by the 1981 Declaration on the Elimination of All Forms of Intolerance and of Discrimination Based on Religion or Belief (the "1981 Declaration")[13] and by a variety of regional international instruments.[14]

The Legal Status of International Law Norms Governing Freedom of Religion or Belief

The Legal Status of Major International Instruments

At the international level, then, a variety of declarations, treaties, and other instruments affirm the right to freedom of religion or belief. It is important to pay attention to the legal status of such instruments. At the international level, there are two primary sources of legal obligations: treaties and customary law.[15] While a treaty such as the ICCPR is clearly binding under international law, United Nations declarations, such as the UDHR and the 1981 Declaration, are merely UN resolutions and are not legally binding in themselves.[16] However, the norms they articulate may be legally effective because (1) they have direct corollaries in binding treaty language or help clarify the meaning of binding treaty language, or (2) they have acquired customary law status.

Thus Article 18 of the UDHR correlates directly with Article 18 of the ICCPR, which incorporates the key language of the earlier UDHR almost verbatim. This is not surprising, since the aim of the ICCPR was to create binding legal treaty obligations that would protect the rights articulated in the UDHR.[17] With respect to clarification of meaning, the provisions of Article 18 of the ICCPR are more specific than the corresponding provision of the UDHR, so the ICCPR clarifies the UDHR and not vice versa.

The 1981 Declaration may have legal effectiveness both because it uses language parallel to that found in operative treaties and because of its clarifying value. Careful comparison of the 1981 Declaration with the language of other binding treaties shows that most of its provisions are virtually identical to binding treaty language. Thus Article 1 of the 1981 Declaration repeats almost verbatim the operative language of paragraphs 1, 2, and 3 of Article 18 ICCPR. The only differences are these:

- Article 1(1) of the 1981 Declaration indicates that the right "shall include freedom to have a religion or whatever belief of his choice," instead of "shall include freedom to have or adopt a religion or belief of his choice," as in Article 18(1) ICCPR.
- Article 1(2) of the 1981 Declaration speaks only of the right to be free from "coercion which would impair his freedom to have a religion of his choice," whereas Article 18(2) uses the locution "have or adopt" instead of simply "have."

These changes were apparently designed to appease communist countries that wanted to affirm the right to hold atheist beliefs and Muslim countries concerned about Muslim teachings proscribing conversion from Islam to other religions. However, careful analysis of the debates leading to the final language of the ICCPR and the 1981 Declaration demonstrates that the aim was to move away from the UDHR's explicit focus on the notion of "changing" religions, while at the same time protecting the right to freedom of choice in this area. No substantive change in the meaning of the provisions was intended, as emphasized by Article 8 of the 1981 Declaration, which affirms, "Nothing in the present Declaration shall be construed as restricting or derogating from any right defined in the [UDHR and the ICCPR]."[18]

Articles 2 and 3 of the 1981 Declaration simply spell out the antidiscrimination norm of Article 26 of the ICCPR in greater detail.[19] Article 4 of the 1981 Declaration parallels Article 2 of the ICCPR in committing countries to take "effective measures to prevent and eliminate discrimination." It goes somewhat further in specifying that states "shall make efforts to enact or rescind legislation where necessary" to this end. In that sense it possibly goes further than the ICCPR,[20] although many would argue that the ICCPR should be construed in the same way.[21] Article 5 of the 1981 Declaration parallels Article 18(4) of the ICCPR, which addresses the rights of parents to "ensure the religious and moral education of their children in conformity with their own convictions," as well as provisions of Articles 14 and 28 of the Convention on the Rights of the Child,[22] which affirm and delimit the rights of children to freedom of religion and education. Article 6 of the 1981 Declaration admittedly goes into much greater detail in specifying types of situations typically covered by international freedom of religion norms. However, all of the examples are reasonable inferences from the general principles articulated in formal treaty language. Article 7, like Article 4 of the 1981 Declaration, parallels Article 2 in calling for effective implementation steps but goes somewhat further in calling for national legislation that will enable everyone to "be able to avail himself of such rights and freedoms in practice."

In short, the eight articles of the 1981 Declaration either track or closely parallel actual treaty language or constitute reasonable inferences from it. In that sense, while formally a declaration without legally binding effect, the Declaration attracts the legal mandate of the treaty provisions it draws so heavily upon. To the extent there are some differences in detail, the 1981 Declaration can clearly be used "as a supplement to the legally binding ICCPR, clarifying the treaty obligations taken on by its signatories.... Thus, the Declaration would have legal effect without carrying legal force."[23]

Customary Law

Turning to the question of whether religious freedom principles articulated in the UDHR and the 1981 Declaration have become customary law, the starting point is to determine whether these principles meet the requirements for acquiring this status. Essentially two requirements must be met: "Customary law results from [1] a general and consistent practice of states followed by them [2] from a sense of legal obligation."[24] That is, there must be a consistent pattern of compliance with the rule, and states must act in this manner in light of *opinio juris*—because they believe they have an obligation to do so. There is now broad support for the notion that the right to freedom of religion or belief as articulated in the UDHR has achieved customary law status.[25]

Perhaps because of its greater specificity and the fact that there was more controversy surrounding the adoption of the 1981 Declaration, the circle of experts asserting that it has achieved customary law status is more limited.[26] Carolyn Evans has identified the key difficulty as a lack of sufficient consensus.[27] She notes that while "[s]tates are often prepared to make forceful statements in international forums that illustrate their sense of obligation in relation to religious freedom, yet State practice is much less likely to follow its publicly voiced principles."[28] She concludes that "the 1981 Declaration is part of a long, slow, and on-going process of generating consensus around the fundamental need to protect religious freedom. These principles are strengthening, but have generally not achieved the status of customary law."[29] In Evans's view, the 1981 Declaration can help clarify the more general religious freedom norm articulated in the UDHR, and it has no doubt contributed to the process of norm crystallization, but the process has not yet reached completion.

On the other hand, as demonstrated earlier, the case of the 1981 Declaration differs from the case of other candidates for customary law status since in substantial part it reflects treaty language that most countries have already assumed. In the end the difficulty is precisely whether norms that have been so widely accepted but have been consciously rejected by at least some of the nonratifiers, may be imposed nonetheless as a matter of customary law despite such conscious opposition. Probably the most one can hope for at this point is that nonratifiers accept the 1981 Declaration as persuasive authority that should guide religion policy and practice in the country. Countries that have refused to ratify the key treaty provisions are equally unlikely to submit to the jurisdiction of international tribunals, so assertion of customary law claims is likely to have at best persuasive impact as a practical matter. This persuasive impact, however, when wielded by effective political leaders and civil society organizations, can be considerable.

Religious Freedom in National Systems

Whatever the resolution of the customary law point may be, support for religious liberty principles extends far beyond ratification of international instruments. The right to freedom of religion or belief articulated in international law is recognized and affirmed in the overwhelming majority of the world's constitutions,[30] including virtually every European constitution and the constitution of every independent country in the Western Hemisphere. Moreover, religious freedom protections have been significantly expanded over the past two decades both in formerly communist countries and in many other countries where the collapse of communism tilted the balance of power in more democratic directions. Furthermore, not only do most of the world's constitutions contain provisions paralleling international law religious freedom norms, but many countries have constitutional or statutory provisions that expressly recognize the place of international norms in their legal systems.[31] In most systems, some form of legal priority is given to international treaties.[32] The precise weight given to them and whether they are directly enforceable without additional legislation varies from system to system.[33] Some systems attach particular importance to human rights treaties.[34] In countries belonging to the Council of Europe, the European Convention for the Protection of Human Rights and Fundamental Freedoms (ECHR), including Article 9 on freedom of religion or belief, as well as the decisions of the European Court of Human Rights (ECtHR) interpreting that provision, have binding effect. In short, the legal systems of most countries clearly recognize the validity of religious freedom norms in principle.

International Norms and Constitutional Change

Significantly, international human rights norms, once adopted and ratified, form a critical background against which new constitutional provisions are assessed. This is true whether the new provisions arise by way of constitutional amendment or at the time a new constitution is drafted and adopted. The general rule with regard to international treaty obligations following a change of regime is the principle of continuity. Specifically this rule holds that "notwithstanding internal alterations in the organization of government, or in the constitutional structure of a particular state, the state itself continues to be bound by its rights and obligations under international law, including treaty rights and obligations."[35] For example, "despite the considerable alterations to its constitution when India emerged as an independent state, it continued as an original member of the United Nations."[36] Similarly, despite the profound social and constitutional change experienced by Iran as a result of its 1979 revolution, the principle of continuity applied.[37] As the examples demonstrate, this principle applies whether regime change occurs as a result of peaceful or revolutionary change.[38] Once accepted, international human rights norms constitute a floor below which regime performance and regime transformation should not be permitted to fall.

The rationale behind the continuity rule is straightforward. Other parties to a treaty are entitled to rely on existing treaty provisions regardless of internal power shifts occurring within other sovereign states. This can be particularly significant at moments of profound constitutional change. Constitutional drafters sometimes act as though they are drafting on a tabula rasa, but at least where their country has previously become a party to international human rights treaties, they are legally bound not to adopt constitutional principles that violate relevant international human rights norms. Unilateral revision of treaty obligations is not permissible. Once a country is bound by a treaty, the obligations imposed by the treaty can be revised only by mutual consent of the parties.[39] Multilateral treaties such as the ICCPR and the International Covenant on Economic, Social, and Cultural Rights are even less subject to unilateral adjustment.

Further, "[a] party may not invoke the provisions of its internal law as justification for its failure to perform a treaty."[40] This is particularly true when a country explicitly seeks, *after* assuming the treaty obligations in question, to create the internal legal norms it plans subsequently to invoke as a basis for ignoring treaty obligations.

The foregoing considerations also have relevance in settings where less radical change is at stake. It is axiomatic that a state has an obligation to perform its treaty obligations in good faith.[41] One of a country's obligations in living up to a treaty is to see that the treaty's terms are fully implemented in its constitution, laws, and practice. A state commits a material breach of a treaty if it repudiates its obligations under the treaty or if it violates "a provision essential to the accomplishment of the object or purpose of the treaty."[42] In a similar vein, unilateral narrowing of treaty obligations is not permissible. In the context of international religious freedom norms, laws or judicial decisions that unduly broaden permissible limitations on religion, thereby narrowing religious freedom protections, may run afoul of this principle.

Positive Developments in the Protection of Religious Freedom

Thus far we have been assessing the status of the law of international liberty by examining progress in norm formulation and norm adoption. Here there is much that is positive to report, particularly when one takes the long view looking back across the centuries. The fundamental standards articulated in key United Nations declarations and treaties have been widely adopted and written into domestic constitutions. International and national tribunals have developed extensive case law implementing religious freedom norms. The norms themselves have achieved a level of legitimacy that is incontestable. Failure to adopt and implement these norms is widely recognized as a failure of justice.

Moreover, significant progress continues to be made on many fronts. Four examples of important developments are representative. First, over the past two decades, substantial progress has been made in recognizing and protecting the rights of religious communities to acquire the legal entity status they require in various legal systems to carry out the full range of their legitimate religious affairs. This can take any of a number of forms: the right to incorporate, to have a religious association recognized, to create a trust or religious corporation, and so forth, depending on the particular legal system involved.[43] The right of access to such legal structures, long taken for granted in the United States[44] and Western Europe,[45] is now firmly entrenched in the case law of the European Court of Human Rights[46] and the commitments of the Organization for Security and Cooperation in Europe.[47]

Second, substantial protections are in place for the widely recognized right to autonomy and self-determination of religious communities in their religious affairs. This right has a lengthy history and is deeply embedded in legal systems with any substantial history of protecting religious freedom.[48] There is now a significant body of case law in the European Court of Human Rights affirming this right, which includes the right to autonomy in determining matters of belief and doctrine as well as matters of ecclesiastical structure.[49] A recent set of cases has also recognized the right of religious communities to autonomy with respect to personnel matters. The case law has protected broad authority of religious communities to terminate employees serving in representative[50] or teaching capacities,[51] but has qualified this right to some extent by insisting on a careful balancing of interests and state supervision where the credibility of a religious community and its teaching mission is less clearly at stake. Thus in *Schüth v. Germany*[52] the European Court of Human Rights sustained a privacy claim brought by an organist at a Catholic church who was terminated for extramarital paternity of a child. The Court held that the German courts (which considered the case) had not adequately balanced all the interests at stake. That is, while the German courts had balanced the church's autonomy interests against the employee's interests in continued employment, they had not adequately considered (1) the decision's impact on the private and family life of the applicant; (2) the fact that Germany's payroll tax system prevented the applicant from concealing from his employer civil status events such as divorce or the birth of a child; (3) the proximity of the employee's work to the proclamation mission of the church; (4) the fact that an individual right was being balanced against a collective right; (5) the fact that one could not automatically assume a lifelong commitment to abstinence from divorce from the signature on an employment contract; (6) the fact that the employee had not publicized the fact that his lifestyle was inconsistent with the moral teachings of the church; and (7) the difficulty for the employee of finding alternative work.[53]

Careful consideration of these factors will make it more difficult in future cases for religious communities to establish religiously based behavior requirements for employees whose tasks are not closely connected to their expressive identity and mission. However, given the European Court's emphasis on the fact that Schüth's work was integrally involved in the celebration of the Eucharist,[54] and that a religious organization may require its employees to respect certain principles,[55] and that it is the role of national courts to make the relevant factual findings in such matters,[56] it is conceivable that the European Court would sustain termination of an employee by a religious organization where an employment contract conditions continued employment on conformity with religious teachings, where the job description explicitly links responsibilities to the expressive dimension of the community's activities, and where a national court adequately considers the kinds of factors described above. That is, a national court reviewing *Schüth* after considering all the factors might reasonably conclude that autonomy considerations justify termination. The holding in *Schüth* does not preclude that possibility.

From the standpoint of expressive organizations, whether religious or ideological, the conduct of employees is critical because of the message it sends concerning the seriousness and authenticity of the organization's beliefs. Failure to protect the right of expressive organizations to maintain their authenticity in this way attacks pluralism at its roots. The European Court's opinion that various additional employee-side interests should be explicitly taken into account is reasonable, and particularly where there is evidence that deviations from the expressive community's ethos are not in fact significant to the community, greater protection of the employee may be warranted. But requiring an expressive organization to retain an employee who acts inconsistently with the normative aspirations of that organization, even if done in the name of protecting broader societal pluralism, in effect requires every organization to be pluralistic in exactly the same way and is wrong-headed for that reason alone. If the employee secures employment based on a commitment that he will abide by the behavioral requirements of an expressive community, the community should have the right to terminate him when that fundamental commitment is breached.

A third development worth noting relates to the right to travel of religious personnel. It is well settled that countries have a strong interest and broad authority with respect to controlling their borders. However, the European Court of Human Rights has repeatedly held that "immigration controls have to be exercised consistently with [European] Convention obligations."[57] Thus the use of border or immigration regulations "to stifle the spreading of the religion or philosophy," "to repress the exercise of [religious freedom] rights," or "to put an end to an applicant's religious activities within its jurisdiction" constitutes an interference with Article 9 (religious freedom) rights.[58] In *Nolan and K. v. Russia*, the European Court held that undisclosed national security reasons were not sufficient to justify exclusion of a member of the Unification Church from Russia.[59] The Court emphasized that the permissible grounds articulated by Article 9(2) ECHR must be narrowly construed and that even if Russia had disclosed a credible national security interest in the case, Article 9(2) "does not allow restrictions on the ground of national security."[60] The Court emphasized that the omission of national security from the list of legitimating grounds for limitation of freedom of religion or belief was "[f]ar from being an accidental omission" and that this "reflects the primordial importance of religious pluralism as 'one of the foundations of a "democratic society" within the meaning of the Convention' and the fact that a State cannot dictate what a person believes or take coercive steps to make him change his beliefs."[61]

Fourth, a particularly significant development relates to a recent and groundbreaking consensus resolution dealing with offenses to religious sensibilities.

For more than a decade the Organisation of Islamic Conference (since a June 28, 2011, official name change, the Organisation of Islamic Cooperation) has succeeded in securing the passage of a series of resolutions condemning "defamation of religion" at the United Nations in the Human Rights Commission,[62] the Human Rights Council,[63] and the General Assembly.[64] These resolutions have attracted increasing criticism in recent years because, while they address an issue of genuine concern, they do so in a fashion that unnecessarily threatens freedom of religion and freedom of expression rights.[65] The difficulty is that they focus on protecting religions, not individuals, with the result that less popular religions and individuals speaking critically about religions are put at risk. Moreover, in practice defamation of religion rules can be used selectively to entrench power of autocratic regimes while allowing offenses against the most vulnerable groups to go unchecked. In a breakthrough consensus resolution passed on March 24, 2011, the Human Rights Council changed its approach and dropped references to the controversial notion of "defamation of religion" in its latest effort to condemn violence, discrimination, and incitement to religious hatred.[66] As noted by Tad Stahnke of Human Rights First,

> This new text adopted by the UN Human Rights Council is a huge achievement because, for the first time in many years, it focuses on the protections of individuals rather than religions. The consensus behind today's resolution should put the divisive debates on defamation of religions behind us. Instead, states need to do more to adopt measures to combat violence and discrimination on the basis of religion or belief, as well as address religious hatred without restricting speech. The resolution is a start, but recent events across the globe remind us that much more work needs to be done.[67]

The new approach retains focus on religious sensitivities, but it does so in a way that focuses on the real problems, while striving to retain sensitivity for individual rights to freedom of expression and freedom of religion or belief.

Erosion Threats in the Religious Freedom Domain

In spite of great progress, however, we continue to live in a world in which substantial shortfalls in implementation of religious freedom norms are pervasive. This is the clear message of important new empirical work and of many of the other chapters in this volume, which describe the problems in more detail. A study published by the Pew Forum on Religion & Public Life at the end of 2009 documents the fact that 32 percent of the countries of the world maintain high or very high restrictions on religion, and since many of the countries involved are among the most populous on earth, 70 percent of the world's population lives in countries with such restrictions.[68] Recent studies also substantiate disturbing levels of religious persecution involving violence or physical displacement. Eighty-six percent of the 143 countries with populations of more than 2 million have documented cases of such problems between July 1, 2000, and June 30, 2007; 36 countries had more than 1,000 cases, and 25 countries had more than 10,000 cases over that period.[69] The UN Special Rapporteur on Freedom of Religion or Belief has lamented increasing incidents of anti-Semitism, Islamophobia, and Christianophobia, as well as a broader litany of religious freedom violations.[70] The Annual Reports to Congress on International Religious Freedom prepared by the U.S. State Department[71] contain seemingly endless accounts of religious freedom violations, as do studies by other credible organizations and experts.[72]

While a large percentage of the violations are attributable to more or less blatant noncompliance with applicable international and constitutional norms—in part a reflection of congenital weakness in the power of international law in particular to generate effective compliance[73] a substantial part of the problem reflects erosion of religious freedom norms themselves. Occasionally this takes the form of narrowing the prima facie coverage of religious freedom protections. This can occur, for example, when a country concludes that only a limited number of religions are entitled to religious freedom protections,[74] or when religious freedom protections are not extended to less popular or nontraditional groups.[75] The fundamental problem, however, is erosion by exception. That is, the difficulty is not that the legitimacy of religious liberty norms themselves is being questioned but that the exceptional circumstances that justify limitations on the right are being given an overly broad interpretation. A variety of social forces are combining to erode religious freedom, and for the most part the entry point for such corrosive forces is the limitation clauses built into international (and domestic) religious freedom norms. With that in mind, we first set forth a brief summary of the limitation clauses and how they are intended to be applied, and then catalogue the array of forces that put pressure on religious freedom protections.

International Limitation Clauses

Because of the reality of conflicting religious claims in a pluralistic world, it has always been understood that the right to freedom of religion is not unlimited. At the international level, these limitations have been carefully spelled out in treaty language, and a large body of case law analyzes boundary questions. Representative in this regard is the language of Article 18 of the ICCPR:

1. Everyone shall have the right to freedom of thought, conscience and religion. This right shall include freedom to have or to adopt a religion

or belief of his choice, and freedom, either individually or in community with others and in public or private, to manifest his religion or belief in worship, observance, practice and teaching....

3. Freedom to manifest one's religion or beliefs may be subject only to such limitations as are prescribed by law and are necessary to protect public safety, order, health, or morals or the fundamental rights and freedoms of others.[76]

The first point to note about the limitation clause, which is contained in paragraph 3, is that it applies only to "manifestations" of religion. This reflects the axiomatic notion that the right to internal freedom of belief, including the right to have or adopt a religion or belief, may not be regulated by the state. This is the so-called *forum internum* that has long been understood to go to the core of human dignity and to deserve absolute protection. The idea here is that the internal forum is jurisdictionally beyond the reach of the state, and claims in this domain are not subject to balancing analysis.

In part this is a practical issue because short of drug therapy or other unconscionable intrusions, the state literally cannot reach this internal domain. But in fact there are ways that the state can interfere with this inner domain of conscience. Identity cards that require disclosure of one's religion, for example, coerce action in the domain of conscience, where otherwise no "manifestation" would occur.[77] Cases involving priest-penitent and similar privileges may turn on internal forum issues. Catholic priests, for example, are bound not to break the seal of the confessional by disclosing to third parties what they have learned. The right to have or adopt or change religions has also been thought to fall within the domain of *forum internum*.[78] One type of erosion of religious freedom protections is to construe *forum internum* protections in a way that narrows them to the vanishing point.

As a practical matter, most religious freedom claims involve "manifestations of religion or belief," and limitations analysis proceeds with manifestations or external conduct in mind. A source of erosion here is that the notion of a manifestation of religion can be construed in an unnecessarily narrow way. This can happen in three ways.

First, the scope of manifestation can be construed narrowly by adopting restrictive interpretations of the types of manifestation mentioned in Article 18(1), which speaks of manifesting religion or belief in "worship, observance, practice and teaching." These terms ought to be viewed as examples of religious conduct, and they should be construed broadly. Unfortunately they are sometimes construed narrowly, as though they cluster exclusively around acts normally associated with worship.

Second, the notion of manifestation can be interpreted narrowly to provide protection only for conduct that directly manifests or actually expresses religious belief. A line of cases in the European Court of Human Rights has followed this unfortunate interpretation.[79] But of course, religious teachings may frequently command conduct that does not necessarily symbolically express religious belief itself. In particular, where the objection is to something the applicant is being coerced to do that is inconsistent with his or her religion, the action required obviously does not actually express the individual's religious belief.[80]

Third, free exercise ought to protect not only conduct that is *commanded* in the strict sense but also conduct that is *motivated* by religious belief. European Court decisions often include language to the contrary,[81] but there are many religious acts that are motivated but not commanded by religion. For example, the vocation to serve as a priest or minister is voluntary, though clearly motivated by religion. Freedom of religion does have limits, but those limits should not be based on artificially narrow conceptions of what "manifestations" of religion are covered.

With this background, we turn to the core structure of permissible limitations under international law. Limitations are permissible only if three rigorous criteria are met.[82]

First, limitations can only be imposed by law, and in particular, by laws that comport with the rule-of-law ideal.[83] Many of the constraints on religious association laws described above flow from this requirement. Thus limitations may not be retroactively or arbitrarily imposed on specific individuals or groups; neither may they be imposed by rules that purport to be laws but are so vague that they do not give fair notice of what is required or they allow arbitrary enforcement.[84] Due process considerations, such as the rights to prompt decisions and to appeals, also reflect this basic rule-of-law requirement.

Second, limitations must further one of a narrowly circumscribed set of legitimating social interests. Recognizing that too often majority rule can be insensitive to minority religious freedom rights, the limitations clause makes it clear that in addition to mustering sufficient political support to be "prescribed by law," limitations are permissible only if they additionally further public safety, public order, health or morals, or the rights and freedoms of others. Significantly, as the UN Human Rights Committee's official commentary on the parallel language of Article 18(3) of the ICCPR points out, the language of the limitations clause is to be strictly interpreted:

> Restrictions are not allowed on grounds not specified there, even if they would be allowed as restrictions to other rights protected in the Covenant, such as national security. *Limitations may be applied only for those purposes for which they were prescribed and must be directly related and proportionate to the specific need* on which they are predicated. *Restrictions may not be imposed for discriminatory purposes or applied in a discriminatory manner.*[85]

The reference to "public order" as a legitimating ground must be understood narrowly as referring to prevention of public disturbances as opposed to a more generalized sense of respecting general public policies. Significantly the term for "public order" in the French version of the ICCPR is not *ordre public* in the sense often used in French public and administrative law to refer to the general policies of the community, but rather *la protection de l'ordre*,[86] terminology suggesting concrete public disturbance and disorder. Further, Article 18 makes it clear that only "*fundamental* rights and freedoms of others" can be a permissible ground for limitations. It would be odd if rights of lesser stature could provide the basis for limiting a right as fundamental and as central to human dignity as the right to freedom of religion or belief.

Third, even if a particular limitation on freedom of religion or belief passes all the foregoing tests, it is only permissible as a matter of international human rights law if it is genuinely necessary. The importance attached to this requirement by the UN Human Rights Committee is indicated by its statement that "[l]imitations may be applied *only* for those purposes for which they are prescribed and must be directly related and proportionate to the specific need on which they are predicated."[87]

The decisions of the European Court of Human Rights in Strasbourg, which has had the most experience adjudicating the meaning of limitation clause language of any international tribunal, have made it clear that in most cases analysis turns ultimately on the necessity clause. In the Court's decisions, public officials defending a certain limitation can often point to legislation supporting it, and the legitimating grounds of Article 9(2) are broad enough that they can be used to cover a broad range of potential limitations. Insistence that limitations be genuinely and strictly necessary puts crucial brakes on state action that would otherwise impose excessive limitations on manifestations of religion. As the European Court has framed the issue, an interference with religion is necessary only when there is a "pressing social need" that is "proportionate to the legitimate aim pursued."[88]

Clearly, when analyzed in these terms, the issue of necessity must be assessed on a case-by-case basis. However, certain general conclusions have emerged. First, in assessing which limitations are "proportionate," it is vital to remember that "freedom of thought, conscience and religion is one of the foundations of a 'democratic society.'"[89] State interests must be weighty indeed to justify abrogating a right that is this significant. Second, limitations cannot pass the necessity test if they reflect state conduct that is not neutral and impartial[90] or that imposes arbitrary constraints on the right to manifest religion.[91] Discriminatory and arbitrary government conduct is not "necessary"—especially not in a democratic society. In particular, state regulations that impose excessive and arbitrary burdens on the right to associate and worship in community with others are impermissible.[92] In general, where laws are not narrowly tailored to further one of the permissible legitimating grounds for limitation, or where religious groups can point to alternative ways that a particular state objective can be achieved that would be less burdensome for the religious group and would substantially accomplish the state's objective, it is difficult to claim that the more burdensome alternative is genuinely necessary. Further, counterproductive measures are obviously not necessary. Third, limitations "must not be applied in a manner that would vitiate the rights guaranteed in article 18,"[93] and restrictions on religious freedom "must not impair the very essence of the right in question."[94]

The limitation clauses of Article 18 ICCPR and Article 9 ECHR are obviously intended to put rather sharp limits on efforts by states to override religious freedom protections. There are of course numerous possibilities for expansive interpretation of limitation cause provisions that can be used to justify encroachments on religious freedom. With respect to the rule-of-law constraint, states are constantly tempted to use vague or imprecise standards when authorizing various types of state regulation of religion. Similarly each of the legitimating grounds can be given excessively broad interpretations. For example, despite the clear statutory history that the "public order" ground was intended to apply only to situations that threatened actual public disturbances, this was used as one of the primary grounds for sustaining the headscarf ban in *Şahin v. Turkey*.[95] Except in situations where wearing a headscarf might trigger a riot—something not at issue in the case—it is difficult to imagine a headscarf causing public disorder of this type. The rights of others, also a ground for the decision in *Şahin*, can also be given an excessively broad interpretation. In fact, only *fundamental* rights ought to be recognized as having sufficient weight to override religious freedom claims, and even then careful and sensitive balancing is necessary. Finally, the type of proportionality assessment needed to assess whether interference with religious freedom is genuinely necessary can be abused. Protecting religious freedom requires vigilance in assuring that the fundamental norm is not devoured by exceptions.

Social Forces Threatening Religious Freedom

The limitations clauses provide the fulcrum in a balancing process increasingly weighted against religious freedom. In this next part of our chapter, we simply catalogue a number of the forces that militate against religious freedom. Some of these are broad social trends that affect the context in which religious liberty argumentation unfolds. Others present opportunities as well as problems. Still others describe specific types of practical problems that need to be resolved. The aim here is not to enter into precise analysis of how these forces should be assessed as they play out in particular cases. Rather we suggest the magnitude of the challenges that lie ahead in protecting religious freedom and provide a road map to major issues needing further research and thought.

Secularization

Earlier assumptions about "secularization" as the inevitable trend of history have come under increasing attack, primarily because in most areas of the world outside of Europe, the thesis—taken in the sense of a predicted end of religion or religious influence in society—is clearly not supported by the evidence.[96] To be sure, the role of religion in society has undergone significant changes in the West over the past century, and secularization is a process that continues to have significant influence.[97] To cite only one of myriad examples, studies conducted in February and April 2010 in the United States showed that one in four eighteen- to twenty-nine-year-olds are unaffiliated with any particular faith, far more than any prior generation at a comparable stage of life. Millennials are far less likely to attend church or view religion as important; instead they tend to turn to other, competing forms of spirituality or drift to agnosticism or atheism.[98] If decreased religiosity is evident in relatively religious America,[99] it is even more striking in Europe.[100] To some extent this reflects disaffection with organized religion and a shift to other forms of spirituality.[101] Highly visible problems such as the recent clergy sex abuse scandals have contributed to negative perceptions of religion in general and organized religion in particular. The fact that elites tend to be more highly secularized than other sectors of society compounds the impact of secularized attitudes on public policy. In some sectors, particularly among militant secularists and atheists, pressures for secularization take the form of calls for freedom *from* religion instead of freedom *of* religion.[102]

Apathy Regarding Religious Freedom

One result of secularization is the development of a pattern of taking freedom of religion for granted. Religious freedom protection has been so effective in much of the Western world that its benefits are simply taken for granted, and problems of its denial are beyond the horizon of urgent political concerns. This makes it much easier for other social issues to take priority and for religious freedom to suffer as a result. Influential commentators question whether religion is unique, necessary, important, or even good.[103] Some conclude that religion and religious institutions are harmful to society, even dangerous. Three general arguments emerge: (1) Religion isn't special: zoning or land use boards should not afford special protections to places of worship, and legislation should not exempt churches any more than labor unions or teachers' organizations. (2) Religion is a private affair that doesn't belong in public: no religious symbols should be worn or displayed; the government should not recognize religious holidays; and religious principles or tenets should not influence legislation. (3) Religion is a bad influence: religious institutions, motivated by money or power like other corporations, should be regulated and held accountable for misdeeds, just as are corporations; religious organizations are intolerant, breeding repression and hate; religious organizations trap adherents (sanctuaries for abuse); and religious belief is irrational. Such views, as they become more accepted by society, naturally lead to diminished support for religious liberty.

Growing Relativism

Modern society is increasingly hospitable to various versions of relativism. As David Kirkpatrick has noted, "Many opinion leaders today reject a moral view of the world based on Judeo-Christian values. In their view there is no objective moral order. They believe no preference should be given to moral goals."[104] This may be a corollary of secularization: the truth value of nonsecular beliefs is questioned, and in particular exclusive truth claims made by particular religious communities are criticized. The ideals of tolerance and mutual respect, which originally called for tolerating and respecting individuals who made divergent and often mutually exclusive truth claims, are reinterpreted to proscribe the holding of exclusive truth claims and to accord toleration only to those who do not hold exclusive truth claims. The idea that persons should be treated equally is reinterpreted to mean that belief systems should be treated equally, not only by states but by everyone. Equality of persons is mistakenly assumed to entail equality of values. Tolerance comes to be understood as accepting rival and even contradictory claims. The irony, of course, is that relativism ends up asserting the self-defeating claim that there are no valid truth claims in the religious or moral domain, which would of course mean that relativism itself cannot be a valid truth claim.[105]

These ideas are connected with a belief that social stability depends on the willingness of members of society to accept a broad range of beliefs. But this misunderstands the fundamental Lockean insight underlying the success of modern regimes that provide strong religious freedom protections. The pre-Lockean view held that religious homogeneity was vital to social stability. This was the theory underlying the *cuius regio, eius religio* formula implemented after the Peace of Augsburg and the Treaty of Westphalia.[106] Relativists assume that allowing people to hold differing and ultimately incompatible views is divisive and leads to loss of social peace. The Lockean insight, in contrast, held that social peace flows not from requiring people to accept the beliefs of others but from knowing that they would be protected in their own beliefs (which might disagree radically with the beliefs of others).[107] It is when people are coerced in matters of religion, not when they are allowed to hold their own strong and even exclusivist views, that violent reactions are most likely. This view is confirmed by recent research showing that government restrictions are a primary factor correlated with religious violence.[108]

Another corollary of relativism is a conception of ecumenism that is critical of evangelizing and robust exchange of views concerning religious belief. Thus a code of conduct for missionary activities adopted by the World Council of Churches denounces as "improper," a "scandal," and "counterwitness" to attempt to "present one's church or confession as 'the true church' and its teachings as 'the right faith'" or to persuade those moving from one church to another "to be rebaptized."[109] The World Council of Churches is, of course, entitled to adopt such a view as its own religiously based view, but other religious communities may take quite different views about their obligations to share their faith, and they should be protected in their right to do so.[110]

One of the paradoxes of relativism is that though one would expect those committed to that belief to be among the strongest supporters of religious freedom, in fact they often care more about undermining religious claims than about protecting the differences represented by the spectrum of religious beliefs. This basic paradox has a number of corollaries. Differing political and philosophical views should be granted full freedom of speech, but granting full freedom of religious speech is questioned.[111] Relativists insist on respect for proliferating lifestyle choices but seem less concerned about protecting traditional religious lifestyles. The difficulty is that while the idea is to open the doors to new visions of society, the number of moral pimps who enter vastly exceeds the number of moral pilgrims. Of course, it is often the case that those holding relativist views exemplify an honest agnosticism about values that is grounded in an underlying integrity and commitment to authenticity. The worry is that relativism can in fact deaden the call of conscience, leading to decadence, loss of respect for religion, disregard for religion, anger and rebellion against religion, and ultimately loss of concern to protect freedom of religion.

Social science does not have particularly good metrics for measuring the costs of decadence, but it is easy to see how full protection of religious freedom could be an early casualty. Moral relativism teaches that any particular religion is just one more comprehensive belief system and that no system has a unique claim to truth. Particular brands of right and wrong are of no particular concern. Religious difference is just a sign of the subjectivity and relativity of values. More, such difference is a source of social conflict that is better left behind. Religion can make no special claim, and thus religious freedom deserves no special protection. The need to protect conscientious claims of religious difference is lost, because in essence there is no difference to protect.

The Rise of Competing (and Sometimes Newly Recognized) Human Rights

For the most part, all human rights, including the right to freedom of religion or belief, are mutually reinforcing. All protect the core value of human dignity. But in recent times conflicts have been increasing. At precisely the time that secularization, apathy, and relativism are attaching lesser importance to religious freedom protections, the increased importance attached to some traditional rights and the emergence of others that have been newly minted has increased the range of situations in which religious freedom rights may be overridden by other claims. Lying behind many of these changes is the rise of an equality paradigm and the partial eclipse of a freedom paradigm that runs through much of human rights law.[112] This is reflected not only in new and expanded conceptions of equality but also in the fact that even classic freedoms such as freedom of expression and freedom of religion or belief are increasingly seen through equalitarian filters. Discrimination emerges as the archetypal harm, and other infringements of freedom are most easily seen to be legally cognizable if they can be translated into the language of unequal or nonneutral treatment. General and neutral laws override religious freedom claims unless they "target" and discriminate against specific religious groups or activities.[113] Prominent in the new equalitarian pantheon are concerns about women's rights,[114] indigenous peoples,[115] and discrimination on the basis of sexual orientation.[116]

Expanding hate crime norms, often passed with the aim of protecting human dignity and equality, have added another area of potential conflict. A particularly notorious case involved a Pentecostal pastor, Åke Green, from Borgholm, Sweden, who was sentenced in 2003 to one month of imprisonment for preaching a sermon that included a comprehensive list of biblical texts on homosexuality. The sermon was published in a local newspaper, and Pastor Green was prosecuted for "agitation against a national or ethnic group." His conviction was ultimately overturned by the Swedish Supreme Court, but only because the Court believed that convicting Green for hate speech would not be held by the European Court of Human Rights to be "proportionate" to the harm involved.[117] Pastor Green thus had a freedom of expression right to preach about the Bible's condemnation of homosexual relations as a sin, even if such views were alien to most Swedish citizens. While Pastor Green's rights were ultimately protected, cases of this type are proliferating.[118]

Also significant is the expanding right of personal privacy. The emergence of modern privacy law in the United States is a well-known and fascinating story of the evolution of rights. Beginning with a famous law review article by Brandeis and Warren,[119] strands of law basically reflecting "the right to be left alone"[120] were first crystallized into tort doctrines using traditional common law analysis and were subsequently elevated and transformed into a constitutionally protected "zone of privacy" discerned by the U.S. Supreme Court in "penumbras, formed by emanations"[121] from more fragmentary constitutional doctrines. This doctrine of constitutional privacy is now used to shield from state condemnation such actions as abortion and homosexual conduct. The right to privacy has ultimately become coterminous with personal autonomy and has evolved to provide support for claims that conduct that was previously thought to be illicit has become legitimate and rightful. While a right to privacy has not necessarily experienced the same judicial evolution in other countries, it is widely recognized in international law and in constitutional norms around the world.

Whatever their provenance, privacy rights can easily come into collision with rights asserted by religious believers and communities. The German religious employment cases cited earlier provide one such example. In the *Obst* and *Schüth* cases,[122] employees claimed that Germany had violated their privacy rights by protecting the autonomy of religious communities to terminate employees who violated agreements to abide by religious teachings. Religious communities attach great importance to these cases because of the critical role that religious personnel play for the credibility, authenticity, and autonomy of religious institutions in carrying out their religious mission. Those defending privacy claims of employees attempt to downplay the significance and legal scope of such concerns. Of course, the religious employment issue is only one of many areas where privacy rights are in tension with religious freedom beliefs. Clashes in this area are likely to continue.[123]

Still another impact involves shifting assumptions about privacy and the appropriate boundaries of missionary work. There is a growing tendency to think that "the right [of a missionary] to attempt to convince people to change their religious beliefs stands in tension with the other party's right to privacy."[124] The classic door-to-door colporteur now faces a variety of practical obstacles to his or her work. What might once have been assumed to be normal missionary activity now risks being seen as an inappropriate invasion of private space. Though ultimately vindicated in *Kokkinakis v. Greece*,[125] a Jehovah's Witness was initially convicted of proselytism for going door-to-door in the effort to share his beliefs.[126] The dissent viewed his conduct as being impermissibly invasive and aggressive.[127] In *Stanislaus v. Madhya Pradesh and Others*,[128] the Supreme Court of India held that the right to "propagate religion" did not require the invalidation of anticonversion legislation because converting another person went beyond mere transmission or spreading of tenets and thus was too intrusive to be protected by the "propagation" provision. Such cases are not technically about privacy rights, but they reflect the shifting boundaries in our contemporary conceptualizations of social space.

The potential conflicts of freedom of religion with other rights are further compounded by the modern tendency to assume that human rights claims can be made not only against the state but also against private individuals. The difficulty is that while it is quite appropriate for the state to be required to be neutral in its treatment of individuals and groups with divergent beliefs, it is quite another thing to require religious individuals to be neutral in the same way. The ability to differentiate among beliefs and those with whom one chooses to manifest one's belief, "either individually or in community with others and in public or private" (Article 18(1) ICCPR), lies at the core of religious relationships. Such differentiations are not wrongful; they lie at the core of what freedom of religion or belief protects.

The challenge in this area is that each of the countervailing rights has legitimacy at some level, and the values at stake may in appropriate circumstances warrant overriding religious freedom. The difficulty is that, in too many cases, the countervailing rights are being construed as automatic trumps, available without further analysis as a justification for negating religious freedom. Such wooden and doctrinaire rejection of religious freedom claims fails to give those claims the respect they deserve, causes unnecessary polarization in society, and has the result of making it difficult or impossible for the religious communities themselves to find more sensitive accommodations of the conflicting interests.[129]

Burgeoning State Regimes

Freedom of religion norms face "erosion by exception" not only because of conflicts with other rights but also because of conflicts with the state itself. The rise of the modern leviathan state—whether in totalitarian or more innocuous welfare or performance state forms—has permanently transformed the context in which religious freedom rights exist. International and constitutional limitation clauses recognize that "pressing social needs" or "compelling state interests" can justify overriding religious freedom claims, at least where the limitations in question are "narrowly tailored" or cannot be achieved in some "less restrictive" way. But state bureaucrats routinely assume that the state interests behind the programs they administer are compelling or pressing. How else can budgets be continually renewed?

Leaving that aside, the sheer pervasiveness of the state accustoms citizens to assume that the state has authority to intervene in any sphere. The fact that many constitutions seek to limit the scope of state authority to enumerated constitutional powers is forgotten. State paternalism is increasingly assumed to be the norm. The result is that if religion is relegated to the private sphere, it must live in a shrinking social space. Even if religion is recognized as having a legitimate public role as well, the thicket of state regulations grows ever thicker, and burdensome compliance demands carry a strong presumption of legitimacy. Moreover as the size of the state grows and an ever increasing percentage of the gross national product is devoted to material welfare objectives, the available resources left to private individuals to support religion and the building of spiritual capital is inevitably diminished. All of these forces change the baseline assumptions and realities within which religious believers and communities seek to assert their freedom.

Identity Politics

The rise of identity politics is another factor affecting religious freedom. This can take many forms. The tension of religious beliefs in relation to the politics of gender and sexual orientation is one manifestation of this new source of pressure on religious communities. The movement in support of indigenous people's rights is another form of identity politics. Defense of "millet system" approaches to religious and personal law tends to lock in protections of indigenous religions.[130] At the international level, reactions against globalization or perceived neocolonialism can place local groups at odds with religions that have international organizations. Bad historical experiences with missionary organizations backed by foreign powers sometimes lead to restrictive policies on religions that have transnational organizations. Negative reactions to what is perceived as decadent Western entertainment serve as a basis for narrowing personal liberties, including religious freedom. In all of these areas, identity politics helps to mobilize political sentiments standing behind the state or social interests that seem to be sufficiently compelling to override religious freedom.

Nationalism and the Impact of Dominant Religions and Ideologies

In a sense nationalism has long been one of the most potent forms of identity politics, and in many countries the historically dominant religion is closely tied to nationalism. In a similar sense religious and ethnic groups almost inevitably engage in identity politics, whether or not that identity is in the majority or minority in a particular national setting. Not surprisingly, then, there is a constant temptation for politicians to cater to religious communities because such communities often form a fairly organized base if their support can be attracted.

This can take many forms. In the Balkans, for example, it was religion that helped to preserve a sense of national identity during the long years of Ottoman rule, and to this day national identity is closely linked to the national branch of Eastern Orthodox prevailing in each country. In the years since the collapse of communism, strong efforts in Russia, Ukraine, Romania, Bulgaria, and other countries in the sphere of Eastern Christianity have sought to reassert the influence of the Orthodox tradition.

In the Islamic world pressures mount for stricter and more extreme enforcement of sharia, particularly in states or provinces where Islam is the prevailing religion. This includes calls for strict enforcement of Islamic sanctions for apostasy and for punishment of groups that deviate from traditional Muslim teachings; the Ahmadiyya, for example, have encountered harsh treatment in countries such as Pakistan and Indonesia.[131] Laws reflecting the call for "defamation of religion" legislation in recent years have often done more to reinforce persecution of other groups than to reduce Islamophobia.[132] At the international level, the growing influence of the Organisation of Islamic Cooperation is a sign of Muslim power.[133] Even where Muslims are not in the majority, fear of fundamentalist groups has led to tightened regulation that ends up spilling over and affecting all religious groups. For example, Central Asian republics have had fairly restrictive legislation since the collapse of communism, but this has become even more restrictive in recent years as a result of fear of groups that new legislation deems to be "extremist."[134]

Not surprisingly, pressures to favor dominant religions almost inevitably have as a consequence that other groups in the society suffer. What is perhaps less obvious is that the dominant religious groups also suffer adverse impacts. More often than not, the dominant religion ends up being "captured" by the state, and authentic religious teaching is distorted as it is exploited to reinforce the legitimacy and the power base of the state.

Consolidation of Power by Authoritarian Regimes

The foregoing problems are compounded in authoritarian regimes. Religious communities other than those supported by the regime are inevitably seen as competing bases for legitimacy and thus a threat to authoritarian power. The religion or ideology favored by the state is almost inevitably captured and manipulated by the state for its own ends. Other religious communities are restricted or repressed.

China provides a typical example for what happens in a secular authoritarian regime. A Communist Party directive on religious matters is representative:

> The fact that our Party proclaims and implements a policy of freedom of religious belief does not, of course, mean that Communist Party members can freely believe in religion. The policy of freedom of religious belief is directed toward the citizens of our country. It is not applicable to Party members. Unlike the average citizen, the Party member belongs to a Marxist political party, and there can be no doubt at all that s/he must be an atheist and not a theist. Our Party has clearly stated on many previous occasions: A Communist Party member cannot be a religious believer: s/he cannot take part in religious activities. Any member who persists in going against this proscription should be told to leave the Party.[135]

There have been some signs of loosening these requirements in recent years, but the quoted policy is indicative of authoritarian patterns. With respect to other religions, the situation is very restrictive. Only five other religions are officially recognized in China, and these are subjected to strong party controls.[136]

Of course, religious regimes can be as repressive as secular authoritarian governments. Saudi Arabia is a case in point.[137] To the extent authoritarian regimes persist, they pose the strongest hazards to religious freedom.[138]

Greater Security Concerns

The events of September 11, 2001, in the United States (and parallel events in Spain and the United Kingdom) have etched into everyone's memory the understanding that there are powerful security concerns that in some cases need to override freedom of religion. The international limitation clauses recognized the need to be able to limit freedom of religion to deal with threats to public safety and public order. But in too many cases this justification for additional state interference with religious freedom (and other human rights) has been carried much too far. Often security concerns have been used as a blank check authorizing virtually any imaginable regulation that is arguably linked to security. It is important to remember in this regard that national security in the abstract is not one of the enumerated grounds that serves as a permissible basis for limiting freedom of religion and cannot, without more, legitimate restrictions on religious freedom.[139] Even when limitations are more tightly linked to public safety or public order issues, there is still a risk that limitations can have the unintended consequence of persecution.[140] Great care must be taken to assure that understandable public safety concerns are not allowed to unduly reduce religious freedom protections.

Conclusion

The challenge of religious tension and conflict is as old as history but, tragically, also as current as every new day's headlines. Each new generation must relearn the virtues of tolerance and mutual respect in a world in which sparks of hatred can ignite firestorms that easily overwhelm more fragile efforts to build bridges of understanding.

Fortunately we now have some of the best tools humankind has ever had to address these challenges. The right to freedom of religion or belief is more widely recognized and better codified than ever before at the levels of international and constitutional law. Its legitimacy as a guarantor of values that lie at the core of human dignity is unquestioned, at least in theory and in public rhetoric. Yet acute problems of noncompliance with this acknowledged ideal are pervasive around the globe, even though pathbreaking new empirical research has shown more clearly than ever before the strength of the correlation of religious freedom protections with countless other social goods.

While much of the problem derives from age-old human traits that seem continually bent on renewing man's inhumanity to man, part of the problem is that a juggernaut of trends and pressures—many of which seem totally disconnected with each other—combine to facilitate "erosion by exception" of freedom of religion or belief. In area after area limitations on freedom of religion that are legitimate and often necessary if narrowly construed are contorted and expanded in the face of seemingly overwhelming pressures. Too often the concrete conflicts regarding isolated religious freedom cases are viewed microscopically, with a narrow vision that fails to take into account the full range of pressures to which the fragile religious freedom right is exposed. In contrast, we portray the pending threats to freedom of religion and belief in the context of the wider social environment. Although we have not attempted to give detailed analyses of the responses needed or strategies to be pursued, our hope is that painting the broader picture will help motivate vigilance in protecting this oldest and in many ways most profound of our fundamental rights.

Notes

1. W. Cole Durham Jr., "Perspectives on Religious Liberty: A Comparative Framework," in *Religious Human Rights in Global Perspective,* ed. Johan D. van der Vyver and John Witte (Boston: Martinus Nijhoff, 1996), 1–44.
2. William H. Maehl, *Germany in Western Civilization* (Tuscaloosa: University of Alabama Press, 1981), 149, 194.
3. Malcolm Evans, "Historical Analysis of Freedom of Religion or Belief as a Technique for Resolving Religious Conflict," in *Facilitating Freedom of Religion or Belief: A Deskbook,* ed. Tore Lindholm, W. Cole Durham Jr., and Bahia Tahzib-Lie (Leiden: Martinus Nijhoff, 2004), 1, 5–6.
4. *Treaty of Osnabrück*, art. 5, section 30. Those who changed religion after the Treaty could be required to leave after three years.
5. See M. Evans, "Historical Analysis of Freedom of Religion or Belief," 5–6.
6. Ibid., 6–7.
7. Ibid., 7–10.
8. The shift was not total, since some vestiges of the minorities approach remain. For example, Article 27 of the International Covenant on Civil and Political Rights protects the rights of minorities "in community with other members of their group, to enjoy their own culture, to profess and practice their own religion, or to use their own language." More recently, on February 1, 1995, the Council of Europe opened for signature the Framework Convention for the Protection of National Minorities. European Treaty Series No. 157.
9. GA Res. 217 (A (III), December 10, 1948, UN Doc. A/810, at 71 (1948)).
10. Ibid., Article 18.
11. GA Res. 2200A, UN GAOR, 21st Sess., Supp. no. 16, at 52, 55, UN Doc. A/6316 (1966), 999 UNTS 171 (1976) (art. 18). Authoritative interpretation of Article 18 of the ICCPR, the key article on freedom of religion or belief, has been provided in a General Comment issued by the UN Human Rights Committee, the body charged under the treaty with responsibility for monitoring performance under the treaty. UN Human Rights Committee, General Comment No. 22 (48). UN Doc. CCPR/C/21/Rev. 1/Add. 4 (1993), reprinted in UN Doc. HRI/GEN/1/Rev. 1 at 35 (1994).
12. The status of the treaty in terms of the number of countries that have signed, acceded to, or succeeded to the treaty is available at http://treaties.un.org/Pages/ViewDetails.aspx?src=

TREATY&mtdsg_no=IV-4&chapter=4&lang=en. The following countries have signed but not ratified the ICCPR: People's Republic of China (1998-10-05), Comoros (2008-09-25), Cuba (2008-02-28), Nauru (2001-11-12), Palau (2011-09-20), São Tomé and Principe (1995-10-31), and St. Lucia (2011-09-22). The following countries have neither signed nor ratified the ICCPR: Antigua and Barbuda, Bhutan, Brunei, Burma (Myanmar), Fiji, Kiribati, Malaysia, Marshall Islands, Micronesia, Oman, Palau, Qatar, Saint Kitts and Nevis, Saint Lucia, Saudi Arabia, Singapore, Solomon Islands, Tonga, Tuvalu, United Arab Emirates, Vatican City (Holy See).

13. Adopted January 18, 1982, GA Res. 55, 36 UN GAOR Supp. (no. 51), UN Doc. A/RES/36/55 (1982).

14. E.g., *American Declaration of the Rights and Duties of Man*, Article III, OAS Res. XXX, adopted by the Ninth International Conference of American States, Bogota (1948): *Novena Conferencia Internacional Americana*, 6 *Actas y Documentos* (1953), 297–302; American Convention of Human Rights, OAS Treaty Series No. 36, at 1, OEAS/serL/V/II.23, Doc. Rev. 2 (entered into force July 18, 1978) (ratified by twenty-five countries); [European] Convention for the Protection of Human Rights and Fundamental Freedoms (ECHR), November 4, 1950, Article 9, 213 UNTS 222 (entered into force September 3, 1953) (ratified by forty-seven countries); Helsinki Final Act, 1(A), Section VII (adopted by the Conference on Security and Cooperation in Europe on August 1, 1975); Concluding Document of the Vienna Meeting 1986 of Representatives of the Participating States of the Conference on Security and Co-Operation in Europe, Held on the Basis of the Provisions of the Final Act Relating to the Follow-up to the Conference, January 17, 1989, 28 ILM 527, 534 (1989), esp. Principles 16–17.

15. Statute of the International Court of Justice, art. 38(1), June 26, 1945, 59 Stat. 2055; *Restatement (Third) of Foreign Relations Law of the United States,* section 102 (1987); see also Sean D. Murphy, *Principles of International Law* (St. Paul, Minn.: Thomson/West, 2006), 65–88.

16. UN Charter, art. 13 para. 1(b).

17. See Derek H. Davis, "The Evolution of Religious Freedom as a Universal Human Right: Examining the Role of the 1981 United Nations Declaration on the Elimination of All Forms of Intolerance and of Discrimination Based on Religion or Belief," (2002) *BYU L. Rev.* 217, 225.

18. For a detailed analysis of the legislative history of the various provisions, see Paul M. Taylor, *Freedom of Religion: U.N. and European Human Rights Law and Practice* (Cambridge: Cambridge University Press, 2005), 27–42. Article 18 of the UDHR proclaimed that the right to freedom of religion or belief includes "freedom to change his religion or belief." While the ICCPR and 1981 Declaration language avoided use of the word "change," Article 8 of the 1981 Declaration confirms what the legislative history also makes clear—namely that the change in language was made to make the opening language more politically palatable but was not intended to imply that the right to change religion was not covered. Indeed it is hard to imagine what freedom of religion means if it does not include the right to change. The UN Human Rights Committee clarifies this point by stating that "freedom to 'have or adopt' a religion or belief necessarily entails the freedom to choose a religion or belief, including, *inter alia*, the right to replace one's current religion or belief with another or to adopt atheistic views, as well as the right to retain one's religion or belief." UN Human Rights Committee, General Comment No. 22 (48) para. 5.

19. Article 2(1) of the 1981 Declaration possibly goes beyond Article 26 ICCPR in that it expressly forbids "discrimination by any State, institution, group of persons or person on the grounds of religion or other beliefs." Article 26 ICCPR is ambiguous as to whether it is intended to prohibit only state discrimination or discrimination by private actors as well.

20. See Brice Dickson, "The United Nations and Freedom of Religion" (1995) 44 *Int'l & Comp. L.Q.* 327, 344–345.

21. See discussion in John H. Knox, "Horizontal Human Rights Law" (2008) 102 *Am. J. Int'l L.* 1, 10–11 (noting that the "four general human rights agreements" [the ICCPR, the International Covenant on Economic, Social, and Cultural Rights, the ECHR, and the American Convention on Human Rights] "specify the allowable limits on certain rights more clearly than the declarations, at the same time revealing that those limits do not apply at all to other rights. They also further marginalize references to private duties."). See also UN Human Rights Committee, General Comment No. 31, UN Doc. CCPR/C/21/Rev. 1/Add13, para. 8 (May 26, 2004).

22. Adopted and opened for signature by United Nations General Assembly Resolution 44/25 on November 20, 1989, 28 ILM 1448; entered into force September 2, 1990. The Convention on the Rights of the Child has been ratified by even more countries than the ICCPR. Only the United States and Somalia have not ratified.

23. Carolyn Evans, "Time for a Treaty? The Legal Sufficiency of the Declaration on the Elimination of All Forms of Intolerance and Discrimination" (2007) *BYU L. Rev.* 617, 629; Davis, "The Evolution of Religious Freedom," 231–232 (noting that the UN Human Rights Committee draws on the 1981 Declaration in clarifying the ICCPR).

24. Restatement (Third) of Foreign Relations Law of the United States (1987), section 102(2).

25. See, e.g., Philip Alston, "The Universal Declaration at 35: Western and Passé or Alive and Universal," 30 *Review of the International Commission of Jurists* 69 (arguing that the Universal Declaration is customary law); Richard Bilder, "The Status of International Human Rights Law: An Overview," in *International Human Rights Law and Practice*, ed. James Tuttle (Washington, D.C.: American Bar Association, 1978), 8 (arguing that the Universal Declaration is customary law); Louis Henkin, *The Age of Rights* (New York: Columbia University Press, 1990), 19 (arguing that the Universal Declaration is customary law); John Humphrey, *No Distant Millennium: The International Law of Human Rights* (Paris, UNESCO, 1989), 155 (arguing that the Universal Declaration is customary law); John Humphrey, "The International Bill of Rights: Scope and Implementation" (1976) 17 *Wm. & Mary L. Rev.* 529 (arguing that the Universal Declaration is customary law); Richard B. Lillich, "Civil Rights," in *Human Rights in International Law: Legal and Policy Issues*, ed. Thedor Meron (Oxford: Clarendon Press, 1984), 116 (arguing that the Universal Declaration is customary law); A. H. Robertson and J. G. Merrills, *Human Rights in the World*, 3rd ed. (Manchester: Manchester University Press, 1989), 96 (arguing that the Universal Declaration is customary law); Louis B. Sohn, "The Human Rights Law of the Charter" (1997) 12 *Texas Int'l L. J.* 133 (arguing that the Universal Declaration is customary law); Patrick Thornberry, *International Law and the Rights of Minorities* (Oxford: Clarendon Press, 1991), 237–238 (arguing that the Universal Declaration is customary law); Humphrey Waldcock, "Human Rights in Contemporary International Law and the Significance of the European Convention," *The European Convention of Human Rights*, Series No. 5 (London: British Institute of International & Comparative Law, 1965), 15 (arguing that the Universal Declaration is customary law). See also Hannum Hurst, "The Emerging Pattern of Church and State in Western Europe: The Italian Model" (1995) *BYU L. Rev.* 317–352 (summarizing statements of constituents of several states and international bodies as well as influential authors holding that the Universal Declaration of Human Rights is customary law).

26. See, e.g., Davis, "The Evolution of Religious Freedom" (arguing that the 1981 Declaration is customary law); Bahiyyih G. Tahzib, *Freedom of Religion or Belief: Ensuring Effective International Legal Protection* (Leiden: Martinus Nijhoff, 1996), 184–185 (arguing that the 1981 Declaration is customary law).

27. C. Evans, "Time for a Treaty?," 631.

28. Ibid.

29. Ibid., 632.

30. See Afghanistan Const. art. 2; Albania Const. art. 24; Algeria Const. art. 36; Andorra Const. art. 11; Angola Const. art. 45; Antigua and Barbuda Const. arts. 3, 11; Argentina Const. s. 14, s. 20; Armenia Const. art. 26; Australia Const. Act s. 116; Austria Const. art 7; Azerbaijan Const art 48; Bahamas Const. arts. 15 cl. 2, 22; Bahrain Const. art. 22; Bangladesh Const. arts. 39, 41; Barbados Const. arts. 11, 19; Belarus Const. art. 31; Belgium Const. art. 19; Belize Const. arts. 3 cl. 2, 11; Benin Const. art. 23, Bhutan Const. art. 7 cl. 4; Bolivia Const. arts. 4, 21, Bosnia and Herzegovina Const. art. 2 cl. 3g; Botswana Const. arts. 3, 11; Brazil Const. art. 5; Brunei Darussalam Const. art. 3 cl. 1; Bulgaria Const. arts. 13 cl. 1, 37; Burkina Faso Const. art. 7; Burundi Const. art. 31; Cambodia Const. art. 43; Cameroon Const. pmbl.; Canada Const. Act, Part 1, s. 2a; Cape Verde Const. arts. 28; Central African Republic Const. art. 8; Chad Const. art. 27; Chile Const. art. 19 cl. 6; People's Republic of China Const. art. 36; Republic of China Const. art. 13; Colombia Const. art. 2; Congo Const. art. 18; Democratic Republic of Congo Const. art. 22; Cook Islands Const. art. 64 cl. 1d; Costa Rica Const. art. 75;

Cote d'Ivoire Const. art.. 9; Croatia Const. art. 40; Cuba Const. arts. 8, 55; Cyprus Const. art. 18; Czech Republic Charter of Fundamental Rights and Basic Freedoms, arts. 15 cl. 1, 16 cl. 1; Denmark Const s. 70, s. 71 cl. 1; Djibouti Const. art. 11; Dominica Const. art. 9; Dominican Republic Const. art. 45; East Timor Const. art. 45; Ecuador Const. art. 66; Egypt Const. art. 46; El Salvador Const. art. 25; Equatorial Guinea Const. art. 13; Eritrea Const. art. 19; Estonia Const. arts. 40, 41; Ethiopia Const. art. 27; Fiji Const. art. 35; Finland Const. s. 11; France Const. art. 1; Gabon Const. art. 1, cl 2; Gambia Const. s. 25, s. 32 Georgia Const. art. 9, 19; Germany Basic Law arts. 4, 140; Ghana Const. art. 21 cl. 1; Greece Const. art. 13; Grenada Const. Order arts. 1 cl 1, 9; Guatemala Const. art. 36; Guinea Const. arts. 7, 14; Guinea-Bissau Const. art. 6 cl. 2; Guyana Const. arts. 40 cl. 1, 145; Haiti Const. art. 30; Honduras Const. art. 77; Hong Kong Basic Law arts. 11, 32; Hong Kong Bill of Rights art. 15; Hungary Const. (1949) art. 60, Basic Law of Hungary (2011) art. 6; Iceland Const. art. 63; India Const. art. 25; Indonesia Const. arts. 28E, 29, 281 cl. 1; Iraq Const. arts. 2 cl. 2, 39, 40; Ireland Const. art. 44; Israel Palestine Order in Council art. 83; Italy Const. art. 19; Jamaica Const. arts. 13, 21; Japan Const. art. 20; Jordan Const. art. 14; Kazakhstan Const. art. 22 cl. 1; Kenya Const. arts. 70, 78; Kiribati Const. art. 11; North Korea Const. art. 68; South Korea Const. arts. 19, 20, cl. 1; Kuwait Const. art. 35; Kyrgyzstan Const. art. 14, cl. 5; Laos Const. art. 30; Latvia Const. art. 99; Lebanon Const. art. 9; Lesotho Const. arts. 4 cl.1, 13, Liberia Const. art. 14; Libya Const. art. 2; Liechtenstein Const. art. 37; Lithuania Const. art. 26; Luxembourg Const. art. 19; Macedonia Const. arts. 16, 19; Madagascar Const. art. 10; Malawi Const. art. 33; Malaysia Const. art. 11; Mali Const. art. 4; Malta Const. s. 32b, s. 40 cl. 1; Marshall Islands Const. art. 2, s. 1; Mauritius Const. arts. 3, 11 cl.1; Mexico Const. art. 24; Micronesia Const. art. 4, s. 2; Moldova Const. art. 31; Monaco Const. art. 23; Mongolia Const. arts. 16 cl. 15; Montenegro Const. art. 46; Morocco Const. art. 6; Mozambique Const. art. 54; Myanmar Const. arts. 34, 354; Namibia Const. art. 21; Nauru Const. art. 11; Nepal Const. arts. 3, 23 cl. 1; Netherlands Const. arts. 6; New Zealand Bill of Rights Act s. 13; Nicaragua Const. art. 29; Niger Const. art. 26; Nigeria Const. art. 38, cl. 1; Norway Const. art. 2; Oman Basic Law art. 28; Pakistan Const. art. 20; Palau Const. art. 4 s. 1; Panama Const. art. 35; Papua New Guinea Const. art. 45; Paraguay Const. art. 24; Peru Const. art. 2; Philippines Const. art. 3 s. 5; Poland Const. art. 53; Portugal Const. art. 41; Qatar Const. art. 50; Romania Const. art. 29; Russia Const. art. 28; Rwanda Const. art. 33; St. Kitts and Nevis Const. art. 11; St. Lucia Const. art. 9; St. Vincent and the Grenadines Const. art. 9; Western Samoa Const. art. 11; San Marino Const. art. 6; São Tomé and Principe Const. art. 27; Senegal Const. art. 8; Serbia Const. art. 43; Seychelles Const. art. 21; Sierra Leone Const. arts. 15, 24, cl. 1; Singapore Const. art. 15; Slovakia Const. art. 24; Slovenia Const. art. 41; Solomon Islands Const. art. 11; Somalia Const. art. 31; South Africa Const. arts. 15 cl. 1, 31; Spain Const. art. 16; Sri Lanka Const. arts. 10, 14 cl. 1, 15; Sudan Const. art. 38; Suriname Const. art. 18; Swaziland Const. arts. 14, 23; Sweden Instrument of Government ch. 2 art. 1 cl. 6; Switzerland Const. art. 15; Syria Const. art. 35; Taiwan Const. art. 13; Tajikistan Const. art. 26; Tanzania Const art. 19 cl. 1; Thailand Const. s. 37; Tibet Const. art. 10; Togo Const. art. 25; Tonga Const. art. 5; Trinidad and Tobago Const. s. 4h; Tunisia Const art. 5; Turkey Const art. 24; Turkmenistan Const. art. 12; Tuvalu Const. arts. 11, 23, 29; Uganda Const. art. 29, 37; Ukraine Const. art. 35; United Arab Emirates Const. art. 32; United Kingdom Human Rights Act art. 13; United States Const. amend. 1; Uruguay Const art. 5; Uzbekistan Const. art. 31; Vanuatu Const art. 5 cl. 1f; Venezuela Const. art. 59; Vietnam Const. art. 70; Zambia Const. pmbl., art.19; Zimbabwe Const. arts. 11, 19. For reliable access to the texts of these constitutions, see http://oceanalaw.com/and%20http://heinonline.org/. Unfortunately these databases are by subscription only; however, these services provide the most up-to-date copies of the world's constitutions.

31. See, e.g., Argentina Const. art. 75 (22) (treaties have primacy over national laws; constitutional status is conferred on a number of treaties, particularly human rights treaties); Armenia Const. art. 6 ("International treaties that have been ratified are a constituent part of the legal system of the Republic. If norms are provided in these treaties other than those provided by laws of the Republic, then the norms provided in the treaty shall prevail. International treaties that contradict the Constitution may be ratified after making a

corresponding amendment to the Constitution."); Cameroon Const. art. 45 ("Duly approved or ratified treaties and international agreements shall, following their publication, override national laws, provided the other party implements the said treaty or agreement"); France Const. art. 55 (1958) ("Treaties or agreements duly ratified or approved shall, upon publication, have an authority superior to that of laws, subject to each agreement or treaty is applied by the other party"); Germany Const. art. 25 ("The general rules of public international law constitute an integral part of federal law. They take precedence over statutes and directly create rights and duties for the inhabitants of the federal territory."); Indonesia's Human Rights Act, art. 7(2) (1999) ("Provisions set forth in international law concerning human rights ratified by the Republic of Indonesia, are recognized under this Act as legally binding in Indonesia"); Netherlands Const. art. 94 ("Statutory regulations in force within the Kingdom shall not be applicable if such application is in conflict with provisions of treaties that are binding on all persons or of resolutions by international institutions"); Constitution of Russian Federation, art. 15(4) ("The commonly recognized principles and norms of the international law and the international treaties of the Russian Federation shall be a component part of its legal system. If an international treaty of the Russian Federation stipulates other rules than those stipulated by the law, the rules of the international treaty shall apply."); Spain Const. art. 10(2) ("The norms relative to basic rights and liberties which are recognized by the Constitution shall be interpreted in conformity with the Universal Declaration of Human Rights and the international treaties and agreements on those matters ratified by Spain"); Tunisia Const. art. 32 ("Treaties do not have the force of law until after their ratification. Treaties duly ratified have an authority superior to laws.").

32. Alfred de Zayas, "Le Droit Constitutionnel et L'internationalisation des Droits de l'Homme," *Recueil des Cours de l'Academie International de Droit Constitutionnel* (2001) 9, http://www .alfreddezayas.com/Lectures/tunis3_fr.shtml.

33. Thus in the Netherlands, Belgium, and Luxembourg a duly concluded treaty takes precedence over domestic law as a whole, including the Constitution. More typically treaties are superior to previously and subsequently adopted legislation. This is the case in France, Spain, Switzerland, Portugal, Greece, Bulgaria, Cyprus, Croatia, and Slovenia. Most states adhere to the rule that treaties simply have the force of law and take precedence over earlier statutes but may be affected by later statutes. This is true in Germany, Austria, Denmark, Finland, Hungary, United States, Ireland, Italy, Sweden, United Kingdom, Turkey, Norway, Iceland, Liechtenstein, San Marino, Romania, Albania, Poland, and Lithuania. Many of these countries in fact take effective steps to minimize the likelihood that conflicts between statutory and treaty obligations will arise. See C. Economides, "The Relationship between International and Domestic Law," paper prepared under the auspices of the European Commission for Democracy through Law (Venice Commission), CDL-STD (1993) 006, http://www.venice. coe.int/docs/1993/CDL-STD(1993)006-e.pdf, section 3. Professor Dinah Shelton argues that legal systems that have survived a period of repression often display a higher attachment to international law in the aftermath. Dinah Shelton, ed., *International Law and Domestic Legal Systems: Incorporation, Transformation, and Persuasion* (Oxford: Oxford University Press, 2011). See also Melissa A. Waters, "'Foreign Authority' through a Narrow Lens: Interpretive Incorporation of Treaties," http://www.law.uga.edu/intl/waters.pdf; Dinah Shelton, "The Boundaries of Human Rights Jurisdictions in Europe" (2003) 13 *Duke J. Comp. & Int'l L.* 95; A. F. M. Maniruzzaman, "State Contracts in Contemporary International Law: Monist versus Dualist Controversies" (2001) 12 *European J. Int'l L.* 309–328.

34. Some states (e.g., Liechtenstein, Russia, and Romania) give priority only to certain types of treaties, such as those that protect human rights. Economides, "The Relationship between International and Domestic Law," section 3.3.

35. I. A. Shearer, *Starke's International Law,* 11th ed. (London: Butterworths, 1994), 305.

36. Ibid., 305–306.

37. See "Case Concerning United States Diplomatic and Consular Staff in Tehran" (the hostages case) ICJ 1979, 7; ICJ 1980, 3.

38. Shearer, *Starke's International Law,* 305–306.

39. See Vienna Convention section 39.

40. Ibid., sections 27, 46. Section 27 notes that "[t]his rule is without prejudice to article 46," which provides that "[a] state may not invoke the fact that its consent to be bound by a treaty has been expressed in violation of a provision of its internal law regarding competence to conclude treaties as invalidating its consent unless that violation was *manifest* and concerned a *rule of its internal law of fundamental importance*." It would be difficult to show that it was "manifest" that Iraq had a rule prohibiting the adoption of legislation subject to an Islamic repugnancy clause at the time it originally ratified the Covenants. Among other things, not long prior to its ratification, it had undertaken significant liberalizing reforms of its family code that suggested the contrary was true.

41. This is fundamental to the law of treaties. See Vienna Convention section 26.

42. Ibid., section 60(3).

43. For a brief description of the types of legal structures available in the United States, Europe, and formerly communist states, and of the international legal norms protecting the rights of access to such structures, see W. Cole Durham Jr., "Legal Status of Religious Organizations: A Comparative Overview" (2010) 8 *Review of Faith & Int'l Affairs* 3–14, http://www.informaworld.com/smpp/section?content=a923076944&fulltext=713240928. See also Durham, "Facilitating Freedom of Religion or Belief through Religious Association Laws," in Lindholm et al., *Deskbook*, 321–405.

44. Durham, "Legal Status of Religious Organizations," 3–5.

45. Ibid., 6–7. See also Lars Friedner, ed., *Churches and Other Religious Organisations as Legal Persons: Proceedings of the 17th Meeting of the European Consortium for Church and State Research* (Höör, Sweden, November 17–20, 2005.

46. Canea Catholic Church v. Greece, 27 EHRR 521 (1999) (App. no. 25528/94, December 16, 1997) (legal personality of the Roman Catholic Church protected); United Communist Party of Turkey v. Turkey, 26 EHRR 121 (1998) (App. no. 19392/92, January 30, 1998); Sidiropoulos & Others v. Greece, 27 EHRR 633 (1999) (App. no. 26695/95, July 10, 1998); Freedom and Democracy Party (ÖZDEP) v. Turkey, 31 EHRR 27 (2001) (App. no. 23885/94, December 8, 1999); Hasan and Chaush v. Bulgaria, 34 EHRR 55 (2002) (App. no. 30985/96, October 26, 2000); Metropolitan Church of Bessarabia v. Moldova, 35 EHRR 13 (2002) (App. no. 45701/99, December 13, 2001); Moscow Branch of the Salvation Army v. Russia, 44 EHRR 46 (2007) (App. no. 72881/01, October 5, 2006); Church of Scientology Moscow v. Russia, 46 EHRR 16 (2008) (App. no. 18147/02, April 5, 2007); Svyato-Mykhaylivska Parafiya v. Ukraine (App. no. 77703/01, September 14, 2007); Kimlya v. Russia (App. nos. 76836/01, 32782/03, October 1, 2009). Note that cases of the European Court of Human Rights and the European Commission of Human Rights are available on the Court's website through the HUDOC search portal, http://www.echr.coe.int/echr/en/hudoc/. The cases involving freedom of religion, conscience, or belief are available in a convenient table on the website of the Strasbourg Consortium, http://www.strasbourgconsortium.org/portal.case.php?pageId=10.

47. Key OSCE Commitments in this regard are spelled out in Principle 16.3 of the Vienna Concluding Document, and are more particularly spelled out in OSCE, *Guidelines for Review of Legislation* (2004), http://www.osce.org/odihr/13993. A summary of specific protections is provided in Durham, "Legal Status of Religious Organizations," 7–8. These include the right to freedom of religion without registering; the right to acquire such status without burdensome bureaucratic obstacles; the right to clear rules to qualify for legal entity status administered in a nonarbitrary and nondiscriminatory fashion; the right to acquire such status without high minimum membership requirements, lengthy residency requirements, and nonneutral substantive review of religious beliefs; the right to acquire such status promptly; and the right to judicial review of denials of such status.

48. For a comparative overview, see Gerhard Robbers, ed., *Church Autonomy: A Comparative Survey* (Frankfurt: Peter Lang, 2002).

49. See, e.g., Hasan and Chaush v. Bulgaria, 34 EHRR 55 (2002) (App. no. 30985/96, October 26, 2000); Metropolitan Church of Bessarabia v. Moldova, 35 EHRR 13 (2002) (App. no. 45701/99, December 13, 2001); Svyato-Mykhaylivska Parafiya v. Ukraine (ECtHR, App. no. 77703/01, September 14, 2007).

50. Obst v. Germany (ECtHR, App. no. 425/03, September 23, 2010).

51. Siebenhaar v. Germany (ECtHR, App. no. 18136/02, February 3, 2011).

52. ECtHR, App. no. 1620/03, September 23, 2010.

53. Ibid., sections 65–74.

54. Ibid., sections 61–63.

55. Ibid., section 70.

56. Ibid., section 65.

57. Nolan and K. v. Russia (ECtHR, App. no. 2512/04, February 12, 2009), citing Abdulaziz, Babales and Balkandali v. United Kingdom, 7 EHRR 417 (1985) (ECtHR, App. nos. 9214/80, 9473/81, 9474/81, May 28, 1985), sections 59–60.

58. Ibid.

59. Ibid., sections 68–75.

60. Ibid., section 73.

61. Ibid.

62. The first such resolution was introduced in 1999, UN Economic & Social Council [ECOSOC], Commission on Human Rights, Pakistan, Draft Resolution "Racism, Racial Discrimination, Xenophobia and all Forms of Discrimination" UN Doc. E/CN.4/1999/L.40 (April 20, 1999). Similar resolutions were passed in 2000 (CHR Res. 2000/84 at 336, UN ESCOR, 56th Sess. Supp. No. 3, UN Doc. E/CN.4/2000/167 (April 25, 2000), which like the 1999 resolution passed with no vote. In 2001 a similar resolution passed with 28 states in favor, 15 opposed and 9 abstaining. CHR Res. 2001/4, at 47, UN ESCOR 58th Sess. Supp. No. 3, UN Doc. E/CN.4/2001/167 (April 18, 2001). The Commission voted to pass similar resolutions in each of the subsequent four years. CHR Res. 2002/9, at 56, UN ESCOR, 58th Sess. Supp. No. 3, UN Doc. E/CN.4/2002/200 (April 15, 2002); CHR Res. 2003/4, at 34, UN ESCOR, 59th Sess. Supp. No. 3, UN Doc. E/CN.4/2003/135 (April 14, 2003); CHR Res. 2004/6, at 28, UN ESCOR, 60th Sess. Supp. No. 3, UN Doc. E/CN.4/2004/127 (April 13, 2004). In 2005 there were 101 votes in favor of the resolution and only 53 opposed. Twenty abstained from the voting. GA 60th Sess. 3rd Comm., Yemen: Draft Resolution: Combating Defamation of Religions, UN Doc. A/C.3/60/L.29 (October 31, 2005).

63. Human Rights Council Resolution 7/22, A/HRC/RES/7/19 (adopted March 27, 2008, with 21 in favor, 10 against, and 14 abstentions); Human Rights Council Resolution 10/22, A/HRC/RES/10/22 (adopted March 26, 2009 with 23 in favor, 11 against, and 13 abstentions); Human Rights Council Resolution 13/16, A/HRC/RES/13/16 (adopted March 25, 2010, with 20 in favor, 17 against, and 8 abstentions).

64. UN GAOR, 64th Sess., 65th plen. mtg., UN Doc. A/64/156 (adopted December 18, 2009, by a recorded vote of 80 in favor, 61 against, with 42 abstentions); UN GAOR, 63rd Sess., 70th plen. mtg. at 17–18, UN Doc. A/63/PV.70 (adopted December 18, 2008, with 86 in favor, 53 against, and 42 abstentions).

65. See, e.g., Joint Declaration on Defamation of Religions and Anti-Terrorism and Anti-Extremism Legislation, Frank La Rue, UN Special Rapporteur on Freedom of Opinion and Expression, Miklos Haraszti, OSCE Representative on Freedom of the Media, Catalina Botero, OAS Special Rapporteur on Freedom of Expression, and Faith Pansy Tlakula, ACHPR Special Rapporteur on Freedom of Expression, p. 2 (December 10, 2008), http://www.osce.org/documents/rfm/2008/12/35705_en.pdf; Annual Report of the United National High Commissioner for Human Rights and Reports of the Office of the High Commissioner and the Secretary-General: Study of the United Nations High Commissioner for Human Rights compiling existing legislations and jurisprudence concerning defamation of and contempt for religions, A/HRC/9/25 (September 5, 2008), paras. 36–37.

66. The action was based on a draft resolution submitted by Pakistan on behalf of the Organisation of the Islamic Conference, "Combatting intolerance, negative stereotyping and stigmatization of, and discrimination, incitement to violence, and violence against persons based on religion or belief," UN Human Rights Council, A/HRC/16/L.38 (March 21, 2011). The resolution was passed as submitted by unanimous vote.

67. Human Rights First, press release, http://www.humanrightsfirst.org/2011/03/24/groundbreaking-consensus-reached-to-abandon-global-blasphemy-code-at-the-united-nations/.

68. Pew Forum on Religion & Public Life, Global Restrictions on Religion (2009) 1, http://pewforum.org/newassets/images/reports/restrictions/restrictionsfullreport.pdf.

69. Brian J. Grim and Roger Finke, *The Price of Freedom Denied: Religious Persecution and Conflict in the Twenty-First Century* (Cambridge: Cambridge University Press, 2011), 18–21.

70. See, e.g., Statement by Heiner Bielefeldt, Special Rapporteur on Freedom of Religion or Belief, 16th Session of the Human Rights Council, Item 3, March 10, 2011, Geneva, http://www2 .ohchr.org/english/issues/religion/docs/HRC16statement_March2011.pdf; Report of the Special Rapporteur on Freedom of Religion or Belief to the General Assembly, AA/HRD/16/53, December 15, 2010, http://daccess-dds-ny.un.org/doc/UNDOC/GEN/G10/177/93/PDF/G1017793.pdf?OpenElement. Annual Reports of the Special Rapporteur to the Human Rights Council, Commission on Human Rights, and General Assembly are available at http://www.ohchr.org/EN/Issues/FreedomReligion/Pages/Annual.aspx.

71. See, e.g., the U.S. State Department's International Religious Freedom Report 2011, http://www.state.gov/j/drl/rls/irf/religiousfreedom/index.htm.

72. E.g., Freedom House (http://www.freedomhouse.org/), Hudson Institute (http://www.hudson.org/), Human Rights First (http://www.humanrightsfirst.org), Human Rights Watch (http://www.hrw.org/), Human Rights Without Frontiers International (http://www.hrwf .org/), and the Organization for Security and Cooperation in Europe (OSCE, http://www .osce.org).

73. See generally Jack L. Goldsmith and Eric A. Posner, *The Limits of International Law* (Oxford: Oxford University Press, 2005); Michael J. Glennon, *The Fog of Law: Pragmatism, Security, and International Law* (Washington, D.C.: Woodrow Wilson Center Press and Stanford University Press, 2010).

74. The People's Republic of China, for example, "recognizes only five official religions—Buddhism, Taoism, Islam, Catholicism, and Protestantism—and considers the practice of any other faith illegal." Preeti Bhattacharji, "Religion in China," Council on Foreign Relations *Backgrounder*, May 16, 2008, http://www.cfr.org/china/religion-china/p16272.

75. There has been pressure in Central Asia to limit religious freedom protections to "traditional religions." Another problem is that some writers seem to think that religious freedom norms protect only religions, and not sects or cults, as though the latter were not themselves religions. This is clearly inconsistent with the view of the UN Human Rights Committee, the body officially charged with supervising compliance with the ICCPR. That body has emphasized that "Article 18 protects theistic, non-theistic, and atheistic beliefs, as well as the right not to profess any religion or belief. The terms belief and religion are to be broadly construed. Article 18 is not limited in its application to traditional religions or to religions and beliefs with institutional characteristics or practices analogous to those of traditional religions. The Committee therefore views with concern any tendency to discriminate against any religion or belief for any reasons, including the fact that they are newly established or represent religious minorities that may be the subject of hostility by a predominant religious community." UN Human Rights Committee, General Comment 22 (48) para. 2.

76. While the analysis that follows focuses on Article 18 ICCPR, it applies equally to Article 9(2) ECHR, which is virtually identical to Article 18(3).

77. This problem was present in the Turkish identity card case, Sinan Işık v. Turkey (ECtHR, App. no. 21924/05, February 2, 2010), although the Court did not rely on internal forum analysis in that case.

78. Tahzib, *Freedom of Religion or Belief*, 71–74.

79. Arrowsmith v. United Kingdom (ECmHR, App. no. 7050/75, October 12, 1978). See Taylor, *Freedom of Religion*, 123–127; Carolyn Evans, *Freedom of Religion under the European Convention on Human Rights* (Oxford: Oxford University Press, 2001), 116. Also see E. M. Barendt, "Arrowsmith v The United Kingdom" (1981) 1 *Oxford J. Legal Studies* 279–284.

80. See Taylor, *Freedom of Religion*, 127.

81. See, e.g., Metropolitan Church of Bessarabia v. Moldova (ECtHR, App. no. 45701/99, December 13, 2001), s. 114; Khan v. United Kingdom (ECmHR, App. no. 11579/85, July 7, 1986); Brett G. Scharffs, "The Autonomy of Church and State" (2004) *BYU L. Rev.* 1217, 1324.

82. The summary of key limitation clause features draws on language drafted by Professor Durham and included in analyses of various legislative measures prepared in his capacity as a member of the OSCE/ODIHR Advisory Council on Freedom of Religion or Belief.

83. See, e.g., Sunday Times v. the United Kingdom, 2 EHRR 245 (1979) (App. no. 6538/74, April 26, 1979); Kokkinakis v. Greece, 17 EHRR 397 (1994) (App. no. 14307/88, May 25, 1993); W. Cole Durham Jr. and Brett G. Scharffs, *Law and Religion: National, International and Comparative Perspectives* (New York: Aspen/Wolters Kluwer, 2010), 232; Malcolm Evans, *Religious Liberty and International Law in Europe* (Cambridge: Cambridge University Press, 1997), 319–320.

84. Religionsgemeinschaft der Zeugen Jehovas and Others v. Austria, 48 EHRR 17 (2009) (App. no. 40825/98, July 31, 2008), section 71; Hasan and Chaush v. Bulgaria, 34 EHRR 55 (2002) (App. no. 30985/96, October 26, 2000). See C. Evans, *Freedom of Religion*, 138–142; Taylor, *Freedom of Religion*, 293–301.

85. UN Human Rights Committee, General Comment No. 22 (48) para. 8 (emphasis added).

86. C. Evans, *Freedom of Religion*, 150; Manfred Nowak and Tanja Vospernik, "Permissible Restrictions on Freedom of Religion or Belief," in Lindholm et al., *Deskbook*, 152–153, n. 23.

87. UN Human Rights Committee, General Comment 22 (48) para. 8.

88. See, e.g., Kokkinakis v. Greece, 17 EHRR 397 (A/26-A) (1994) (A/26-A) (App. no. 14307/88, May 25, 1993), section 49; Wingrove v. United Kingdom, 24 EHRR 1(1997) (App. no. 17419/90 November 25, 1996), section 53; Manoussakis and Others v. Greece, 23 EHRR 387 (1997) (App. no. 18748/91, September 26, 1996), sections 43–53; Serif v. Greece, 31 EHRR 20 (2001) (App. no. 38178/97, December 14, 1999), section 49; Metropolitan Church of Bessarabia v. Moldova, 35 EHRR 13 (2002) (App. no. 45701/99, December 13, 2001), section 119.

89. Metropolitan Church of Bessarabia v. Moldova, 35 EHRR 13 (2002) (App. no. 45701/99, December 13, 2001), section 114.

90. Ibid., section 116.

91. Ibid., section 118; Manoussakis and Others v. Greece, 23 EHRR 387 (1997) (App. no. 18748/91, August 29, 1996), sections 43–53.

92. Metropolitan Church of Bessarabia v. Moldova, 35 EHRR 13 (2002) (App. no. 45701/99, December 13, 2001), section 118.

93. United Nations Human Rights Committee General Comment No. 22 (48) (Article 18), adopted by the UN Human Rights Committee on July 20, 1993. UN Doc. CCPR/C/21/Rev. 1/Add.4 (1993), reprinted in UN Doc. HRI/GEN/1/Rev. 1 at 35 (1994) para. 8.

94. Decision, Republic of Korea [2007] UNHRC 5; CCPR/C/88/D/1321-1322/2004 (January 23, 2007) (UN HRC).

95. 41 EHRR 8 (2007) (App. no. 44774/98, June 29, 2004), affirmed by Grand Chamber, 44 EHRR 5 (2007) (App. no. 44774/98, November 10, 2005).

96. See, e.g., Peter L. Berger, ed., *The Desecularization of the World: Resurgent Religion and World Politics* (Washington, D.C.: Ethics and Public Policy Center, 1999).

97. For a discussion of the issue, see "After Secularization," special double issue of (2006) 8 The *Hedgehog Review: Critical Reflections on Contemporary Culture* nos. 1–2, http://www.iasc-culture.org/THR/hedgehog_review_2006-Spring-Summer.php, especially Steve Bruce, "Secularization and the Impotence of Individualized Religion," http://www.iasc-culture.org/THR/archives/AfterSecularization/8.12CCasanova.pdf; José Casanova, "Rethinking Secularization: A Global Comparative Perspective," http://www.iasc-culture.org/THR/archives/AfterSecularization/8.12CCasanova.pdf; Grace Davie, "Is Europe an Exceptional Case?," http://www.iasc-culture.org/THR/archives/AfterSecularization/8.12DDavie.pdf; Paul Heelas, "Challenging Secularization Theory: The Growth of 'New Age' Spiritualities of Life," http://www.iasc-culture.org/THR/archives/AfterSecularization/8.12FHeelas.pdf; David Novak, "Secularity without Secularism: The Best Political Position for Contemporary Jews," http://www.iasc-culture.org/THR/archives/AfterSecularization/8.12JNovak.pdf; Slavica Jakelic, "Secularization, European Identity, and 'The End of the West,'" http://www.iasc-culture.org/THR/archives/AfterSecularization/8.12MJakelic.pdf.

98. See Robert D. Putnam and Daniel E. Campbell, *American Grace: How Religion Divides and Unites Us* (New York: Simon & Schuster, 2010), 139–140.

99. Ibid., 122–123.

100. See Grace Davie, "Christian, but Not as We Know It," *Guardian*, June 1, 2009, http://www .guardian.co.uk/commentisfree/belief/2009/jun/01/europe-christianity-religion.

101. See, e.g., Frederick M. Gedicks, "Spirituality, Fundamentalism, Liberty: Religion at the End of Modernity" (2005) 54 *DePaul L. Rev.* 1197, 1216–1217.

102. For example, in the United States, the Freedom From Religion Foundation (http://www .ffrf.org/) is increasingly visible in political and legal news.

103. Typical in this regard is a recent statement by Sam Harris:

> One of the greatest challenges facing civilization in the twenty-first century is for human beings to learn to speak about their deepest personal concerns—about ethics, spiritual experience, and the inevitability of human suffering—in ways that are not flagrantly irrational. Nothing stands in the way of this project more than the respect we accord religious faith. Incompatible religious doctrines have balkanized our world into separate moral communities, and these divisions have become a continuous source of human conflict. The idea that there is a necessary link between religious faith and morality is one of the principal myths keeping religion in good standing among otherwise reasonable men and women. And yet, it is a myth that is easily dispelled. (Sam Harris, "The Myth of Secular Moral Chaos," *Council for Secular Humanism,* http: //www.secularhumanism.org/index.php?section=library&page=sharris_26_3)

104. David D. Kirkpatrick, "The Right Hand of the Fathers," *New York Times Magazine*, December 20, 2009.

105. On self-defeating arguments of this type, see John Finnis, *Natural Law and Natural Right* (Oxford: Clarendon Press, 1980), 73–75.

106. See the first section of this chapter.

107. See John Locke, *A Letter Concerning Toleration* (first published in 1689; cited edition: Indianapolis: Bobbs-Merrill, 1990), 68–69; Durham, "Perspectives on Religious Liberty," 7–12 (describing the Lockean revolution in religious liberty).

108. Grim and Finke, *The Price of Freedom Denied,* 215–222.

109. World Council of Churches, *Towards Common Witness—A Call to Adopt Responsible Relationships in Mission and to Renounce Proselytism* (1997), 3–5.

110. For an overview of a range of codes of missionary conduct prepared in recent years, see Matthew K. Richards, Are Svendsen, and Rainer Bless, "Voluntary Codes of Conduct for Religious Persuasion: Effective Tools for Balancing Human Rights and Resolving Conflicts?" (2011) 6 *Religion and Human Rights* 151–183.

111. Amos N. Guiora, *Freedom from Religion* (Oxford: Oxford University Press, 2009), 27–39.

112. W. Cole Durham Jr. and Brett G. Scharffs, "State and Religious Communities in the United States: The Tension between Freedom and Equality," in *Church and State: Towards Protection for Freedom of Religion*, 362 (Japanese Association of Comparative Constitutional Law, Proceedings of the International Conference on Comparative Constitutional Law, September 2–4, 2005).

113. In this sense the U.S. Supreme Court's decision in *Employment Division v. Smith*, 494 U.S. 872 (1990) transformed free exercise of religion into an equality norm.

114. See, e.g., Durham and Scharffs, *Law and Religion,* 331–368; Martha Minow, "Should Religious Groups Be Exempt from Civil Rights Law?" (2007) 48 *BC L Rev* 781, 784–785, 801–807; Lindholm et al., *Deskbook.* 455–560.

115. Among nations that were the targets of Western colonialism or crusades, there is some-times a bitter view of the suppression of early missionary tactics. On behalf of Africa, one scholar asserts that proselytizing has racial overtones, and that "unless groups are given protection against invasion and control by others, their cultural and ethnic identities could be quashed by more powerful cultures and political systems. The violent advocacy of pros-elytizing religions in Africa could be seen as a negation of [the rights of indigenous peoples] particularly because religion is often the first point of attack in the process of acculturation." Makau Mutua, "Proselytism and Cultural Integrity," in Lindholm et al., *Deskbook,* 651,

655–656 ("[C]entral to [Christianity and Islam, both of which assert the absolute and universal truth of their faiths,] is the belief in the racial superiority of the proselytizers; the other is quite often depicted as inferior.").

116. See, e.g., Lawrence v. Texas, 529 U.S. 558 (2003); Perry v. Schwarzenegger, no. 3:09-cv-02292 (ND Cal.); Christian Legal Society v. Martinez, 131 S.Ct. 2971(2010); Schalk and Kopf v. Austria, ECtHR App. no. 18984/02, June 24, 2010 (holding that Article 12 imposes no obligation on governments to grant marriage rights to same-sex couples.); J. M. v. United Kingdom, ECtHR, App. no. 37060/06, September 28, 2010 (finding discrimination on the basis of sexual orientation by authorities who set inequitable child maintenance payments for divorced mother who had formed new same-sex relationship); Alekseyev v. Russia, ECtHR App. nos. 4916/07, 25924/08, and 14599/09, October 21, 2010 ("The Court reiterates that sexual orientation is a concept covered by Article 14... [and] that in the present case [applicants banned from holding gay rights parades] there has been a violation," sections 108, 110).

117. See The Pastor Green Case, Supreme Court of Sweden, Case no. B 1050-05 (November 29, 2005).

118. See, e.g., Stacey v. Campbell, 2002 B.C.H.R.T. 35 (2002) (a pastor was sued under hate crimes law and brought before the British Columbia Human Rights Tribunal for "express[ing] his view of religious teachings concerning homosexuality" in a paid newspaper ad); Islamic Council of Victoria v. Catch the Fire Ministries, VCAT no. A392/2002 (Vict. Civ. Adm. Trib. December 17, 2004) (finding pastor liable for "vilifying" Islam during a religious seminar); Ben El Mahi and Others v. Denmark, ECtHR, App. no. 5853/06, December 11, 2006 (inadmissible) (for Moroccan Muslims' complaints of discrimination by Denmark in permitting publication of offensive caricatures of the Prophet Muhammad, the Court judged that it had "no competence to examine the applicants' substantive complaints under the Articles of the Convention relied upon").

119. Louis D. Brandeis and Samuel D. Warren, "The Right to Privacy" (1890) 4 *Harv. L. Rev.* 193. This article, coauthored by a future U.S. Supreme Court justice, has been heralded as "the most influential law review article" in American history, laying the foundation for what ultimately became the constitutional right to privacy. Harry Kalven Jr., "Privacy in Tort Law—Were Warren and Brandeis Wrong?" (1966) 31 *Law & Contemp. Probs.* 326, 327 (1966), quoted in Benjamin A. Bratman, "Brandeis and Warren's 'The Right to Privacy' and the Birth of the Right to Privacy" (2002) 69 *Tenn. L. Rev.* 623, 623.

120. This phrase was borrowed from Michigan Supreme Court Justice Thomas Cooley's treatise on torts. *Cooley on Torts* (2nd ed., 1888) 229.

121. Griswold v. Connecticut, 381 U.S. 479, 484 (1965).

122. See discussion accompanying notes 50, 51, and 52.

123. On January 11, 2012, the U.S. Supreme Court issued its opinion in the important religious employment case, Hosanna-Tabor Evangelical Lutheran Church and School v. EEOC, 131 S.Ct. 1783 (2012). While the *Hosanna-Tabor* case did not directly raise privacy issues, its 9–0 opinion in favor of the Petitioner religious organization, giving broad scope to the "ministerial exception," will have significant implications for privacy cases as well. "[I]t is impermissible," wrote Chief Justice Roberts for the unanimous Court, "for the government to contradict a church's determination of who can act as its ministers."

124. Joel A. Nichols, "Mission, Evangelism, and Proselytism in Christianity: Mainline Conceptions as Reflected in Church Documents" (1998) 12 *Emory Int'l L. Rev.* 563, 565.

125. 17 EHRR 397 (1994) (App. no. 14307/88, May 25, 1993).

126. Ibid., section 9.

127. In his dissent in *Kokkinakis*, Judge Valticos characterized proselytism as a "rape of the beliefs of others" and asserted that Greek law criminalizing it "cannot in any way be regarded as contrary to Article 9 of the Convention. On the contrary, it is such as to protect individuals' freedom of religious belief."

128. 1977 AIR 908 (January 17, 1977).

129. See, e.g., Minow, "Should Religious Groups Be Exempt from Civil Rights Law?," 839 (arguing that religious groups should be allowed some flexibility to deal with sexual orientation issues).

130. "Millet systems" are legal systems adopted originally by colonial regimes and used currently in various states (e.g., Israel) as a means of preserving indigenous cultures. The religious law of a denomination applies to adherents of that denomination and defines the rules for marriage, divorce, the age of majority, and the like.

131. The websites of the Ahmadiyya Muslim Community of the United States of America, http://www.ahmadiyya.us/, and the Lahore Ahmadiyya Movement, http://ahmadiyya.org/, track difficulties experienced by members of this religious movement.

132. Assassinations of those defending individuals charged with blasphemy in Pakistan may have highlighted this phenomenon and helped to turn the tide against the defamation of religion initiative in the Human Rights Council in March 2011. See UN Resolution A/HRC/16/L.38, introduced by Pakistan, discussed in text accompanying notes 65–67.

133. The thirty-seventh annual conference of the Organisation of the Islamic Conference on May 18, 2010, was held in Tajikistan, the first time a CIS Central Asian country has ever hosted the meeting. A Tajik political scientist opined that Tajikistan has been building an alliance with OIC members in hopes that OIC will become a major investor in the Tajik economy. The OIC has a combined US$5 trillion in economic potential. Rukshona Ibragimova, "Islamic Conference Foreign Ministers Meet in Dushanbe," Central Asia Online, http://centralasiaonline.com/cocoon/caii/xhtml/en_GB/features/caii/features/main/2010/05/18/feature-04.

134. Elizabeth A. Clark, "Liberalism in Decline: Legislative Trends Affecting Religious Freedom in Russia and Central Asia," 22 *Transnational Law & Contemporary Problems* (2013) (forthcoming).

135. Central Committee of the Chinese Communist Party, *The People's Republic of China: Document 19: The Basic Viewpoint on the Religious Question During Our Country's Socialist Period* (March 31, 1982).

136. See note 73.

137. See U.S. State Department International Religious Freedom Report 2009—Saudi Arabia, http://www.state.gov/g/drl/rls/irf/2009/127357.htm.

138. See, e.g., Arch Puddington, "Freedom in the World 2010: Erosion of Freedom Intensifies," Freedom House Report, http://www.freedomhouse.org/template.cfm?page=130&year=2010.

139. Nolan and K. v. Russia, ECtHR, App. no. 2512/04, February 12, 2009, sections 64–66; UN Human Rights Committee, General Comment 22 (48), *supra* note 11, 8.

140. Brian J. Grim and Roger Finke, "Religious Persecution in Cross-National Context: Clashing Civilizations or Regulated Economies?" (2007) 72 *American Sociological Review* (4), 633, 638.

2

Leveraging Legal Protection for Religious Liberty

ANGELA WU HOWARD

Law embodies a worldview. A law or court decision always embeds a certain assertion about how the world works and who we are. In order to engage the people behind the law, it is vital to understand that worldview. And all lawyers eventually confront the realization that judges and lawmakers, with all their specialized education and knowledge, are subject to the same social pressures, cultural assumptions, and personal biases as others. This simple insight helps us grasp the challenges we encounter when trying to leverage legal protection for religious liberty.

Religious freedom law is at its core a narrative of the human person. It hinges on assumptions about who human beings are, where rights come from, what their contours are. Say, for example, one believes that religious liberty is merely a species of tolerance writ large. A judge, legislator, or police chief who merely tolerates can be counted on to make a self-interested judgment in order to keep a temporary truce among constituents, even at the cost of negating the fundamental rights required to make peace enduring. Such decisions, based primarily on short-term contingencies without reference to stronger philosophical principles, lead in the long term to jurisprudential instability (by setting bad precedent in the courts of law) and to weakness in the public discourse (by demeaning public reason). If, on the other hand, one believes religious liberty to flow from something intrinsic to personhood itself, something tied to unchanging truths at the core of who we are, then the same judge, legislator, or police chief is better equipped to make a courageous decision and to defend it—even at risk to his or her reputation or short-term goals.

Using case studies from the United Nations, Indonesia, India, Europe, and Malaysia, the chapter analyzes how positive law interacts in practice with the protection of religious freedom. In particular, it addresses the importance of grounding human rights, including the freedom of religion, in philosophical first principles. Finally, the chapter details some challenges of deploying legal levers to protect religious freedom.

The Leverage and Limits of Legal Analysis

Calling attention to the letter of the law can be a powerful way to reveal the spirit of a society. That is because the letter of the law reaches a level of particularity that other forms of rhetoric typically do not. General discussions of unfairness, injustice, and violations of rights can help elevate sympathy for human injustices. But they also allow power brokers to retort with equally general justifications for the status quo. Legal analysis on the other hand, by focusing on the technical details of the law and their real-life repercussions, can expose hidden agendas or unintended consequences that threaten freedoms at stake.

"Defamation of Religion" at the United Nations

Take the debate over "defamation of religion" at the United Nations. The notion of "defamation of religion" was first introduced to the United Nation's Commission on Human Rights in 1999 by Pakistan on behalf of the Organisation of the Islamic Conference (OIC) under the agenda item on racism. In its original form, the draft resolution was introduced with the title "Defamation of Islam."

According to the statements made by Pakistan as it presented the draft resolution, it wanted the Commission to stand up against what the OIC felt was a campaign to defame Islam. The OIC argued that such a campaign was inciting manifestations of intolerance toward Muslims similar to anti-Semitic violence in Europe preceding World War II. The impetus for a resolution combating the "defamation of religion" was reinvigorated after the September 11, 2001, terrorist attacks, when many Muslims experienced a social backlash against their faith. The murder of the Dutch anti-immigration film director Theo van Gogh, the 2005 publication of twelve cartoons parodying the Prophet Mohammad in the Danish newspaper *Jyllands-Posten* and subsequent mob attacks on European embassies in Islamic countries, and Geert Wilders's 2008 production of the Dutch film *Fitna*, which depicted Islam as violent and hateful, only intensified this debate.

Critics argued that the resolution was unbalanced in its sole focus on Islam and that the concept of "defamation of religion" was primarily aimed at stifling legitimate debate about Islam. Governments that had long traditions of liberal free speech laws, including the United States and the European Union, consistently opposed the resolution. However, every year that it was raised, the resolution passed by a landslide—until 2006, when lawyers began pointing out specific *legal* problems with the resolution.[1]

Armed with a detailed legal review, civil society groups changed the terms of the debate. UN member states tend to vote in regional blocs, such as the OIC, the Grupo de Estados Miembros de América Latina y el Caribe, and the Western Europe and Others Group. However, the OIC bloc did not have enough votes to pass the resolutions by themselves. What other countries were supporting the OIC's resolutions, and why?

There were, of course, some politics at play. Voting at the UN on any resolution is a horse-trading game, and in addition to a resolution's merits, there are geopolitics, international trade, and diplomatic favors involved. But the Becket Fund for Religious Liberty, a public interest law firm, conducted a voting analysis of the previous years' resolution and saw that some of the yes votes for the resolution made less sense than others. For example, several Latin American countries had generally strong records of free speech laws and usually voted with the United States and Europe on other, similar matters, but were voting in favor of the "defamation of religion" resolution. When the Becket Fund consulted with non-OIC governments about why they were voting in favor of the resolution, we discovered many of the foreign ministers, ambassadors, and UN functionaries could say little more than that "defamation of religion" sounded like a bad thing. But once they delved deeper into a legal analysis, they recognized the problems of the "defamation of religion" approach.[2]

Legal advocates pointed out that the measures contradicted the foundations of human rights law in two ways: one, they protected religions and ideas instead of religious believers or the people who hold the ideas; and two, they further empowered states rather than individuals and dissenting communities. In application, the "defamation of religion" measures failed to remedy the sociological problems of intimidation, mistreatment, and abuse of vulnerable religious minorities that the measures purported to redress. Laws corresponding to "defamation of religion" achieved nothing that existing laws against assault, blackmail, defamation against persons, and incitement to violence couldn't achieve—except to stifle peaceful dissent and speech.

Indeed, the word *defamation* was shown to be a misnomer. Normal defamation laws are meant to protect individuals from public slander or libel that would negatively affect their livelihoods, or inhibit someone from harming another with mistruths. These laws are closely aligned with the rights of persons, not the rights of states. In this manner, the traditional defense in a defamation lawsuit is the truth: the defendant accused of defamation would demur by arguing that the statement he made (e.g., that a person had an affair or that he defrauded his business partner) was factually true and thus, though harmful to that person's reputation, was nonetheless nonactionable. But "defamation of religion" measures do not protect the right of persons to make factually true statements. Rather, they protect beliefs, ideas, and philosophies. This sort of scheme denies the fact that different religions present conflicting truth claims. (Indeed one important feature of religious freedom is to protect the ability of persons to explore varying truth claims.) The defense of truth in a "defamation of religion" suit is then subject to whatever ideas, worldviews, or religious beliefs the judging authority holds to be true. "Defamation of religion" measures are thus distinct from traditional defamation laws because they do not protect persons, good faith speech, or dissent. "Defamation of religion" requires the state to determine which ideas are acceptable, as opposed to which facts are true. A fundamental rule of law problem presents itself in the notion of "defamation of religion", inasmuch as belief cannot be empirically proven true.[3]

Pakistan's Penal Code 295, for example, states that defiling Islam or its prophets deserves the death penalty; defiling, damaging, or desecrating the Qur'an will be punished with life imprisonment; and insulting another's religious feelings can be punished with ten years of prison. Although such laws may be premised on the idea of protecting the image and reputation of Islam, in actuality such laws "are often used to intimidate reform-minded Muslims, sectarian opponents, and religious minorities, or to settle personal scores."[4] In the process they severely hinder the quest for religious truth.

Further, enforcement of "defamation of religion" measures, including antiblasphemy and antivilification laws, is typically left to the unbridled discretion of local officials who are free to act on their own prejudices, usually to the detriment of minorities and dissenters. In Iran an academic and member of the pro-reform Mojahedin of the Islamic Revolution was sentenced to death for calling for the reformation of religion to discourage people from "blindly following" religious leaders. In Egypt a professor at Cairo University was declared an apostate for teaching his students to read certain parts of the Qur'an metaphorically. In other instances antiblasphemy laws punish mere trivialities. In November 2007 a Sudanese court sentenced a British teacher to fifteen days in jail for "insulting religion" when her class named a teddy bear Mohammed, after a popular student who was also named Mohammed. The teacher was pardoned and deported the following month after intense diplomatic pressure.

Rather than providing protection for vulnerable religious minorities, as the OIC had argued they would, "defamation of religion" measures end up empowering majorities against dissenters and the state against individuals. Protecting "bad" speech—peacefully expressed—is a safeguard for protecting all "good" speech. But once the state is empowered to restrict expression in one sphere on vague grounds, the door is opened to even more oppressive restrictions.

Merely presenting this kind of detailed legal critique of "defamation of religion" began to swing votes. In 2007, less than a year after legal advocates started submitting their analyses, yes votes in Geneva were outweighed by no and abstention votes for the first time since 1999. The vote at the General Assembly in New York, where the resolution had been proposed since 2005, also began to turn in the other direction, going from a one-time high of 111 yes votes in 2006 to 86 yes votes in 2008. The trend against the resolution continued until 2011, when the resolution's language shifted from protecting beliefs to protection of believers.[5] This is a prime example of how legal analysis revealed a state of affairs that had previously been obfuscated by general discussions about defamation and religion.

Anticonversion Laws in India

At the national level, legal analysis has illuminated a complex discourse in India, where a major challenge to religious freedom is state-level anticonversion laws.[6] Such state laws were established at different times but are very similar in their content. While there are a few variations in wording, the anticonversion laws all seek to prevent conversions "carried out" by "forcible" or "fraudulent" means or by "allurement" or "inducement." Such words tend to engender sympathy for these laws; few people like the idea of force, fraud, or coercion, and most think the law should protect people from such things. Proponents of anticonversion laws justify them by citing the use of violent or coercive tactics in conversion attempts.

The application of legal analysis, however, exposes why, in practice as well as in principle, anticonversion laws of this sort produce more problems than they solve. Applying similar arguments that attain with the defamation of religion resolutions, we can see that there are already laws in force against assault, false imprisonment, blackmail, defamation, and fraud. The anticonversion laws target only ideas being preached or otherwise persuasively shared, not the forced imposition of religion. This raises the question of what the laws are actually trying to achieve.

If it can be shown that a law as written is based on faulty sociological assumptions or that it does not achieve the goals its proponents claim, then it is possible to achieve one of two things: reveal the lawmaker's true motives or encourage lawmakers to recognize the disconnect between the means they are using and the ends they truly hope to achieve.[7] Either way, the conflict at the heart of the debate is revealed.

A legal textual reading of the Orissa anticonversion law of 1967, on which all the other state laws are based, also helps clarify what the impact of these laws really is. The law reads, "No person *shall convert* or *attempt to convert*, either directly or otherwise, any person from one religious faith to another by the use of force or by inducement or by any fraudulent means nor shall any person abet any such conversion."[8]

First, note the implicit understanding of conversion. Many of the arguments in favor of anticonversion laws suppose that conversion is a physical act that one person can visit upon another. The anticonversion law assumes that the act of conversion is a *transitive* action that occurs when one person causes another person to switch from one religion to another in an instant.

This is in contrast to the experience of conversion either as a primarily internal, individual transformation of the heart, conscience, and belief system and/ or is something that takes place over time through actions (such as prayer, study of scripture, sacraments, fellowship with other believers, or attending religious services) that may transform the person over a period of time. Anticonversion laws act primarily as barriers to these *manifestations* of religious belief, including rites of conversion such as baptism, or other outward expressions of a person's newly chosen faith. (Thus some anticonversion laws in India also require converts to register and obtain permission for conversion.)

The Orissa law primarily affects people who might influence the convert instead of the convert himself. It does so in a sweeping manner. The law's prohibitions on conversion "directly *or otherwise*" and on any person who would "*abet any such conversion*" encompass a broad range of actions and impose a virtually indiscernible standard by which people must avoid words and actions that might lead to a conversion. On its face, the standard created violates a general principle of law: that a law should not be overly broad or vague, that it must have enough specificity to be obeyed.

Force is defined as "a show of force or threat for injury of any kind including *threat of divine displeasure or social excommunication*." In this definition the inclusion of the "threat of divine displeasure" is not only vague but also prohibits the transmission of many core religious teachings which lawmakers may or may not originally have envisioned restricting. Virtually all religions, including Hinduism, Buddhism, Christianity, Islam, and Judaism, appeal to the character of a higher divinity that judges people's acts and omissions. Like the "defamation of religion" resolution, the anticonversion law's overbreadth and vagueness could be read to outlaw truth claims.

Inducement in the Orissa law is defined as "the offer of any gift or gratification, either in cash or in kind, and shall also include the grant of any benefit, either pecuniary or otherwise." Under this definition, fulfilling religious obligations toward the poor, or simple acts of kindness toward someone of another faith, can be considered violations of the laws. This definition of inducement in effect criminalizes the philanthropic or charitable activity of many religious groups.

All of these things are evident from a simple textual analysis, on paper alone. But here is the real point: behind all the terminology and definitions lies a story—or many stories. There is the story of colonialism and lingering perceptions of Christianity and Christians as a foreign import. There is the story of the struggle to form a cohesive national identity in one of the most religiously diverse countries in the world, and of the rise of Hindu nationalism in the decades surrounding the passing of the anticonversion laws. There is the story of the poorest parts of a developing country in which many of the schools and hospitals that grant a benefit, "pecuniary or otherwise," are Catholic. There is the story of mass conversions of lower castes to Buddhism, Christianity, Islam, or another faith that promises more equality and dignity than the old order. There is the story of missionaries destroying idols, calling the old gods "devils," in language meant to provoke. There is the story of converts renouncing their long-prescribed role in an economic landscape that depends on the lowest paid workers. There is the story of caste discrimination that crosses religious boundaries, and of the Hindus who object to the characterization that caste is inherent in the Hindu faith.

These stories all have varying degrees of accuracy. But they all play into the public discourse, the national psyche, the worldview of lawmakers, police, and judges and that complex background represents some of the contemporary challenges of leveraging legal protection for religious liberty.

Indonesian Blasphemy Act

The power of worldviews is illustrated in court as well as in diplomacy. One way to view a trial is as a conversation between the prosecutor, defense, and judge. This kind of conversation was on display in the Indonesian Constitutional Court during a landmark challenge to the national blasphemy law in 2010.

The Indonesian Blasphemy Act imposes up to five years' imprisonment for the practice of religions that "deviate from" state-sanctioned religions. Like all laws, this one has several stories. It was first enacted in 1965 as part of an effort to root out communism and unify Indonesia. Since its enactment, the Blasphemy Act has been invoked against Muslims, Christians, indigenous Javanese, atheists, and others whose beliefs do not fall neatly into acceptable religious beliefs as interpreted by the Indonesian government.

Over the course of several weeks' trial, the Constitutional Court judges heard testimony from a series of expert witnesses. Defenders argued that the blasphemy law was necessary to maintain theological purity among Muslims by guarding them against heresies. They argued that national unity and public order required that people not be permitted to say things that would divide the public opinion or offend others, as acts of blasphemy led to reprisals of violence and rioting in protest against the alleged blasphemer.

On the other side, challengers argued that the Blasphemy Act was detrimental to genuine theological discourse. They argued that the "public order" limitations on freedom of expression were narrow and should not be read to prohibit sincere and peaceful speech, even if it is upsetting to others. They presented constitutional analyses of provisions on freedom of religion, freedom of speech, and freedom of association. They presented arguments regarding Indonesia's duties under international human rights instruments. Challengers also argued that the Blasphemy Act was disproportional to its aim and presented evidence on its unintended consequences. For example, the law had been invoked to imprison Muslims accused of whistling during prayers or reciting Qur'anic verse in a native tongue instead of in Arabic.

In the end the Court ruled in favor of the Blasphemy Act. The Court's decision stated that unchecked "religious freedom" would result in so much heresy that it would deteriorate Indonesia's high regard for religious faith and the orthodox beliefs of its Muslim population. They pointed to Europe and America as examples of societies that Indonesia did not want to emulate in their essentially "secular" characters. During proceedings there had been particular confusion over whether or not religion could be taught in American state-run schools without violating what they thought of as America's system of "strict separation between church and state." Although teaching about religion in state-run schools in America is perfectly constitutional, in its final decision the Court mentioned the lack of religious instruction in these schools as influential in its reasoning. In Europe, nondevotional religious instruction in government schools is quite common, but in the Indonesian context, the sui generis American situation came to represent the "secular West," even though religion generally plays a larger role in the American public discourse than in Europe.

The judges of the Indonesian Constitutional Court had a worldview, a narrative of what other countries are like, what Indonesian society should be, and what role the state should play in the spiritual formation of its citizens. Personally vested in the kind of society that Indonesia should be, the judges understood America and other countries that actively promote religious freedom to be societies in which religious faith is not welcome in the public square. They shared the defending lawyers' belief that Indonesia was a Muslim country, though not an Islamic state, and could not be treated like other, "secular" countries. They believed that human beings need strong guidance about their beliefs and that clerics chosen by the government could best serve that role. The judges were also influenced by the practical reality that in Indonesia, large public protests and violent riots had become common and, in some cases, difficult for local law enforcement to quell. The easiest path to social peace seemed to be to prevent the rioters from being upset in the first place.

The Indonesian lawyers challenging the law knew that their case was an uphill battle. Public opinion, particularly of orthodox Muslim leaders, was strongly in favor of the law. What came as a surprise to the lawyers was how fixed the judges' narrative turned out to be. In the middle of the trial, the lawyers themselves were seeking answers to questions about public policy in America. In an effort to persuade the Court to adhere to a prevailing international norm favoring religious freedom, they presented evidence on religious freedom in other countries. But they had not anticipated how reluctant the Court would be to emulate the practices of societies and countries that they regarded as being not religious enough, or antireligious, regardless of whether the principles espoused regarding religious freedom were themselves good.

In the end the Indonesian lawyers felt that the strongest arguments against the blasphemy law—that the law would place the state in the position of theologian with police power, therefore having a chilling effect on sincere public discourse over religion, and invariably being used against the minority and dissenting voices that most need state protection—had not really been explored by the Court. Rather the proceedings had been dominated by discussions over whether Indonesia wanted to be like other countries that it deemed insufficiently religious. The worldviews and narratives of actors consequently obscured a more serious inquiry into the actual impact of the antiblasphemy law on Indonesian society.

Anticonversion and Interreligious Violence in Orissa, India

Narratives that obfuscate can lead to catastrophic results. I was in India in 2008 when violence broke out in Orissa, the state that passed India's first anticonversion law, and what happened subsequently was a lesson in why first principles are so important. The narratives surrounding the violence, which continued for almost six weeks, operated to reinforce the very forces that produced the violence.

A venerated Hindu swami who was active in campaigns against cow slaughter and conversions to Christianity had been gunned down. Local police blamed the extreme Maoist Naxalite movement active in the area, citing death threat notes the Naxalites had sent to the swami and the style of the execution. But some leaders in the Hindu nationalist movement blamed Christians, who had confronted the swami before; they announced their certainty on national television. Within days clashes broke out as mobs attacked Christian streets and villages. Over the course of six weeks, thousands of Christian homes and churches were burned, fifty thousand people were displaced, and over sixty Christians and a Hindu teacher who worked at a Christian missionary school had been burned alive or hacked to death.

The issue of conversion had been a primary one in Orissa politics. The swami and other Hindu nationalists had campaigned against what they said were mass and aggressive conversions of Orissa's Hindus to Christianity, and the issue had become a platform in local elections. But when I visited Orissa's hardest-hit district, Kandhamal, it was difficult to find any Christians who were recently converted or whose families had not already been Christian for many generations. Nevertheless the prevailing rhetoric surrounding the violence in Orissa was about the contemporary threat of conversions. After the violence subsided, the governor of Orissa emerged with a five-point plan to prevent future incidents of communal violence. None of them included public education to teach that violence is an inappropriate response to conversion or aggressive prosecutions of those who had perpetrated the violence. One of the five points was to enforce existing anticonversion laws, presumably in an effort to appease the Hindu nationalists. The "solution" of enforcing anticonversion laws in order to quiet religious violence left intact the trope that *conversion* rather than *violence* was the real problem in Orissa. The conversion narrative had easily obscured the duty of the state to protect its citizens from violence regardless of the motivation for the violence.

Another common, if contradictory, narrative that I heard was that the violence was not in fact about religion at all. Orissa is India's second poorest state, and Kandhamal its poorest region. Tribal rivalries, sometimes over public benefits, had a long and complex history, and unemployment was widespread. Many said the violence was tribe against tribe, Pano against Kandh; the Panos happened to be primarily Christian, and the Kandha were primarily Hindu. Most of the hospitals and schools were run by Catholic missionaries, and people discussed how the missions had primarily benefited Christian Panos. What at first looked like religiously motivated violence might instead have been tribal rivalries arising from a complex system of caste and tribe-based economic benefits.

However, interviews revealed that when the mobs approached the villages, witnesses uniformly reported that they were chanting slogans against Christians or seeking Christian pastors, not targeting or seeking Panos. Interviews also revealed that some Kandha were Christian, and the mobs were not distinguishing between Kandh and Pano when attacking homes identified as Christian. Christians were compelled, on point of death, to renounce their faith and embrace Hinduism during and after attacks,[9] undermining the narrative that the real problem was tribal and unrelated to religion.

To be sure, religion does act as a proxy for other tensions, and religious identity can serve as a group signifier based on ethnicity, tribal affiliation, or socioeconomic class. However, this can become an excuse for officials to dismiss religious freedom violations. Moreover even if the initial motivation for persecution is not primarily religious, it implicates religious freedom when houses of worship and religious communities become targets. It was impossible to discuss the violence in Orissa and recourse for its victims without confronting each of these collateral narratives. First principles have room to present themselves for debate much more productively once narratives are sifted through for clarity and distractions eliminated.

First Principles and Postural Errors

Two propositions lie at the heart of modern human rights law: first, that all human beings have inherent dignity that should be respected regardless of their life situation, and second, that they should have protection from the fickle will of the state. Like other human rights, religious freedom necessarily implicates the action or inaction of the state. But states often commit what I term "postural errors," which inevitably undercut religious freedom. Below I outline four of these errors.

Deciding Religious Doctrine

The state necessarily mediates between competing interests of its citizens and competing claims of the common good. It can create a safe space in which all of its citizens, religious or not, can participate in a vibrant public discourse. But there is one role it is not as well equipped to play: that of the enforcing theologian. Almost all religious freedom conflicts can be resolved in processes that do not involve the state's pronouncing on or enforcing a) theological truths (whether Jesus was divine or merely human, whether Mohammed was the last prophet of God, whether Buddha was a god, and attendant consequences); b) certain religious matters internal to particular religious communities (whether Hindu temples should be governed by vote or appointment); or c) religious doctrines (whether Jews should keep kosher, whether Muslim women must wear headscarves, whether it is necessary for Sikhs to carry the kirpan). The modern state is better equipped to protect the ability of religious communities and individuals to govern themselves according to their own religious beliefs—and safely interact with others according to their conscience. As the work of my co-contributor Brian Grim illustrates, violations and religious strife tend to flow from states arrogating to themselves theological roles.

This is not to say that it is incompatible for a state both to be inspired by theological truths and to respect religious freedom. Laws concerning, for example, the different degrees of murder, if they are to go beyond the purely utilitarian, might be further illuminated, understood, refined, and supported in the general population by religious defenses of the sanctity of human life. Laws on religious freedom are best understood, though need not be solely understood, with an understanding of the need for a repository of man's conscience, and even his freedom to violate his own conscience, in the course of an exploratory, truth-seeking life. Positive law can benefit from religious explorations of the nature of man's conscience, judgment, understanding, responsibility, and practical reason. As well, to suggest that the state's primary role is not as enforcing theologian does not mean that states need never engage with religious affairs, as though religion is an incomprehensible realm that lawmakers must never have anything to do with. A properly formed law responds to the reasons for the law itself – we want laws to be successful in bringing about the state of affairs the legislature envisaged; to this end, lawmakers must accurately understand the world which the law is regulating, and a religious belief or practice might substantially shape that world. The state's accurate knowledge and understanding of religious matters, of religious believers' motivations, and of the circumstances of their lives may, in some circumstances, be essential to really insuring the freedom of religious believers.

Such philosophical principles of good lawmaking are to be distinguished from those of a state that enforces particular religious doctrines. Instead of seeking to answer theological questions, the state's responsibility in enacting laws concerning religious freedom is best understood as a responsibility to create and protect the possibility for its citizens peacefully to debate and possibly vehemently to disagree over those questions.

Communitarian Values versus Individual Rights

States also sometimes attempt to justify religious freedom violations by pitting communitarian values against individual rights. State authorities sometimes argue that individuals may not violate the will of their communities or that the individual owes a duty to the community as a whole. The communitarian values that states champion might be theocratic (those of a state religion), secular (those resulting from state neutrality that brooks no public expression of religion), or theological (those represented by a state preference for one religious viewpoint or community over others).

But the dichotomy between communitarian values and individual values is a false one. Individuals are indeed shaped by their communities, and religion does indeed have social dimensions requiring public and associational expression. However, this does not negate an individual's conscience, nor does it imply that an individual claim will *always* trump an apparently competing public interest. The consideration of public interest and a claim of competing individual conscience is a complex task that includes considerations of the common good, practicability, and human dignity. It deserves more than a swift dismissal of either based on the existence of the other.

The Exception of Public Order

Some states use a claim to public order to negate religious freedom rights entirely. Authorities often claim to be balancing religious freedom against state interests such as public order. But when treated as a trump, the interest in public order can swallow up the freedom itself.

The Human Rights Committee, a body of independent experts tasked by the United Nations to monitor implementation of the International Covenant on Civil and Political Rights (ICCPR),[10] the UN's primary civil rights treaty, is empowered to hear individual and interstate complaints alleging violations of the ICCPR. It stipulates that permissible state restrictions of these freedoms must be very narrowly tailored, such that "when a State party imposes certain restrictions on the exercise of freedom of expression, *these may not put in jeopardy the right itself.*"[11]

Though pragmatic concerns play a part in good governance, public order does not mean a state has carte blanche to override fundamental freedoms. It is a limited *exception* to the space that fundamental freedoms occupy, not the *rule* through which a freedom derives its roots.

State Sovereignty

A fourth defensive argument put forth by states is that advocacy for international religious freedom should be bound by state sovereignty. For example, in 2005 a U.S. appellate court affirmed the deportation of a Chinese man who had applied for asylum in the United States after being arrested in China, beaten, and charged with the crime of holding unregistered church services. The United States Court of Appeal for the Fifth Circuit stated that China was within its rights to regulate religion and that the applicant had been punished for breaking the law in his country rather than persecuted on the basis of his religious beliefs.[12] The ruling evinced a fundamental miscomprehension of religious freedom rooted in the inherent dignity of the applicant, not in the whims of the state, and a mistaken belief that "rule of law" is a sufficient value, on its own and as a mere procedural formality, to overcome any violations of an asylum seeker's conscience or fundamental rights.

The principle of state sovereignty has its place in international law. Certainly a ruling in one country might not attain in another jurisdiction. And for the most part there are no effective enforcement mechanisms for international religious freedom law rulings. However, claims of sovereignty are an unsatisfactory shield for bad state actions.

Challenges of Advocacy in the Field

In this section I briefly outline some practical challenges to advocacy in the field. In traditional common law litigation, the precedential nature of a court decision ensures that a change in the law ripples far beyond one case. This is a double-edged sword. It means any one case can set a good precedent, but it can also set a poor one. While it is always the right time to advocate for victims of torture or unjust imprisonment, in hindsight cases should not have been brought to court when they were, even though the cause was just, as they were likely to set bad precedents.

In the case of the constitutional challenge to the Indonesian blasphemy law, although the lawyers bringing the challenge were well prepared with knowledge of Indonesian constitutional law and the principles of religious freedom, they were ill-equipped to deal with the political climate that dictated the court's interests. An insurmountable array of players in the Muslim-majority country was lined up in opposition. Many judges of the Constitutional Court had publicly declared their support for the law before they were even assigned to the case. Every major Muslim group, as well as the state's ministries of religious affairs, internal affairs, and human rights, had all expressed strong support for the blasphemy law.

Similarly, cases at the European Court of Human Rights challenging bans on the Muslim headscarf in certain public venues in France and Turkey failed one after another. These cases involved a complex dialogue, a debate that pitted a strict secularist vision of the state against an individual whose religious conscience dictated visible religious clothing that is displeasing to the state. Invariably, as plaintiff after plaintiff petitioned the Court to declare that her religious freedom was violated by an impermissible state ideology, it was the individual who lost to the state ideology of *laïcité*.[13] The Court sidestepped the question of the impact on the individual by focusing on the right of states to determine their own political characters.

There is one case in the European Court of Human Rights that stands as an exception to the string of losses and demonstrates the value of strategic litigation positioning even in the wrong political climate. That is the case of Merve Kavakçı, an elected Muslim member of the Turkish Parliament who was physically removed from Parliament for wearing her headscarf.[14] She brought her case to the Court, but in addition to pressing her case on religious freedom grounds, she also argued that Turkey's actions in forbidding her to take her seat in Parliament violated the people's right to vote. The Court's decision assiduously avoided the question of Kavakçı's religious freedom. Instead it ruled in her favor, but only on her "right to vote" claim. This was hardly a vindication of Kavakçı's freedom of religion. But the case did reveal an unresolved tension: the Court was in the uncomfortable position of both refusing to say that Kavakçı's rights had been violated but also admitting that Turkey's action with regard to Kavakçı was wrong. In the end, it was a strategic decision that had not been at the heart of Kavakçı's grievance—the application under the right to vote—that exerted pressure on the Court that it was unable to escape. The Court's failure to vindicate her religious freedom claims nevertheless revealed an uncomfortable tension in its jurisprudence.

In countries with developing legal systems, a nuts-and-bolts problem that is a particular plague is undertrained and overburdened advocates.[15] The religious groups most in need of representation are usually also the most vulnerable and marginalized, with the least economic or educational resources. They often lack a local pool of skilled advocates who can provide reliable fact-finding. Not only do good facts build the skeleton of a strong case, but the way they are stated and shaped can present either a compelling or a discrediting story that isolates why a policy, interpretation of the law, or popular support for the law should or should not stand.

Advocates in international religious freedom need to understand the local context, and that requires costly investment on the ground, often going to remote, difficult-to-reach places. Human rights officers stationed at embassies abroad do not always manage to reach those places and must sometimes rely on the accurate reporting of private parties for their information.

There is a desperate need for training of local leaders to provide the documentation legal advocates need. For example, sworn witness declarations, or affidavits, are extremely difficult to obtain. It is often necessary when working with local counsel to go back to basics. The basic elements of an affidavit include an avowal of who the person making the statement is (name and some identifying information, such as birth date—details that confirm to the reader the statement giver is a real individual), how the person came to have the knowledge he or she did (a statement that the person was an eyewitness and on the scene at the time of an incident), and a dated signature. These elements are entirely missing in many of the declarations that we receive. It is a painstaking process to return to victims and local advocates and request more details, especially when every piece of information obtained requires time, resources, and sometimes personal risk.

There are some situations where the law bar of a country is extremely well-developed, and aside from contributing international attention to a case, there is little a foreign lawyer can contribute in terms of strategy or knowledge. However, in countries with less developed legal systems, one of the most strategic investments religious freedom lawyers can make is to train other advocates.

Conclusion

This chapter's survey of the status and challenges of legal advocacy for international religious freedom suggests the follow lessons:

1. Religious freedom must be grounded in first principles, especially in the acknowledgment of the inherent dignity of the human person.
2. Laws embody a worldview of their own. The letter of the law can explain a legislator's view of the nature of conversion; the reasoning of a court decision can reveal a judge's priorities; a constitution can show what role lawmakers believe states should have in controlling theology.

3. Legal analysis achieves a level of particularity that general rhetoric cannot. Uncovering how a law fails to achieve its purpose, or that it is overly broad such that it suppresses peaceful dissent, can focus discussions in a manner that talking about injustice generally cannot.

4. The wrong narratives can obscure real issues, distracting the legal advocate from pressing critical points, and, when adopted by states, undermining the ability to govern well.

5. When deciding whether to bring a case, consider its precedential value. Some cases may not succeed despite the soundness of its arguments; the political climate can determine the outcome of court cases, whatever the legal merits.

6. Religious freedom advocacy needs, but often lacks, the necessary local resources, and often the most vulnerable communities are the ones with the least capital.

One particular case brings many of these lessons together.

In 1998 a young woman born into an ethnic Malay family fell in love, got engaged, and went to the national marriage registry to obtain a marriage license. Based on the ethnic origins of her name, the civil servants there presumed her faith was Muslim, and on that presumption said that they could not issue a marriage license, as by law, Muslims could not be married through the civil registry. She sued for discrimination under the federal constitution of Malaysia, which provides that "every person has the right to profess and practice his religion." She lost.

The woman is named Lina Joy, and in 2006 she made international headlines when she took her case up to the nation's highest court, asking Malaysia's civil government to recognize her conversion from Islam to Christianity.

Ethnic Malays in Malaysia have traditionally been Muslim, and the 1976 Law Reform Act mandates that Muslim marriages are subject to sharia law. Despite her protestations that she was a Catholic and had been for many years, the civil marriage registry pointed to her Malay name and insisted that it had no authority to issue her a marriage license. She then changed her name from Azlina binti Jailani to Lina Joy through the National Registration Department because, she said, God had given her much joy. With her new, non-Malay name, Lina Joy approached the civil marriage registry again—but by then the national identity card regulations had changed so that her identity card now stated that she was a Muslim despite her affirmative declaration that she was a Christian. The registration department refused her application to have the statement removed, and instead suggested that she obtain an order from the sharia court stating that she had become an apostate. But the only ethnic Malays who had applied to sharia courts for such statements in Malaysia had been denied, and some had been sentenced to sharia "rehabilitation camps."

Without other options, Lina Joy filed suit in civil court. She was optimistic. Malaysia's federal constitution provides equal protection and freedom of religion for all citizens. There were also federal provisions for sharia governance in enumerated areas of the law, mostly in "personal" matters such as marriage, divorce, and inheritance, but even there sharia applied only to Muslims, and Lina Joy was not a Muslim. Surely the civil law would apply to her.

The trial court dismissed her application, arguing that ethnic Malays are constitutionally defined as Muslim, thereby making conversion from Islam illegal. The judge also reasoned that allowing an exemption would encourage future converts. The court of appeals subsequently wrote that allowing Lina Joy's conversion would "consequently be inviting the censure of the Muslim community." Ignoring her years of Catholic study, church attendance, and the baptism certificate she presented as proof of her sincerity, Chief Justice Ahmad Fairuz Sheikh Abdul Halim said in his decision, "You can't at whim and fancy convert from one religion to another." What he meant was that Lina Joy could not convert without the approval of her community.

Judge Richard Malanjum, the only non-Muslim among the three judges, dissented, arguing that because the National Registration Department had required special approval only for Muslims, it violated the equal treatment provision in Article 8 of the Federal Constitution. In its perverse way the ruling against Lina Joy was discriminatory only against those born into Islam. By then Lina Joy had waited ten years to hear the Malaysian government tell her that it knew what she believed in, or ought to believe in, better than she did.

A powerful narrative led Lina Joy into this legal quagmire. It involved political parties that leveraged religious demographics against one another; it involved a hybrid legal system that sought to satisfy the demands of both civil and religious law; it was born of postcolonial rhetoric about Christianity being foreign to Malays; and most of all, it involved very human judges who did not view conversion as something an individual could undertake without communal approval and who felt pressure from the large crowds gathered in the courthouse every day of the proceedings, chanting slogans against Lina Joy's case.

Lina Joy's story raises crucial questions that often arise in religious freedom cases. Should the state decide whether Islam permits conversion? Should that decision, whoever makes it, be accorded the police power to back it up? What pragmatic influence should be accorded the potential of public rioting in reaction to the decision? Should communitarian values trump an individual conscience?

Little did Lina Joy know that her cause would uncover a profound tension in Malaysia law. But it did. The dual nature of the Malaysian court system means that whomever the state regards as Muslims are subject to sharia law and required to study Islam, marry within their faith, and raise their children as Muslims. This has led in one case to one man, married to a Hindu woman, attempting to gain custody of his children by secretly converting to Islam and shifting the forum for their divorce proceedings to the sharia court, where non-Muslims such as his wife have limited legal personality.

The real battle in Malaysia is not between sharia and civil courts. It is between those who believe that religion is something transitive that can be imposed by one person onto another, and those who believe that the wellspring of religious experience is the conscience, the interior mind and soul of a person, imprinted by God—even as religion has external, communal expression and inspiration. It is the narrative of the human being—whether he has an inherent dignity, a conscience to be respected by the state—that is at play.

After death threats, Lina Joy fled her country in order to live peacefully according to her conscience. But there are many countries in which conversion brings not only government-backed social censure, as in Lina Joy's case, but also sentences of death, and where the pursuit of conscience brings not just onerous regulations but imprisonment and torture. As dispassionate as legal analysis must be at times, behind each case is a human face, a story in which the personal has reluctantly become political, and the consequences can be severe. There is one narrative that should compel above all others: a passion for what is just, what is right, and what is true, irrespective of national, cultural, and geographic boundaries. This is the vision of the human person as having an inviolable dignity that should be protected, no matter her beliefs and however unpopular her views.

Notes

1. See, e.g., Becket Fund for Religious Liberty, *Statement at the Second Regular Session of the UN Human Rights Council*, October 4, 2006; Becket Fund for Religious Liberty, *Intervention at the Fourth Regular Session of the UN Human Rights Council*, March 27, 2007.
2. Some countries had given the resolution more thought, but not necessarily in a more heartening way. At one meeting with the Becket Fund, a diplomat from a South Asian country argued that the "purpose of the human rights system is to protect state sovereignty." We will revisit this trope later.
3. In a court case brought in Victoria, Australia by Muslims attempting to enforce an antivilification law very similar to "defamation of religion" measures, the plaintiffs argued that "truth is not a defense" when the defendant, a Pakistani Christian pastor, attempted to read from the Qur'an during his court testimony to show that his statements regarding Islam were Qur'anic.
4. U.S. Department of State, International Religious Freedom Report 2006, "Pakistan."
5. The UN Human Rights Committee subsequently released General Comment 34, which judged that prohibitions on expression related to religion could not "prevent or punish criticism of religious leaders or commentary on religious doctrine and tenets of faith."
6. At the national level, although the plain text of the Indian Constitution protects noncoercive proselytism, the Supreme Court of India has held that the right to propagate religion does not include the right to "convert" another person to one's religion because this violates that convert's freedom of conscience. The landmark 1977 case of the *Rev. Stanislaus v. State of Madhya Pradesh* established that the right to propagate permits only the transmission of religion by the exposition of its tenets, presumably excluding any apologetical or persuasive religious speech. See Rev. Stanislaus v. State of Madhya Pradesh, AIR 1977 SC 908 (1977).

7. Returning to the "defamation of religion" case study, the OIC promotes the "defamation of religion" concept as a defense against anti-Muslim bigotry, but within the OIC states, blasphemy laws (while disproportionately harsh on religious minorities) are brought mostly against professing Muslims. Much of the persecution and prosecution has resulted from state action against the expression of religious minorities and dissenters who promote viewpoints that are often considered offensive to the local majority religious populations rather than from "defamation of religion."

8. Orissa Freedom of Religion Act, No. 21, art. 3 (1967) (emphasis added).

9. See Vijay Simha, "In the Name of God," *Tehelka*, September 13, 2008, http://www.tehelka .com/story_main40.asp?filename=Ne130908CoverStory.asp; Somini Sengupta, "Hindu Threat to Christians: Convert or Flee," *New York Times*, October 13, 2008, http://www.nytimes. com/2008/10/13/world/asia/13india.html?pagewanted=1&_r=2&sq=orissa&st=cse&scp=1.

10. See ICCPR, G.A. Res. 2200A (XXI), 21 U.N. GAOR Supp. (No. 16) at 52, U.N. Doc. A/6316 (1966), 999 U.N.T.S. 171, *entered into force* March 23, 1976.

11. See UN High Comm'r for Human Rights, HRC, *General Comment No. 10: Freedom of expression (Art. 19)*, (June 26, 1983) [*General Comment* 10]; UN High Comm'r for Human Rights, HRC, *General Comment No. 11: Prohibition of propaganda for war and inciting national, racial or religious hatred (Art. 20)*, (July 29, 1983); UN High Comm'r for Human Rights, HRC., *General Comment No. 22: The right to freedom of thought, conscience and religion (Art. 18)*, CCPR/C/21/ Rev.1/Add.4 (July 30, 1993). Emphasis added on General Comment 10.

12. Xiaodong Li v. Gonzales, 420 F.3d 500 (5th Cir. 2005). The Fifth Circuit eventually vacated its own judgment after the Department of Homeland Security withdrew its case and petitioned for reopening "based on new evidence." Xiaodong Li v. Gonzales, 429 F.3d 1153 (5th Cir. 2005).

13. See, e.g., Şahin v. Turkey, App. No. 44774/98 (2005) (grand chamber); Dogru v. France, App. No. 27058/05 (2008) (judgment); Kervanci v. France, App. No. 31645/04 (2008). See also Aktas v. France, App. No. 43563/08 (dec.), Bayrak v. France, App. No. 14308/08 (dec.), Gamaleddyn v. France, App. No. 18527/08 (dec.), Ghazal v. France, App. No. 29134/08 (dec.), J. Singh v. France, App. No. 25463/08 (dec.), and R. Singh v. France, App. No. 27561/08 (dec.). The European Court of Human Rights dismissed these cases concerning the expulsion of pupils from French schools "for wearing conspicuous symbols of religious affiliation." According to the Court's press release of July 17, 2009, announcing these decisions, "The Court pointed out that the expulsion measure could be explained by the requirements of protecting the rights and freedoms of others and public order rather than by any objections to the pupils' religious beliefs."

14. Kavakçı v. Turkey, App. No. 71907/01 (2007).

15. An excellent, practical, step-by-step guide to international religious freedom advocacy is Knox Thames, Chris Seiple, and Amy Rowe, *International Religious Freedom Advocacy: A Guide to Organizations, Law, and NGOs* (Waco, Texas: Baylor University Press, 2009).

3

Restrictions on Religion in the World

Measures and Implications

BRIAN J. GRIM

Nearly 70 percent of the world's 6.8 billion people live in countries with high restrictions on religion, the brunt of which often falls on religious minorities.
—Archbishop Silvano Tomasi, *Vatican Representative to the United Nations, addressing the Human Rights Council in Geneva, March 12, 2010*

Seventy percent of the world's 6.8 billion people live in countries with a high or very high degree of restrictions on religion.
—Joint letter to U.S. President Obama *signed by leaders of more than twenty-five Muslim, Jewish, Sikh, and Christian organizations as well leading human rights organizations and scholars, April 1, 2010*

About 70 percent of the world's people live under regimes that restrict religious freedom.
—Representative Frank R. Wolf, *addressing the U.S. House of Representatives, April 15, 2010*

The common element in each of these three statements is that they are citing the main finding of a December 2009 report by the Pew Research Center's Forum on Religion & Public Life.[1] This same Pew report was covered extensively by U.S. and international media, including CNN, the BBC, Reuters, the Associated Press, and various country news outlets. For instance, Turkey's *Today's Zaman* carried the headline "Turkey Is among 33 *Countries* Whose Governments Impose *High Restrictions*." In this chapter I discuss the study and its findings and some of its implications for future research.

The Report and Its Findings

Overview

Global Restrictions on Religion, a 2009 study by the Pew Forum, finds that sixty-four nations—about one-third of the countries in the world—have high or very high restrictions on religion.[2] Some restrictions result from government actions, policies, and laws. Others result from hostile acts by private individuals, organizations, and social groups. Both kinds of restrictions are relatively low or moderate in about two-thirds of all countries. But because some of the most restrictive countries are very populous, nearly 70 percent of the world's 6.8 billion people live in countries with high restrictions on religion, as shown in Figure 3.1.

This overall finding is based on a series of more than thirty measures phrased as questions, such as "Is public preaching limited by any level of government?" and, on the social side, "Is there mob violence related to religion?" We answered the questions for each country by combing through two separate years of sixteen widely cited and publicly available reports on international religious freedom by the U.S. State

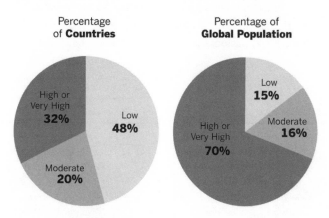

Global Restrictions on Religion

A minority of countries have high restrictions on religion, but these countries contain most of the world's population.

Percentage of **Countries**

High or Very High **32%**
Low **48%**
Moderate **20%**

Percentage of **Global Population**

Low **15%**
Moderate **16%**
High or Very High **70%**

Note: Totals may not add to 100% due to rounding.

Pew Forum on Religion & Public Life
Global Restrictions on Religion, December 2009

Figure 3.1: Global Restrictions on Religion. A minority of countries have high restrictions on religion, but these countries contain most of the world's population. Note: Totals may not add to 100% due to rounding. Pew Forum on Religion & Public Life, *Global Restrictions on Religion, December 2009*.

Department, the U.S. Commission on International Religious Freedom, the United Nations Special Rapporteur, the Council of the European Union, and numerous reports by other organizations, including Human Rights Watch and the Hudson Institute.[3]

I developed this methodology in consultation with other members of the Pew Research Center staff, building on a methodology that I developed at Penn State University while working with Professor Roger Finke and the Association of Religion Data Archives.[4] The goal was to devise quantifiable, objective, and transparent measures of the extent to which governments and societal groups impinge on the practice of religion. This research goes beyond previous efforts to assess restrictions on religion in several ways, including that the Pew Forum coded (categorized and counted) data from sixteen published sources, providing a high degree of confidence in the findings. The Pew Forum's coders looked to the sources only for specific, well-documented facts, not for opinions or commentary.

Global Overview

Although high restrictions are found in a minority of countries, the extent of restrictions is broad. Every country studied has some restrictions on religion, and there may be strong public support in particular countries for laws aimed, for example, at curbing "cult" activity (as in France), preserving an established church (as in the United Kingdom), or keeping tax-exempt religious organizations from endorsing candidates for elected office (as in the United States). But many of the restrictions measured involved some force or coercion. For instance, as shown in Figure 3.2, national or local governments harassed or intimidated

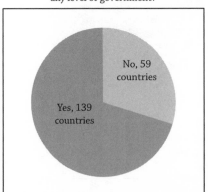
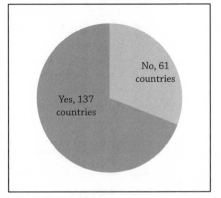

Figure 3.2: Governments: Was there harassment or intimidation of religious groups by any level of government? Private: actors: Was there harassment or intimidation of religious groups by individuals or groups in society? Pew Forum on Religion & Public Life, *Global Restrictions on Religion, December 2009.*

religious groups in 137 countries, and private actors (including individuals and social groups) harassed or intimidated religious groups in 139 countries. The brunt of these restrictions is often felt most directly by religious minorities.

Before discussing overall scores for countries, let me review a few findings on the extent of different types of restrictions. First, government restrictions:

- In 66 percent of countries, some level of government interfered with worship or other religious practices, including religious expression and affiliation.
- In nearly 50 percent of countries, members of one or more religious groups were killed, physically abused, imprisoned, detained, or displaced from their homes by some state or local government actor.
- In more than 25 percent of countries, there was widespread government intimidation of one or more religious groups.
- In nearly 25 percent of countries, the national government did not intervene in cases of discrimination or abuse against religious groups.
- In more than 80 percent of countries, governments clearly discriminated against one or more religious groups by giving preferential support or favors to some religious group(s) and not others.
- In 60 percent of countries, registration requirements for religious groups adversely affected their ability to operate, or the requirements clearly discriminated against certain religious groups, as shown in Figure 3.3.

Considering social hostilities involving religion:

- More than 70 percent of countries experienced crimes, malicious acts, or violence motivated by religious hatred or bias.
- In nearly 90 percent of countries, public tensions between or within religious groups were present, and these tensions involved violence in more than 60 percent of countries, as shown in Figure 3.4.
- In more than 10 percent of countries, these tensions included acts of sectarian or communal violence between religious groups, also shown in Figure 3.4.
- In more than 50 percent of countries, religious groups themselves attempted to prevent other religious groups from being able to operate.
- In nearly 33 percent of countries, individuals were assaulted or displaced from their homes in retaliation for specific religious activities considered offensive or threatening to the majority faith, including preaching and other forms of religious expression.
- In 30 percent of countries, religion-related terrorist groups were active in recruitment or fundraising. Such groups committed violent acts in nearly 10 percent of countries, as shown in Figure 3.5.

Figures 3.6 and 3.7 show how these restrictions play out across the world. The region with the highest level of restrictions is the Middle East and North Africa,

Registration Requirements

Does any level of government ask religious groups to register for any reason, including to be eligible for benefits such as tax exemption?

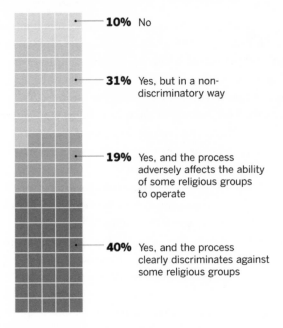

10% No

31% Yes, but in a non-discriminatory way

19% Yes, and the process adversely affects the ability of some religious groups to operate

40% Yes, and the process clearly discriminates against some religious groups

GRI.Q.18
Pew Forum on Religion & Public Life
Global Restrictions on Religion, December 2009

Figure 3.3: Registration Requirements. Does any level of government ask religious groups to register for any reason, including to be eligible for benefits such as tax exemption? GRI.Q.18. Pew Forum on Religion & Public Life, *Global Restrictions on Religion, December 2009.*

which has nearly five times the median level of government restrictions and more than seven times the level of social hostilities involving religion as are found in the Americas region, which has the lowest overall average on both measures. The Asia-Pacific region has the second highest average level of government restrictions, more than three times the average of the Americas and more than half again as high as Europe's average. Sub-Saharan Africa has, on average, slightly lower government restrictions than Europe.

The situation in the Asia-Pacific region is mixed, however, because it includes some countries and territories with low restrictions, such as Japan and Taiwan, but also some countries with very high government restrictions, such as China

Tensions Between Groups

Did violence result from tensions between religious groups?

Sectarian Violence

Were there acts of sectarian or communal violence between religious groups?

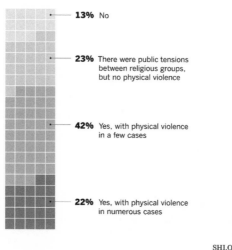

13% No

23% There were public tensions between religious groups, but no physical violence

42% Yes, with physical violence in a few cases

22% Yes, with physical violence in numerous cases

SHI.Q.6
Pew Forum on Religion & Public Life
Global Restrictions on Religion, December 2009

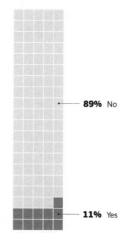

89% No

11% Yes

SHI.Q.3
Pew Forum on Religion & Public Life
Global Restrictions on Religion, December 2009

Figure 3.4: Tensions between Groups: Did violence result from tensions between religious groups? SHI.Q.6. Pew Forum on Religion & Public Life, *Global Restrictions on Religion, December 2009*. Sectarian Violence: Were there acts of sectarian or communal violence between religious groups? SHI.Q.3. Pew Forum on Religion & Public Life, *Global Restrictions on Religion, December 2009*.

and Burma. Of the ten countries with very high government restrictions, only two are in the Middle East and North Africa (Saudi Arabia and Egypt), while seven are in Asia (Iran, Uzbekistan, China, Burma, the Maldives, Malaysia, and Brunei). Only one is in sub-Saharan Africa (Eritrea). A similar picture is seen when looking at the eleven countries with very high levels of social hostilities involving religion. Six are in Asia-Pacific (India, Pakistan, Afghanistan, Indonesia, Bangladesh, and Sri Lanka) and four are in the Middle East and North Africa (Iraq, Israel, Sudan, and Saudi Arabia). One is in sub-Saharan Africa (Somalia).

Comparing the countries with highest government restrictions with the countries with highest social hostilities involving religion shows that only one country, Saudi Arabia, is in the very high category on both lists (see Table 3.1). Contributing factors to this high scores for Saudi Arabia include the ever-present religious police, or *muttawa,* who operate with official approval but rely on volunteers to help enforce a strict interpretation of Islam. Also exacerbating the religious hostilities in Saudi society is the contention between Sunnis and Shias.

Terrorist Groups

Were religion-related terrorist groups active in the country?

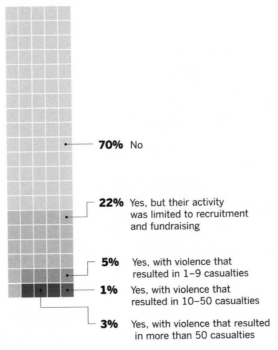

70% No

22% Yes, but their activity was limited to recruitment and fundraising

5% Yes, with violence that resulted in 1–9 casualties

1% Yes, with violence that resulted in 10–50 casualties

3% Yes, with violence that resulted in more than 50 casualties

Note: Totals may not add to 100% due to rounding.

SHI.Q.4
Pew Forum on Religion & Public Life
Global Restrictions on Religion, December 2009

Religion-related terrorism is defined as politically motivated violence against noncombatants by sub-national groups or clandestine agents with a religious justification or intent.

Figure 3.5: Terrorist Groups. Were religion-related terrorist groups active in the country? Note: Totals may not add to 100% due to rounding. *Religion-related terrorism* is defined as politically motivated violence against noncombatants by subnational groups of clandestine agents with a religious justification or intent. SHI.Q.4. Pew Forum on Religion & Public Life, *Global Restrictions on Religion, December 2009.*

Though Sunnis far outnumber Shias and control the country, Shias are concentrated in the region with the highest levels of oil production.

One country many observers might find surprisingly absent from the lists is North Korea. The sources clearly indicate that North Korea's government is among the most repressive in the world with respect to religion as well as other civil and political liberties. For instance, the U.S. State Department's 2008

Government Restrictions on Religion by Region

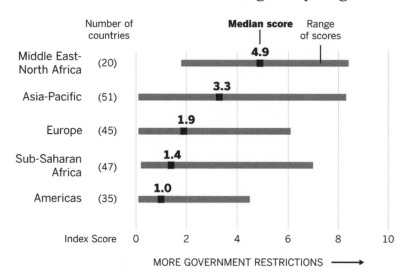

Pew Forum on Religion & Public Life • *Global Restrictions on Religion, December 2009*

Figure 3.6: Government Restrictions on Religion by Region. Pew Forum on Religion & Public Life, *Global Restrictions on Religion, December 2009.*

Report on International Religious Freedom states that "genuine freedom of religion does not exist" in North Korea. But because North Korean society is effectively closed to outsiders and independent observers lack regular access to the country, the sources are unable to provide the kind of specific, timely information that the Pew Forum categorized and counted ("coded," in social science jargon) for their quantitative study. Therefore the Pew Forum's report does not include scores for North Korea.

The highest overall restrictions are found in countries where government restrictions on religion and social hostilities involving religion are both high. In *Global Restrictions on Religion*, we plotted the twenty-five most populous countries by their scores on both measures; the results are shown in Figure 3.8, where social hostilities are measured on the vertical scale and government restrictions are measured on the horizontal scale. If a country has both high government restrictions and high social hostilities, it appears on the top right square of the figure, as do Pakistan, Indonesia, Egypt, and Iran. Since Saudi Arabia has a relatively small population, it is not included on this chart, but if it were, it would be located in the top right square.

While government restrictions and social hostilities tend to exist in tandem, there are some notable exceptions.[5] China and Vietnam have extremely high

Social Hostilities Involving Religion by Region

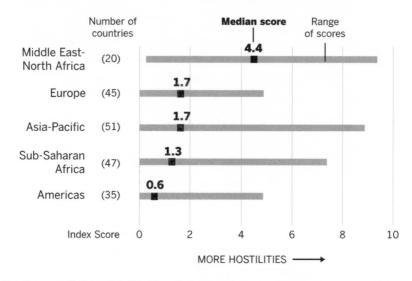

Pew Forum on Religion & Public Life • *Global Restrictions on Religion, December 2009*

Figure 3.7: Social Hostilities Involving Religion by Region. Pew Forum on Religion & Public Life, *Global Restrictions on Religion, December 2009.*

Table 3.1: **Countries With Very High Government Restrictions on Religion or Social Hostilities Involving Religion**

Government Restrictions	Social Hostilities
Very High	Very High
Top 5% of scores	*Top 5% of scores*
Scores from 6.7 to 8.4	Scores from 6.8 to 9.4
Saudi Arabia	Iraq
Iran	India
Uzbekistan	Pakistan
China	Afghanistan
Egypt	Indonesia
Burma (Myanmar)	Bangladesh
Maldives	Somalia
Eritrea	Israel
Malaysia	Sri Lanka
Brunei	Sudan
	Saudi Arabia

Religious Restrictions in the 25 Most Populous Countries

This chart shows how the world's 25 most populous countries score in terms of both government restrictions on religion and social hostilities involving religion. Countries in the upper right have the most restrictions and hostilities. Countries in the lower left have the least.

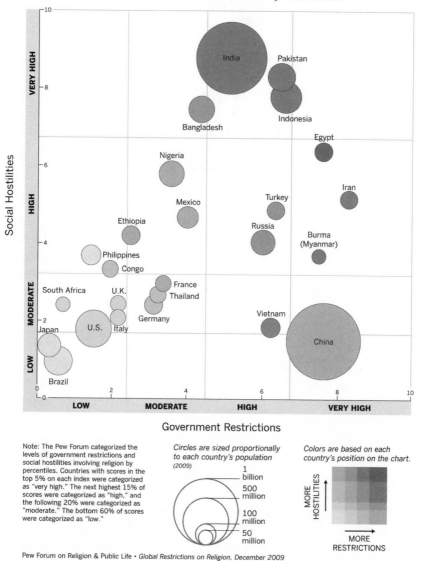

Note: The Pew Forum categorized the levels of government restrictions and social hostilities involving religion by percentiles. Countries with scores in the top 5% on each index were categorized as "very high." The next highest 15% of scores were categorized as "high," and the following 20% were categorized as "moderate." The bottom 60% of scores were categorized as "low."

Circles are sized proportionally to each country's population (2009)

1 billion
500 million
100 million
50 million

Colors are based on each country's position on the chart.

MORE HOSTILITIES
MORE RESTRICTIONS

Pew Forum on Religion & Public Life • *Global Restrictions on Religion, December 2009*

Figure 3.8: Religious Restrictions in the 25 Most Populous Countries. This chart shows how the world's 25 most populous countries score in terms of both government restrictions on religion and social hostilities involving religion. Countries in the upper right have the most restrictions and hostilities. Countries in the lower left have the least. Note: The Pew Forum categorized the levels of government restrictions and social hostilities involving religion by percentiles. Countries with scores in the top 5% on each index were categorized as "very high." The next highest 15% of scores were categorized as "high," and the following 20% were categorized as "moderate." The bottom 60% of scores were categorized as "low." Pew Forum on Religion & Public Life, *Global Restrictions on Religion, December 2009*.

restrictions on religion imposed by the government but relatively few restrictions coming from people and groups in society. Although social tensions over religion appear to be on the rise in Chinese society, particularly in the Tibet and Xinjiang Autonomous Regions, China is on the low end of the Social Hostilities Index for the period covered by this study, which may help explain the religious growth and dynamism present in China today.

On the other end of the spectrum, you can see India in the top-center part of Figure 3.8, indicating that social hostilities tend to be higher than government restrictions, though both tend to be high. Nigeria is another example of a country where social hostilities are a more potent force than government restrictions on religion. In the bottom left-hand corner of Figure 3.8 is a cluster of countries. Only two of the twenty-five most populous countries are low on both measures: Japan and Brazil. The United States falls into the moderately restrictive category in terms of social hostilities, primarily due to frequent, religiously biased hate crimes. For instance, each year law enforcement officials report about 1,400 religiously biased hate crimes in the United States, spread across nearly all fifty states. In sum, the scatter plot provides a way to understand the main sources of restrictions on religious groups within a given country.

Comparing Government Restrictions and Social Hostilities

Further analysis of the two main ways in which religion is restricted—by government actions and by hostilities in society—reveals a number of important patterns.[6] Some are evident in Figure 3.9, which compares these two measures for the fifty most populous countries as well as for the six countries with smaller populations that score very high on either index (Brunei, Eritrea, Israel, Maldives, Sri Lanka, and Somalia).

As Figure 3.9 shows, nearly all of the countries high on both measures of restrictions (upper right) are in the Middle East–North Africa region or in Asia. Many of the restrictions in these countries are driven by groups pressing for the enshrinement of their interpretation of the majority faith, including through sharia law in Muslim societies and through Hindutva movements in India, which have sought to define India as a Hindu nation.

A look at the lower left portion of Figure 3.9 shows that the most populous European countries—including France, Germany, Italy, Poland, Ukraine, and the United Kingdom—generally have moderate or low levels of government restrictions as well as of social hostilities. But fewer than a dozen of the world's fifty most populous countries are in the low range on *both* measures. In the United States, which has relatively few government restrictions on religion, the level of social hostilities involving religion is near the bottom of the moderate range, somewhat higher than in a number of other large Western countries, such

Religious Restrictions in the 50 Most Populous Countries

This chart shows how the world's 50 most populous countries and selected others score in terms of both government restrictions on religion and social hostilities involving religion. Countries in the upper right have the most restrictions and hostilities. Countries in the lower left have the least.

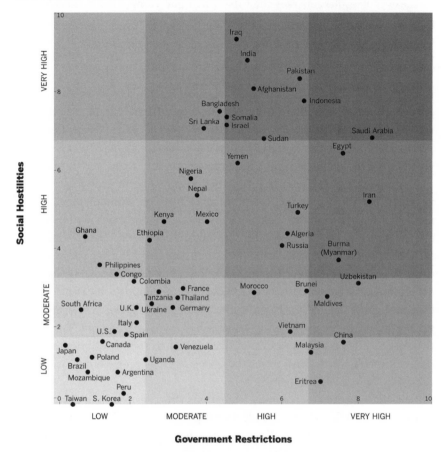

Note: The Pew Forum categorized the levels of government restrictions and social hostilities involving religion by percentiles. Countries with scores in the top 5% on each index were categorized as "very high." The next highest 15% of scores were categorized as "high," and the following 20% were categorized as "moderate." The bottom 60% of scores were categorized as "low."

Pew Forum on Religion & Public Life • *Global Restrictions on Religion, December 2009*

Figure 3.9: Religions Restrictions in the 50 Most Populous Countries. This chart shows how the world's 50 most populous countries and selected others score in terms of both government restrictions on religion and social hostilities involving religion. Countries in the upper right have the most restrictions and hostilities. Countries in the lower left have the least. Note: The Pew Forum categorized the levels of government restrictions and social hostilities involving religion by percentiles. Countries with scores in the top 5% on each index were categorized as "very high." The next highest 15% of scores were categorized as "high," and the following 20% were categorized as "moderate." The bottom 60% of scores were categorized as "low." Pew Forum on Religion & Public Life, *Global Restrictions on Religion, December 2009.*

as Canada, Brazil, and Argentina. As already noted, only one country, Saudi Arabia, is in the very high category on both the Government Restrictions Index and the Social Hostilities Index.

The overall results generally show that where government restrictions on religion are high, so are social hostilities involving religion, though with some exceptions. It is important to remember, however, that our study is just a snapshot of a particular time period, and situations can and do change. For instance, although Malaysia was among the countries with the highest government restrictions, it had low social hostilities involving religion during the time period studied. However, had the recent social violence surrounding the dispute over whether Christians can use the name "Allah" for God happened during the study period, Malaysia's social hostility score would have been higher.

When all 198 countries and self-administering territories are plotted on a chart comparing their government restriction and social hostility scores, it is apparent that the two measures tend to move together. Running through Figure 3.10 is a regression line that plots how scores on one index are related, on average, to scores on the other index. The upward slope of the line indicates that higher scores on one index generally are associated with higher scores on the other. Many countries are clustered in the lower left corner, showing that they are low on both types of restrictions. Though the remaining countries are fairly dispersed, most still follow the direction taken by the regression line, and very few are located in the upper left or lower right corners of the graph. This means that, in general, it is rare for countries that are high in social hostilities to be low on government restrictions, or for those that are high on government restrictions to be low in social hostilities.

Nevertheless there are notable exceptions. In a few nations government restrictions on religion are considerably higher than social hostilities. These countries—including China, Vietnam, Uzbekistan, and Burma—tend to have either communist or authoritarian backgrounds, and religion is often viewed by the government as a potential threat to its authority.

Countries that follow the opposite pattern—that is, where social hostilities are considerably higher than government restrictions—tend to have large segments of the population that want to protect the special place of a particular religion, such as Buddhism in Sri Lanka, Hinduism in Nepal, Islam in Bangladesh, and Orthodox Christianity in Ethiopia.

Some Implications

Understanding the Connection between Restrictions and Violence

My colleague Roger Finke and I published an analysis of the relationship between restrictions on religion and religion-related violence in the *American Sociological*

Religious Restrictions in 198 Countries

This chart shows how the world's 198 countries and self-administering territories score in terms of both government restrictions on religion and social hostilities involving religion.
Correlation = .586 (p<.001, two-tailed); r-square = .34

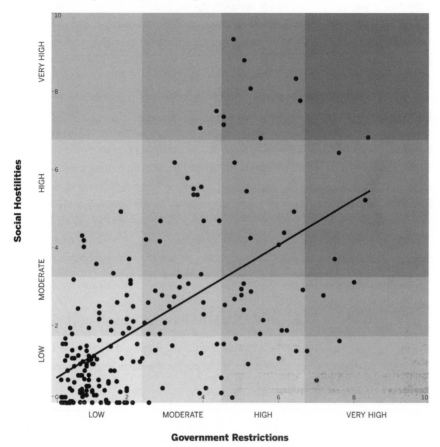

Government Restrictions

Note: The Pew Forum categorized the levels of government restrictions and social hostilities involving religion by percentiles. Countries with scores in the top 5% on each index were categorized as "very high." The next highest 15% of scores were categorized as "high," and the following 20% were categorized as "moderate." The bottom 60% of scores were categorized as "low."

Pew Forum on Religion & Public Life • *Global Restrictions on Religion, December 2009*

Figure 3.10: Religious Restrictions in 198 Countries. This chart shows how the world's 198 countries and self-administering territories score in terms of both government restrictions on religion and social hostilities involving religion. Correlation = 0.586 (p<.001, two-tailed); r-square = 0.34. Note: The Pew Forum categorized the levels of government restrictions and social hostilities involving religion by percentiles. Countries with scores in the top 5% on each index were categorized as "very high." The next highest 15% of scores were categorized as "high," and the following 20% were categorized as "moderate." The bottom 60% of scores were categorized as "low." Pew Forum on Religion & Public Life, *Global Restrictions on Religion, December 2009*.

Review, which we develop further in our book, *The Price of Freedom Denied.*[7] Our statistical analysis shown in Figure 3.11 finds that social and governmental restrictions on religion are associated with more violence and conflict, not less. Specifically we found that social restrictions on religious freedom lead to government restrictions on religious freedom; that the two act in tandem to increase the level of violence related to religion; and that this in turn cycles back and leads to even higher social and government restrictions on religion, creating the *religious violence cycle.*

One unique aspect of these statistical findings is that *social* restriction of religious freedom (or social religious intolerance) tends to drive government restrictions more than vice versa. Examples include the social pressures in India for anticonversion laws; calls for sharia law in northern Nigeria and parts of Indonesia; expulsions of evangelicals in Chiapas, Mexico; and numerous religious rebellions from China's long history, including the Taiping Heavenly Kingdom Rebellion. One of the clearest historical examples of the way social restrictions of religious freedom can feed into the religious violence cycle is the Holocaust. Research has shown that the Nazi government's violence toward Jewish people reinforced existing social prejudices, creating a cycle of violence that was banally carried out with the support of many in German society.[8]

Does Religious Freedom Matter in the Broader Scheme of Things?

In 2007 a survey of thirty-four nations by the Pew Research Center Global Attitudes Project found that, on average, 93 percent of respondents reported that

Figure 3.11:

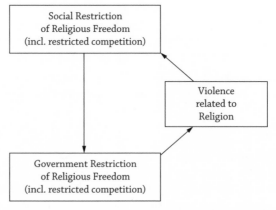

The Religious Violence Cycle[i]

Structural Equation Model, 143 countries, populations > 2 million
Grim and Finke (2007), *American Sociological Review* 72(4):649

"living in a country where I can freely practice my religion" is "somewhat or very important," whereas fewer than 2 percent indicated that it wasn't important at all. The importance of religious freedom was remarkably high across global regions, ranging from 84 percent in Eastern Europe to 98 percent in Africa.[9] Since the level of restrictions on religion is high at the same time as is the desire for religious freedom, this topic is in need of further careful study.

Religious Freedoms and Other Freedoms

Although the focus of most research to date has been on the restriction of religion and its inverse, religious freedom, an initial review of the data indicates that religious freedom is embedded within a much larger bundle of civil liberties.[10] Indeed the level of restrictions on religion is correlated with restrictions on freedom of the press, fewer democratic processes, and other issues.[11] In *The Price of Freedom Denied* we note that at the core of religious expression is the freedom of speech, and at the core of freedom to worship is the freedom to assemble. To claim freedom of speech without allowing for freedom to express religious beliefs quickly erodes freedom of speech in other areas. Likewise, allowing for restrictions on the assembly of religious groups opens the door for curtailing the activities of other groups. The denial of religious freedoms is certainly intertwined with the denial of other freedoms.

Because religious freedoms are intertwined with other civil liberties, the outcomes of these liberties can also be expected to be closely associated. Nobel Laureate Amartya Sen, an economist at Harvard, argues that human freedom is not just the *general* opportunity for freedom in the abstract but the *specific* processes within a country that result in better lives. In our book we analyze reverse-coded measures of restrictions on religion so that high scores are an indication of religious freedom. The results are shown in Table 3.2, which displays the relationships of religious freedom to other civil liberties and indicators of the well-being of a country's residents. The associations between religious freedoms and other civil liberties, press freedoms, and political freedoms are especially striking. The highly significant and strong correlations (exceeding 0.6) suggest that that the freedoms are closely intertwined.

Additional research produced similar findings. A recent study of 101 countries conducted by the Hudson Institute's Center for Religious Freedom, using entirely independent data from the Pew Forum and from the ARDA at Penn State, also found that religious freedom in a country is strongly associated with other freedoms, including civil and political liberty, press freedom, and economic freedom, as well as with multiple measures of well-being. That study found that wherever religious freedom is high, there tend to be fewer incidents of armed conflict, better health outcomes, higher levels of earned income, prolonged democracy, and better educational opportunities for women.

Table 3.2: **Correlation of Religious Freedom with Other Freedoms and Well-being within Countries**

Higher GDP	.16
Higher earned income for men	.16
Higher earned income for women	.20
More foreign direct investment	.25
Lower income inequality	.25
Overall livability	.28
Higher % of GDP spent on public heath	.29
Economic freedom	.31
Lower poverty	.35
Lower levels of armed conflict	.36
Longevity of democracy	.40
Lower % of GDP spent on military	.42
Gender empowerment	.48
Civil liberties	.61
Freedom of the press	.61
Political freedom	.61

Number of countries compared varies depending on data availability from the ARDA and the United Nations. All correlations are statistically significant. (*Note:* the larger the number, the stronger the direct correlation.)

Of course, correlations make no claims on the causal order, but they do suggest that religious freedom is an integral part of a "bundled commodity" of human freedoms. Both religious freedoms and this bundle of freedoms are associated with many positive outcomes. Yet the relationship of religious freedoms to other civil liberties and social outcomes is still poorly understood and is in need of further serious study. Such studies are now possible in a way that was not just a few years ago, thanks to these new data that are now beginning to provide measures of restrictions on religion and social hostilities involving religion *over time*. Time series data are particularly important when trying to disentangle the many factors that might or might not be causally related. While understanding the relationship between religion and social conflict has received initial attention, other questions can now be empirically studied. Economists and other social scientists can better examine and evaluate the relationship between religion and economic development. Social, political, and human rights issues that are closely tied to religion can now be studied, ranging from gender roles to the formation of democracy and the likelihood of state failure. Finally, these new data will also permit theories about change in the religious life of countries to be tested. Indeed the work of understanding the relationship of restrictions on religion to other social outcomes is just beginning.[12]

Notes

1. Signatories to the Obama letter represented a diverse range of leading scholars and advocacy groups, including, among others, Salam Al-Marayati, executive director, Muslim Public Affairs Council; Radwan Masmoudi, founder and president, Center for the Study of Islam and Democracy; Sayyid M. Syeed, national director, Office of Interfaith and Community Alliances, Islamic Society of North America; John L. Esposito, founding director, Prince Alwaleed bin Talal Center for Muslim-Christian Understanding, Walsh School of Foreign Service, Georgetown University; Abba Cohen, Washington director and counsel, Agudath Israel of America; Marc D. Stern, acting co-executive director, American Jewish Congress; Abba Cohen, Washington director and counsel, Agudath Israel of America; Manjit Singh, chairman, Sikh American Legal Defense and Education Fund; James E. Winkler, general secretary, United Methodist Church, General Board of Church and Society; Jim Wallis, president and chief executive officer, Sojourners; Larry Cox, executive director, Amnesty International USA; and Thomas O. Melia, deputy executive director, Freedom House.

2. This section includes excerpts from the full report. The methodology and country indexes and individual scores on each question can be found at www.PewForum.org. Portions of this section were also presented in my briefing to the U.S. House of Representatives Foreign Affairs Subcommittee on International Organizations, Human Rights, and Oversight, February 3, 2010.

3. For a full description of the methodology, see the report at www.PewForum.org. For a comparison of the coded social hostilities involving religion with other measures from public opinion surveys and expert opinion, see Brian J. Grim and Richard Wike, "Cross-Validating Measures of Global Religious Intolerance: Comparing Coded State Department Reports with Survey Data and Expert Opinion," *Politics & Religion,* April 2010.

4. For a description of the work at Penn State, see Brian J. Grim, "The Cities of God versus the Countries of Earth: The Regulation of Religious Freedom (RRF)," paper delivered at the Association for Study of Religion, Economics, and Culture national conference, October 21, 2004; Brian J. Grim and Roger Finke, "International Religion Indexes: Government Regulation, Government Favoritism, and Social Regulation of Religion," *Interdisciplinary Journal of Research on Religion* 2, no. 1 (2006): 1–40; Brian J. Grim, Roger Finke, Jaime Harris, Catherine Meyers, and Julie VanEerden, "Measuring International Socio-Religious Values and Conflict by Coding U.S. State Department Reports," in *JSM Proceedings of the American Association of Public Opinion Research, Survey Research Methods Section* (Alexandria, Va.: American Statistical Association, 2006).

5. Although it is very likely that more restrictions exist than are reported by the sixteen primary sources, taken together the sources are sufficiently comprehensive to provide a good estimate of the levels of restrictions in almost all countries.

6. This section is taken from the Pew Forum's report *Global Restrictions on Religion, December* 2009.

7. Brian J. Grim and Roger Finke, *The Price of Freedom Denied: Religious Persecution and Conflict in the 21st Century* (New York: Cambridge University Press, 2010).

8. William I. Brustein, *Roots of Hate: Anti-Semitism in Europe before the Holocaust* (Cambridge: Cambridge University Press, 2003). Also see Hannah Arendt, *Eichmann in Jerusalem: A Report on the Banality of Evil* (New York: Viking, 1963).

9. See "World Publics Welcome Global Trade—But Not Immigration," Pew Global Attitudes Project, October 4, 2007, http://pewglobal.org/reports/pdf/258topline.pdf. Question wording: "How important is it to you to live in a country where you can practice your religion freely? Is it very important, somewhat important, not too important or not at all important?" Countries covered: *The Americas*: Argentina, Bolivia, Brazil, Chile, Mexico, Peru, Venezuela; *Eastern Europe*: Bulgaria, Czech Republic, Poland, Russia, Slovakia, Ukraine; *Middle East*: Egypt, Jordan, Kuwait, Lebanon, Morocco, Palestinian territories, Turkey; *Asia*: Bangladesh, India, Indonesia, Malaysia, Pakistan; *Africa*: Ethiopia, Ghana, Ivory Coast, Kenya, Mali, Nigeria, Senegal, South Africa, Tanzania, Uganda. The question was not asked in Western Europe.

10. Portions of this section come from Grim and Finke, *The Price of Freedom Denied*.

11. See Pew Forum Transcript, http://pewforum.org/events/?EventID=223.

12. See Brian J. Grim, "Religion, Law and Social Conflict in the 21st Century: Findings from Sociological Research," *Oxford Journal of Law and Religion*, Vol. 1, No. 1 (2012), pp. 249–271, for a discussion of three additional questions: Does official favoritism of one religion correlate with more or less conflict involving religion? Do constitutional protections for religious freedom coincide with increased or decreased restrictions? And do laws prohibiting blasphemy, apostasy or defamation of religion relate to more or to less overall contentions involving religion?

PART TWO

RELIGIOUS MARKETS, PLURALISM, AND THE STATE

4

Religious Pluralism, Political Incentives, and the Origins of Religious Liberty

ANTHONY GILL

Not Just an Idea, but an Action

Religious liberty is a wonderful idea. It speaks directly to the innate human desire to think what we want, worship how we please, and assemble how we choose. The classic liberal writings of John Locke, Algernon Sidney, and William Penn certainly inspired the authors of the U.S. Constitution.[1] In turn, the First Amendment served as a template for future constitutional declarations of religious liberty throughout the world. In the contemporary world, the United Nations' *Universal Declaration of Human Rights* and subsequent *Declaration on the Elimination of All Forms of Intolerance and Discrimination Based on Religion and Believe* (Resolution 36/55) present rhetorical models from which national governments can draft their own laws regarding religious freedom. International watchdog groups such as Forum 18, the International Religious Liberty Association, and Freedom House not only monitor how closely nations adhere to the principles of religious liberty, but they also serve as an ideological beacon promoting the intellectual concept of freedom as an inherent good.

Unfortunately not all wonderful ideas are adopted into policy or law. While it is true that nearly every national constitution currently in existence has some basic guarantee of religious freedom, the reality of the situation is that the vast majority of governments still place onerous legal and bureaucratic obstacles in the way of religious organizations or provide favored status to a particular denomination, thereby disadvantaging other groups.[2] While some of these regulations may simply be the cost of doing business in modern, highly bureaucratic states, many are intentionally crafted to limit the rights and free exercise of religious minorities. Physical persecution of religious minorities is also a common occurrence, with governments either actively participating in such activities or looking askance and failing to prosecute when individuals are harassed, beaten, or killed for their spiritual beliefs.[3] For good ideas to be adopted, government officials must be willing to take legislative action in writing those ideas into law and enforcing their application.

If religious liberty is such a universally accepted ideal, and if most national constitutions claim adherence to this ideal, why do violations still occur? Alternatively, and more to the subject of this chapter, what prompts political leaders to implement policies that increase the level of religious liberty within a society? The ideas are there; what needs to be explained is the action (or inaction) of legislating and enforcing the idea of religious liberty. I will argue that legislation aimed at increasing religious freedom within a country is not merely the result of a good idea taking hold among politicians; it is the result of political calculations based on the self-interest of legislators and other decision makers within society. Don't get me wrong (as many critics have been wont to do): I firmly agree that ideas matter.[4] If no one in a society believed religious liberty was a good idea, such a policy would not likely get passed into law. However, new legislative ideas rarely go uncontested, as there are always opposing ideas and interests at the bargaining table. To understand why one policy idea gets implemented and not another, it is essential to look at the *political interests* of those who write (and lobby for) the laws. Understanding the *political* origins of religious liberty helps us to explain why religious freedom flourishes in some nations but is lacking in others.

The argument here is fairly simple and straightforward. Political leaders will favor policies of religious liberty when it enhances their hold on power, enriches the nation's economy and increases tax revenue to the state, and minimizes social conflict.[5] Likewise where policymakers see religious freedom as deleterious to any of those goals, they will not promote religious liberty and may well roll back any freedoms that various religious groups enjoy. As such, my thesis explains both the increase and the decrease in religious freedom, an important feature of the theory considering that there is no guarantee religious freedom invariably marches forward.[6] The other critical ingredient for ensuring policies favorable to religious freedom is the existence of religious pluralism. This is somewhat paradoxical, if not ironic, given that religious liberty is crucial in cultivating denominational pluralism, yet without such pluralism there is very little political incentive to guarantee freedom. Meet chicken and egg: Which one must come first? The rise of religious diversity in a society where freedom for minorities is not guaranteed again relies on the role of political incentives. If policymakers see no particular political advantage in enforcing restrictive laws against minorities, religious pluralism will naturally increase (often to the chagrin of leaders of the dominant faith). The rise of religious pluralism and its symbiotic relationship with religious freedom is largely the story of the United States and Latin America, the two cases we focus on below.

The Political Origins of Religious Liberty

Before I explain the political logic underlying the legal creation of religious free-dom in a society, it is important to conceptualize such freedom as a matter of government regulatory policy. This sounds cold and calculating, the stuff of pub-lic administration, instead of lofty and noble, the stuff of philosophical debates. However, this shifts attention away from conceptualizing religious liberty merely as a good idea and forces us to look at the legislative actions that guarantee (or restrict) such freedom. While a simple constitutional declaration respecting the rights of individuals and groups to believe as they choose and practice their beliefs in accordance with their traditions is a necessary condition for religious liberty, it is certainly not sufficient. There are myriad ways in which a govern-ment can restrict the ability of individuals or groups to practice their faith.[7]

In the realm of public choice economics,[8] any governmental law or regulation that imposes a cost on an individual or business is a restriction of liberty, as the coercive power of the government is being used to limit the range of choices available to those individuals or groups. For instance, if a government requires an auto manufacturer to make cars that meet a certain fuel-efficiency threshold, the government is limiting the freedom of that business to make the product it chooses and concurrently limits the range of choices and freedom of consumers. Likewise requiring a homeowner to apply for a permit to cut down a tree on his property and pay a fee for that activity is also a limitation on that individual's freedom. Whether or not we feel that such laws and regulations are good for society as a whole is not at issue here. All but the most extreme anarchists would agree that some governmental restrictions on human choice are necessary for a well-functioning society. Laws against murder obviously restrict the freedom of individuals who want to kill others, but such laws are certainly beneficial in reducing fear and allowing other freedoms to flourish. Nonetheless it is still important to realize that any governmental action—which, as Max Weber reminded us, is invariably based on coercion—limits freedom. This conceptual-ization opens up a whole new door for understanding the subtle ways in which governments limit religious freedom, either for reasons that seem plausibly good for society (e.g., banning human sacrifice) or may be more nefarious (e.g., prohibiting sacred texts from being printed and distributed).

Throughout history, and beyond outright bans of spiritual practice, govern-ments have used a wide array of laws and regulations to inhibit the freedom of all or selected religions.[9] Such actions include restrictions on foreign missionar-ies, prohibitions on importing religious books (including the Bible), limiting the ability of religions to own or access various media outlets (e.g., newspapers, radio), employment mandates,[10] and voting eligibility or office-holding require-ments. Perhaps the most onerous set of restrictions apply to property.[11] If a religious group cannot obtain an identifiable piece of property wherein they can meet on a regular basis, the chances that they will grow or even maintain their membership will be severely limited. Zoning policy and regulations on property use can significantly affect membership; forcing a religious group to locate in a sparsely populated rural area miles away from the town it wishes to serve can guarantee the failure of that group.[12] Registration requirements for religious groups wanting to receive tax exempt status or special guarantees on property rights are an area where political leaders can manipulate to favor one denomination over another; more stringent requirements for new denominations (e.g., having a large membership or a long historical presence within a nation) tend to favor existing faiths and limit the choices available to worshippers.[13] Speaking of favoritism, laws that give one denomination preferential subsidies or official status relative to others raises the costs of belonging to those nonfavored confessions. After all, who would want to have a portion of their taxes go to pay the official state religion and then have to tithe for another religion? Preferential access to schools, hospitals, prisons, and the military for one religion but not others can also make it more difficult for minority faiths to gain a foothold within a society.[14]

Now that we have a basic knowledge of the various ways governments can raise the costs of doing religious business, the key question becomes why a political leader would want to impose costly restrictions on religions or, alternatively, relax such regulations? The latter question is akin to enhancing the level of religious liberty within society. Given that the historical norm has been regimes wherein one particular religion was favored to the exclusion of others, the question of the origins of religious liberty are a bit more puzzling. Why would political rulers want to deregulate a sector of society (the religious marketplace) that exists under tight government control? To better understand why this might occur, we need to lay out the preferences and incentives of the various actors in the regulatory game. These actors include both the politicians who write the rules and regulations and the individuals and entities affected by them, namely religions. We begin with the latter group.

Within the Western world, Christianity has been the favored faith since the reign of the Roman emperor Constantine (306–37). Even after the split of Christianity into Eastern Orthodoxy and Roman Catholicism, one Church always remained dominant within its territorial realm. And while Martin Luther's Reformation successfully challenged the hegemony of the Vatican in Western Europe, the Reformation's promise of decoupling religious and secular authority eventually gave way to the political establishment of Protestant monopolies.[15] From the vantage point of a hegemonic religion, the preferred religious regulatory regime is one that favors itself and prohibits the entry of upstart sects.[16] In other words, dominant confessions will prefer highly limited religious freedoms for any other denomination, including the outright prohibition of other faiths. Minority faiths, on the other hand, will prefer a greater degree of liberty so that they may proselytize more openly, attract adherents, and gain a foothold in the nation's culture. Religious minorities will be one of the key actors lobbying for greater religious freedom; they are the couriers for the *idea* of religious liberty. Without minority religious groups, there will be no voice for legal changes. How minority religions can ever gain entry into a highly restricted religious market is an important topic that we will take up below.

On the other side of the equation stand government leaders who make policy affecting religious liberties. Political scientists have long held that the primary goal motivating any ruler—be it an elected democrat or a self-anointed dictator— is the desire to remain in power.[17] Without power, a ruler could not achieve his subsidiary goals. These subsidiary goals include increasing tax revenue, encouraging economic growth, maintaining social order, and minimizing the costs of rule.[18] All of these secondary goals enhance the ability of obtaining the primary goal of remaining in power. Increased tax revenue from a growing economy allows rulers to buy support among the population via patronage or provide public services that please constituents. Minimizing social unrest and seeking ways to have the populace obey laws without having to rely on a huge police force frees up more tax revenue for patronage or other goals. Of course, political leaders may have all sorts of specific policy goals, ranging from the altruistic (e.g., expanding health care) to the not so altruistic (e.g., absconding with tax money), but the primary goal of retaining power and secondary goals of revenue collection and social stability tend to focus the policy calculus of most politicians.

When it comes to these goals for politicians, creating an aura of moral authority goes a long way toward reducing the costs of rule and enhancing one's leadership tenure. If people pay their taxes without cheating and obey the other laws of the state because they consider such actions the legitimate and just thing to do, then a leader need not rely on a costly coercive apparatus or large amounts of side payments to keep citizens loyal. This is where religious authority becomes important. To the extent that religious leaders are highly respected sources of moral authority within society, a secular ruler has a strong incentive to seek the favor of the clergy. The blessing of a pope, rabbi, or imam can serve to reassure the populace that their secular leaders are trustworthy and should be obeyed. It is not surprising that kings and presidents throughout the ages have sought public approval from prominent religious figures. In return for such a blessing, religious leaders frequently receive funding for their faith and protection from competitors—that is, restrictions on the religious freedom of minority sects.

To see how the logic behind this bargain works in practice, one need only consider the case of the New England Puritans during the 1600s and 1700s.[19] As a separatist religious faction in Britain, they fought vigorously for their own freedom of worship without interference from the established Church of England.[20] As their efforts to present a more faithful version of Anglicanism failed, they chose to avail themselves of an exit option, fleeing to the new British colonies in North America. After becoming the dominant religious group in the Massachusetts Bay Colony they were rather reluctant to extend liberties to Quakers, Presbyterians, and folks like Roger Williams. Civil and religious authority was closely aligned in the New England colony for much of the seventeenth and eighteenth centuries, with Puritan clergy legitimizing colonial governors and colonial governors keeping Quakers like Mary Dyer from hanging around their territory.[21] Thus in this case we see how a minority religious group that is a voice for freedom when facing a hegemonic state religion can itself become a force against religious liberties when it obtains majority status. We also see how political actors willingly align with the majoritarian confession and provide it with funding and protection from competitors in exchange for religious legitimation.

Cases of church-state bargains being struck between the dominant faith and the regime are not merely remnants of the past; they still exist today. While it is easy to think of secular Europe as a place where church-state separation and religious freedom reigns, in reality the current regulatory landscape for religions reflects the shadow of such church-state bargains made centuries ago.[22] Official state churches still exist in many nations, including England, Scotland, Denmark, Norway, and Greece. In other countries, such as the Netherlands, Lithuania, Russia, and Germany, a small number of historical confessions are given special privileges relative to religious minorities. And in virtually every European nation, a kaleidoscope of regulatory hurdles still exist for nontraditional faiths and foreign missionaries, making it incredibly difficult for these religions to compete on an equal legal footing with historically dominant churches.[23]

If the dominant state of affairs throughout history has been one wherein a state grants favored status to a single denomination and restricts the freedoms of competing religious groups, and if this bargain is so attractive to both parties, why would a government ever want to deregulate the religious landscape and allow for the expansion of religious minorities? In other words, what are the political origins of religious liberty? The answer lies in the incentives facing politicians. Where a close association between a single faith and the state hinders the ability of the political authorities to rule effectively—including staying in power, collecting revenue, enhancing economic growth, and maintaining social stability—political leaders will see it in their best interest to promote religious freedom, or at least not enforce the restrictions on such liberties. And as noted earlier, it is essential to have minority religions in society willing and able to press for such freedoms. But if the typical state of affairs is for a government to officially sanction just one religion and exclude all others, how could religious pluralism ever develop? Where would the upstart sects so critically needed to lobby for religious liberty come from?

As the sociologist Rodney Stark has pointed out, religious preferences in society are naturally diverse[24]. No one religion can satisfy everyone's tastes and preferences for style of worship, theological emphasis, organizational structure, and so on.[25] Some individuals prefer very formal and ritualistic worship, while others love to whoop and holler. Stark further argues that monotheistic religions are prone to schism, as theological debates naturally arise within any population. And schism is all the more likely when a single faith must rely on government coercion to tamp down competing sects. The close arrangement between church and state in such situations usually results in corruption within the leadership of the church, giving rise to reform movements that try to purify the faith. The history of Christianity dating back to its inception is rife with schism and competition; eliminating the presence of minority sects is a virtual impossibility. Even before the Reformation, the presence of competing theologies was apparent in movements inspired by such figures as Jan Hus and John Wycliffe. These minority sects find space to grow and religious pluralism materializes when secular rulers have no incentive to enforce the laws of religious conformity.

Enforcing religious conformity can be a costly endeavor for rulers, both financially and in terms of their political power. If religious minorities are productive and well-placed within society, stamping them out could cause a significant loss of political support for a ruler and/or a drop in tax revenue and economic growth. It is widely believed that Constantine's decision to end the persecution of Christians and given them legal rights similar to pagans in the early fourth century was related to the fact that both his mother and important military leaders that he depended on were practicing Christians. Both the Edict of Nantes (1598) and the Acts of Toleration (1688) were legal changes meant to quell violent civil unrest and economic turmoil in France and Britain, respectively. As the historian Roland Bainton observed about the situation in France, "Henry IV...had come to the recognition that the welfare of the state is to be preferred to the victory of one religion" (1936, 431). Likewise Megan Armstrong argued that King Henry's "duty to foster the spiritual development of his subjects as well as their economic prosperity" led him to call a truce to the Wars of Religion wracking France (2004, 11).[26] In England similar religious strife led to a political and economic calculation on the part of the monarchy and the passage of the Acts of Toleration. "The ill effects of persecution and civil war upon trade, the fact that dissent was especially prevalent among the commercial groups, and the supposed connection between Dutch prosperity and the religious freedom which obtained there exerted considerable influence in the direction of religious toleration."[27] With no incentive to enforce a denominational monopoly, political leaders let the natural religious pluralism of society grow. Minority religious voices, in turn, created increased lobbying pressure for expanded and more secure liberties. Unfortunately, though, as the case of France and the revocation of the Edict of Nantes in 1685 reveals, religious freedoms once run are never fully guaranteed; political calculations aimed at securing support from key segments of society can lead to a reversal of hard-won liberties.[28]

Thus the key to understanding the origins of religious liberty, and its potential reversal, relates to the political and economic interests of the ruler and the level of competition within the religious economy. Religious pluralism, which naturally arises when restrictions on minority sects are not enforced, enhances the likelihood that religious freedom will be enacted and maintained. Nonetheless, as in the case of France's Edict of Nantes, there is no guarantee that religious pluralism per se will preserve religious freedom. The other important component of religious liberty is the calculus of political leaders. The religious marketplace is most likely to be deregulated if it enhances the political power of rulers as well as positively affecting the ability of the regime to collect tax revenue, encourage economic growth, and dispel civil unrest. To see how this has played out historically, let us briefly turn to an examination of how religious liberty came to be in North and South America.

The Rise of Religious Freedom in the Western Hemisphere

The United States

Putting the popular myth of the Pilgrims aside, the Massachusetts Bay Colony in North America was not founded on the principle of religious freedom. The English Crown's concern over establishing colonies in the New World lest their Spanish and French rivals obtain valuable territory was a more pressing reason behind settlements in North America. It worked out favorably, however, that the king could defuse some of the religious tensions at home by shipping off spiritual dissenters to the American colonies. And once those dissenters made it to the shores of America, they became the top dogs and were exceedingly reluctant to guarantee the freedom to worship to others not of their ilk. To the south of Massachusetts, Anglicans tended to predominate and were similarly loath to grant liberties to religious outsiders. For the most part, then, the British colonies comprised two major religious blocs. Nonetheless religious minorities found cracks within and between these blocs with which to flourish.

The colony of Maryland began its history as an outpost for British Catholics. The great irony, though, was that its charter required toleration of non-Catholic denominations. Within a few decades of its founding, enough Anglicans had moved into the territory to vote for making the Church of England the established faith of the colony and limiting the freedom of Catholics.[29] Greater success at securing religious freedom was found in Rhode Island, Pennsylvania, and New York. All three of these colonies were settled neither by Anglicans nor Congregationalists (Puritans).[30] The reason for the early implementation of religious freedom in these colonies relates specifically to the political and economic interests of the colonial leaders at the time. There were, of course, ideological justifications for their statutes; noble and lofty rhetoric is the main stuff of political communication. However, underneath the surface of these justifications lurked more material motivations.

First and foremost, colonies require colonists. Attracting settlers to a desolate wilderness is no easy task. Any slight inconvenience that might be heaped upon a prospective settler (e.g., being arrested for practicing the wrong religion) only makes the goal of recruitment that much more difficult. While there were plenty of Anglicans to settle the southern colonies (e.g., Virginia, the Carolinas) and Congregationalists for New England, there were not as many Quakers for Pennsylvania. As W. W. Sweet observed for several of the colonies settled by religious minorities:

> [T]he Catholic proprietor of Maryland and the Quakers [sic] proprietors of New Jersey, Pennsylvania, and Delaware were undoubtedly liberal-minded gentlemen, and were sincere in their desire to establish in their several colonies a refuge for persecuted religious groups...but they likewise had vast tracts of land for sale. They were all engaged in a great business enterprise and if their vast wilderness estates were to prove profitable, people in large numbers must be attracted to take up land, establish homes and pay quit rent to the proprietors. (1935, 46–47)

Rhode Island, where the founder Roger Williams first fashioned himself as a Baptist and then a nondenominational seeker, naturally had the same incentive.

New Amsterdam (its name before the English renamed it New York in 1664) was originally settled as a Dutch trading colony. It would have been political and economic suicide for them to bear down on Congregationalists to the north or Anglicans to their south. Indeed the economic self-interest of New Amsterdam simply required that they open their trading port to anyone who wanted to do business, regardless of creed or national origin.

> Turning a profit was the basic aim [of New Amsterdam, or New Netherland]; the idea of establishing an outpost of Dutch society in North America was never first in the minds of the directors of the W.I.C. [West India Company]....[T]he W.I.C....launched a series of experiments to attract immigrants to New Netherland....New Netherland's commercial character gave birth, very early, to a situation of religious pluralism and the accompanying de facto toleration of a wide variety of religious viewpoints....The growing desire of the Dutch W.I.C. to populate the province added Jews and Quakers to this religious mélange.[31]

The ability of any colony to require strict adherence to one denomination, and pay mandatory taxes to that denomination, was made all the more difficult by the ease of exit available to the population; there was plenty of land for the taking in the colonies. Given that the primary demographic of initial settlers was young males, who are notoriously unchurched, too much religious coercion by civil magistrates simply meant that workers and entrepreneurs would pull up stakes and move. Granted, the economic power of being in a city was a major attraction for laborer and businessman alike, but the opportunity to find new opportunities elsewhere made it difficult for even places like Congregational-dominated New England to keep people locked down to one religion; over time the initial restrictions on minority faiths put in place by the Puritans faded into de facto tolerance.

While the needs of settlement initially drove the toleration of different religions in these territories, the desire to facilitate commerce and economic growth kept the drive alive. Even the New England colonies, which contained the most pious colonists in the British Americas, found that expanding religious freedom was in their own economic self-interest. As early as 1659 the United Colonies of New Haven, Massachusetts, Connecticut, and Plymouth threatened a trade embargo on Rhode Island if that colony continued to allow Quakers to make their home there. Although concerned with such a threat, the Rhode Island government stood its ground and forced their New England neighbors to back away from their threat, realizing that trade with Providence was much more valuable than their desire for religious conformity.[32] William Penn, one of the great theorists of liberty in early American thought, himself made the explicit connection between economic prosperity, government revenue, and religious freedom:

> But as it [persecution] has many Arguments for it, that are drawn from the Advantages that have and would come to the Publick by it, so there are divers Mischiefs that must unavoidably follow the Persecution of Dissenters, that may reasonably disswade from such Severity. For they must either be ruined, fly, or conform; and perhaps the last is not the Safest. If they are Ruin'd in their Estates and their Persons Imprisoned, modestly compute, a Fourth of the Trade and Manufactury of the Kingdom sinks; and those that have helped to maintain the Poor, must come upon the Poor's Book for Maintenance. This seems to be an Impoverishing of the Publick.[33]

The case was similar in Virginia, where in the mid-1700s non-Anglican religious groups sought to obtain licenses for meetinghouses. When they were blocked by the colonial government from doing so, a number of businessmen came to their defense, arguing that such restrictions on religious dissenters would only lead them to take their business elsewhere.[34]

Over the course of the seventeenth and eighteenth centuries, religious diversity increased in the colonies largely for the reasons noted above: the need to attract immigrants and merchants and easy exit for dissenters. By the eve of the Revolutionary War, two major religious blocs still existed in the colonies, but their hold on their respective territories was far from hegemonic. The First Great Awakening scattered Methodists and Baptists throughout the southern colonies and New England. Catholics, still a small minority, were making their presence felt in the border areas of French Canada. When war broke out with England, national unity took precedence over denominational conflict. Even the much-despised Catholics were granted a newfound respect and toleration so as to assure the support of the French in the war, a situation that one Catholic historian termed a "necessary virtue."[35] And again when it came time to piece together the disparate colonies into a unified nation, it was readily apparent that no one denomination could claim dominance, or even a majority. A "balance of power" existed among the many faiths of the colonies, and this balance necessitated a laissez-faire policy with no religious establishment and with a guarantee for the free exercise of conscience. It should be duly noted that the First Amendment, with its prohibition on an established church and guarantee of free exercise, only applied to the federal government. Established churches still existed in Massachusetts, Connecticut, and Delaware following the ratification of the Constitution. However, growing religious pluralism eventually necessitated the expansion of religious liberty within these states, and by 1832 Massachusetts ended the last religious establishment in the United States.

Latin America

Religious pluralism and freedom came much later to Latin America than to the United States. The political, economic, and religious context of Spanish and Portuguese settlement guaranteed a Catholic monopoly from 1500 to roughly the early 1900s. First, Spain and Portugal avoided the Protestant Reformation and the schismatic religious landscape that accompanied it. Their colonies did not become dumping grounds for dissenting sects, as did Massachusetts. As the Catholic Church was the only confession in the motherland, it naturally became the only official faith in the colonies.[36] Second, the political economy of Iberian settlement was much different from that in the British colonies. Instead of establishing small farming communities and trading outposts, the Latin American colonies were dominated by a resource-extraction and plantation (*latifundio*) economy that resembled European feudalism. Trade between the regional colonial centers was substantially less than the level of commerce among the North American colonies. As such, immigration and the need to attract merchants of all denominational stripes were not imperatives driving religious policy in the region. Catholic priests could sleep safely knowing their hegemonic status was secure during the colonial period. Indeed the Vatican had entered into an agreement, the *patronato real* (royal patronage), with the Iberian monarchs that guaranteed no spiritual competitors would be allowed in the territory.[37]

Latin American independence, occurring in the first three decades of the nineteenth century, was inspired to a significant extent by both the founding of the United States and the French Revolution. Liberal-minded revolutionaries such as Simón Bolívar and Manuel Belgrano not only carried with them a desire to imitate the political structure of the United States, but they also were tinged by the anticlerical attitudes of the Jacobins in France. The latter were somewhat natural given that the upper tiers of the Catholic Church had been chosen by the Spanish monarchy and were seen as antagonistic toward the independence cause.[38] Nonetheless the leaders of the various separatist movements realized that the Church was a crucial player in securing the loyalties of the population. This was perhaps best exemplified in the crosscutting tensions felt by Bolívar, the Great Liberator, who was one of the more forceful advocates of religious freedom in the new nations of Latin America.

> Bolívar was an exception among the great leaders of Latin American independence, for he advocated separation of Church and State.... [Bolívar] had drunk deeply of the teachings of the French philosophers and religion at best rested but lightly upon him.... Notwithstanding his liberal religious views and his unflagging efforts to have them incorporated into the organic laws of Venezuela and New Granada, Bolívar recognized the political importance of clerical support of the Revolution.... He therefore was careful not to antagonize the clergy and put aside personal opinion for the sake of the general good.[39]

For the most part, independence did not bring a substantial increase in religious freedom in the new states of Latin America. The lack of Protestants in the region meant that the topic of freedom for minority religions was a moot point. Church-state relations centered on how much control national governments would have over the Catholic Church, with most political leaders favoring a continuation of the colonial patronage policies wherein secular leaders exercised veto power over the appointment of bishops. Debates about religious liberty, in essence, were limited to the scope of institutional autonomy granted to the Church by secular politicians.

The next significant change in church-state relations in Latin America occurred during the middle decades of the nineteenth century. Facing severe financial crises brought about by fiscal mismanagement and years of political turmoil, many states saw the property of the Church as a valuable asset that they could expropriate and sell to private investors, raising revenue quickly and creating a new source of taxed property (as Church real estate was traditionally tax-exempt). A weakened Church, facing episcopal vacancies and a serious shortage of clergy, could do little but yield to these actions. But again this represented not a real advancement in terms of religious freedom but rather an alteration of the institutional relationship between the state and the dominant religious organization at the time. The Church lost control of much of its property, but in return it received some limited autonomy in selecting its own personnel.[40] It would take the gradual growth of religious pluralism during the next century to force real changes that reflected an advance in true religious freedom.

The growth of religious pluralism in Latin America varied by country, was largely unforeseen, and resulted from political pressures to open up commerce with Protestant nations in Europe and North America. One of the first nations to introduce religious freedoms for minority faiths was Chile. Prior to the construction of the Panama Canal, Chile was the most inaccessible country to foreign trade in the region. "It was a standard policy of Chilean governments to maximize overseas trade.... [I]t therefore was necessary to handle foreigner's religious sentiments with some care. Guarantees of freedom of worship for foreign nationals were written into commercial treaties concluded with the United States (1833), France (1852), and Britain (1855)."[41] Similar treaties linking religious freedom with trade were negotiated with Mexico, Colombia, Brazil, and Argentina.[42] It should be noted that these early policies were drafted primarily for the benefit of foreigner traders, not missionaries or local citizens seeking to set up a new denomination. Governments still exercised creative ways to limit the influence of non-Catholic sects domestically, including prohibitions on the distribution of the Bible and forbidding Protestant services from being held in Spanish.[43] Despite these restrictions, Protestant missionaries were able to make their way slowly into various societies and begin converting individuals, including indigenous folk who would then become pastors for these new churches. Once Protestants began indigenizing their churches, it became difficult for governments to prevent their growth. It was one thing to deport foreign missionaries; it was just not possible to deport one's own citizens. Moreover most of these new churches provided valuable social services to communities (e.g., literacy training, food banks for the poor), and their members tended to stay out of politics, which was significant for politicians benefiting from the status quo. Latin American politicians had much more important things to worry about than whether their citizens were going to the correct church or not. Over time countries that provided small legal openings for Protestants early on in their histories (e.g., Brazil, Chile, Nicaragua, El Salvador) discovered that by the mid-twentieth century they had sizable populations of non-Catholics. These mostly Protestant constituencies became strong advocates for expanded religious freedoms following the return to democratic forms of government in the 1980s and 1990s.[44]

The important lesson here is that real religious freedom came slowly to the region rather than in one fell swoop. In many ways this gradual growth in freedom may have more staying power than a large change brought about overnight.[45]

It was not smooth sailing for Protestants in all countries, however. In certain countries, most notably Argentina and Colombia, the Catholic Church was able to leverage political turmoil in the mid-twentieth century to its advantage and throw its weight in with politicians that rolled back many of the liberties for minority religions that had been introduced earlier. In Argentina Catholic bishops forged an alliance with Juan Perón during the 1950s that allowed them to impose greater restrictions on foreign missionaries.[46] Although that relationship soured in short order, the Argentine episcopacy still found supporters in the two separate military regimes that held power between 1966 and 1983.[47] In Colombia a period of political violence in the 1950s, known appropriately as *La Violencia,* allowed the Catholic Church to negotiate a truce between the warring factions and secure a more favorable position for itself relative to Protestants.[48] In Mexico the decision by the Catholic hierarchy to side with the conservatives during the Mexican Revolution (1910–20) led to a constitutional provision that effectively made the Catholic Church and other religions illegal in the nation. This had the effect of slowing the growth of Protestantism, or perhaps made it less visible.[49] The spillover of Pentecostalism on the southern border from Guatemala and Protestant missionaries operating just across the U.S. border led to an increase in religious pluralism over time. When Mexico finally began liberalizing its political system in the 1990s, this de facto growth of religious pluralism led to a situation where it was difficult to exclude non-Catholics from new constitutional freedoms, making churches legal once again.[50] Despite freedom for minority faiths taking a step backward in these three nations, it became impossible to ignore the growing presence of Protestantism, and by the beginning of the twenty-first century a reasonable degree of religious liberty was in place throughout the region, with the exception of communist Cuba.[51]

For the most part the expansion of religious pluralism and freedom has been a boon to all faiths in the region. The growing presence of Protestant competitors to Catholic hegemony forced many Catholic hierarchs to engage in a substantial amount of self-reflection and criticism. Initially the Church responded to the presence of new faiths by trying to have them banned by the government, much the way Ford and General Motors attempted to have steep tariffs placed on Toyotas and Hondas in the 1970s. However, given that politicians were preoccupied with more pressing matters (e.g., collapsing economies, communist insurgencies), such a response was not tenable in the long run. The second and more effective response was for the Catholic clergy to become more engaged with their parishioners. Being a centuries-old monopoly meant that Catholic priests became a bit lax in their pastoral effort, taking for granted that everyone in society was Catholic. But as Protestant missionaries quickly discovered, a population that rarely had contact with a Catholic priest (due to a shortage of seminarians) did not have deep Catholic loyalties.

Interestingly the area where the Catholic Church was the weakest institutionally was among the poor. This was not the result of careless disregard, as some may think; it is difficult to find a priest or bishop who truly despises the downtrodden. Instead it was merely a response to an institutional reality. Lacking an adequate number of priests to tend to the entire Latin American population, bishops naturally spent their resources in areas where they got the most return for their investment: among the middle and upper classes. It was these folks who, after all, had money to tithe, which in turn could be devoted to charitable services for the poor. But the neglect of the poor opened a door for Protestant missionaries seeking to attract converts. It was an early strategy of these missionaries to provide a number of material services for the poor, such as medical assistance, literacy training, and other community improvement projects. Not to be outdone, the Catholic Church—in the nations that were experiencing the greatest degree of Protestant competition[52]—began importing more clergy from the United States and Europe and engaged in a new "preferential option for the poor" (see Gill 1998).[53] The result has been a reawakening of Latin America's religious landscape; not only are more people attending Protestant services than ever before, but active lay participation in Catholicism is at an all-time high.[54] To the extent that religious participation yields a number of positive externalities for society (e.g., more charitable giving, lower levels of criminal deviancy, a stronger sense of community), this certainly is a beneficial development for Latin American society, much the way that Alexis de Tocqueville viewed it as beneficial for the United States. Score yet another success for religious freedom and pluralism, unless of course you are Richard Dawkins.

Conclusion: Denominational Pluralism and the Future of Religious Freedom

The process of democratization that swept across Latin America in the last two decades of the twentieth century has largely been consolidated today. Combined with a vibrant and growing environment of religious pluralism, led principally by Pentecostal churches, Latin Americans now enjoy a measure of religious freedom unparalleled in the region's history. Likewise in the United States worshippers of all stripes enjoy freedoms that are historically rare and that remain the envy of many other peoples around the world. In large part these hard-won liberties appear to be firmly rooted in the laws of these nations, and it appears unlikely that there will be a major reversal of religious freedoms in the Western Hemisphere anytime soon. Denominational pluralism acts a strong check on the designs of any one faith that may seek to use the powers of government to limit the rights of others. In short, religious diversity is critical to the emergence and maintenance of religious freedom, and once such pluralism is unleashed it is difficult to put back into the bottle.

Nonetheless denominational pluralism, as we have seen, is not the only factor in promoting an environment of religious freedom. One must look closely at the incentives of those who make the laws. As I have argued, a desire by political actors to maintain power, enhance tax revenue, and promote economic growth greatly affects the likelihood that laws and regulations will be crafted that affect the rights and freedoms of religious groups. These political interests still drive how religions are regulated today. While a wholesale reversal of policies guaranteeing religious freedom is unlikely in Latin America, governments of their own design and for their own reasons often find ways to make public worship difficult for many individuals. For example, even in the United States, where religious liberty seems to stand on a solid foundation, local governments facing budgetary shortfalls have been quick to deny building permits to churches that pay little or no taxes and favor more commercial uses that are more likely to fill the coffers. The growth of homeschooling cooperatives that often use the building space of large churches has also led some local governments to place restrictions on the use of church property as a means of slowing the flight of students from public schools.[55] In countries such as Russia, freedoms for religious minorities that seemed to have been established following the collapse of the Soviet Union have withered away as a whole series of new laws and regulations have made it difficult for non–Russian Orthodox groups to establish a presence.[56] Venezuela has also seen an increase in the harassment of religious groups that are seen as antithetical to Hugo Chávez's increasingly autocratic rule.

In the final analysis the lesson here is that religious liberty cannot be conceived simply as a good idea. It is a reality that individuals must fight for and defend on a daily basis. In this struggle it must be remembered that there are multiple political and economic interests at play and that a successful effort to ensure liberty requires being able to connect the principles of religious freedom to the self-interests of crucial actors who may not necessarily see the benefit of expanding freedom for all.

Notes

1. Arlin M. Adams and Charles J. Emmerich, *A Nation Dedicated to Religious Liberty: The Constitutional Heritage of the Religious Clauses* (Philadelphia: University of Pennsylvania Press, 1990), 3.
2. Jonathan Fox, *A World Survey of Religion and the State* (Cambridge: Cambridge University Press, 2008).
3. Brian J. Grim and Roger Finke, *The Price of Freedom Denied: Religious Persecution and Conflict in the 21st Century* (Cambridge: Cambridge University Press, 2010).
4. See Anthony Gill, *The Political Origins of Religious Liberty* (Cambridge: Cambridge University Press, 2007),57–59, for an explicit discussion on how I view the role of ideas in social scientific arguments. Various reviews of my 2007 book seem to overlook that extensive passage

and criticize me for thinking that ideas play no role in determining social outcomes. This is simply not the case, and you have been forewarned.

5. Some of these goals may be contradictory at times. It may well be the case that a particular ruler can enhance his own position of political power by exacerbating conflict within society.

6. The revocation of the Edict of Nantes is a classic case in point. Following nearly a century of legally guaranteed freedoms for French Protestants, King Louis XIV rescinded his predecessor's declaration, resulting in the persecution and flight of thousands of Huguenots (see Joseph Bergin. *Crown, Church and Episcopate under Louis XIV* (New Haven: Yale University Press. 2004). Similarly in 1997 the Russian government reversed a half-decade-old policy whereby all religious groups were on an equal footing and created a category of historically favored denominations. This policy had the effect of making the life of foreign missionaries remarkably difficult (see Jeremy T. Gunn. "The Law of the Russian Federation on the Freedom of Conscience and Religious Associations from a Human Rights Perspective," in *Proselytism and Orthodoxy in Russia: The New War for the Souls*, edited by John Witte Jr. and Michael Bourdeaux (Maryknoll, NY: Orbis Books.1999).

7. While it is virtually impossible to prevent an individual from believing what he wants, short of some coercive brainwashing technique, restrictions on religious liberty largely affect how people practice and express their beliefs publicly. However, there is a literature that demonstrates that religious practice and belief are closely linked; the more one actively engages in one's faith tradition, the stronger one's beliefs become (cf. Laurence Iannaccone."Religious Practice: A Human Capital Approach." *Journal for the Scientific Study of Religion* 29 (3)(1990) 297–314).

8. Public choice economics is the study of how various rules and institutions, most frequently governmental institutions, affect the cost-benefit calculus of individuals within a society. See Gordon Tullock and James Buchanan. The Calculus of Consent (Indianapolis: The Liberty Fund. 2010 [1962]) for the quintessential primer to this topic.

9. See Gill, *The Political Origins of Religious Liberty*, 12–22, for an inclusive list. Also consult Brian J. Grim and Roger Finke, "International Religion Indexes: Government Regulation, Government Favoritism, and Social Regulation of Religion," *Interdisciplinary Journal of Research on Religion* (2006); and Jonathan Fox. *A World Survey of Religion and the State. (Cambridge: Cambridge University Press. 2008).*

10. Government rules that require religious groups to hire individuals who may disagree with their spiritual mission and/or that require groups to offer certain health benefits that run counter to spiritual teachings (e.g., insurance for contraception) to employees can force a religious group to simply close shop.

11. Anthony Gill, "Septics, Sewers, and Secularization: How Government Regulation Flushes Religiosity Down the Drain," ARDA Guiding Paper Series, 2010.

12. King Charles II of England (1660–85) implemented the Five-Mile Act, which prevented any nonconforming religion from locating within a radius of five miles of a town. Given that transportation was difficult at the time, such a rule was equivalent to a death sentence to any non-Anglican denomination (Clyde L. Grose. "The Religion of Restoration England." *Church History* 6 (3) (1937) 226–227.

13. In 2003 the government of the Czech Republic changed registration requirements for churches. In order to gain official recognition, and hence tax-exempt status, a church must be able to show membership of at least 10,000 people. This rule favored the Catholic Church and other traditional denominations that had an episcopal structure and raised the costs to small, independent start-up churches. See Petr Pajas. "The Impact of New Czech Laws on Churches." *The International Journal of Not-for-Profit Law* 6 (1). (2003).

14. See See Scott E. Isaacson. "A Practical Comparison of the Laws of Religion of Colombia and Chile." *The International Journal of Not-for-Profit Law* 6 (1) (Internet edition 2003).

15. The one thing that did change, though, was that the costs of creating schismatic movements decreased, and fissiparity has been the defining feature of Protestant Christianity ever since Luther.

16. Gill, *The Political Origins of Religious Liberty*.

17. David Mayhew, *Congress: The Electoral Connection* (New Haven, Conn.: Yale University Press, 1974); Barbara Geddes, *Politician's Dilemma: Building State Capacity in Latin America* (Berkeley: University of California Press, 1994); Ronald Wintrobe, *The Political Economy of Dictatorship* (Cambridge: Cambridge University Press, 2000).

18. I recognize that there are some trade-offs between these goals, particularly increasing tax revenue and economic growth. However, this is neither the time nor the place to lay out this debate. See Mancur Olson, "Dictatorship, Development, and Democracy," American Political Science Review 87, no.3 (1993) for a good discussion of these trade-offs. See also Gill, *The Political Origins of Religious Liberty,* 47–50.

19. See Carla Gardina Pestana. *Quakers and Baptists in Colonial Massachusetts* (Cambridge: Cambridge University Press. 1991).

20. Technically the Puritans saw themselves as the more faithful component of the Church of England and sought to reform what they saw as a corrupt religious hierarchy. Nonetheless as time went on it was clear that they represented a significant schismatic movement and hence an alternative competitor to the official established church.

21. Although the Puritan-dominated government of Massachusetts kept expelling Mary Dyer from their territory, they did give her one last chance to hang around Boston Commons—at her public execution.

22. Stephen V. Monsma and J. Christopher Soper, *The Challenge of Pluralism: Church and State in Five Democracies,* 2nd ed. (Lanham, Md.: Rowman & Littlefield, 2008).

23. Rodney Stark and Laurence R. Iannaccone, "A Supply-Side Reinterpretation of the 'Secularization' of Europe," *Journal for the Scientific Study of Religion* 33, no. 3 (1994): 230–52; Jonathan Fox, "The Last Bastion of Secularism? Government Religion Policy in Western Democracies, 1990–2008," paper presented at the annual conference of the International Studies Association, New Orleans, 2010.

24. Rodney Stark, *For the Glory of God: How Monotheism Led to Reformations, Science, Witch-Hunts, and the End of Slavery* (Princeton: Princeton University Press, 2003).

25. This has been one of the more controversial suppositions within the economics of religion literature, with many critics claiming that a single religious preference tends to dominate a culture and is a key component of nationalism. For example, Latin American nations are defined by their reverence for Roman Catholicism, and looking at various Latin American societies during the early part of the twentieth century one would assume that there was only a single religious preference. However, upon closer inspection it becomes apparent that this supposed single preference is largely due to laws making it impossible for competing churches to proselytize. Once these laws are liberalized, religious pluralism quickly becomes commonplace. See Anthony Gill, *Rendering unto Caesar: The Catholic Church and the State in Latin America* (Chicago: University of Chicago Press, 1998); Gill, *The Political Origins of Religious Liberty*.

26. To emphasize that religious liberty is not simply a unilinear trend in society, the Edict of Nantes was revoked roughly a century later by Louis XIV after prodding by his Catholic advisor Cardinal Marazin. See Joseph Bergin. *Crown, Church and Episcopate under Louis XIV* (New Haven: Yale University Press. 2004).

27. W. K. Jordan, *The Development of Religious Toleration in England: From the Beginning of the English Reformation to the Death of Queen Elizabeth* (Cambridge, Mass.: Harvard University Press, 1932) 22.

28. A situation similar to that of France's experiment with religious freedom in the seventeenth century occurred recently in Russia. Following the collapse of the Soviet Union in 1991, a spirit of laissez-faire prevailed in the religious marketplace. Preoccupied with more pressing economic and political concerns, Boris Yeltsin simply declared a Nugentonian free-for-all with respect to religious liberty. Foreign missionaries immediately poured into the country, creating significant competition for the institutionally hobbled Russian Orthodox Church. In response the Moscow patriarch embarked on a campaign to curtail the freedoms of these new religious groups and convinced the Russian government—struggling to pull together an economy spiraling out of control—to make Orthodoxy the favored confession and clamp down on denominations that were directly competing; in exchange the patriarch offered

religious endorsement of the government. Judaism, Islam, and Buddhism were also granted privileged status, as none of those traditional faiths was seen as a proselytizing threat to the Orthodox Church's base. See Gill, *The Political Origins of Religious Liberty*, 80–81, 201–213.

29. Jay P. Dolan, *The American Catholic Experience: A History from Colonial Times to the Present* (Notre Dame, Ind.: University of Notre Dame Press, 1992).

30. It might be possible to say that Rhode Island was settled by a Puritan, Roger Williams. He was so puritanical that he thought the Puritans were not sufficiently pure. Williams followed a theology that argued for a strict separation of religious authority and the civilian magistrates, which, of all the major figures of the colonial period, including William Penn, places him as the one actor most solely motivated by an ideational concern for religious freedom. However, separation of church and state is not necessarily equivalent to religious freedom, as church and state may be institutionally and financially separate yet there still could exist laws restricting the rights of various religious groups. Williams did allow for religious freedom in Rhode Island, partially on ideological grounds but also out of an understanding for the need to attract settlers to his colony and to maintain good relations with the neighboring New England colonies.

31. George L. Smith, *Religion and Trade in New Netherland: Dutch Origins and American Development* (Ithaca, N.Y.: Cornell University Press, 1973), 12–13.

32. Thomas J. Curry, *The First Freedoms: Church and State in America to the Passage of the First Amendment* (Oxford: Oxford University Press, 1986, 22–23).

33. William Penn, *The Political Writings of William Penn,* introduction and annotations by Andrew R. Murphy (Indianapolis: Liberty Fund, 2002), 317.

34. For more detailed evidence on the link between immigration, trade and public revenues, and religious freedom, including additional citations on the topic from William Penn, see Gill, *The Political Origins of Religious Liberty,* 91–113; Rhys Isaac, "Religion and Authority: Problems of the Anglican Establishment in Virginia in the Era of the Great Awakening and the Parsons' Cause," *William and Mary Quarterly* 30, no. 1 (1973): 27.

35. Charles P. Hanson, *Necessary Virtue: The Pragmatic Origins of Religious Liberty in New England* (Charlottesville: University Press of Virginia, 1998).

36. Unofficially religious pluralism in the guise of "folk Catholicism" flourished. As the Catholic Church was woefully understaffed in the colonies and could not enforce an orthodox theology, indigenous populations amended official Catholicism with various native elements and/ or cultic worship of Christian saints or other figures. The strong devotion to the Virgin of Guadalupe, involving the worship of the Virgin Mary and the story of how she appeared to a Mexican boy, is a classic example of this de facto pluralism under the patina of a single, unified faith.

37. This deal came with significant trade-offs for the Church, namely a substantial loss of autonomy when it came to picking religious officials in the colonies.

38. The loyalties of the colonial episcopacy were not as clear-cut as one might assume, though. When liberal forces came to ascendancy in the Spanish Parliament in the early 1800s, and when the Spanish king was deposed by Napoleon's forces, several bishops felt compelled to join the more conservative elements of the independence cause out of sheer self-preservation. Nonetheless the roots of anticlericalism ran deep in colonial Latin America, as the Catholic hierarchy was clearly viewed as a remnant of the Old World. See J. Lloyd Mecham, *Church and State in Latin America: A History of Politico-Ecclesiastical Relations* (Chapel Hill: University of North Carolina Press, 1966); Gill, *Rendering unto Caesar,* 20–24.

39. One should be careful to avoid judging historical figures by today's normative standards. While Bolívar certainly favored separation of church and state, which is a key component of religious liberty, especially if it is associated with only one denomination, it is unclear to the extent that he would have granted outright freedoms to other denominations. Since non-Catholic churches were virtually nonexistent in the region at the time, excepting a few British and Dutch trading outposts, this was never a question Bolívar or others had to wrestle with at the time. See Mecham, *Church and State in Latin America,* 45.

40. In a modification of the *patronato real*, secular governments agreed not to select episcopal appointments directly. Instead the Vatican got to choose who would fill vacant sees as long as

the candidates met with the implicit approval of the national president or legislature. Given the relative lack of candidates and the desire of political leaders to get the positions filled so as to have somebody to bless their governments, this new policy generally favored greater institutional autonomy for the Church.

41. Simon Collier, "Religious Freedom, Clericalism, and Anticlericalism in Chile, 1820–1920," in *Freedom and Religion in the Nineteenth Century*, ed. Richard Helmstadter (Stanford: Stanford University Press, 1997), 310.

42. Wilkins B. Winn, "The Efforts of the United States to Secure Religious Liberty in a Commercial Treaty with Mexico, 1825–1831," *The Americas* 28, no. 3 (1972): 311–32; Wilkins B. Winn, "The Issue of Religious Liberty in the United States Commercial Treaty with Colombia, 1824," *The Americas* 26, no. 3 (1970): 291–301; Gill, *Rendering unto Caesar,* 152.

43. Collier, "Religious Freedom, Clericalism, and Anticlericalism in Chile," 305; Gill, *The Political Origins of Religious Liberty,* 133–137.

44. Gill, *The Political Origins of Religious Liberty,* 135–146.

45. Compare the Latin American cases with Russia, where a dramatic opening in religious freedom in 1991 gave way to the door slamming shut for all but a few favored denominations in 1997 (see Gill The Political Origins of Religious Liberty, 200–213). The connection between the rapidity with which religious (or any) freedoms are guaranteed and their staying power suggests itself as an interesting research topic.

46. Santiago Canclini, *Los Evangélicos en el tiempo de Perón: Memorias de un pastor bautista sobre la libertad religiosa en la Argentina* (Buenos Aires: Editorial Mundo Hispano, 1972).

47. Gill, *Rendering unto Caesar.*

48. James E. Goff, *The Persecution of Protestant Christians in Colombia, 1948–1958*, SONDEOS No. 23 (Cuernavaca, Mexico: CIDOC, 1968).

49. The history of Protestantism in Mexico remains to be written. The freezing of the religious marketplace in the 1920s meant that most scholars paid little attention to religious developments in the country, particularly with respect to Protestant denominations.

50. Anthony Gill, "The Politics of Regulating Religion in Mexico: The 1992 Constitutional Reforms in Historical Context," *Journal of Church and State* 41, no. 4 (1999): 761–94.

51. The other exception may be Venezuela, where Hugo Chávez has increasingly tightened his grip on every aspect of society. While not much has been written about his regime's policy toward religious groups, particularly religious minorities, I have heard from various informal sources that Protestant missionaries have faced increased levels of harassment.

52. As a brief aside, one should not fall into the trap of viewing competition merely as a zero-sum proposition, wherein the success of one group means the failure of the other. Religious competition certainly contains an element of a zero-sum game to the extent that conversion results in one person leaving one church to join another. But there are positive-sum aspects to competition as well. As multiple churches compete in the religious marketplace, they can learn different pastoral strategies from one another: which techniques work and which ones fail. This enhances the ability of all churches to better serve the needs and desires of their congregants. Just as athletic competition helps to improve the proficiency of an athlete irrespective of whether or not he or she wins on the field, so too does religious competition yield stronger institutions.

53. While the connection between Protestant competition and the Church's "preferential option for the poor" may seem tendentious, that connection was nonetheless admitted to by numerous Catholic officials, including the likes of Padre Alberto Hurtado, who is on his way to being beatified as the first saint of Chile (Alberto Hurtado. *¿Es Chile un país católico?* (Santiago, Chile: Editorial Los Andes. [1941] 1992); see also Maryknoll Fathers."Proceedings of the Lima Methods Conference of the Maryknoll Fathers". Maryknoll House, Lima Peru, 23–28 August 1954. (Maryknoll, NY: Maryknoll Fathers. 1954); Helmut Gnadt Vitalis. *The Significance of Changes in Latin American Catholicism since Chimbote 1953.* (Cuernavaca, Mexico: CIDOC.1969); and Guillermo Cook. *The Expectation of the Poor: Latin American Base Ecclesial Communities in Protestant Perspective.* (Maryknoll, NY: Orbis Books. 1985). See Gill, *Rendering unto Caesar,* for this argument. GuillermoTrejo. "Religion Competition and Ethnic Mobilization in Latin America: Why the Catholic Church Promotes Indigenous Movements

in Mexico." American Political Science Review 103 (3): 323–42. (2009). provides an independent test of, and shows support for, Gill's thesis on the role of competition in sparking the Catholic Church to pay greater attention to the poor.

54. R. Andrew Chesnut, *Competitive Spirits: Latin America's New Religious Economy* (Oxford: Oxford University Press, 2003).

55. See Gill, "Septics, Sewers, and Secularization."

56. Mark Elliott and Sharyl Corrado, "The 1997 Russian Law on Religion: The Impact on Protestants," *Religion, State & Society* 27, no. 1 (1999): 109–34.

5

Oligopoly Dynamics and the Triple Religious Markets in China

FENGGANG YANG

In the study of church-state relations and religious change, the contrasting models of religious monopoly and pluralism have been the main axis of theoretical constructions. When such theories, which are based on European and American experiences, are applied to non-Western societies, blurred or even distorted panoramas are probably inevitable. We get a distorted picture of the world if we see only Europe and America facing each other across the Atlantic Ocean. If instead we face away from the Atlantic in either direction, we notice a variety of Muslim countries, Asian nations, and numerous distinct cultures. And we see that the dominant type of church-state relations in the world today is neither monopoly nor pluralism but oligopoly—the dominance of a select few religions in a society. In an attempt to take a truly global perspective, I propose to adopt the lenses of oligopoly to understand the dynamics of church-state relations and religious change in society in the world today.

In this chapter I will first describe the four types of church-state relations in human history, then clarify the key concepts of pluralism, plurality, and pluralization and suggest some theoretical propositions of the oligopoly dynamics. I will then trace the historical origin of the pluralistic legal arrangement in the United States, which has been seriously challenged but upheld because of the cultural and civic arrangements for religious freedom. The theoretical concepts and propositions will then be applied to understand China as one of the cases of religious oligopoly, which manifests in the triple religious market.[1]

Four Types of State-Religion Relations

There have been four types of state-religion relations in human history: religious monopoly, pluralism, oligopoly, and total ban of religion by the state.

Many scholars have explored religious pluralism and religious monopoly as antitheses.[2] However, many countries have never had a religious monopoly or pluralism. Instead they maintained religious oligopoly. In religious oligopoly the state allows more than one religion to operate legally, but other religions are banned or subject to repression.[3] China is an example par excellence. For millennia China has allowed multiple religions to operate, yet the government has maintained restrictive regulations and suppressed heterodox and sectarian religious movements. Under communist rule since 1949, China officially allows only five religions: Buddhism, Daoism, Islam, Catholicism, and Christianity (Protestantism). But China is not the only country that maintains religious oligopoly. In Indonesia the Ministry of Religious Affairs extends official status to six religious groups: Islam, Catholicism, Protestantism, Buddhism, Hinduism, and Confucianism. Iran recognizes Islam, and its constitution states that "within the limits of the law" Zoroastrians, Jews, and Christians are the only recognized religious minorities who are guaranteed freedom to practice their beliefs.

China once imposed a total ban of religion. All churches, temples, and mosques were closed down during the Cultural Revolution. The Maoists tried hard to eradicate religion and replace it with an atheist ideology. Total ban of religion has happened rarely, but not uniquely. As far as I know, at least one other country once banned all religions: Albania under the communists. The Soviet Union and other communist countries had at least some churches, mosques, or temples open for religious activities throughout the communist era. To my knowledge, a total ban of religion is not practiced in any country today. Nevertheless it is an important type for the full understanding of religion and society. The failures of such experiments in China and Albania may have implications for various secularist experiments in other societies.

From the perspective of the state, the range from total ban to pluralism may be regarded as quantitative: banning all, banning all but one, banning all but a few, or banning none.[4] Brian Grim and Roger Finke[5] compiled cross-national data that include a question about state-religion relations: "To what extent is there a favored (or established) religion in the country?" Many countries today grant legal status to only a selected few religions (see Table 5.1). The left column of Table 5.1 is my categorization of the four major types of state-religion relationships. The table shows that about 20 percent of countries are pluralistic and slightly more countries monopolistic. The majority, almost 58 percent, are more or less oligopolistic. Even if we adopt a stricter criterion of formal regulations, about 50 percent of the countries in the world today are oligopolistic. This global fact of religious oligopoly should serve as the starting point for constructing or reconstructing a theory of church-state relations and religious change in society.

Table 5.1. **Four Types of State-Religion Relations**

"To what extent is there a favored (or established) religion in the country?"

Religious policy/law		Number of countries	Percentage
Pluralism	All religious brands are treated the same	40	20.4
Oligopoly	Cultural or historical legacies only	16	8.2
	Some brands have special privileges or government access	56	28.6
	One religious brand has privileges or government access	41	20.9
Monopoly	One single state or official religious brand	43	21.9
Total Ban	*All religions are banned*	(2)	
TOTAL		196	100.0

Note: "Cross-National Data: Religion Indexes, Religious Adherents, and Other Data," http://www.thearda.com/. This data file assembles data from multiple sources, but many of the measures are from the ARDA's coding of the 2003 U.S. State Department's International Religious Freedom Reports. This coding produced data on 195 different countries and territories (for a list of countries coded, see Brian J. Grim and Roger Finke, "International Religion Indexes: Government Regulation, Government Favoritism, and Social Regulation of Religion," *Interdisciplinary Journal of Research on Religion* 2 [2006]) but excluded the United States. Additional data on religious regulation and favoritism in the smaller countries not covered by the State Department Reports were provided by researchers at the World Christian Database. In addition this project assembled (with permission) other cross-national measures of interest to researchers on religion, economics, and politics. They include adherent information from the World Christian Database, scales from Freedom House and the Heritage Foundation, and various socioeconomic measures from the United Nations. Measures for religious persecution (AESTIMA) and ethnic identity (DETHNIC) were added to this file in August 2007.

Pluralism, Plurality, and Pluralization

In the sociology of religion, there have been ongoing debates about religious pluralism, including heated debates on the relationship between religious pluralism and religious vitality. The old wisdom, known as the secularization theory, was that religious pluralism would lead to religious decline because it undermines the plausibility of religion.[6] "New paradigm" scholars argue that religious pluralism is associated with religious vitality because it bolsters competition among religious groups.[7] While the negative correlation between religious pluralism and religious vitality has been rejected by most scholars,[8] including Peter Berger himself,[9] the positive correlation between religious pluralism and religious participation has been subject to fierce dispute.[10] This debate has involved painstaking technicalities of measurements and statistical procedures. However, the involved scholars have made little effort to clarify the concept of pluralism itself. What is pluralism? Is it accidental or inevitable?

As a first step toward clarification, it is necessary to distinguish the descriptive and normative uses of the term *pluralism*. James A. Beckford (1999) suggests using "diversity" for the former and "pluralism" for the latter. Robert Wuthnow substantiates these distinctions succinctly in his presidential address to the Society for the Scientific Study of Religion: "If diversity is concerned descriptively with the degree of heterogeneity among units within a society, pluralism refers to the normative evaluation of this diversity and with the social arrangements put in place to maintain these normative judgments."[11] In light of this distinction, the dispute appears to surround descriptive diversity. However, the persisting use of *pluralism* instead of *diversity* indicates that the involved scholars might hold, consciously or unconsciously, a normative position, either regarding pluralism as a good thing or a bad thing, thus arguing for its positive effect on religious vitality or the lack of it, respectively.

The descriptive and normative dimensions of pluralism may indeed be entangled, so much so that adopting two seemingly unrelated terms may not be the best approach for conceptualization and theorizing. Following the lead of some scholars,[12] I would adopt a set of related words with the same root—plurality, pluralization, and pluralism—to define the interconnected status, process, and configuration on the *social* level:

> Plurality (diversity) describes the *status* or *degree* of religious heterogeneity within a society.
> Pluralization is the *process* of increasing plurality within a society.
> Pluralism refers to the *social arrangements* favorable to a high or increased level of plurality.

I would further differentiate the "social arrangements" of pluralism into legal, civic, and cultural arrangements. The pluralistic legal structure that legitimizes religious freedom is favorable to increased plurality. In modern times the legal structure appears to be the key to pluralization, or the lack of it. On the other hand, most of the existing religions seem to have a natural tendency to seek their own monopoly in society, attempting to ally with state powers to achieve and maintain monopoly whenever possible. Without the intellectual understanding and a certain level of social consensus that legitimize and justify individual freedom of religion and group equality of religions, and without civic organizations in the civil society that keep in check the state agencies and religious organizations, the pluralistic legal structure cannot be implemented or maintained in practice. Therefore the civic and cultural arrangements are foundational to attain and retain the legal arrangement for pluralism.

We must keep in mind that pluralism has also been used to refer to a position on the individual level, a philosophical or theological position regarding the relationship between one's own religion and other religions. Besides pluralism, other philosophical or theological positions include relativism, exclusivism, and inclusivism.[13] Wuthnow distinguishes the individual and social pluralism this way: "A pluralist [person] is someone who can see and appreciate all points of view, a person who is presumably tolerant, informed, cosmopolitan, and a pluralist society is one in which social arrangements favor the expression of diverse perspectives and lifestyles."[14] We may call these *individual pluralism* and *social pluralism*, respectively. The problem of secularization theory, especially in the form articulated by Berger in the 1960s, is that it confuses individual pluralism and social pluralism. Empirical evidence has shown that the social arrangements of religious pluralism do not necessarily lead to individual pluralism or relativism. In the United States and many other pluralistic societies, there are many fundamentalists and evangelicals who squarely reject theological or philosophical pluralism. At the same time many of these people affirm the social pluralism that guarantees their freedom of religious belief and practice. Therefore the pluralistic society in reality has created sufficient social space for individuals to choose and hold one of the philosophical or theological positions or attitudes. In this chapter I will focus on social pluralism.

Applying this set of social-level descriptive terms on the world today, we may begin with these basic statements (propositions) regarding the relationship between religion and society in modern times:

1. Religious pluralization is the general trend in modern societies.
2. More and more states have adopted the legal arrangement for pluralism.
3. The civic and cultural arrangements of pluralism tend to lag behind the adoption of the pluralistic legal arrangement.

Pluralization happens in many societies but is more common in the modern world. A tribal or relatively isolated society may maintain a substantial level of religious homogeneity. However, modern economic, political, and social changes and structures have created spiritual and intellectual conditions favorable to pluralization, which takes place either through invention of new sects (denominations) or through importation of foreign religions. Globalization further increases the interconnectedness of societies and eases religious diffusion across the world. In the globalizing world, people of different religious traditions become neighbors either physically through migration or virtually through the mass media and the Internet.

Modernization and globalization under the influence of liberal democratic principles that originated in the modern West have resulted in the adoption of the pluralistic legal arrangement by an increasing number of countries. However, the intellectual understanding of this pluralism remains limited in most societies, resulting in the lack of civic and cultural arrangements for religious pluralism. The report by the Pew Forum on Religion & Public Life *Global Restrictions on Religion* distinguishes government restrictions and social hostilities to plural religions.[15] The two indexes tend to move together (are positively correlated); that is, "higher scores on one index generally are associated with higher scores on the other." Historically speaking, the United Nations Universal Declaration of Human Rights in 1948 may have promoted the adoption of religious freedom in the constitution or basic law of UN member countries.[16] However, the understanding of religious freedom may not be shared by the citizens at the time of constitutional adoption, nor does the underdeveloped civil society provide the necessary social and cultural support for upholding it. While some people strive for pluralism, others try hard to resist it. If pluralization is indeed the general trend, however, the resistance stands to lose over time. To gain a better understanding of the process of pluralization, we need to turn to its historical development.

Accidental and Deliberate Pluralism

An important trigger of pluralization in modern times is the separation of church and state, an innovation first attempted in the United States. After the thirteen colonies joined to form the United States of America, the First Amendment to the Constitution was ratified in 1791. Regarding religion, it states, "Congress shall make no law respecting an establishment of religion, or prohibiting the free exercise thereof." This legal arrangement of religious freedom includes disestablishment (no state religion) and deregulation (no prohibition of any religion). It might have happened accidentally due to the unusual religious and cultural conditions in those states at the time: "The thirteen colonies which formed the United States were populated with settlers from Western Europe (and slaves from Africa) adhering to several different religions. . . . Although the vast majority were Protestant Christians, they belonged to different denominations which were not at all united. Therefore, all the religions were minority religions; no one dominated."[17] Until 1791 most of the colonies had an established church or a privileged Protestant denomination, but none of them was acceptable as the established church in the other states of the new nation. In this sense the American experiment of the separation of church and state was accidental. It took almost fifty years before "the last traces of privilege of the Congregational Church disappeared in the state of Massachusetts."[18]

This pluralistic legal arrangement propelled the trend of pluralization in the United States. While the denominations at the founding of the country have persisted, a number of Protestant sects emerged. On the other hand, the new nation was very much Protestant Christian in its collective conscience, although it was a secular state in legal and legislative terms. It took about a hundred years before the United States faced the first real challenges of pluralism. That was when southern, central, and eastern European immigrants arrived in large numbers around the turn of the twentieth century, and among them many were Catholics and Jews and some were Orthodox Christians. This substantial pluralization challenged the nation to redefine its collective identity. It took about half a century before Americans came to terms with this new plurality. While the state maintained the pluralistic legal structure, the nation settled for a Judeo-Christian cultural identity, well illustrated in Will Herberg's seminal work, *Protestant-Catholic-Jew* (1955).

Since the 1960s the United States has been facing greater challenges of pluralism. First, amid the social turmoil and problems of race, ethnicity, gender, the Vietnam War, political ideology, and so on, numerous new religious movements emerged and attracted many young people. Social reactions to these movements included the anticult and deprogramming frenzy. Second, after 1965 immigrants have come from Latin America, Asia, and the Mideast. Not only are they viewed as racially different, but many have brought different religions, including Hinduism, Buddhism, Islam, and a variety of other religions.[19] Consequently it is probably not an exaggeration to say that any religion that ever existed anywhere in the world has followers or practitioners in the United States today. The increasing presence of non-Judeo-Christian and nonconventional religions has brought many challenges to American society, among which is the burning question of national identity, as squarely raised by the political scientist Samuel Huntington in *Who Are We? The Challenges to American National Identity* (2004).

Responding to these new challenges, some people have called to enlarge the inclusion, by talking of "Abrahamic religions" or "one nation under God," while others have appealed to the Protestant Christian roots of the nation. Meanwhile many people have come to reexamine the very notion of pluralism. Is pluralism a good thing for American society? Although some scholars have championed it,[20] others have sounded more cautious.[21] Some legal cases and political contentions have challenged the pluralistic legal arrangement itself. Worrying about this ongoing trial of pluralism, some scholars argue that "disestablishment and protection of religious freedom are never permanent. In the United States, they remain in danger of being overturned at any time by those with particular religious beliefs."[22] In my view, however, because the civil and cultural arrangements of pluralism are in place, and because civil society is well developed in the United States, the overturning of the legal separation of state and religion is unlikely to happen. Pluralization seems irreversible.

Even though the innovative experiment of pluralism started accidently, the idea of church-state separation seems infectious, just as innovations have a natural tendency of diffusion.[23] Of course, the diffusion of state-religion separation has been a slow and long process, full of challenges, twists, and turns, as many European and Asian countries can attest.

Religious Oligopoly in Historical and Contemporary China

For centuries multiple religions existed in imperial China. Confucianism, a cultural tradition that has a religious dimension or is quasi-religious, had been the orthodoxy, but Daoist and Buddhist sects existed alongside Confucianism as ordinary and supplementary heterodoxies.[24] Following the revolution in 1911 that overthrew the imperial Qing Dynasty, China became the first republic in Asia. Around that time, facing Western imperialism and the pressure to construct the modern nation-state, some individuals in Chinese elites considered establishing Confucianism as the monopolistic national religion or state religion (*guo jiao*), as did the Britons with Anglicanism and the Japanese with Shinto. After fierce debates and struggles, the American model eventually prevailed. The new Republic of China adopted the principle of religious freedom in its constitution, even though there was a lack of understanding of the meaning of pluralism among the populace as well as among the elites. In the following decades wars and political turmoil destabilized China. Eventually the Chinese Communist Party took power in mainland China in 1949. The Republic of China under the Kuomintang (the Nationalist Party) withdrew to the island of Taiwan and imposed martial law for almost four decades. Only after martial law was lifted in 1987 were people able to practice the freedom of religion decreed in the Constitution of the Republic of China. Today many religions and religious groups and sects freely operate in Taiwan. In mainland China freedom of religious belief has been retained in the Constitution of the People's Republic of China. In practice, however, religions have been subjected to repression and eradication.

Following the establishment of the People's Republic of China (PRC) in 1949, the atheist ideology compelled the Chinese Communist Party (CCP) to impose control over religion. First, the party-state banned the heterodox sects of Chinese traditions. Hundreds of sectarian groups, including the once prominent Yiguandao and numerous so-called redemptive societies, were suppressed as antirevolutionary and reactionary *hui-dao-men*. Second, the party-state adopted a more tactical approach of co-opting major religions that had massive followings and international connections. Through tremendous government maneuvers, the party-state managed to form "patriotic" associations for the five religions, namely the Buddhist Association of China (1953), the Islamic Association of China (1953), the Christian Three-Self Patriotic Movement Committee of China (1954), the Daoist Association of China (1957), and the Catholic Laity

Patriotic Association of China (1957), which was later renamed the Catholic Patriotic Association of China. Thereafter these patriotic associations have served as an integral part of the control mechanism of the CCP's religious policy.

Soon after that, amalgamation was imposed upon each of the five religions. Existing denominational and sectarian systems were banned. Protestant Christians were forced to hold unified services that included believers of all Protestant denominations. Many temples, churches, and mosques were closed down or converted for nonreligious uses. Those remaining open had to reduce the frequency of religious activities, and their clergy were forced to become physical laborers. Resistant religious leaders were imprisoned or sent to labor camps. Religious sites disappeared and activities diminished in the following years. Some prefectures and counties rushed to declare themselves "no-religion prefectures" and "no-religion counties."

In 1966 Chairman Mao Zedong single-handedly launched the Great Proletarian Cultural Revolution to purge the "bourgeois elements" believed to be permeating the party and society at large. The remaining religious venues were shut down. Many religious buildings were actually torn down, statues of gods and religious artifacts were smashed, and religious scriptures were burned.

Following the death of Mao in 1976, Deng Xiaoping gradually emerged as the paramount leader within the CCP. Under his leadership the CCP set a new course for the country, focusing on modernization and economic development. In order to rally people of all walks around the central task of economic development, the pragmatic CCP began to loosen control over various aspects of social life. Beginning in 1979 a limited number of Protestant and Catholic churches, Buddhist and Daoist temples, and Islamic mosques reopened for religious services.

In 1982 religious toleration was formally inscribed in a new edict of the CCP, titled "The Basic Viewpoint and Policy on the Religious Affairs during the Socialist Period of Our Country." It has become better known as Document No. 19.[25] This central document has served as the basis for religious policy since then. It grants legal existence to Buddhism, Daoism, Islam, Protestantism, and Catholicism under the government-sanctioned patriotic associations, but not to any group outside of the five religious associations, nor to other religions.

Since 1982 the party-state has promulgated circulars, enacted ordinances, and issued administrative orders (Potter 2003) that have increasingly tightened its control over religious organizations. For example, in 1991 the CCP issued Document No. 6, which calls for strengthening the religious affairs administration, including expansion of the number of Religious Affairs Bureau cadres down to the township level of government. In 1994 the State Council published two ordinances that require all religious groups to register with the government and prohibit foreigners from proselytizing in China. In 1996 the CCP and the State Council issued a joint decree to curb the building of temples and outdoor Buddha statues and constrict authority to grant new building permits for religious venues to provincial governments. In 1999 Falun Gong was banned as an "evil cult" (*xie jiao*), and its core leaders were jailed, although the movement's founder took refuge in the United States. After the initial crackdown on Falun Gong, the National People's Congress Standing Committee adopted the Legislative Resolution on Banning Heretic Cults in October 1999, which presented a form of legitimacy to the crackdown on Falun Gong and other *qigong* or cultic groups. In the following years provincial governments issued numerous temporary or draft ordinances and administrative orders aimed at controlling religious groups. Eventually these administrative orders were consolidated into the State Council's Regulations of Religious Affairs that took effect on March 1, 2005.

The religious oligopoly of the five religions in contemporary China is maintained by interwoven control apparatuses, as listed in Document No. 19, "including the united front department [of the CCP], the religious affairs bureau [of the state], the nationalities affairs commission, the political-legal ministry, the ministries of propaganda, culture, education, science and technology, and health, and the people's associations of the Workers' Union, the Communist Youth League, and the Women's Union." The circular stresses the importance for all these party or state departments to "seek unity of thinking, unity of cognition, and unity of policy, divide work with responsibility, act in close coordination, take this important work into hands earnestly, and do it persistently and seriously."

Regarding the division of work and responsibility, the major control apparatuses are the United Front Departments of the party and the Religious Affairs Bureaus of the government. The United Front Department of the CCP Central Committee has a division of religious affairs, which is charged with making religious policies and rallying religious leaders around the CCP. The day-to-day administration of religious affairs lies in the Religious Affairs Bureau (RAB) of the State Council, including approving the opening of temples, churches, and mosques, approving special religious gatherings and activities, and approving the appointment of leaders in the religious associations. The RAB is sometimes combined with the Commission of Ethnic Affairs at the provincial and county levels, and the provincial- and lower-level RAB chief is often an associate director of the CCP's United Front Department of the corresponding level.

Since the restoration of the Religious Affairs Bureau of the State Council in 1979, significant increases in the number of religious affairs cadres have occurred in 1988, 1994, 1998, and 2004. By the end of 1995 there were 3,053 religious affairs officials on the county level or above. Meanwhile more functions have been added to the RAB of the State Council, including the Research Center of Religion in 1988, *China Religion* magazine, and the Religious Culture Press in 1994. In 1998 the RAB of the State Council was renamed the State Administration of Religious Affairs (SARA) and given increased administrative status within the central government system.

Besides the United Front Department and SARA/RAB, religious associations must also register with the Ministry of Civil Affairs, but the registration must be approved first by the RAB. The Ministry of Public Security (police) deals with all illegal religious activities, including any illegal activities of the five official religions and all activities of all other religions. The Ministry of State Security also watches some religious groups and active leaders, especially since the early 1990s, when Chinese authorities intensified the fight against infiltration by foreign religious organizations and foreign political entities using religion. Since the crackdown on Falun Gong and banning "evil cults," more resources have been put into religious control and atheist propaganda, including publishing the new magazine called *Science and Atheism* and books of atheism, organizing atheist and anticult associations and exhibitions, and organizing study sessions by the CCP and Communist Youth League branches. An anticult ministry has been developed under the secretive name of the 610 Office. (It is said that the name came from the CCP directive on June 10, 1999, that established this ministry.) The 610 Office has been added to provincial, prefectural, and even county governments.

In practice the SARA/RAB usually rules through the so-called patriotic religious associations. The associations of the five official religions are nongovernmental organizations in name, but they function as an extension and delegation of RAB. For example, in principle the provincial-level Three-Self Patriotic Movement Committee (TSPM) holds the power to ordain ministers, but no one can be ordained without prior approval by the provincial RAB. The prefecture- or county-level TSPM appoints the senior pastor of local churches, but the appointment must first be approved by the same level RAB and United Front Department. More important, the national, provincial, prefectural, and county TSPMs are separate organizations independent from each other. That is, the local TSPMs are not under the leadership of the provincial or national TSPMs. TSPMs report to the RAB on the same level and the one immediately above. When a church plans to organize meetings or activities involving people beyond the local administrative region, it has to apply to the higher-level RAB. If the activity involves people from another county, it has to be approved by the prefectural RAB; if from another prefecture, then from the provincial RAB; if from another province or another country, then from the SARA. These rules and mechanisms apply to all five religions.

Once the total ban of religion was lifted in 1979, however, a religious upsurge outpaced regulatory expansion in spite of the state's accelerated efforts of control. Economic development remains the central task of the CCP's top leadership, and many local governments have often used this to justify a pragmatic approach to various religions. In other words, many of the governmental agencies have tried to use religion for economic development, such as building temples for tourism and allowing more churches in order to attract overseas investments. In the reform era, the economic consideration often prevails, which exacerbates the frustrations of religious affairs cadres, who are losing control of the religious organizations.

Triple Religious Markets under Heavy Regulation

All countries under communist rule, past and present, enacted heavy regulations on religion, with the intention of reducing and eventually eliminating religion. Suppressive regulation may lead to the decline of one form of religiosity—participation in formal organizations—but other forms of religiosity, including beliefs and noninstitutionalized practices, are more difficult to control. In effect, oligopolistic heavy regulation leads not to religious reduction but to complication of the religious market, resulting in a tripartite market with different dynamics. The heavily regulated market may be subdivided into the red, black, and gray markets.[26]

> DEFINITION 1. A red market comprises all legal (officially permitted) religious organizations, believers, and religious activities.

The red market is not equally open to all religious groups. The religious organizations have to comply with the commands of the political authorities. They are stained red, that is, colored with the official communist ideology. The red stain is reflected in the rhetoric of the clergy, theological discourses, and practices of the religious groups.[27]

> DEFINITION 2. A black market comprises all illegal (officially banned) religious organizations, believers, and religious activities.

Black market exchanges are conducted underground or in secrecy.

> DEFINITION 3. A gray market comprises all religious and spiritual organizations, practitioners, and activities with ambiguous legal status.

The groups, individuals, and activities in a gray area of religious regulation may be perceived as both legal and illegal or neither legal nor illegal.

The gray market is the most difficult to demarcate because of its ambiguous and amorphous nature. Broadly speaking it includes two types of groups and practices: (1) illegal religious activities of legally existing religious groups and (2) religious or spiritual practices that manifest in culture or science instead of religion.

Type 1 religious practices of the gray market are conducted by legal religious suppliers and consumers evading restrictive regulation. For example, a regulation may prohibit proselytizing outside the premises of a religious building or to children. Defying the regulation, family members and friends of an otherwise legal religious group might gather at home to discuss their beliefs and, in the process, socialize their children into the religious faith. Religious groups and individuals may provide social services with the implicit intention to proselytize. Regulating these kinds of activities requires more elaborate rules regarding legal boundaries, and in enforcing such rules authorities must exert great care to delineate ambiguous boundaries or borderline zones. Meanwhile religious suppliers and consumers can be very creative in responding to adverse rules. Creativity in evading regulations also makes it difficult for researchers to document and quantify the extent of gray market religiosity.

Type 2 religious activities of the gray market include various forms of informal or implicit religion and spirituality. These activities have been studied by scholars as folk religion, popular religion, quasi-religion, New Age occult religions, magic, yoga, client and audience cults, or new spiritualities.[28] Not all scholars agree that each of these activities should be classified as religious, but sociologists of religion generally agree that, regardless of classification, these spiritual alternatives compete for adherents with conventional religions. While it is difficult for scholars to define alternative spirituality, it is almost impossible for authorities to regulate it. Rather than professing religious belief, alternative spiritualists may insist that their practices are culturally or scientifically based. For example, shamanism may be practiced as ethnic or folk dances, and spiritual healing may be carried out in the name of an alternative medicine. As culture or science, such activities arguably fall outside the boundaries of religious regulation. However, authorities may nevertheless try to bring such practices under control, especially when religious dimensions of the practices become more obvious. As part of the gray market, informal spiritual practices are a constant challenge to regulators and researchers alike.

Three propositions about the triple market of religion are most important for the understanding of the oligopoly dynamics:

PROPOSITION 1. To the extent that religious organizations are restricted in number and in operation, a black market will emerge in spite of high costs to individuals.

The black market is a logical consequence of heavy regulation, which seeks to eliminate illegal groups. In spite of regulation and suppression, however, history recounts myriad religious virtuosos who sought and practiced proscribed religions regardless of circumstance, and clandestinely if necessary.[29] There are always people who are willing to pay a high price for their religion, including sacrificing one's life in this world. When the state bans certain religious exchanges to the extent that the religious needs of certain people are not met in the red market, a black market will emerge to fill in.

> PROPOSITION 2. To the extent that a red market is restricted and a black market is suppressed, a gray market will emerge.

The risks and costs of black market religion can be high, including inconveniences and disadvantages, discrimination, monetary fines, labor camps, and prison terms. At the same time, red market religious groups are limited in number and inaccessible to many people. Moreover approved religious groups are commonly red-stained because of restrictions imposed by political authorities, which often results in "sanitized" or "watered-down" religious preaching and services.[30] When people cannot find satisfaction in the red market and are unwilling to risk black market penalties, a gray market fills the gap.

> PROPOSITION 3. The more restrictive and suppressive the regulation, the larger the gray market.

The relative size of each of the triple markets largely depends on the severity of regulation and the effectiveness of enforcement. In a minimally regulated economy like the United States, the open market can meet the religious needs of most people. In a heavily regulated economy, the high-cost black market draws only a small number of devout believers, and the red market is either inaccessible or unappealing to large numbers of people. Unable or unwilling to engage in either the open market or the black market, many people resort to the gray market to meet their religious needs, resulting in a large gray market.

Proposition 3 may appear counterintuitive. Unrelenting atheist education in communist-ruled societies appeared to have reduced the need for religion in the populace. However, the rebound of religiosity in almost all post-Soviet societies shows that the artificial reduction in religious need was mostly illusory, or temporary at best.[31] Some professed atheists during the Soviet period were discreet religious believers.[32] Perhaps more people practiced alternative forms of gray market spirituality, such as popular religion,[33] shamanism,[34] or the personality cult of Lenin[35] as a substitute for "real" religion.

In China during the Cultural Revolution, the red market did not exist, the black market was severely suppressed, and most forms of gray market religion—especially popular religion and alternative spiritualities—were repressed as well. However, one form of gray market religion reached its peak during this period: the Mao personality cult, or "political religion,"[36] had hundreds of millions of sincere worshippers. Mao was glorified as "the great savior of the people" (*renmin de da jiuxing*) and "the Red Sun" (*hong taiyang*). People danced and sang to Mao's statue and confessed sins and made vows before Mao's portrait. The *Little*

Red Book of Mao's words was revered. Studying Mao's quotes was institutionalized into the daily schedule of government officials, school students, factory workers, and village farmers. Even mathematics and science lessons in all textbooks began with the words of Chairman Mao. In post-Mao China *qigong* replaced Maoism as an unconscious outlet for religious zealotry.

To summarize these propositions in dynamic terms: increased religious regulation will lead not to reduction of religion per se but to a triple religious market. Although participation in formal religious organizations may decline, other forms of religiosity will persist and tend to increase. Moreover, given its ambiguous nature, a gray market in a heavily regulated society is likely to be large, volatile, and unsettled, making religious regulation an arduous task and impossible to enforce.

The Red Market

Since 1949, except for the thirteen radical years between 1966 and 1979, the Chinese government has granted legal status to five religions under the control of patriotic associations: Buddhism, Daoism, Islam, Protestantism, and Catholicism. Since the mid-1990s the authorities have repeatedly claimed that there are about 100 million religious believers. This is less than 9 percent of the population (1.3 billion). If this low proportion is even remotely close to reality, people who wish for religion's demise certainly have a good reason to celebrate. But the reality is that the 100 million religious believers are probably only those within sight of the authorities, that is, the red market of religion. Many more religious people have stayed away from the red market but engage in religious belief and practice in the black and gray markets.

The red market is not a free market. Many restrictions are imposed on the government-sanctioned churches, temples, and mosques. Some restrictions are explicit in law, others are implicit in CCP circulars, and many are arbitrarily decided by local officials. Explicitly, Article 36 of the Constitution of the PRC (in effect since 1982) maintains, "The state protects normal religious activities. No one may make use of religion to engage in activities that disrupt public order, impair the health of citizens, or interfere with the educational system of the state." The key word here is *normal*. "Normal religious activities" are defined by the officials in charge. What is normal in other countries may not be normal in the eyes of the Chinese authorities. For example, religious education of children is a common practice in almost all countries; in China, however, providing religious education to children under eighteen is mostly prohibited. Christian churches cannot lawfully hold Sunday school for children or baptize youth under eighteen. Of course, exceptions can be made when politically necessary, such as when a child was identified as the reincarnation of the Tibetan Buddhist Panchen Lama. Religious initiation and education have been allowed for several boy lamas. In 2001 some Christians filed a lawsuit against the local RAB in Wenzhou, Zhejiang, contending for equal rights to comparable religious practice for their children.[37] Although the ban is still in effect, nowadays many religious groups have offered programs for youth and children. The red market has been enlarging despite regulatory restrictions.

The Black Market

When existing churches and temples in the red market cannot meet religious needs, many people will seek alternatives. The religious black market was first created by the regime's antireligious policy in the 1950s, when the government made great efforts to create the national patriotic religious associations. Many believers refused to join them because of theological and political considerations.

A major segment of the black market contains underground Catholics. The animosity between the Roman Catholic Church and the CCP goes back to the founding of the PRC in 1949. Madsen (2003, 471) states:

> In 1949, the Vatican, led by the strongly anti-communist Pope Pius XII, forbade Chinese Catholics, under pain of excommunication, to co-operate in any way with the new Chinese regime.... Because of the Vatican's strict stance against any cooperation with communism,... it was particularly difficult to find any Catholic bishops or priests who would accept leadership positions within the CPA [Catholic Patriotic Association]. Indeed, one requirement of accepting such a position was to sever one's allegiance to the Vatican, which for Catholics would have been seen as a major betrayal of their identity.

The CCP authorities received little cooperation from the Catholic clergy. After persistent and heavy-handed maneuvers, the authorities succeeded in establishing the China Catholic Laypeople Patriotic Association (*zhongguo tianzhu jiaoyou aiguohui*).[38] Only after sentencing the most prominent Catholic leaders, such as Archbishop Ignatius Gong Pinmei of Shanghai, to long prison terms did the authorities find five bishops willing to assume leadership roles within the patriotic association. These bishops went on to consecrate several other bishops without Vatican approval. "Most Catholics," however, "both clergy and laity, refused to participate in institutions controlled by these bishops. They carried on their faith in secret, sometimes under threat of severe punishment."[39]

Today the underground Catholic Church is well organized. An underground Catholic Bishops Conference operates parallel to the officially sanctioned China Catholic Bishops Conference within the China Catholic Patriotic Association.[40] Recent estimates put the total number of Catholics in China at 12 million.[41]

About 4 million are associated with the officially sanctioned Catholic Church. "Perhaps six to eight million Catholics are associated with the so-called 'underground church.'"[42]

Initially, Protestant Christians of sectarian groups, including the Little Flock and the True Jesus Church, and some independent congregations refused to join the Protestant TSPM. Once again, the authorities responded by jailing the stubborn leaders. The best known among them were Wang Mingdao in Beijing and Watchman Nee in Shanghai. Subsequently, many Protestants agreed to join the TSPM. In 1957, however, they reversed course when, dictated by the authorities, the TSPM Committee coerced all believers into the union worship service. All Protestants—Episcopalians, Methodists, Baptists, and sectarian members—were forced to disband their denominations and come together for unified worship. All church properties were centralized under the TSPM Committee. As a reaction, many Christians, especially those of sectarian backgrounds, completely stopped attending church. As devout believers, however, they would not stop gathering for worship. They simply resorted to gatherings at private homes or in the wilderness.[43] These underground "house churches" became seeds of revivals in the 1980s and 1990s.[44]

Although many churches have reopened since 1979 under the auspices of the TSPM, many "house churches" continue to stay underground. Dissenters criticize the TSPM mostly for its unconditional political submission and the liberal theology among its top leaders. As evangelical Christians, they cannot abide by the regulation that prohibits evangelism outside of church premises, as dictated by Document No. 19. Because their existence and activities are illegal, the house churches "are vulnerable to much more coercive and punitive state action, including physical harassment, detention, fines, and labor re-education or criminal proceedings and prison sentences."[45]

Chinese authorities have officially singled out dozens of interprovincial Christian sectarian and cultic groups and taken resolute measures, including hunting down and jailing leaders and the most active members, tearing down buildings, confiscating possessions, and fining and reeducating (deprogramming) loyal followers. Many more congregations and groups active within only one province are also banned. Non-Christian groups founded in other countries, such as the Unification Church, the Children of God, and the True Buddha Sect, have been present in China as well.

No estimates exist regarding underground Buddhists, Daoists, and Muslims. In cities like Shanghai, scholars have observed numerous private Buddhist temples and chapels at private homes; their operation is similar to the Protestant house churches. Many Daoist ritual specialists (*huo ju dao shi*) are active in Shanghai and in the provinces along the Yangtze River.[46] They are comparable to the Protestant self-proclaimed evangelists (*zi feng chuan dao ren*), who are subject to crackdowns. Among ethnic separatists there are also Tibetan Buddhists[47] and Uyghur Muslims.[48] The authorities have carried out repeated and severe crackdowns on the separatists.

The costs of engaging in the black market of religion in China are very high. Once found by the authorities, leaders and believers may suffer psychological abuse, physical torture, monetary fines, temporary detention, labor camps, prison terms, and even death penalties. In spite of these dangers, black-market religion cannot be wiped out. Sectarian groups such as the Shouters have been banned since the early 1980s, but thirty years later they are still active in many parts of China. After some leaders were rounded up, new leadership and groups sprang up. Moreover novel groups keep emerging. Yet the high costs are unbearable to most people. When religious needs cannot be met in the red market, and the potential costs are too great in the black market, many people seek alternatives in the gray market.

The Gray Market

The gray market of religion is very complex. Boundaries between the gray market, red market, and black market are vague, elastic, and constantly shifting. In any society, informal religious and spiritual activities are difficult to document, and the political restrictions in China present additional obstacles to data collection. Here I can offer only broad brush strokes to illustrate the gray market's huge size and complexity.

The first type of gray market religion is explicitly religious, including illegal activities of legal religious organizations and individuals and ambiguous groups and activities sponsored by government agencies or officials. It is worth noting that government-sanctioned religious groups and individuals have undertaken illegal religious activities. The authorities have imposed various restrictions on the five religions supervised by the patriotic associations. For instance, no proselytizing is allowed outside premises of religious buildings; however, most religions proselytize, and the urge to proselytize is difficult to suppress. Some local officials of the RAB seemed to be aware of certain illegal activities of legally recognized ministers, but many watched them with "one eye closed" unless the activities became too conspicuous. For example, the government-sanctioned Nanjing Theological Seminary has had faculty members and students discreetly preaching at underground house churches. In 1999 three of these students were ordered to quit school; in 2000 a faculty member, Ji Tai, was fired.

Since the mid-2000s some house church Christians have taken their cases to court, arguing that the Chinese Constitution guarantees the freedom of religious belief and there is no explicit law clearly banning such religious practices outside the five patriotic associations. Following a series of such legal challenges, more and more house churches have come aboveground. Although they are not recognized by the government as legal, most of the time most of them are left undisturbed by the authorities. A significant segment of the black market has been turning gray.

Similarly the clergy in the Catholic Patriotic Association also engages in activities that the government considers illegal. Although the authorities forbid Catholics from having organizational connections with the Vatican, more than two-thirds of the bishops in the government-sanctioned church have quietly received "apostolic mandates," or official approval, from the Vatican. Consequently "[t]here is now no clear distinction between an open church which the government controls politically and an underground church which it does not."[49] The authorities have failed to stop part of the red market from turning gray.

Another manifestation of the explicitly religious type in the gray market is, ironically, sponsored by certain government agencies or individual officials, who do so mostly for political or economic reasons. For example, in order to bring Taiwan closer to mainland China through direct links of transportation and commerce, a goal adamantly resisted by Taiwanese authorities, Chinese authorities restored and rebuilt Mazu temples in Meizhou, Fujian, the legendary birthplace of the girl who eventually came to be worshipped as the goddess Mazu or Tianhou. Part of the intent was to encourage Mazu worshippers in Taiwan to take homage trips, which would put pressure on the Taiwanese government to open direct links with the mainland.

A major reason that government agencies support temple revivals is to attract overseas Chinese investments and businesses. "Build the religious stage to sing the economic opera" (*zongjiao datai, jingji changxi*) is the plain intention, and many local governments have put this strategy into practice, essentially pouring oil on the fire of religious revivals. Falling into this category are some Huang Daxian (Wong Tai Sin, in Cantonese) temples. In 1984, when Lang and Ragvald (1993) started their study of the Huang Daxian temple in Hong Kong, no Huang Daxian temple existed in mainland China because all of them had been destroyed in the 1950s and 1960s. By 2001, however, at least a dozen Huang Daxian temples had been rebuilt in Guangdong and Zhejiang provinces. Moreover six of the ten temples documented in the study "were founded with the support and sometimes at the initiative of agencies of the local government."[50]

The agencies involved in temple-reviving projects include the Tourist Bureau, the Cultural Affairs Bureau, and the Preservation of Historic Sites Bureau of a local government. By 1996 the construction of temples and outdoor Buddha statues had become so widespread that the central government issued a circular to curb the craze. Consequently many temples were torn down, some were converted to secular uses, and others were co-opted into the existing Daoist or Buddhist patriotic association. This shows the ambivalence of the authorities, who, on the one hand, hope to promote economic development and, on the other hand, want to uphold the atheist ideology. It also reflects the complex orientations and priorities of various bureaus at different levels of government.

When explicitly religious organizations and activities are restricted and curbed, many individuals resort to more implicit forms of religion, expressed as culture and as health science. When they carry out activities in the name of culture or science, no religious regulation applies, even if most scholars in the West normally classify such groups and activities as religious.

In traditional Chinese society, alongside the institutional religions, there existed so-called diffused religion;[51] that is, religious elements intimately merged with the secular institutions and social life. Between 1949 and 1979 the authorities tried hard to extract and expel religious elements from secular institutions. Since 1979, however, diffused religion has come back. Such elements mostly returned in the name of culture, for culture is a neutral or positive concept without ideological weight. Since the mid-2000s it is further legitimized in the name of preserving nonmaterial cultural heritage.

The government has restored many temples in order to reap the economic benefits of tourism. It has also restored temples dedicated to ancient and legendary kings of Yan, Huang, Yao, Shun, and Yu, with the intention of strengthening cultural ties with all Chinese in the world. Many villages and towns have revived popular practices, including building temples dedicated to historic heroes and immortals that have become tutelage gods. They hold dedication ceremonies, temple fairs, and festival celebrations. These temples and activities are difficult to classify as either Daoist or Buddhist, although they often include Daoist gods and Buddhas or Bodhisattvas in their pantheons. Some may be more organized than others, such as the Three-in-One cult (*sanyi jiao*) in Fujian,[52] but most remain informal. The whole village often supports the construction of such temples, and retired officials frequently organize the projects. Most villagers and clansmen participate in the celebration of festivals and fairs related to the temple. As such, these activities are regarded as part of the local cultural tradition or folklore rather than religion. Revived local communal religions have been observed in southeastern China,[53] northwestern China,[54] and northern China,[55] and they are spreading all over the country. In addition many households maintain an ancestral altar or a shrine dedicated to gods and goddesses. Many clan ancestral temples (*ci tang*) have been rebuilt as well. Many restaurants and businesses in cities throughout China conspicuously display an altar for the Tudi (earth god) or Caishen (wealth god).

A more widespread manifestation of implicit religion was *qigong* in the name of health science. The word *qigong* means, literally, "the power or exercise of *qi*" (air or breathing). Simply put, *qigong* is a form of physical exercise, meditation, and healing. Not all *qigong* groups or practices are religious. The *qigong* phenomenon in the PRC has been extremely complex, entangled with traditional Chinese medicine, modern scientism, body politics, and now international relations.[56] A detailed examination of *qigong* is beyond the scope of this chapter, but suffice it to say that most *qigong* groups and practices are a form of implicit religion. First, almost all large *qigong* groups offer an explanatory system that uses Buddhist and/or Daoist concepts and theories. Only a very few rudimentary *qigong* practices resemble the martial arts (*wu shu*) or general physical exercises (*ti cao*) in claiming no supernatural elements. Second, most *qigong* masters claim to be the heirs of certain ancient Daoist or Buddhist lineages and assert that they have been sent by certain mystical masters to "go out of the mountains" (*chu shan*) and spread the *gong*. Third, the practices often involve meditating over religious images or cosmic principles, reciting mantras, and/or reading scriptures. For political and cultural reasons, *qigong* masters and practitioners insisted that they were not religious in order to avoid religious regulations. However, to some extent they are comparable to New Age religions, occult religions, magic, yoga, or "client and audience cults" in the West.[57] Some groups such as the Falun Gong are well-organized new religious movements (NRMs).

Between 1979 and 1999 there were tens of thousands of *qigong* teachers and masters and thousands of *qigong* groups with many followers. Some large *qigong* groups established "cultivation and education bases" (*xiulian peixun jidi*) and "research centers" (*yanjiu zhongxin*) with magnificent buildings and organized hundreds or thousands of "cultivation points" (*liangong dian*), most of which were in public parks or streets. The largest and most effective ones became powerful economic enterprises and organizations with enthusiastic cadres.

Qigong groups also commonly adopted the latest scientific terms, thus insisting that they were related to science instead of religion. In fact top-ranked scientists holding high-level political positions helped *qigong* take off with a bang in the 1980s. The most enthusiastic supporters of *qigong* included Qian Xuesen (Tsien Hsue-shen), the father of China's aerospace science, and General Zhang Zhenhuan, head of the National Defense Science and Engineering Commission. General Zhang later headed the China Qigong Scientific Research Council (*qigong kexue yanjiu hui*), which provided institutional legitimacy for many *qigong* groups. When a new *qigong* master emerged, if he managed to take a photo with Qian, Zhang, and/or other top officials, he would instantly become a great master and soon attract hundreds and thousands of followers. Such photos with political figures not only serve publicity purposes but also provide legitimacy and protection.

Before 1999 most *qigong* groups existed in some sort of legitimate form, such as being affiliated with either the Physical Education and Sports Bureau or the Science and Technology Association (*keji xiehui*). Some of the less religiously oriented *qigong* masters were housed in hospitals as specialty physicians. However, the ambiguous nature of *qigong* groups had caused dissension within the party ranks from the very beginning. Since 1981 top party ideologues such as Yu Guangyuan (1997) have continually voiced strong criticisms of the so-called paranormal power (*teyi gongneng*) and called for restriction. Beginning in about 1990 a few overly religious *qigong* masters were prosecuted and jailed.

Among the largest *qigong* groups, Falun Gong came into existence late. Soon after its launching in 1992, however, it swept the country, partly because of its increasingly religious overtones in a receptive culture.[58] Initially it registered with the China Qigong Scientific Research Council. However, its religious overtones quickly caused concerns, and Falun Gong was subsequently deregistered in 1996. Some Falun Gong leaders then sought to affiliate with the China Buddhist Association but failed. At this time Falun Gong had gained millions of followers all over China and had spread globally to the United States, Australia, and other countries as well. In 1999 Falun Gong made a bold move by gathering over 10,000 followers to surround Zhongnanhai, the headquarters of the CCP and the central government, to demand official legalization. The authorities responded with a determined crackdown and banned it as an "evil cult" (*xie jiao*). Following this, Zhong Gong, Xiang Gong, and other large *qigong* groups were all tagged as evil cults and were banned. Their key leaders were prosecuted, properties confiscated, and practices prohibited. In fact all *qigong* groups were disbanded or deregistered at this time. Finally, the China Qigong Scientific Research Council was officially deregistered by the State Civil Affairs Department in summer 2003. The group practice of *qigong* in the park in the morning, once a universal scene all over China, has disappeared.

Making *qigong* illegal has blackened a significant part of the gray market. However, with millions of followers in each of the major *qigong* groups, the ban cannot halt *qigong* practice completely. Suppressed in the public sphere, some *qigong* practitioners went underground, just as some Christians did in the 1950s. Falun Gong followers persist despite severe crackdowns, but the number of practitioners has greatly decreased. Most of the former *qigong* practitioners seem to have stopped practicing; some have converted to Buddhism or Christianity.

After a pause of several years, some *qigong* groups have managed to reemerge, albeit under new names and with great caution. For example, Guolin New Qigong followers now practice in public parks under the name Guolin Fitness Way (*guolin jianshen fa*). The religious or supernatural words are removed or significantly toned down, at least in public. Currently several major *qigong* groups are quietly regrouping through Internet websites, exploring ways to go public again. In 2004 the *jianshen qigong* (health-oriented *qigong*) regained legal status under the supervision of the China Physical Education and Sports Bureau. A major challenge for the regulators is determining how to distinguish and certify health *qigong* masters from the rest.

How large is the gray market of religion in China today? Based on the estimates in previous sections, we can say that there are about 100 million people engaged in the red market and around 200 million people engaged in the black market. If these estimates are accurate, about 1 billion people are neither in the red market nor in the black market of religion. Are these 1 billion Chinese really irreligious, or are they simply engaged in the gray market of religion? Without surveys based on national probability sampling, it is impossible to tell one way or the other. If the majority of the Chinese population is at least open toward supernatural beliefs but only small minorities have been recruited into either the government-approved religions or the underground ones, there exists a huge gray market with hundreds of millions of potential religious consumers. Perhaps many of them have unmet religious needs or are waiting to be awakened. Many may consciously or unconsciously engage in the gray market of implicitly religious groups or spiritual entrepreneurs. Such a huge gray market is destined to be a fertile ground for NRMs.

The boundaries of the tripartite market are not clear-cut and are constantly shifting. During the eradication period from 1966 to 1979, no red market existed. All religious organizations and activities were repressed so severely that religion could exist only in the black or gray markets. Since 1979 some religious groups have been legalized. However, deciding which religious groups are to be allowed or banned is a constant challenge for regulators and regulation enforcers. CCP agencies, the central government, and provincial and local governments are not always on the same page in regard to particular religious groups and activities. For example, some local governments encouraged and even sponsored restoring temples for the purpose of attracting overseas investment, but the central government curbed the frenzy by tearing down most of the new buildings. However, some of the temples built this way were co-opted into patriotic religious associations and were therefore moved from the gray market into the red market. Throughout the 1980s and 1990s *qigong* groups were allowed or even encouraged by various government officials. Since 1999, however, all *qigong* groups have been disbanded, thus turning these gray market groups black. In recent years many Christian house churches in the black market have turned gray with ambiguous legal status.

When stronger regulations blacken previously gray market segments, two consequences are inevitable: the black market is enlarged, and the gray market is emptied. Criminalization will likely reduce the total number of religious adherents of some sects because not all want to practice in the underground, but the emptied gray market opens up space for new and innovative suppliers. The level of volatility in the gray market increases as charismatic and entrepreneurial individuals and groups rise to fill the emptied niches. The ambiguity of gray market practices makes it difficult to regulate or enforce regulations.

Oligopoly Dynamics

Oligopoly is the most prevalent type of state-religion relationship in the world today, but it remains understudied because of the lack of conceptualization. The few studies of oligopoly dynamics indicate that the theories or propositions generated from studies of pluralism or monopoly are not applicable without substantial modification.[59]

For example, according to Stark and Finke (2000), a religious monopoly breeds a lazy clergy, and consequently a less religiously mobilized population. In comparison, a deregulated religious economy "will tend to be very pluralistic," one in which more religious "firms" compete for a share of the market.[60] Thus, they assert, "[t]o the degree that religious economies are unregulated and competitive, overall levels of religious participation will be high."[61] Religious change in the United States appears to provide strong evidence of deregulation effects. Since the First Amendment to the U.S. Constitution was adopted, the rate of religious adherence in the U.S. population steadily increased, from 17 percent in 1774 to 62 percent in 1990.[62]

However, oligopoly economies are both regulated and competitive. There is competition among the government-sanctioned religions, but the competition seems different in kind from that in pluralistic societies.[63] First of all, they compete for government favoritism. They also compete for followers against other religions. A strong factor in the growth of some religious groups seems to be government favoritism, and competition for such political favoritism is common. Meanwhile religious leaders still need to mobilize other resources to succeed in the marketplace, as they are in competition with other officially sanctioned religions and nonsanctioned religious groups as well.

Therefore an important modification to the proposition is necessary. Increased restrictive regulation in oligopoly does not necessarily lead to the decline of overall religious participation. Rather, heavy regulation "leads to complication of the religious market, resulting in a tripartite market with different dynamics."[64] Under increased religious regulation, although participation in formal religious organizations may decline, other forms of religiosity will persist. This appears true in Europe as well. In the relatively more regulated markets of contemporary Western Europe, participation in institutional religion is lower than in the less regulated U.S. religious market. On the other hand, however, there are more new religious movements per capita in Europe than in the United States. On average there are 1.7 NRMs per million people in the United States, but 3.4 NRMs per million in Europe, even though the number of NRMs in Europe tends to be undercounted.[65]

Even though Stark and Finke (2000) recognize this contrast, they fail to theorize in this regard. This is due to a blind spot in their perception that is based almost exclusively on North American and Western European experiences. Their conceptualization does not include religious oligopoly as a distinct type of state-religion relationship.

Moreover, in oligopoly, pluralization is probably inevitable, even though it may be a slow and difficult process. Under heavy regulation, underground religions will persist regardless of the severity of suppression, as there are always religious "virtuosos" who practice the religion regardless of the social costs.[66] Meanwhile the gray market "is likely to be large, volatile, and unsettled, making religious regulation an arduous task and impossible to enforce."[67] Weighing the social and political benefits of religious restrictions and their financial, political, and human costs, a rational choice on the part of the state is to relax restrictions and grant legal status to more religions.

In China, in addition to the five major religions recognized by the central government, some local governments have begun to legalize certain minor religions in recent years, including Orthodox Christianity in the northeastern province of Heilongjiang, Mazu and Three-in-One in the southeastern province of Fujian, and Huangdaxian in the southern provinces of Zhejiang and Guangdong. Various new religions originating abroad, including Mormonism, the Unification Church, and Baha'i, have been working to gain official recognition.

Conclusion

How much can the state control religion through regulation? Obviously the efficacy of state power has been exaggerated in regard to Western societies (claiming that deregulation would lead to the demise of religion)[68] and to China (believing state suppression would eradicate religion). The triple-market theory shows that market forces are at work, and religious groups and believers may not respond in ways that the regulators want. Heavy regulation cannot effectively reduce religion. It can only complicate the religious market by pushing religious organizations and believers into the black and gray markets. Under heavy regulation, the gray market is not only huge, it is also volatile, providing fertile ground for NRMs. For regulators and regulation enforcers, the gray market creates an unmanageable state of religious affairs.

It is insufficient to explain the complexity of religious dynamics in oligopolistic society using principles or propositions of free market economics. It is necessary to adopt a political-economic approach, which has been called for by some sociologists,[69] but there have been few theory-driven empirical studies so far.

There are other important questions about religious oligopoly that should be studied. Given the prevalence of religious oligopoly in the world today, we must examine the justifications for it. Is pluralism necessarily a good thing? Could oligopoly be a better configuration in state-religion relations? What are the most important arguments and counterarguments regarding maintaining an oligopoly that privileges one dominant religion? In China today there are discussions within certain elite circles about making up a state religion, perhaps something based on Confucianism, to take the place of the failing communist ideology, as well as about preserving Chinese cultural traditions against the "foreign" religions of Christianity and Islam. A strong motivation for such suggestions is to preserve the distinct Chinese culture and nourish the Chinese national identity amid rapid globalization and Westernization. Similar arguments may be found in Russia and other countries that face the same challenges of globalization and the hegemonic Western culture. To take a detached, scientific approach, we may ask: Is oligopoly a necessary stage toward pluralism? What does it take to progress beyond this stage? There are ample historical and contemporary cases for us to work on in order to achieve a better understanding about oligopoly dynamics. Such theory-driven empirical studies will have important practical implications as well as theoretical significance.

Notes

1. The first part of the theoretical construction of this article was first presented at the plenary session "Religious Pluralism as a Challenge for Contemporary Society" of the thirtieth conference of the International Society for the Sociology of Religion, July 27–31, 2009, Santiago de Compostela, Spain. It then was developed in an article published as "Oligopoly Dynamics: Consequences of Religious Regulation," *Social Compass* 57, no. 2 (2010): 1–12. The second part of the theoretical construction and description of religion in China was published in Fenggang Yang, "The Red, Black, and Gray Markets of Religion in China," *Sociological Quarterly* 47, no. 1 (2006): 93–122 and Fenggang Yang, "Oligopoly Dynamics: Official Religions in China," in *The Sage Handbook of the Sociology of Religion*, ed. James Beckford and Jay Demerath (London: Sage, 2007). This chapter is a refined and summarized synthesis. I would like to thank Allen Hertzke for helpful suggestions.

2. Peter Berger, *The Sacred Canopy: Elements of A Sociological Theory of Religion* (New York: Doubleday, 1967); R. Stephen Warner, "Work in Progress toward a New Paradigm for the Sociological Study of Religion in the United States," *American Journal of Sociology* 98, no. 5 (1993): 1044–93; Rodney Stark and Roger Finke, *Acts of Faith: Explaining the Human Side of Religion* (Berkeley: University of California Press, 2000); Grace Davie, *The Sociology of Religion* (London: Sage, 2007).

3. Speaking in economic terms, open market competition without government interference may also result in oligopoly or monopoly of the market, but this article focuses on the oligopoly as a result of state regulations.

4. Yang, "The Red, Black, and Gray Markets of Religion in China," 95–96.

5. Brian J. Grim and Roger Finke, "International Religion Indexes: Government Regulation, Government Favoritism, and Social Regulation of Religion," *Interdisciplinary Journal of Research on Religion* 2 (2006): article 1.

6. Berger, *The Sacred Canopy*.

7. Warner, "Work in Progress," 1044–93; Stark and Finke, *Acts of Faith*.

8. Davie, *The Sociology of Religion*.

9. Peter Berger, *The Desecularization of the World: Resurgent Religion and World Politics* (Washington, D.C.: Ethics and Public Policy Center, 1999).

10. Mark Chaves and Philip Gorski, "Religious Pluralism and Religious Participation," *Annual Review of Sociology* 27 (2001): 261–81; David Voas, Daniel Olson, and Alasdair Crockett, "Religious Pluralism and Participation: Why Previous Research Is Wrong," *American Sociological Review* 67, no. 2 (2002): 212–30; James Montgomery, "A Formalization and Test of the Religious Economies Model," *American Sociological Review* 68, no. 5 (2003): 782–809; Michael McBride, "Religious Pluralism and Religious Participation: A Game Theoretic Analysis," *American Journal of Sociology* 114, no. 1 (2008): 77–108.

11. Robert Wuthnow, "Presidential Address 2003: The Challenge of Diversity," *Journal for the Scientific Study of Religion* 43, no. 2 (2004): 162.

12. David W. Machacek, "The Problem of Pluralism," *Sociology of Religion* 64, no. 2 (2003): 145–61; and Peter Berger, "Concluding Remarks," Constituting the Future: A Symposium on Religious Liberty, Law, and Flourishing Societies, Istanbul, April 20–22, 2009.

13. Buster G. Smith, "Attitudes toward Religious Pluralism: Measurements and Consequences," *Social Compass* 54, no. 2 (2007): 333–53.

14. Wuthnow, "Presidential Address 2003," 162–63.

15. Pew Forum on Religion & Public Life, *Global Restrictions on Religion,* 2009, http://pewforum .org/newassets/images/reports/restrictions/restrictionsfullreport.pdf.

16 On December 10, 1948, the General Assembly of the United Nations adopted and proclaimed the Universal Declaration of Human Rights. Following this historic act the Assembly called upon all member countries to publicize the text of the Declaration and "to cause it to be disseminated, displayed, read and expounded principally in schools and other educational institutions, without distinction based on the political status of countries or territories." Article 18 of the Declaration states, "Everyone has the right to freedom of thought, conscience and religion; this right includes freedom to change his religion or belief, and freedom, either alone or in community with others and in public or private, to manifest his religion or belief in teaching, practice, worship and observance."

17. William V. D'Antonio and Dean R. Hoge, "The American Experience of Religious Disestablishment and Pluralism," *Social Compass* 53, no. 3 (2006): 346.

18. Ibid., 346–47.

19. R. Stephen Warner and Judith Wittner, eds., *Gatherings in Diaspora: Religious Communities and the New Immigration* (Philadelphia: Temple University Press, 1998); Helen Rose Ebaugh and Janet S. Chafetz, eds., *Religion and the New Immigrants: Continuities and Adaptations in Immigrant Congregations* (Walnut Creek, Calif.: AltaMira Press, 2000); Dianna L. Eck, *A New Religious America: How a "Christian Country" Has Become the World's Most Religiously Diverse Nation* (San Francisco: Harper San Francisco, 2001).

20. Eck, *A New Religious America*; Dianna L. Eck, "AAR 2006 Presidential Address: Prospects for Pluralism: Voice and Vision in the Study of Religion," *Journal of the American Academy of Religion* 75, no. 4 (2007): 743–76.

21. Wuthnow, "Presidential Address 2003," 159–70; Robert Wuthnow, *America and the Challenges of Religious Diversity* (Princeton, N.J.: Princeton University Press, 2007).

22. D'Antonio and Hoge, "The American Experience of Religious Disestablishment and Pluralism," 354.

23. Everett M. Rogers, *The Diffusion of Innovations,* 4th ed. (New York: Free Press, 1995).

24. Max Weber, *The Religion of China* (1916–17; New York: Free Press, 1951); C. K. Yang, *Religion in Chinese Society* (Berkeley: University of California Press, 1960).

25. There have been a number of annotated English translations of the Chinese Constitution, CCP documents, and government ordinances, and explanatory analyses of them. See, for example, Donald E. MacInnis, *Religion in China Today: Policy and Practice* (New York: Orbis Books, 1989); Julian F. Pas, ed., *The Turning of the Tide: Religion in China Today* (Hong Kong: Oxford University Press, 1989); Human Rights Watch/Asia, *Continuing Religious Repression in China* (New York: Human Rights Watch, 1993), and *China: State Control of Religion* (1997); Pitman B. Potter, "Belief in Control: Regulation of Religion in China," *China Quarterly* 174, no. 2 (2003): 468–87; Mickey Spiegel, "Control and Containment in the Reform Era," in *God and Caesar in China: Policy Implications of Church-State Tensions,* ed. Jason Kindropp and Carol Lee Hamrin (Washington, D.C.: Brookings Institute Press, 2004).

26. Yang, "The Red, Black, and Gray Markets of Religion in China," 93–122.

27. Jianbo Huang and Fenggang Yang, "The Cross Faces the Loudspeakers: A Village Church Perseveres under State Power," in *State, Market, and Religions in Chinese Societies,* ed. Fenggang Yang and Joseph B. Tamney (Leiden: Brill Academic Publishers, 2005); Fenggang Yang and Dedong Wei, "The Bailin Buddhist Temple: Thriving under Communism," in Yang and Tamney, *State, Market, and Religions.*

28. Rodney Stark and William Sims Bainbridge, *The Future of Religion: Secularization, Revival and Cult Formation* (Berkeley: University of California Press, 1985); Arthur L. Greil and Thomas Robbins, eds., *Between Sacred and Secular: Research and Theory on Quasi-Religion* (Greenwich, Conn.: JAI Press, 1994); Wade Clark Roof, *Spiritual Marketplace: Baby Boomers and the*

Remaking of American Religion (Princeton, N.J.: Princeton University Press, 1999); Paul Heelas and Linda Woodhead, *The Spiritual Revolution: Why Religion Is Giving Way to Spirituality* (Oxford: Blackwell, 2005).

29. Stephen Sharot, *A Comparative Sociology of World Religions: Virtuosos, Priests, and Popular Religion* (New York: New York University Press, 2001); Max Weber, "The Social Psychology of the World Religions," in *From Max Weber: Essays in Sociology*, ed. Hans H. Gerth and C. Wright Mills (London: Routledge and Kegan Paul, 1948); Max Weber, *Economy and Society* (1921; New York: Bedminster Press, 1968).

30. Huang and Yang, "The Cross Faces the Loudspeakers"; Yang and Wei, "The Bailin Buddhist Temple."

31. Andrew Greeley, "A Religious Revival in Russia?," *Journal for the Scientific Study of Religion* 33, no. 3 (1994): 253–72; Mary L. Gautier, "Church Attendance and Religious Belief in Postcommunist Societies," *Journal for the Scientific Study of Religion* 36, no. 2 (1997): 289–97; Paul Froese, "Hungary for Religion: A Supply-Side Interpretation of the Hungarian Religious Revival," *Journal for the Scientific Study of Religion* 40, no. 2 (2001): 251–68; Paul Froese, "After Atheism: An Analysis of Religious Monopolies in the Post-Communist World," *Sociology of Religion* 65, no. 1 (2004): 57–75; Paul Froese, "Forced Secularization in Soviet Russia: Why an Atheistic Monopoly Failed," *Journal for the Scientific Study of Religion* 43, no. 1 (2004): 35–50.

32. John Anderson, *Religion, State and Politics in the Soviet Union and Successor States* (Cambridge: Cambridge University Press, 1994); Olga Tchepournaya, "The Hidden Sphere of Religious Searches in the Soviet Union: Independent Religious Communities in Leningrad from the 1960s to the 1970s," *Sociology of Religion* 64, no. 3 (2003): 377–88.

33. Moshe Lewin, "Popular Religion in Twentieth-Century Russia," in *The Making of the Soviet System: Essays in the Social History of Interwar Russia*, ed. Moshe Lewin (New York: Pantheon Books, 1985).

34. Marjorie Mandelstam Balzer, ed., *Shamanism: Soviet Studies of Traditional Religion in Siberia and Central Asia* (New York: M. E. Sharpe, 1990).

35. Nina Tumarkin, *Lenin Lives! The Lenin Cult in Soviet Russia* (Cambridge, Mass.: Harvard University Press, 1983).

36. Jinping Zuo, "Political Religion: The Case of the Cultural Revolution in China," *Sociological Analysis* 52, no. 1 (1991):99–110.

37. John Pomfret, "Evangelicals on the Rise in Land of Mao: Despite Crackdowns, Protestant Religious Groups Flourishing in China," *Washington Post*, December 24, 2002.

38. Guangwu Luo, 1949–1999 *Xin Zhongguo Zongjiao Gongzuo Dashi Gailan* (A Brief Overview of Major Events of Religious Affairs in New China 1949–1999) (Beijing: Huawen Press, 2001).

39. Richard Madsen, "Catholic Revival during the Reform Era," *China Quarterly* 174, no. 2 (2003): 472.

40. Ibid., 473.

41. Ibid., 468.

42. Ibid., 472.

43. David Aikman, *Jesus in Beijing: How Christianity Is Transforming China and Changing the Global Balance of Power* (Washington, D.C.: Regnery, 2003).

44. Jonathan Chao and Rosanna Chong, *A History of Christianity in Socialist China, 1949–1997* (Taipei: China Ministries International Publishing, 1997).

45. Daniel H. Bays, "Chinese Protestant Christianity Today," *China Quarterly* 174, no. 2 (2003): 492; see also Ryan Dunch, "Protestant Christianity in China Today: Fragile, Fragmented, Flourishing," in *China and Christianity: Burdened Past, Hopeful Future*, ed. Stephen Uhalley Jr. and Xiaoxin Wu (New York: M. E. Sharpe, 2001).

46. Xuezeng Gong, ed., *Minzu Zongjiao Jiben Wenti Duben* (Basic Questions Regarding Ethnicity and Religion: A Reader) (Chengdu, China: Sichuan People's Press, 2001); Fenggang Yang, "Between Secularist Ideology and Desecularizing Reality: The Birth and Growth of Religious Research in Communist China," *Sociology of Religion* 65, no. 2 (2004): 101–19.

47. Raoul Birnhaum, "Buddhist China at the Century's Turn," *China Quarterly* 174, no. 2 (2003): 428–50.

48. Dru Gladney, "Islam in China: Accommodation or Separatism?," *China Quarterly* 174, no. 2 (2003): 451–67.

49. Madsen, "Catholic Revival," 483.

50. Graeme Lang, Selina Ching Chan, and Lars Ragvald, *The Return of the Refugee God: Wong Tai Sin in China*, CSRCS Occasional Paper No. 8 (Hong Kong: Chinese University of Hong Kong, 2002), 14.

51. Yang, *Religion in Chinese Society*.

52. Kenneth Dean, *Lord of the Three in One* (Princeton: Princeton University Press, 1998).

53. Kenneth Dean, *Taoist Ritual and Popular Cults of Southeast China* (Princeton: Princeton University Press, 1993); Dean, *Lord of the Three in One*; Khun Eng Kuah, *Rebuilding the Ancestral Village: Singaporeans in China* (Aldershot, England: Ashgate, 2000); Kenneth Dean, "Local Communal Religion in Contemporary South-East China," *China Quarterly* 174, no. 2 (2003): 338–58.

54. Jun Jing, *The Temple of Memories: History, Power, and Morality in a Chinese Village* (Stanford: Stanford University Press, 1996).

55. Zhentao Zhang, *The Cult of Houtu and the Music Associations of Hebei Province*, CSRCS Occasional Paper No. 7 (Hong Kong: Chinese University of Hong Kong, 2001); Lizhu Fan, "The Cult of the Silkworm Mother as a Core of Local Community Religion in a North China Village: Field Study in Zhiwuying, Baording, Hebei," *China Quarterly* 174, no. 2 (2003): 359–72.

56. Jian Xu, "Body, Discourse, and the Cultural Politics of Contemporary Chinese Qigong," *Journal of Asian Studies* 58, no. 4 (1999): 961–92; Nancy N. Chen, *Breathing Spaces: Qigong, Psychiatry, and Healing in China* (New York: Columbia University Press, 2003); Nancy N. Chen, "Healing Sects and Anti-cult Campaigns," *China Quarterly* 174, no. 2 (2003): 505–20; David A. Palmer, *Qigong Fever: Body, Charisma, and Utopia in China* (New York: Columbia University Press, 2007).

57. Stark and Bainbridge, *Future of Religion*.

58. Beatrice Leung, "China and Falun Gong: Party and Society Relations in the Modern Era," *Journal of Contemporary China* 11, no. 3 (2002): 76184; Yunfeng Lu, "Entrepreneurial Logics and the Evolution of Falun Gong," *Journal for the Scientific Study of Religion* 44, no. 2 (2005): 173–85.

59. Yang, "The Red, Black, and Gray Markets of Religion in China," 93–122; Yang, "Oligopoly Dynamics," 619–37; and Yunfeng Lu, *The Transformation of Yiguan Dao in Taiwan: Adapting To a Changing Religious Economy* (Lanham, Md.: Lexington Books, 2008).

60. Stark and Finke, *Acts of Faith*, 198.

61. Ibid., 199.

62. Roger Finke and Rodney Stark, *The Churching of America, 1776–1990: Winners and Losers in Our Religious Economy* (New Brunswick, N.J.: Rutgers University Press, 1992).

63. Yang, "Oligopoly Dynamics," 619–637.

64. Yang, "The Red, Black, and Gray Markets of Religion in China," 97.

65. Stark and Finke, *Acts of Faith*, 255.

66. Sharot, *A Comparative Sociology of World Religions*; Weber, "The Social Psychology of the World Religions," 267–301; Weber, *Economy and Society*.

67. Yang, "The Red, Black, and Gray Markets of Religion in China," 99.

68. See Roger Finke, "Religious Deregulation: Origins and Consequences," *Journal of Church and State* 32, no. 3 (1990): 609–26.

69. Chaves and Gorski, "Religious Pluralism and Religious Participation," 261–81.

6

The Status of and Challenges to Religious Freedom in Russia

ROMAN LUNKIN

In Russia the authorities treat the many religions and denominations unequally. This was the case back in the times of the Russian Empire, when only a few non-Russian natives were granted religious freedom, particularly those who were historically affiliated with Buddhism and Islam. This was also the case in the Soviet era, when the state initially attempted to destroy all religious communities and later implemented an official antireligious policy, according to which it began to classify religious believers into two groups: those loyal to the government and dangerous dissidents. In Russian society today there remains a paradoxical discrepancy between the policy advanced by the authorities and the actual religious situation. We see this in the gap between the provisions of law and the actual attitudes and deeds of government officials, law enforcement officers, and the press toward the faithful of different religions. Unlike other periods in Russian history, however, the post-Soviet phase of the country's development has finally provided an opportunity for the freedom of religion and belief to emerge, rooted in the growing civil society engagement of people with diverse religious perspectives.

The revival, or rather the boom of religiosity in Russia in the 1990s led to unparalleled religious diversity, restored interest in religion in general and in Orthodox Christianity in particular, and fostered hopes that new legislation would be based on the principle of freedom of conscience. At the same time, in this new stage of Russian history, the ideological stereotypes and complexes rooted in the prerevolutionary and Soviet periods were embraced by the state. This produced the tendency to label adherents of nontraditional religions "sectarians" and harass them, as well as to identify the religious figures who were most loyal to the government, ultimately creating the foundation for the new regime's legitimacy by promoting the Russian Orthodox Church (ROC) as a symbol and pillar of state ideology. From the mid-1990s on, representatives of the Moscow Patriarchate joined with the ruling elite in attempts to suppress the freedom of religious competitors by employing xenophobic slogans that manifested support for the "traditional" religions and opposition to "sects," foreign missionaries, and Western influence in general.

Contrary to previous periods in Russian history, however, this time around the gradual return to a familiar form of authoritarian Soviet-type government did not fully disrupt nascent democratic developments. By the middle of the first decade of the millennium, things began to turn in another direction: the more the state and ROC officials attempted to control or pressure society, the more open was the public response. Despite a very complicated historical heritage, Russia has the opportunity to become a democratic country capable of overcoming its many complexes—from its self-image as a "country of immense spirituality" to its inferiority complex in relation to Western living standards. Russian citizens are facing social and moral crises but lack trust in government officials to deliver the promised modernization. While society remains atomized, with only a small intellectual class truly active in the public arena, nascent social movements are rising in Russia to challenge state repression of religious freedom. Given this situation, patriotic myths about Holy Russia, about Moscow being the Third Rome, and the superior spirituality of Russia, which have served as pretexts for restricting religious freedom, are losing practical meaning. People are becoming disillusioned—so much faster than in the Soviet era—with such official ideology, which does not deliver what it promises.

From Absolute Freedom to Legislative Pressure

From the very moment Soviet ideology collapsed, Russia has followed a tortuous path of contradictory impulses. The adoption of religious freedom was a natural development in the period of perestroika and glasnost led by Mikhail Gorbachev. The celebration of the Millennium of the Baptism of Russia (in 1988) became an important symbolic act by the state and marked the return of churches and monasteries to the Russian Orthodox Church. However, party reformers did not need the support of Orthodox Christianity as an ideology and did not seek to make the ROC one of the symbols of the government. Having rejected the communist ideology, leaders of the perestroika movement had hoped to create a secular state with room for any religion practiced in any way, as long as it did not interfere with social accord.

In accordance with these orientations, a sweeping Law on Freedom of Conscience was adopted for the USSR in 1990 and replicated for the Russian Federation later that year. The first law of its kind in Russia, it provided broad religious liberty protections. Remarkably it eliminated any restrictions on registration and activities of religious associations. Precisely because of such liberalism, however, the 1990 Law on Freedom of Conscience was heavily criticized, especially by the ROC, which claimed (and still claims) that it opened the gates for "foreign sects and missionaries" to flood into the country with preachers that brought "a spirituality that is alien to Russia."[1]

So early in the new democratic regime in Russia, there were attempts, led by President Boris Yeltsin, to revise the liberal religious law. The Moscow Patriarchate played a significant role in this process. Secular authorities were seeking historically grounded ideological support to enhance their legitimacy. At the same time, the top religious officials of the ROC demanded penitence and the rectification of the injustice the Church suffered in the decades of Soviet persecution. This entailed ROC demands for the restitution of its property and buildings, as well as government support for its operations. In addition the ROC sought to curb revelations of it activities during the Soviet era. In 1992 investigations of KGB archives by the Commission of the Supreme Soviet of the Russian Federation, which uncovered collaborations between the members of the Moscow Patriarchate and the Soviet secret services, were halted. Patriarch Alexey II paid a personal visit to the Supreme Soviet to request that the Commission be liquidated and that the archives be restricted—requests that were fulfilled shortly thereafter.

Beginning in 1993 a number of legislative bills were proposed to eliminate the principle of the equality of religions. Among them were bills that supported the traditional religions (Orthodox Christianity, Islam, Buddhism, and Judaism), granting them various privileges while applying restrictions to the activities of religious minorities and foreign missionaries, thereby amending the 1990 law. This ongoing political struggle, which led to the adoption of the revised Law on the Freedom of Conscience in 1997, received extensive coverage both in English and Russian media sources that emphasized how it undermined religious liberty.[2] As we will see, its impact was considerably diffused and at times paradoxical.

First, there was no consolidated opinion among the authorities (the presidential administration and the State Duma Committee for Relations with Nongovernmental Organizations and Religious Associations) regarding the necessity of the restrictions on the activities of religious minorities. The most discriminatory proposals were rejected as a result of efforts by human rights advocates, the leaders of non-Orthodox religious associations, democratically minded deputies of the State Duma, and members of the Yeltsin administration. For example, Metropolitan Kirill (currently patriarch), who was at that time the head of the Department for External Church Relations, was actively involved in drafting the bill and proposing a fifty-year rule for all religious associations.[3] Under the proposal, to receive the status of a legal entity an organization must prove that it had existed in Russia for at least fifty years. But in the final law the required term of existence was eventually set at fifteen years.

The restrictions imposed by the 1997 law caused a storm of criticism in the West and in Russia, coming from both the legal and the human rights community. The law essentially divided organizations into traditional (Orthodoxy, Islam, Buddhism, Judaism) and nontraditional (all the rest).

Procedures involved in the establishment of an organization were changed substantially, in some cases restricting the eligibility of founders and members. For example, the right to establish a local religious organization was recognized as applying only to Russian citizens (Article 9). Foreign nationals and stateless citizens (including displaced persons) may be participants in a religious organization provided that their permanent residence is within the Russian Federation (Article 3).[4] Positively the law introduced a new definition of religious group as a voluntary association of individuals formed for the collective practice and proliferation of their faith, which can operate without official state recognition (Article 7). On the one hand, this legal provision vested in the religious associations the right to operate legally without being subject to state registration or interference. On the other hand, it required a fifteen-year "probation" period of activity within the territory of the Russian Federation for religious associations to enjoy such rights (Article 11, §5).[5]

In order to overcome the negative consequences of the required fifteen-year period, three prominent lawyers, A. V. Pchelintsev, V. V. Ryakhovsky, and G. A. Krylova, prepared a legal complaint for submission to the court on behalf of the Proslavleniye Pentecostal Church in Abakan, Republic of Khakassia. Around the same time, a similar complaint was received by the court from the members of a religious community of Jehovah's Witnesses in the city of Yaroslavl. Both complaints were combined into a single legal appeal heard by the Constitutional Court on October 21, 1999. In both cases the Court was tasked with considering the constitutional validity of certain provisions of Article 27 of the Law of 1997, which restricted the rights of local religious organizations that did not belong to more centralized structures and have no documents to prove they had been active in the Russian Federation for at least fifteen years. On November 23, 1999, the Court found that the disputed provisions of the law were indeed of constitutional validity. However, the judges felt compelled to provide an interpretation of these provisions that, in essence, reversed their effect.

According to the decision of the Constitutional Court, the disputed provisions are constitutionally valid but do not apply to "those religious organizations established before the coming into force of this Federal Law, as well as local religious organizations that are integrated within the centralized structure of a religious organization." This "implies that such religious organizations are entitled to rights as legal entities in full, without having to confirm the fifteen-year minimum term of existence on the territory of the Russian Federation or without undergoing an annual registration." Following this decision, any community can essentially register under a centralized religious organization, thereby obtaining the full rights of a legal entity.

The combined efforts of public figures and religious leaders (especially of Protestant and Catholic denominations) helped to overcome almost all the negative consequences of the Law of 1997, which otherwise seemed to banish religious freedom in Russia. The required fifteen-year period applied only to a relatively small number of independent religious groups, as well as certain new religious movements, which tended to make do without receiving mandatory registration.

With respect to the provision of the 1997 law on mandatory reregistration of all religious associations, the deadline for groups to undergo this process was eventually extended to 2001. Most of the non-Orthodox communities managed to complete this procedure in a timely fashion. Ironically parishes of the Russian Orthodox Church experienced the greatest difficulties because church officials were not ready to complete the long and complex forms for so many thousands of congregations.

It is also worth noting that in the 1990s many regions of Russia adopted separate local laws to regulate missionary activity, including toughening the requirements for missionaries and introducing mandatory notification of the authorities about their activities. However, following the adoption of the Law of 1997 most of the local laws on missionary activities were repealed as a part of the process of "bringing the legislation of the entities of the Russian Federation in line with that of the Federal legislation." (At present the only existing local law on missionary activity that remains is in the Belgorod region.)

The effect of the Law of 1997 and its place in the establishment of religious freedom in Russia was most clearly expressed in the words of the American scholars Christopher Marsh and Wallace Daniel:

> The Law of 1997 cannot be seen as a final and lasting piece of legislation but as a legislative response to an existing situation. The law did not represent a thought-out, consistent or well prepared legislative solution but rather a short-term legal stopgap that was a part of a natural process where Russia has to choose its path, trying different options and directions without any established laws and legislative standards. The way these laws and standards would evolve, how they would be interpreted and applied and how relevant they would be towards religious organizations in the following decade will say a lot about the efforts taken on the part of Russian citizens and authorities in order to organize a new political, social and religious order.[6]

This assessment explains why a law intended to favor Orthodoxy and restrict its competitors instead propelled the principle of freedom of conscience in Russia.

The first decade of religious struggle in independent Russia ultimately led to policy that would allow religious groups to exist in accordance with democratic standards. That is why the Law on Freedom of Conscience of 1997 eventually became a symbol of stability, given the constantly evolving threats to the freedom of conscience and the numerous attempts to undermine it. The law initially sparked informal, extralegal discrimination of nontraditional religious communities, with the result that religious minorities were deprived of their leases, expelled from social institutions, and subject to suppression of missionary and social activities. But legal appeals against this discrimination spurred better juridical practice on the freedom of conscience in Russia and provided grounds for numerous complaints to the European Court of Human Rights.

The first complaint was filed in 2001 by the Moscow branch of the Salvation Army, which in 1999 was refused the right to reregister because the Department of Justice in Moscow claimed it was a "paramilitary" organization. In 2006 the European Court ruled in favor of the Salvation Army, but it wasn't until 2009 that the organization was finally permitted to complete the reregistration procedure in Moscow.[7]

Ultimately the Constitution of the Russian Federation, along with judicial interpretations of the 1997 Law on Freedom of Conscience, constrained attempts to change the secular character of the state or to harshly discriminate against the country's religious minorities. But compliance of officials with the Constitution and the law varied, and real and unlawful discrimination of religious groups occurred, especially in the Putin era.

Putin's Decade: The Failure of Authoritarianism

After 2000, by the force of historical inertia, both the state and the church began gravitating even closer toward each other, leading to the integration of the Russian Orthodox Church into the current political and ideological agenda. During the presidential term of Vladimir Putin, the Russian Orthodox Church Abroad (ROCA) was reunited with the Moscow Patriarchate under the auspices of the Russian government and the president of the Russian Federation as a "symbol of unity of the Russian world." Later a particular understanding of "spiritual security" was introduced for the purpose of fighting against missionaries' activity and a number of religious minorities.[8]

The toughened policies introduced under President Putin shuttered many social and humanitarian programs of non-Orthodox churches. This policy touched all humanitarian programs of religious organizations that got aid from abroad. Procedures to clear humanitarian aid shipments were also tightened, especially those conducted by Protestant churches. For many non-Orthodox Christians and new religious movements, it became difficult to rent space for their worship services, obtain land plots, or build their houses of worship. At the same time, in many regions there were explicit attempts to hamper all existing construction works commenced by local religious groups. Muslims, more than any other non-Christian religious group, received the most monitoring from the authorities. Official Muslim communities already recognized by the government received more scrutiny, while independent Muslim groups felt more pressure from law enforcement agencies, which conducted repeated audits.

The clamping down on foreign influences and sects effectively set the tone for the Kremlin's policy and became one of the main phobias during Putin's presidential term, although these ideas had been voiced before he came to power and are still in place now that he has left office. For example, the Concept of National Security of Russia (1997) asserted the "crucial role of the Russian Orthodox Church and churches of other denominations in the maintenance and preservation of our spiritual values." That document contained a statement heavily influenced by the Moscow Patriarchate, which read as follows: "It is important to consider the destructive role played by various religious sects and the damage that they cause to the spiritual life of our society, thereby posing a direct threat to the lives and health of the citizens of Russia, which is often used to conceal illegal activities." In 2000 the updated Concept of National Security, adopted under Putin's presidency, listed fighting against sectarian and missionary activity among the state's measures to counteract foreign threats. It reads as follows:

> In order to enhance the national security of the Russian Federation, we must protect our cultural and spiritual legacy, morals, historical traditions and social standards, . . . form state policies on the spiritual nurturing and moral education of our people, ban the use of airtime and electronic media for broadcasting programs that promote violence and the exploitation of base and immoral subjects, as well as counteract the negative influence of foreign religious organizations and missionaries.

After Putin's term, however, the Strategy of National Security of Russia until 2020, adopted in 2009 under President Dmitry Medvedev, regarded religious questions of secondary importance (but significantly called for the need to fight against religious intolerance).[9]

In the course of Putin's presidential term, administrative measures against missionaries and religious minorities intensified. In 2002 the campaign to deport all foreign preachers from Russia reached its peak, with a record-high number of eighteen religious figures deported. Between 2000 and 2008 there were about a hundred missionaries deported from Russia for various reasons or without being given any reason at all.[10] While deportees included Catholics, Mormons, Muslims, and Buddhists, most were members of evangelical Christian associations and missions. The most active clergy also tended to be deported, often without being given any explanation. Among the deportees were such prominent religious figures as Father Stefano Caprio, the rector of a Catholic parish in the city of Vladimir, and the missionary-evangelist Leo Mårtensson of the mission The Light of the East and author of the translation of the Gospel into the Adyg language (he carried out his work in the Republic of Adygea and the Krasnodar region). Paul Kim, a Korean American whose visa was revoked by the authorities in February 2002, was also among those deported; he was the founder of the National Kalmyk Church of Evangelical Christian Missionary Union. Talipov Tahir of Latvia, a Baptist and founder of an independent Tatar evangelical community, was deported in late November 2003; he had served as the leader of the church in Tatarstan since the beginning of the 1990s. The accusation made against Talipov was that the views upheld by his church "do not correspond with the interests of the country and are of an extremist nature, thereby undermining the stability of interfaith relations and the interethnic situation in Russia."

Another example, which took place in 2005–6, involved four groups of American citizens invited by the Resurrection Church of Evangelical Christian Baptists (the church is part of the Russian Union of Evangelical Christians-Baptists), who were deported from the city of Ivanovo. They were detained while attending a religious meeting with local church members in the church sanctuary, at which time they were presented with a deportation order. The local television channel ran coverage of the situation, showing film footage accompanied by commentaries that the detained American missionaries and church members (one of them a former U.S. senator) used their religious visas to come to Russia and lure children into their church. Local newspapers printed a press release from the regional Office of the Federal Security Service (FSB) regarding the deportation of the group of missionaries, claiming that they had violated visa regulations.[11]

Work on a new draft law aimed at restricting missionary activity also began during the presidency of Putin and marked a continuation of the antimissionary policies. The road to creating this draft law began in 2000, when Putin adopted the Concept of National Security of Russia, which contained a chapter on "spiritual security" and the necessity to retain control and monitoring of missionary activity within the country. Following the adoption of the Concept, the government of the Russian Federation charged the Ministry of Justice of the Russian Federation with the responsibility of drafting the bill. In 2006 the Ministry presented the draft law "On Amendments to a Number of Federal Laws to Counter Illegal Missionary Activity" for the consideration of and approval by numerous religious organizations. This draft was immediately and unanimously rejected by all religious groups, including Protestants, Catholics, Muslims, and Jews, at the session of a government commission on religious associations, which was being supervised by Medvedev at that time. The draft was even rejected by Orthodox

Christians, because proposed regulations on missionary activity would have been too complicated for activists of the Russian Orthodox Church. For example, all missionaries would have to execute several documents, not proselytize vulnerable people (in hospitals, for example), and refrain from providing religious education to children who attended church without their parents.

The preexisting law On the Freedom of Conscience and Religious Organizations explicitly allowed missionary activity by ministers of religious organizations and the members of its governing bodies. The draft bill of 2006 proposed amending that law so that ministers must carry a document certifying their status, while "other persons" must carry a written permit issued by the governing body providing evidence of their "permission to preach." In addition all missionaries must submit a number of documents to the respective territorial agencies of the federal registration body. These documents include a notice of intention to conduct missionary activity, personal identification documents, and certification issued by the governing body of the religious organization. Foreign nationals are required to submit a visa or proof of their registration. The draft bill of 2006 also states that any form of preaching within one hundred meters of a building belonging to a religious organization of a different denomination is prohibited. The prohibition of missionary activity "directed at people who are experiencing difficult life situations and involving any promise to help them resolve such a situation" was a unique precedent in Russian legislation. In the history of restrictions on religious activity in Russia there was never such a legal limitation on ministering to people in trouble. In the Soviet period, to be sure, atheist officials accused religious leaders of exploiting vulnerable people with promises of help, but that was not a part of legislation.

The increasing expression of state support for Orthodox Christianity, along with the constant pressure on religious minorities, became staples in the rhetoric of government officials. In turn leaders in the Russian Orthodox hierarchy proposed a number of initiatives to help enhance the importance of the Orthodox Church within society and government. For instance, in the sphere of education a new subject called "the fundamentals of Orthodox Christian culture" was introduced in schools, along with the recognition of theology as a distinct scientific discipline. Both the increasing political activity of the Russian Orthodox Church and statements made by Orthodox hierarchs ended up provoking the first open protest against the propagation of the ROC's values by state authorities. This opposition was led by intellectuals of Russian society. In July 2007 ten academicians of the Russian Academy of Science took a stand against the growing influence of the Russian Orthodox Church and sent an open letter to President Putin, demanding that authorities cease the process of clericalism within Russian society and curb the interference of the Orthodox Church in all spheres of public life. Among those involved in this protest, the letter was signed by

Nobel Laureates Jaures Alferov and Vitaly Ginzburg. Both scientists referred to sociological data in asserting the following:

> If we assume that all atheists who are of Russian nationality are to be considered Orthodox, then Orthodox Christianity will certainly claim the majority. However, if we exclude all atheists then, alas, Orthodoxy will become a minority. Well, this is beside the point. Is it really necessary to treat people of other religious denominations with such contempt? Does this itself not resemble a form of Orthodox chauvinism? In the end, it would be nice if the Church's hierarchy took a moment to think about its own policies and what it is leading to—the consolidation of the country or its collapse?

This letter was followed by a similar letter written by a number of scientists and teachers, as well as letters from parents who stood against the introduction of the mandatory school subject "the fundamentals of Orthodox Christian culture." (According to a law passed in the Belgorod region in 2006, the subject called "Orthodox Christian culture" officially became mandatory.)

Despite Putin's efforts, authorities ultimately failed to fully curb religious freedom in Russia. The law on missionary work was not adopted, and the Russian Orthodox Church did not become the official state church. As well, no serious restrictions at the legislative level were imposed on the rights of religious minorities. Moreover those religious groups (e.g., Catholics, Lutherans, Baptists, Pentecostals) that have held their registration and property since the 1990s have retained their legal status since that time. As the second largest congregation after Orthodox Christians, Protestants marked a significant event in 2006 when one of their bishops, Sergei Ryakhovsky, a leader of the Pentecostal Church, was selected as a member of the Public Chamber of Russia (an arm's-length high-profile advisory body composed of public figures). To this day he continues to represent the Protestant movement there, and evangelical believers generally are among the most vigorous defenders of democratic values in Russia.[12]

Of course, religious minorities have faced obstacles renting premises and building houses of worship, and missionaries have been deported and humanitarian programs closed. It appears, however, that some restrictions were temporary, and although minorities have been frightened they continue to develop their missions.

Despite the fact all officials claim their commitment to Orthodoxy, Putin's presidency saw almost no initiative of the Russian Orthodox Church come to full fruition, whether in the sphere of education, the army, or property-related issues. Thus with respect to religion, authoritarian trends in the Putin era proved to be somewhat weak, with government actions inconsistent and contradictory and the promotion of Orthodox ideology by authorities superficial and often empty.[13]

Orthodox Christianity and Society in Medvedev's Era

The degree of continuity in religious policy from the Putin to the Medvedev presidency varies by context and policy. Like Putin, the new head of state declared his adherence to the Orthodox faith. But the biography of the new president suggests that, for the first time since the 1990s, the country is now headed by a person of the new era. Dmitry Medvedev essentially belongs to the "perestroika generation" because he was only twenty in 1985. His personality developed during an epoch characterized by a religious boom and peak interest in the role of faith, particularly Orthodoxy, in the construction of the new Russia. It is rare that representatives of the ROC speak about politicians in the way they do of Medvedev. They say, "He is a man of faith, an Orthodox believer." Indeed the apparently authentic Orthodoxy of Medvedev stands in striking contrast to the calculating Putin, a rigid statesman and former KGB operative largely distanced from faith.

Medvedev's policy aspires to see the ROC play an active role in building civil society in Russia, but it exhibits a certain pragmatism. Under Medvedev the state directs considerable energy to support of spiritual enlightenment, including religious education under the ROC's framework, ROC-initiated social projects (formally in collaboration with local authorities), cultural projects involving youth, movies, children's camps, Orthodox grammar schools, and more. But through these measures the state is gradually redirecting the ROC toward engagement in social priorities. This should give rise to a new stage in development of ecclesiastical life, from the restoration of buildings to missionary work and religious education.

Medvedev is also a supporter of two essential characteristics of a democratic state: voluntarism and the involvement of various religious associations (not only the ROC) as social partners of the state. In this respect his reaction to the controversial issue of teaching "the fundamentals of Orthodox Christian culture" in public schools is instructive. When this religious issue was raised during his first Internet conference, on March 5, 2007, he replied:

> It is obvious that nothing in this sphere can be compulsory in a secular state. At the same time, the school should respond to suggestions coming from students' parents and from students, with respect to teaching the basics of this or that religion or of world religions. In my opinion, in order not to upset the balance which, thank God, has been achieved on this question, it seems to me that it is important to observe the principle of voluntarism here, so that the corresponding school subjects are taught on a voluntary and optional basis.[14]

This declaratory embrace of democratic standards, the value of freedom, and commitment to strengthening civil society was sometimes reflected in religious policy, but not always in real life. Medvedev claimed, for example, that his support of religious education, military clergy, and restitution of church property was based on the opinion of the representatives of traditional religions in Russia (ROC, Islam, Buddhism, Judaism). But while these measures potentially touch all religious organizations of Russia, they were essentially worked out by the ROC. Moreover it was during Medvedev's presidency that the state took a number of concrete decisions in support of the ideological, financial, social, cultural, and educational initiatives of the ROC, which were actively proposed to the government by Patriarch Kirill, who was newly elected at the beginning of 2009 (after the death of Patriarch Alex II in December 2008). So there is some tension between the real policy of the president and his adherence to the democratic standards in the sphere of freedom of religion and belief.

At the same time, the Russian Orthodox Church's aspiration to receive privileges from the state in every sphere—from the army and education to property rights and placing Orthodox symbols in all sorts of institutions—has been a source of public disputes. Led by Patriarch Kirill, such initiatives have sparked opposition in civil society, especially by representatives of other faiths. Previously skepticism regarding the role of Orthodoxy in Russia was especially evident among pockets of the intelligentsia. Nowadays, however, disputes surrounding the transformation of the ROC into some kind of state symbol, with all its privileges, have come to involve those citizens who have never even given thought to it before. Such disputes even involve people who call themselves Orthodox.

From mid-2009 through early 2010 a number of steps sought to advance the Russian Orthodox Church to a preeminent financial and ideological position among religious associations and public organizations. This reinforcement of the ROC has no parallels in the history of Russia, as this strengthening is occurring in a purportedly secular state (as proclaimed by the Russian Constitution), and is finding its support exclusively in the levers of power. These initiatives were enacted at the request of the ROC and Patriarch Kirill in support of the interests of the ROC. And they are being executed by administrative methods, thereby bypassing Russian legislation and excluding the need for dialogue with other faiths or society as a whole. This approach is now provoking a backlash.

In July 2009 President Medvedev consented to suggestions made by a number of traditional religious associations, the first and foremost being the ROC, and instructed the Ministry of Defense to restore the institution of the military clergy in Russia. It was declared that, during the first stage, priests were to appear in military divisions serving abroad. During the second stage (effective January 1, 2010), ROC priests would be appointed to serve all armed forces units right down to the brigade level. The Armed Forces of the Russian Federation also introduced the position of assistant commander of a military unit, charged with working with the faithful among military servicemen.

This military program was introduced without public discussion and without clear normative and legal justification. The rights and duties of priests have not been outlined, nor has their area of responsibility and competences been defined. Moreover the ideological campaign behind Medvedev's order ignored Article 8 of the Federal Law on Status of Military Servicemen, which stipulates that the state "bears no responsibility to satisfy the needs of the military with regards to their religious beliefs and religious practices." According to federal law, the creation of religious associations within a military unit is also not permitted.

Critics noted other contradictions. In February 2010 the Institute on Religion and Law sent a written appeal to the minister of defense of the Russian Federation, A. E. Serdyukov, pointing out that "according to current statements made by representatives of the Moscow Patriarchate and the Administration of the Ministry of Defense of the Russian Federation, the introduction of the institution of military clergy actually contradicts the constitutional principle of equality of all religions before the law." In addition recommendations issued by the Ministry of Defense at hearings in the Public Chamber of the Russian Federation contained gross errors and offensive statements toward those religious associations that do not number among the declared four traditional religions of Russia.[15]

Nonetheless the Ministry of Defense proceeded to implement Medvedev's order. In April 2010 it declared that it would establish a department for working with the faithful among military personnel, to be headed by a priest from the ROC. The Ministry of Defense acknowledged that the recommendation regarding the appointment of military priests had come from the Russian Orthodox Church only and that the duties of Orthodox priests would also include preaching to believers from other faiths.[16]

In the summer of 2009 President Medvedev also supported the introduction of subjects in public schools on religious themes, first and foremost "the Fundamentals of Orthodox Christian culture." The pilot project involved the addition of a choice of three subjects (secular ethics, basics of the world religions, and basics of one of the traditional religions—Orthodoxy, Islam, Buddhism, and Judaism) to the school curriculum in nineteen regions. This experiment, put on a fast-track mode, caused both tacit and open discontent, not only among representatives of the Ministry of Culture, but also among the majority of school-teachers. In January 2010 one of the country's leading scientists, the deputy head of the Ethics Department of the Philosophical Faculty of St. Petersburg State University, Vadim Perov, refused to write the textbook on the basics of secular ethics for the experimental course "the Fundamentals of Orthodox Christian culture and secular ethics." He considered the timeline allocated for its preparation to be overly rushed, and he found the subject matter unsuitable for students of the fourth and fifth grades. The Orthodox textbook, which was written in just a couple of months, was provided by Deacon Andrey Kraev. It has been subject to extensive criticism by both scientists and teachers.

In April 2010 the textbooks were published and the experiment began against the backdrop of unceasing public discussion. In a number of regions the majority of parents have chosen to enroll their children in the course "the basics of secular ethics" instead of the course on Orthodox Christianity. According to opinion polls of parents of students throughout all of the regions participating in the pilot project, an average of 30 percent of all parents ended up choosing "the Fundamentals of Orthodox Christian culture" for their children, and about the same number each have chosen either "secular ethics" or "the basics of world religions."[17] Representatives of the ROC have been disappointed by such results. Moreover Old Believers (for example, the Pomorskaya Ancient Orthodoxy Church) recommended that members choose the course on secular ethics *instead* of any studies based on the textbook prepared by the Moscow Patriarchate.

It also became obvious that the informal restitution of Orthodox religious buildings and valuables would soon enter a new stage. At the beginning of 2010 representatives of the ROC declared that new draft legislation on transfer of assets of a religious nature to religious associations was ready for submission to the State Duma and for public discussion (99 percent of this project pertains to the ROC). The draft legislation apparently resulted from consultations between representatives of the Patriarchate, which have been accelerated under Patriarch Kirill, and the Ministry of Economic Development and Trade. The bill develops a mechanism for the restoration or transfer of ownership of church property and religious objects to the ROC. Part of the impulse was that many buildings that used to belong to the ROC prior to the Revolution of 1917 have not yet been transferred back to the Church's ownership. The necessary preconditions for the approval of this draft are as follows: simultaneous approval of laws that will allow federal and regional authorities to finance the restoration, renovation, and maintenance of cultural and historic monuments that have been transferred to the ownership of the Moscow Patriarchate of the ROC and also indemnification of property registration expenses to the Church. The new law, if approved, will establish a uniform order and will oblige the state to transfer property rights to the Church at all levels: federal, regional, and municipal.

One more piece of draft legislation, also meant to support the ROC, has come to light. This bill concerns support for the social work carried out by religious associations. At the request of the Moscow Patriarchate, deputies from the United Russia Party have included the right of religious organizations to apply for state aid in the presidential draft law for supporting noncommercial organizations. In February 2010 the bill was approved by the State Duma of the Russian Federation. According to this law, religious organizations will also be able to receive what is known as "socially oriented status." It comes as no surprise that the legal advisor to the Moscow Patriarchate, Ksenia Chernega, immediately declared that such a socially oriented status may be obtained only by select religious associations.

The picture is made complete with draft legislation on missionary activity long in the works within the Ministry of Justice of the Russian Federation. The Ministry has recommended amending the federal law On the Freedom of Worship and on Religious Organizations to regulate missionary activity. The proposal has sparked indignation by both religious figures and human rights activists. The first objection to this bill is that the amendments contradict international norms on religious freedom. Second, they contradict the provisions of the Russian Federation Constitution and the Law on Freedom of Worship (about every person's right to exercise and propagate his faith). Third, in failing to provide an accurate definition of missionary work and introducing fines for preaching in public places that turn out to be heavier than those for creating a public disturbance, the proposal is humiliating for the faithful of religious associations. It is well known that the Moscow Patriarchate fundamentally supports regulating missionary activity. At the same time, its representatives would like to correct some provision in the legislation that may directly affect the ROC itself. According to proposed legislation, a fine may be imposed on the head of a religious association if any of its members preach without proper documents. In addition there is a fine for "not preventing a minor from participating in meetings of a religious association." In other words, one should either turn unfamiliar children away from churches or hope that nobody will inform on the religious organization that the children may have attended without first receiving written permission from their parents. So at the beginning of February 2010 representatives of the Ministry of Justice declared their intention to improve the draft, which had previously been published on the official website of the Ministry of Justice on October 12, 2009. Consequently the adoption of a law on restricting missionary activity has once again been postponed.

The public response to the ROC's initiatives ranges in acuteness and radicalism, from concerns about the general protection of freedom of conscience to aversion toward the overwhelming role that the ROC is playing in contemporary Russia. Despite the diversity of reactions to the political onslaught of Orthodox Christianity initiated by Patriarch Kirill, it is possible to say that all reactions constitute a prominent display of civil consciousness. At the very least, a democratically expressed, patriarchy-criticizing reaction often finds more open and voluntary supporters than any other opposition to state authorities. In many cases, state support for the ROC is perceived as ideological coercion by the authorities, an unwanted intervention by the state in the affairs of citizens. Therefore the actions of the Moscow Patriarchate of the ROC, even those that are within the limits of Russian Federation legislation and are technically harmless, can still be met with a vehemently hostile reaction.

One demonstration of the growing intensity of such disputes is the clash between the ROC and museum employees, who will be the first to feel the brunt if museums are expelled from monastic premises and religious movables, such as ancient icons, are returned to the ROC. Archpriest Vsevolod Chaplin claimed that museum personnel's opposition to the ROC is rooted in their selfish mercenary interests. Speaking on the Soyuz television channel on March 5, 2010, he made this unsubstantiated assertion: "It happens very often, despite the beggarly salaries of museum employees, that museums' management is pretty well off, using the opportunities to organize trade in those places with heavier traffic by visitors, to lease and sublease premises, to arrange junkets and any sort of well-paying pleasure events." The chairman of the Synod Information Department, Vladimir Legoida, also distorted the concerns of museums. He argued that the proposal for the transfer of rights does not at all concern museum funds, although disputes have arisen regarding the ROC's claims to part of the funds from vacating museum premises. Speaking on the radio station Govorit Moskva, Legoida even denied that the ROC has any claims or conflicts in this regard. He stated, "I cannot imagine a situation when priests and the congregation would insist on the transfer of, for instance, icons to the actual detriment of their preservation." The museum community also took great offense with Father Vladimir Vigiljansky of the press office of the Moscow Patriarchate, who accused museum employees of destroying the twelfth-century Bogoljubskaya icon at the Vladimir Uspensky Cathedral in the Knyaginin Monastery. Yet it was the monastery itself that violated all the storage requirements, while not letting museum staff come anywhere near the icon.

For the first time ever, authoritative experts on Russian church art expressed acute anxiety over the existing practice of transferring church buildings and museum artifacts to the ROC. At a roundtable discussion held on January 18, 2010, by the RIA Novosti news agency, art experts stated, "[I]n the course of transferring a huge amount of property to the Church, the larger part of which is made up of historical monuments, it appears that the State and the ROC have concluded agreements between themselves and have therein disregarded Russian society, which includes a professional experts community." The abrupt decision by Prime Minster Putin to transfer the Novodevichy Monastery, a main branch of the Historical Museum, to the Moscow Patriarchate of the ROC was a bolt out of the blue for the employees of its museum, who were not even informed about this decision.[18] Quickly 150 representatives of the museum community signed an open letter to President Medvedev, requesting that the museum's treasures not be transferred to the ROC. Their appeal reads as follows:

> The prospective transfer of ancient churches with frescos and icons, together with the icons and precious liturgical utensils contained within museum funds for Church use, will remove them from the cultural life

of the larger society and may result in their destruction. As representatives of the community of museum restorers and keepers of ancient values, we urge you to speak openly against the rash and doubtful legislative initiative put forth, which is capable of causing irreparable damage to the cultural heritage of Russia.[19]

Under public pressure the Ministry of Culture endorsed the revision of the legislative proposal to transfer museum property to religious associations.

Criticism of official Orthodox Christianity has arisen from other societal strata. For example, an unexpectedly turbulent reaction was caused by Patriarch Kirill's visit to the National Nuclear Studies University's Moscow Engineering and Physics Institute on March 4, 2010. A student group wrote a letter to the university rector, expressing indignation over the dismantling of a revered monument dedicated to students in front of the university building and its replacement with a cross prior to Patriarch Kirill's arrival. In addition students opposed the establishment of a chapel within the university and the delineation of students into Orthodox and non-Orthodox groups. The students' address to the rector emphasized:

The above mentioned facts are in severe violation of the University Charter, which does not stipulate conducting religious ceremonies, not to mention using the University means for the construction of cult objects for any religion whatsoever. Furthermore, the Charter is violated due to the fact that students and university staff are involved in executing the ceremony of "consecrating" the Cross installed on its territory.

Similar conflicts between leaders of the ROC and students or the public have begun to arise in some regional dioceses, and the authorities generally do not oppose such public actions.[20]

Just a year after the installation of Patriarch Kirill, Orthodox political initiatives have sparked acutely negative citizen reaction. In the late Soviet years, Orthodox Christianity was regarded with hope and as a resort of spiritual freedom. Now the ROC faces open mistrust and suspicion. The politicization of Orthodoxy—the administrative imposition of symbols and holidays, the state reference to Orthodox Christianity and its necessity, the need to suppress smaller nonconventional religions, and insults aimed at the critics of the ROC— have effectively split society and have aggravated those contradictions that already existed. For instance, state authorities insist that they are building a legal democratic state and that the ROC's position is rooted in resistance to Western values. At the same time Patriarch Kirill preaches more about Orthodoxy as a social and political ideology than as a Christian faith. His speeches are filled with statements about the social crisis, the strength of the state, Russian patriotism, and the threat of Western liberalism.[21]

Under the presidency of Medvedev, Orthodox Christianity has come to assume a prominent place in mass media and political life. But this has sparked intense public discussion, which has prevented severe diminution of religious freedom. It has also educated citizens about the value of freedom of conscience and faith. However, the process of strengthening civil society and democratic standards is both slow and not uniform and is dependent on historical peculiarities associated with developments of a given region.

Religious Freedom in Numerical Terms

One of the most important factors influencing the emergence of religious freedom in Russia is that the country is gradually ceasing to be perceived as a state with just one or even four traditional religions. This is particularly important against the background of public discussion on the role of religion.

Contrary to common impressions, religious diversity in Russia almost compares to the somewhat motley religious picture in the United States or European countries. Russia is by no means a monoreligious country with one dominating religion. Ever since the end of the 1980s, Russian society has been subject to the same processes of globalization as other countries of the world. On the one hand, this has fostered a secular consciousness for many indifferent to faith, who perceive religion as just another symbol of a people's national or cultural identity. On the other hand, this has expanded the general religious outlook and increased spiritual options for Russian citizens.

The available statistical data give only a very general idea about the presence of the various religions in Russia. One must probe deeper to gain an understanding of the real role and influence that faiths play in the social and political life of the country. According to the Federal Registration Service, as of January 1, 2009, there were 12,727 organizations of the Russian Orthodox Church of the Moscow Patriarchate registered in Russia and 120 organizations that belonged to other Orthodox jurisdictions. The corresponding figure was 278 for Old Believers, 232 for the Catholic faith, 3,885 for Islam, 203 for Buddhism, and 294 adhering to Judaism.[22]

Protestantism is the second largest Christian faith in Russia, with a total of 4,493 officially registered churches as of January 1, 2009. Tremendously diverse, these include Evangelical Baptist Christians, Christians of Evangelical Faith (Pentecostals), Evangelical Christians, Lutherans, Adventists, Methodists, Reformed, Presbyterians, Anglicans, and Mennonites, as well as a number of nondenominational congregations. But Protestants also have the highest number of unregistered communities, especially Pentecostals and Baptist

Evangelists. Estimates put the number of functioning Protestant congregations at 8,000 to 9,000.[23]

In order to gauge the real number of adherents to this or that religion in Russia, it is necessary to apply several criteria. If we proceed on the basis of the ethnic principle of religious adherence (e.g., all Russians are Orthodox, all Jews adhere to Judaism, all peoples of the Caucasus and Tatars are Muslims, etc.), the tally would indicate that there are 120 million Orthodox believers, 600,000 Catholics, more than 1 million followers of the Armenian Apostolic Church, 14 million Muslims, 230,000 adherents of Judaism, and 900,000 Buddhists. (These data are based on the all-Russian census of 2002.)

If we proceed on the basis of people's identification of themselves as Orthodox, Protestant, or Muslim, the numbers can be broken down as follows: 75 million to 85 million people of Orthodox faith (as various polls indicate that 60 to 70 percent of Russian respondents say they are Orthodox), up to 1 million Catholics, 1.5 million to 1.8 million Protestants, fewer than 1.5 million Old Believers, 6 million to 9 million Muslims, up to 50,000 adherents of Judaism, about 550,000 Buddhists, and no more than 300,000 followers of new religious movements.

If we draw on sociological data on numbers actually practicing the faith, however, we get a dramatically different picture. Estimates of the number of ROC practicing believers are much lower than those for identification, ranging from a high of 15 million to a low of 3 million. For Protestants the figure is at least 2 million, for Muslims about 2.8 million, for Buddhists 500,000, for Catholics up to 200,000, for new religious movements 300,000, and under 100,000 each for Judaism and the Old Believers.[24]

These figures help us understand how difficult it is to see who is actually Orthodox in the purportedly Orthodox Russia. By identifying the number of people who consciously profess Orthodox Christianity *and* are actual churchgoers, sociologists have estimated that these "traditional believers" constituted only 3 percent of the population in 1991. This figure rose to 7 percent by 1999 and 8.8 percent by 2005. It turns out, however, that even this modest percentage inflates the core faithful, since 15 percent of these "traditional believers" do not believe in the existence of an afterlife, 30 percent do not acknowledge the resurrection of the soul after death, and 13 percent have never undergone the sacrament of communion.[25] Moreover church services for such major holidays as Christmas and Easter are actually attended by only about 2 percent of the population, and Orthodox Lent is fully observed by only about 4 percent of those who identify themselves as Orthodox.

The Federal Orthodox-oriented policy, in essence, divides Russia into Orthodox Christian and non–Orthodox Christian regions and further divides religions into those that are traditional (Orthodox Christianity, Islam, Judaism, and Buddhism) and those that are nontraditional. But the policy of mainly supporting the Moscow Patriarchate of the ROC and discriminating against the rights of other believers appears to be both innately contradictory and counterproductive. It runs contrary to the Constitution of the Russian Federation and to the democratic declarations made by representatives of the highest ranks of power and therefore cannot be implemented in full, at least not officially. The majority of Russian citizens say they support "a strong state" and Orthodox Christianity, but such declarations often have no real backing and are associated with no particular set of values, ideas, hopes, or aspirations. The former patriotic state ideology, which pursued the goal of strengthening the state, is paradoxically undermining the main principles of the present Russian government.

The rigid pro-Orthodox policy is distorting religious affairs in Russia, as even the relatively Orthodox and Russian regions tend to have a very heterogeneous religious structure.[26] Indeed in a number of major regions—Kaliningrad, northwestern Russia, some Ural areas, Siberia, and the Far East, as well as the ethnic republics—Moscow's rigid state ideology and Orthodoxy seem unconnected to real life and potentially destructive.[27]

Conclusion

Despite authoritarian initiatives, discrimination, and campaigns against other faiths, at both the regional and the federal level, there currently exists more freedom for the faithful of different denominations in Russia than at any previous period in the country's history (with the exception of the brief time immediately following the law on religion of 1990). To be sure, the public is slower to accommodate religious freedom than is otherwise desirable. And ideological clichés (such as the "peril" from the West and imagery of adherents of other faiths as belonging to criminal and destructive "sects") unfortunately still hold some meaning for the bureaucracy and are often broadcast in the mass media.

Nonetheless the freedom of religion is gradually becoming a value in Russia, often paid for dearly by a number of active citizens. This value, which was previously accessible only to Orthodox Christianity or the selected traditional religions (or during the Soviet period to atheists), was essentially unattainable for marginal dissidents who did not even have the right to receive higher education. In the past twenty years the gap between the Russian Orthodox Church, which was among those severely affected during the Soviet era, and other religious faiths has narrowed. In parallel with the revival of the Orthodox Church, many religious movements have successfully developed in recent years and are prospering.

Unfortunately the authoritarian habits of Russian officials, especially those of the FSB, linger. These authorities still carry out senseless discriminatory campaigns in the name of national security. In 2009 a campaign was launched against the Jehovah's Witnesses. Its literature was identified as extremist and imports banned, and Russian officials began inspections in the Witness prayer houses throughout the country. Similarly in April 2010 a Russian local court designated as "extremist" literature of the Church of Scientology. These wild and senseless campaigns, however, are more the exception than the rule, as other religious organizations openly develop their missions.

Despite all the senseless persecutions, state officials cannot stem the growing religious diversity of Russia. And opposition among intelligentsia, students, and the general public is rising against administrative actions that deny this pluralism. Religious life on the ground fosters growing public support for the freedom of religion and belief, which will gradually advance in legislative policy and law enforcement. This should happen in spite of historical myths about Russia's "distinctive way" and the use of such myths in justifying authoritarian practices, and in spite of the phobias and complexes (i.e., the superiority of the traditional religions as opposed to the purportedly crazy Western "sects") that still plague the Russian state.

Notes

1. These are common phrases employed by Russian Orthodox Church authorities.
2. Christopher Marsh and Wallace Daniel, "Russian Law on Freedom of Conscience 1997: in Context and Retrospect," *Journal of Church and State*, no. 49 (Winter 2007): 19–26; W. Cole Durham Jr., Lauren B. Homer, Pieter van Dijk, and John Witte Jr., "The Future of Religious Liberty in Russia: Report of the De Burght Conference on Pending Russian Legislation Restricting Religious Liberty," *Emory International Law Review* 8, no. 1 (1994); "Russian Federation Federal Law on Freedom of Conscience and on Religious Associations," *Emory International Law Review* 12, no. 1 (1998); W. Cole Durham Jr. and Lauren B. Homer, "Russia's 1997 Law on Freedom of Conscience and Religious Associations: An Analytical Appraisal," *Emory International Law Review* 12, no. 1 (1998); Anatoly Pchelintsev, "Religiia i prava cheloveka," in *Religiia i prava cheloveka: Na puti k svobode sovesti*, vol. 3, ed. Lyudmila M. Vorontsova, A. V. Pchelintsev, and Sergei B. Filatov (Moscow: Nauka, 1996); Lyudmila M. Vorontsova and Sergei Filatov, "Russkii put' i grazhdanskoe obshchestvo," *Svobodnaia mysl'*, no. 1 (1995).
3. A. A. Krasikov. "Russkaya Pravoslavnaya Tserkov: Ot sluzhby gosudarevoi k ispytaniu svobodoi," in *Novye tserkvi, starye veruyushie—starye tserkvi, novye veruyushie: Religiya v postsovetskoi Rossii*, ed. Kimmo Kaariainen and Dmitrii Furman (Moscow, 2007), 134–229.
4. See Anatoly Pchelintsev, "Fizicheskie litsa kak subjekty prava na sozdanie religioznogoobjedineniaya," *Konstitucionnoe i municipalnoe pravo*, no. 21 (2009): 8–11.
5. Anatoly Pchelintsev, "Critical Problems of Freedom of Religious Affiliation and the Activity of Religious Associations," in *Twenty Years of Religious Freedom in Russia*, ed. A. Malashenko and Sergei Filatov, Carnegie Moscow Center (Moscow: ROSSPAN, 2009), 70–130.
6. Christopher Marsh and Wallace Daniel, "Russian Law on Freedom of Conscience 1997: In Context and Retrospect," *Journal of Church and State*, no. 49 (Winter 2007): 19–26. Also see the Russian translation of that article in *Russian Review of Keston Institute*, www.keston.org.uk.
7. See the press release of Slavic Center for Law and Justice, http://www.sclj.ru/court_practice/detail.php?ID=1190.
8. Roman Lunkin, "Religion in Russia's Federal Regions: Pragmatism or Witch-Hunt?," *Frontier* (Keston Institute), no. 5 (2004): 37–44.
9. Roman Lunkin, "Klerikalizatsiaya kak vyzov gozbezopasnosti," credo.ru portal, at http://www.portal-credo.ru/site/?act=fresh&id=954.
10. Roman Lunkin, "The Russian Security Service versus Western Missionaries," in *East-West Church & Ministry Report* (Global Center, Samford University) 12, no. 4 (2004): 1–3. Also see

"FSB protiv missionerov: Podarok dlya samogo slabogo," December 24, 2003, http://www
.portal-credo.ru/site/?act=fresh&id=163.

11. See "Osobennosti natsionalnoy deportacii," April 1, 2006, http://www.portal-credo.ru/
site/?act=press&type=list&press_id=474. For complete information about the violations of
religious freedom in Russia, see the website of Slavic Center for Law and Justice and Institute
of Religion and Law (www.sclj.ru) and the analytical news website www.portal-credo.ru.

12. Roman Lunkin, "Protestantism and Human Rights: Creation of the Alternative to the
Authorities," paper presented at the fourth annual Lilly Fellows National Research Conference,
November 11–14, 2005, Samford University, http://www.samford.edu/lillyhumanrights/
papers/Lunkin_Protestantism.pdf.

13. My research on religious policy and the situation in the Russian provinces is based on field
sociological surveys conducted during the project Encyclopedia of Religious Life in Russia
Today by the Keston Institute (Oxford, Xenia Dennen, president). These sociological surveys
were carried out in more than seventy regions of the Russian Federation, extending from
1998 until the present time. This project resulted in the publication of a book of articles,
Religiya i obshestvo: Ocherki sovremennoi zhizni Rossii, ed. Sergei Filatov (Moscow: Letniy Sad,
2002); encyclopedias on religious movements, *Sovremennaya religioznaya zhizn Rossii*, vols.
1–4, ed. Michael Bourdeaux and Sergei Filatov (Moscow: Logos, 2003–6); and a synopsis of
the regional situation, *Atlas of Religious Life in Russia Today*, vols. 1–3, ed. Michael Bourdeaux
and Sergei Filatov (Moscow: Letniy Sad, 2005–6). Some articles about the situation in Russia
are now being published by the *Russian Review of the Keston Institute* (www.keston.org.uk).

14. Stenogram of the public Internet conference of President Dmitry Medvedev, March 5, 2007,
http://voprosy.yandex.ru/db/answers.xml.

15. The hearing took place on December 9, 2009, as cited in "Review of Religious Matters in the
Armed Forces of the Russian Federation" on the topic "Society, Religion and the Army."

16. The letter of the Russian Ministry of Defense on the establishment of the institution of military clergy, dated March 23, 2010.

17. "The Report on Religious Education in Russian Schools in 2009," http://irhrg.ru/files/book_
OPK_monitoring.pdf.

18. On Christmas Eve of 2009 Prime Minister Putin informed the patriarch of the transfer of the
monastery to the ROC, which shocked Marina Shvedova, head of that branch of the Historical
Museum.

19. February 19, 2010, document in author's possession.

20. The websites that regularly shed light on the situation in Russia are www.portal-credo.ru,
www.religiopolis.org, http://religion.sova-center.ru, and the website of the Slavic Center for
Law and Justice and the Institute of Religion and Law, www.sclj.ru.

21. Sergei Filatov, "Religiozno-obshestvennaya zhizn Rossii v 2009," *Russian Review of Keston
Institute*, http://www.keston.org.uk/russianreview-41.php.

22. *Religii v Rossii*, ed. O. Vasilieva and V. Shchmidt (Moscow: Russian Academy of State Service,
2009), 99–108.

23. Roman Lunkin, "Traditional Pentecostals in Russia," *East-West Church & Ministry Report*
(Global Center, Samford University) 12, no. 3 (2004): 4–7; Roman Lunkin, "The Charismatic
Movement in Russia," *East-West Church & Ministry Report* (Global Center, Samford University)
13, no. 1 (2005): 1–5.

24. Roman Lunkin and Sergei Filatov, "Statistika rossiyskoi religioznosti: Magya tsifr i neod-
noznachnaya realnost," *Sociologicheskie issledovaniaya*, no. 6 (2005): 35–45.

25. See the results of that sociological survey: *Novye tserkvi, starye veruyushie—Starye tserkvi,
novye veruyushie. Religiya v postsovetskoi Rossii*, ed. Kimmo Kaariainen and Dmitrii Furman
(Moscow, 2007).

26. Roman Lunkin, "Russkie regiony Rossii: Steepen pravoslavnosti i politicheskie orientacii,"
Sociologicheskie issledovaniaya, no. 4 (288) (2008): 27–37.

27. Sergei Filatov, "The Vibrant Blossoming of the Enchanting Garden of Russian Spirituality:
Twenty Years of Growth of Religious Diversity in Post-Soviet Russia," in *Twenty Years of
Religious Freedom in Russia*, ed. A. Malashenko and Sergei Filatov, Carnegie Moscow Center
(Moscow: ROSSPAN, 2009), 8–40.

PART THREE

CHURCH-STATE CHALLENGES
IN DEMOCRATIC STATES

7

From Solidarity to Freedom

The Mixed Fortunes of Churches in Postcommunist Eastern Europe

JONATHAN LUXMOORE

When the nations of Eastern Europe marked the twentieth anniversary of the collapse of communist rule in autumn 2009, they had much to be proud of. In countries previously under one-party rule, democracy and human rights are now firmly rooted, along with stable institutions and market economies that have brought growth and prosperity for many. With the Iron Curtain now a distant memory, the region's Christians could also afford to celebrate. In the space of two decades, ecclesiastical infrastructures have been rebuilt and novel approaches adapted to pastoral mission in pluralistic societies.

Yet there will be challenges to face in the next decade, in many cases reflecting problems inherited from the communist era. The replacement of austere one-party states with fractious but vibrant democracies signaled a major advance for religious freedom in the world and removed a powerful, long-standing barrier to the survival and development of religious communities. It also raised questions, however, which are still not fully answered. How would the experience of communist-era restrictions affect the self-perception and self-confidence of churches and religious associations, as well as their ability to work together and offer positive, coherent values to postcommunist societies? How would the baneful record of property confiscations, of suppressed institutions, of stifled educational, publishing, and charitable initiatives impact their ability to rebuild? How would the legacy of repression and intimidation influence their capacity to build relations of mutual forgiveness, understanding, and solidarity? How would the dominance of a hostile ideology color habits of thought and behavior? How would revived religious devotions and practices fare in the face of new forms of secularization? How would countries with distinctive, contrasting church-state traditions ensure equal rights for both majority and minority faiths, allowing personal freedom and autonomy to flourish within the framework of reborn national identities?

Although dramatic images from 1989 have dominated memories, the changes in Eastern Europe happened over longer stages and can be traced to systemic fault lines present in the communist system from the very beginning. Most accounts highlight a complex interaction of economic stagnation, ideological meltdown, Western pressure, and imperial overstretch. They also point to a fractious combination of reform from above and rebellion from below and to a chain of intended and unintended consequences that quickly spiraled into a full-scale transformation.

Yet even today the picture is unclear and can be presented in a variety of ways. Evidence suggests governments both East and West were skeptical about the possibilities of far-reaching change and caught out by the speed of events. Trotsky's definition of revolution as "the forcible entry of the masses into the realm of rulership over their own destiny" was played out in Eastern Europe, this time against the communist vision that was supposed to inspire them.[1] Each nation in the region can credibly claim to have led the way in 1989. For Poles, it was prepared by government-opposition roundtable talks and semi-democratic elections on June 4, which took place on the day pro-democracy Chinese demonstrators were massacred in Beijing's Tiananmen Square. For Hungarians, it was the symbolic cutting of border fences with Austria in May and the opening of the Iron Curtain to East German refugees during the summer. For Lithuanians, Latvians, and Estonians, it was the human chain of clasped hands that stretched between the three capitals in August. For Czechs, Slovaks, and Romanians, it was the sudden, dramatic uprisings—one entirely peaceful, the other partly violent—that erupted in November and December. For East Germans, it was the televised opening of the Berlin Wall on November 9, which graphically and visually captured the revolutionary moment in simple, comprehensible images.

Whichever version is preferred, the role of the Catholic, Orthodox, and Protestant communities of Eastern Europe was crucial, especially in giving a moral stamp of approval to opposition movements and in mobilizing the "people power" of hearts and minds that ultimately brought the communist system down. This was most evident in Poland, where the Catholic Church helped sustain the movement for human rights and legality when the Solidarity movement was crushed under martial law, offering vital sanctuary to myriad groups, publications, and social initiatives. In 1989 the Church was represented in all key negotiations, arranging and facilitating talks and mediating and guaranteeing the agreements that paved the way for a peaceful handover of power.

In neighboring Czechoslovakia, the Catholic Church provided a large network of underground groups, which expanded in the mid-1980s into mass opposition, something the country's small, isolated human rights groups could never have achieved. In Lithuania, where the underground *Chronicle of the Catholic Church*, edited and circulated by clergy and laypeople, became the Soviet Union's longest-running samizdat journal, Church leaders provided decisive moral support for the Sajudis democracy movement. In Hungary, Christian base communities were a key element of the nascent civil society that emerged in the 1980s. In Romania, where the Winter Revolution was sparked by the arrest of a Calvinist pastor, Laszlo Toekes, much-persecuted Greek Catholic priests and laity had been active underground for decades, as in neighboring Ukraine. When violence flared, a Catholic archbishop, Ioan Robu, spoke of "the presence of God on the streets," of "a faith which has lived on, through concealment and humiliation, and is now expressing itself in simple, open words and deeds."[2]

Some Eastern Europeans saw 1989 as a triumph for the "liberty, equality, and fraternity" proclaimed by the French Revolution exactly two centuries before and for the spirit of defiance shown by earlier national uprisings. They also detected a major shift in the Catholic Church's position. In contrast to bloody events in previous centuries, the Church had unequivocally welcomed the new spring tide of human liberation. But it had tried to give the ideals of liberty and emancipation a deeper Christian interpretation, which went beyond secular political dimensions. It had also cautioned against false notions of freedom and an uncritical acceptance of Western norms and values.

Behind all of this stood the epic figure of Pope John Paul II, who had openly backed Solidarity in Poland when local church leaders were reticent, bringing millions into the streets. The pope had kept the movement united and peaceful around a clearly articulated set of objectives and set out the moral and spiritual parameters of a reunited Europe—as the analogy put it, "breathing with both lungs." In this way he was a catalyst for forces already emerging by the 1980s, while also helping direct them with an acute understanding of power politics. The pope knew that agreements with communist regimes were worthless unless backed up by powerful pressure. He was also aware that Christians lacked the strength and self-confidence to exert this pressure by themselves and had to find common ground with other "people of goodwill." Above all, he grasped that the modern world functioned not through governments but through people—people whose creative, revolutionary energies could be mobilized to break through the barriers of power and ideology. Communism could not be intimidated by confrontation or appeased by diplomacy. But it could be undermined by the power of values, by a moral victory over fear and hatred which ultimately became a political victory. Having shunned mass social protests in the past, the Church now saw them as a creative tool, natural allies in the godly cause of human rights and social justice.

Ironically this was readily acknowledged by communist leaders. Poland's communist strongman, General Wojciech Jaruzelski, has recorded how the pope's teachings "reawakened hopes and expectations of change." Mikhail Gorbachev, the last Soviet Communist Party ruler, has spoken of how John Paul II contributed to his own "understanding of communism," acknowledging that the end of communist rule would have been "impossible" without him. The Soviet ideologist Vadim Zagladin has admitted that the peaceful coexistence of religious faiths refuted his party's claims and highlighted the dangers posed by ideological fundamentalists claiming a "monopoly of truth." "We tried to bury religion and Christianity more than once—with what result?" Zagladin told his Vatican interlocutors in 1990. "None at all, except that these attempts introduced a hardening of hearts in our life and inhumanity in personal relationships."[3]

As Zagladin belatedly conceded, Christians had faced heavy restrictions under communism. These quickly crumbled during the crucial months of 1989–90. Places of worship were rededicated, priests and ministers reappointed, religious orders revived, and publications relaunched, while parish life began to return to normal, aided by populations eager to explore again the long-closed world of religion and faith.

Some Christians had to wait longer. The Baltic states, Russia, and Ukraine still belonged to the Soviet Union and could count on religious freedom only when they became independent in 1991. For the Yugoslav republics of Croatia, Slovenia, and Bosnia-Herzegovina, meanwhile, communism gave way to a bloody Balkan war which dragged on until NATO's intervention in Kosovo in 1999.

Elsewhere in Eastern Europe, tough struggles still lay ahead. Throughout the 1990s the churches had to campaign to assert their rights and freedoms and to ensure the emerging postcommunist legal order reflected Christian principles. Today in the ten former communist states now part of the European Union—five predominantly Catholic, three Protestant, and two Orthodox by tradition—the churches' mission is protected, helped by Western-style constitutions and treaties with the Vatican, which enjoys full diplomatic ties with every postcommunist state. If religious freedom is no longer an East-West issue, however, attitudes to church and faith vary widely, while disputes continue over their place in local societies and cultures. Meeting in Zagreb in February 2009, Roman Catholic cardinals and bishops from Eastern Europe warned that communism's "psychological burden" was still being felt. "Communism left profound wounds in the lives of individuals and society as a whole—help is sought, and God and the church are needed for healing these wounds," their statement declared. "The church in Europe is called upon to conduct dialogue with everyone, protect freedom of conscience and confront new emerging ideologies . . . and to continue devoting great attention to questions of the protection of life and family, the upbringing of children and young people, and the necessity for reconciliation in society and among nations."[4]

While the hardships of communism may be well recorded, the subsequent history of Eastern Europe's churches deserves to be studied too for what it says about the strengths and weaknesses of religious faith and how this faith can be expected to measure up in future.

In eastern Germany, formerly the German Democratic Republic, the impact of four decades of official atheism is still evident. Catholics nominally made up

10 percent of East Germany's 16.2 million inhabitants when the state was reunified with the western Federal Republic in October 1990, compared to 88 percent nominally belonging to Protestant churches, although the region is now considered one of Europe's least religious. Although two-thirds of Germany's 82.3 million inhabitants still claim membership in Christian churches, the overwhelming majority are concentrated in western *Lande*.

In 2009, a decade after Germany's Roman Catholic Bishops Conference relocated from Bonn to Berlin along with the federal government, the Church's Berlin archdiocese confirmed that it had been forced to close or merge almost half its 208 parishes in order to pay off a $140 million debt to banks and credit institutions. A church spokesman, Stefan Forner, said local Catholics had made donations after a fundraising appeal by Cardinal Georg Sterzinsky, while Germany's other dioceses had agreed to write off what was owed them. He stressed, however, that the recovery had also required the mass sell-off of unused churches and buildings, as well as a 40 percent reduction in clergy and church administrators.[5]

Germany's reunification is widely believed to have depressed overall religious affiliations. Despite the April 2005 election of a German pope who has visited his homeland three times, in August 2005, September 2006, and September 2011, the number of Germans formally choosing to leave the Roman Catholic and Evangelical churches by giving up the traditional church tax has risen, with 123,585 Catholics leaving Germany's twenty-seven dioceses in 2009, compared to 121,155 in 2008. Church baptisms and weddings have dropped by around half in the past two decades, with 13.4 percent of Roman Catholics currently attending Mass, compared to 22 percent in 1989. Priestly and ministerial vocations have also fallen, with the largest numbers studying at Roman Catholic seminaries in Regensburg, Freiburg, and Cologne and the fewest in the eastern German dioceses of Goerlitz, Erfurt, and Magdeburg. Speaking in November 2009, when the twentieth anniversary of the opening of the Berlin Wall was celebrated with a Festival of Freedom, Cardinal Sterzinsky said Germans should remain eternally thankful that their country had been reunited without confrontation and bloodshed. But the euphoria had long since passed, he added, including expectations of a Christian revival. "Although Germany's East and West have since developed at the same pace in many areas, fundamental differences remain between us," the cardinal said. "Those brought up in the West are more individualistic, whereas people from eastern Germany, as before, are more collectivist in outlook. Life has a different feel here."[6]

Even in staunchly Catholic Poland, Christians still face problems at the hands of politicians seeking to curb or undermine their Church's influence. Although long-running disputes over abortion, religious education, and other issues are now largely settled, ex-communist politicians from the opposition Democratic Left Alliance—whose leader, Grzegorz Napieralski, came third in Poland's 2010 presidential election—have gained third place in voter-intention surveys on a pledge to "de-clericalize the state" by barring clergy from state ceremonies and withdrawing the Roman Catholic Church's budget allocations. The party, which was in power in 1993–97, has also threatened to act against clergy business activities and tax exemptions if returned to power, as well as scrapping Poland's 1993 concordat with the Vatican.

Although at least 90 percent of Poland's 38 million inhabitants still call themselves Roman Catholics, admissions to the Church's eighty-four seminaries plummeted by 30 percent in the years 2006–9, while recruitment to female religious orders has halved, falling 15 percent in 2008 alone. Although still high by Western standards, church attendance is also on the decline, dropping 4 percent in 2008, according to the Church's Statistics Institute.[7]

Some Poles blame a spate of controversies since the death of Pope John Paul II, who was revered throughout the region. The country's Roman Catholic, Orthodox, and Lutheran churches have had to tackle claims that they were heavily infiltrated by the communist secret police, allegations that culminated in the shocking January 2007 resignation of Archbishop Stanislaw Wielgus of Warsaw on the day of his installation. In November 2008 the Polish government's Anti-Corruption Office launched an investigation after reports that Roman Catholic parishes and religious orders had made millions of *zloties* reselling land awarded to them at knock-down prices in compensation for communist-era confiscations. In January 2011 Poland's Roman Catholic bishops pulled out of a controversial church-state property commission after their two chief representatives were charged with corruption and untruthfulness. Many Poles had criticized the commission, whose decisions could not be appealed, for failing to consult interested parties and obtain independent valuations.[8]

Several high-profile court cases have gone against the Roman Catholic Church, while Polish parliamentarians have also been ready to vote *against* it on issues such as the legalization of in vitro fertilization. In October 2011 a newly formed anti-clerical movement won third place in national elections on a pledge to "secularize the state," suggesting dormant conflicts could again be revived. The Bishops Conference insists the negative publicity is far outweighed by the Church's positive contributions. Any religious decline, it argues, reflects demographic changes and mass migration, as well as social and cultural pressures that are an inevitable by-product of Westernization. It will take many years for the effects of decline to be felt in a Church that still accounts for a quarter of all Roman Catholic priestly vocations in Europe and is still sending clergy abroad to prop up depleted Church personnel in countries from Russia to France. When 140,000 people attended the June 2010 beatification of Father Jerzy Popieluszko (1947–84), the Solidarity movement priest who was murdered by communist secret police agents, it was a sign of the Church's continuing capacity to rally huge numbers.

"There are plenty of problems and nothing is finally resolved—but we are at least a lot more aware of the issues and challenges we face," explained Krzysztof

Zanussi, a Polish member of the Vatican's Papal Council for Culture. "We still yearn for the unity and togetherness we experienced during that great moment of transformation two decades ago. But in today's civil society, people have far greater possibilities to take responsibility for their lives and gain satisfaction and fulfillment. This is an indisputable achievement."[9]

In neighboring Slovakia, the rights of the Roman Catholic Church, comprising 69 percent of the population of 5.4 million in a 2001 census, were codified under a Vatican concordat in 2000, which was followed up by further accords regulating the Church's finances and confirming its right to teach religion in state schools and operate army, police, and prison chaplaincies. However, disputes have periodically flared over aspects of Catholic teaching.

In February 2006 Slovakia's center-right government collapsed when its premier, Mikulas Dziurinda, shelved an agreement allowing doctors and judges to opt out of abortions and divorce cases, after opponents warned it would violate women's rights and infringe European Union norms. Relations became tenser, however, with the subsequent Social Democrat–led coalition, headed by Premier Robert Fico, which insisted on a secularizing program. In December 2007 the twenty three members of the Roman Catholic Bishops Conference protested planned cuts in religious education and warned in a pastoral letter that a government project for sex education in schools would force "a permissive and individualistic ethos on Slovak society."[10] In summer 2009 the bishops condemned calls for state funding of IVF and protested plans by the UN Population Fund to open a regional office in Bratislava with rent-free accommodation from the Fico government. They also deplored a U.S. firm's bid to open Europe's largest megacasino, with similar government backing, on the border with Austria. Opponents of the casino project, who gathered 100,000 signatures, said a required amendment to Slovakia's gambling law had been approved by ministers and legislators without proper information.[11]

Slovakia's churches have faced challenges in extending pastoral care to their country's large Roma, or Gypsy, population, as well as over provisions for ethnic Hungarians, who make up a tenth of the population. In January 2009 the Roman Catholic bishops rejected a petition calling for a special Hungarian diocese, insisting the move would disrupt parish life and fuel Hungarian separatism in the country, which was known as "Upper Hungary" and ruled from Budapest until 1918.

The Slovak Church can be thankful that popular devotions among Roman Catholic, Lutheran, and Orthodox communities still remain strong. The neighboring Czech Republic, by contrast, is considered predominantly nonreligious, with declared Roman Catholics falling from 40 to 27 percent of the country's 10.5 million inhabitants in the decade after the 1989 Velvet Revolution. Only 5 percent of citizens currently attend Catholic Masses, according to Church data, and even smaller numbers turn out for Protestant services. The Czech Republic is also the only postcommunist country in Eastern Europe without treaty-level protection of Church rights. In 2002 a concordat was signed and ratified by the Vatican, only to be voted down the following year by Czech parliamentarians and blocked by President Vaclav Klaus, on the grounds that its provisions gave Roman Catholics unfair privileges.

Relations have long been tense anyway over demands for compensation for Catholic properties confiscated under communist rule and for measures to end the Church's fiscal dependence on the state. In November 2007 the center-right government of Premier Mirek Topolanek agreed after talks with Church negotiators to draw up a comprehensive settlement that would have allowed a third of communist-seized properties to be returned to religious orders and compensation for the rest, totaling 83 billion Czech crowns ($4.5 billion), to be paid out over sixty years to dioceses and parishes. Direct payments to the Church from the state budget—including clergy salaries, which were also state-funded under communism—would have been steadily reduced over the next decade under the law, finally terminating in 2018 and vitiating the Church's need for further state money.

In June 2008, however, rebel MPs from the governing Civic Democratic Party questioned the validity of the move and voted with Social Democrat and Communist deputies to delay the bill indefinitely by setting up a new parliamentary commission. In April 2009, when the Topolanek government lost a no-confidence vote, the commission recommended scrapping the project altogether. It was a move with "no rational justification whatsoever," Cardinal Miloslav Vlk of Prague told his Church's *Katolicky Tydenik* weekly, a "populist step" to gain election votes which wrecked the best chance in years of a final agreement.[12]

Church leaders are disappointed that *no* solutions were found after the Czech Republic joined the European Union with seven other ex-communist countries in May 2004 and that the disputes have dragged on since it became the first former Warsaw Pact country to hold the EU's rotating presidency in January–June 2009. Although two hundred churches, monasteries, and convents were given back to the Roman Catholic Church in the 1990s, often in derelict condition, some have had to be sold at below-market prices after the Church's nine dioceses became unable to maintain them. In 2008 Christian protesters tried to stop the twelfth-century Church of St. Michael in Prague's Old Town, where the martyred Bohemian reformer Jan Hus (1369–1415) once preached, from being used by a private developer for techno parties and strip shows. In March 2009 the Prague archdiocese lodged a constitutional appeal when the Supreme Court ruled after a seventeen-year legal battle that the city's fourteenth-century gothic St. Vitus Cathedral should belong to the state rather than the Church. The cathedral dispute was resolved in June 2010 by a new church-state accord, allowing the landmark to remain state property but be used by the Church in perpetuity. The Roman Catholic Church's new primate, Archbishop Dominik Duka, who succeeded Cardinal Vlk in April 2010, has predicted that the accord will ensure a "strong foundation for church-state co-operation," while also opening the way for a new government to redraft the long-awaited concordat with the Vatican. The Czech Republic's Ecumenical Council, grouping eleven non-Catholic churches, is hopeful the move will push forward parallel agreements on its own rights and properties.[13]

The Roman Catholic Church has had to face other controversies, including allegations that several still-serving bishops collaborated with the former communist State Security (StB) secret police. In February 2007 the Bishops Conference deplored "media aggressiveness" on the issue and demanded an end to the use of StB material "to settle personal accounts." Some Czech Christians are confident a visit by the pope in September 2009 has since helped create an atmosphere of greater mutual trust and respect. "I want to invite people to the church, acquaint them with the Bible and overcome the prejudices—my maxim is to go out to those who've accepted baptism but no longer see the sense of life," Archbishop Duka told a TV interviewer on the eve of his installation. "Most people here aren't anti-clerical, anti-church or atheist—they believe in something. While some think God offers nothing, others trust the faith must still have value. So I see my challenge as opening the church with greater confidence to society."[14]

In Croatia, where Roman Catholics nominally make up 88 percent of the 4.4 million inhabitants, the Church clashed repeatedly over social and educational issues with the center-left president Stjepan Mesic, who stood down at the end of 2009 after almost a decade as head of state. In February 2009 the Church's leader, Cardinal Josip Bozanic, demanded a "new and courageous evangelization" against the "dictatorship of relativism." The Iron Curtain had fallen, he added, but "its pieces are very resistant"; they were being used by "the sons of lies" to "sow the seed of division and confusion." "Although we have the impression the system stopped functioning in its previous form, it has transformed, presenting itself as poisoned earth where fruit should have sprung up," Cardinal Bozanic told a gathering of Eastern European church leaders in Zagreb. "Despite the fall of communism, its structure has remained in legislation and judicial power, in the economy, education and culture, and especially in the veil of silence that has been hung over events of the recent past."[15]

In August 2009 President Mesic sparked fresh controversy by accusing the Roman Catholic Church of enjoying a "privileged position" and calling for Christian crosses to be banned from public buildings to reflect Croatia's status as a "secular state." A rival candidate in the country's presidential election, Miroslav Tudjman, the son of Croatia's first postcommunist head of state, condemned Mesic's demand as an "attack on the Catholic church and religious feelings of Croats." Meanwhile, in a November pastoral letter, the Bishops Conference said it believed the next head of state should be someone who "respects and protects

Christian principles and the principles of natural law," as well as defending "human life from conception to natural death, the dignity of marriage and the family, and the free choice of religious instruction in school."[16]

In a gesture to the government of Jadranka Kosor, Croatia's first woman premier, the Church later agreed, in consultation with the Vatican, to return part of its 2010 state budget allocation to help alleviate economic recession in the country, which must improve minority rights and facilitate the return of refugees from the 1991–93 breakup of Yugoslavia as a precondition for accession to the European Union. "Every year, our church receives a certain amount from the state budget, pursuant to the international Concordat on financial questions between the Holy See and Republic of Croatia," the Bishops Conference explained in a statement. "The work of the Catholic church is recognized as being of general value to society in the cultural, educational, social and ethical areas. . . . Up to the present, the church has also used a large share of the funds received from the state budget for charitable purposes. It will continue to do so in future."[17]

Father Laszlo Lukacs, a veteran commentator in neighboring Hungary, thinks some churches are still suffering the effects of rules and regulations hurriedly introduced two decades ago. He too remembers the surprise that greeted the events of 1989, as liberal reformers often ran ahead of the churches themselves in their demands for restoring religious rights. The very suddenness posed problems. Hungary's own 1990 Law on Religious Freedom was hurriedly drafted by the last communist government and allowed any sect or cult with at least a hundred members to register as a church with full legal rights. Having had seventeen registered denominations under communist rule, the country soon had over seven hundred. Another law was rapidly enacted on church properties confiscated under communist rule, transferring responsibility from the state to local authorities. Although well-intentioned, this made it much harder in practice for church leaders to reclaim them.

Under a 1997 treaty with the Vatican, the Hungarian government agreed to return buildings to the Roman Catholic Church up to a value of $550 million, while offering index-linked payments in compensation for others. Although the restitution was expected to be completed by the end of 2011, many fiscal problems remain unresolved. The same treaty promised the Church's two hundred schools and colleges the same subsidies as their state counterparts, but this has been vigorously opposed by liberal and ex-communist parliamentarians, who have accused the predominant church of seeking to reimpose a "Catholic cultural monopoly."

In 2003 Hungary's Roman Catholic and Protestant leaders successfully appealed to the Constitutional Court against another law making state subsidies to religious communities dependent on how many citizens covenanted taxes to them. In 2005 they were forced to seek constitutional arbitration again, this time against planned education cuts that would have forced many church schools to close. Although state schools are required by law to allocate time and facilities for religious classes, this has involved a "daily struggle," according to Father Lukacs, who acted as the spokesman for Hungary's Bishops Conference and has also edited the country's Roman Catholic *Vigilia* journal for over two decades.

In April 2011 the center-right government of Premier Viktor Orban pushed through a new constitution, which opens with the words "God bless Hungarians" and notes that the country's citizens "recognize the key role of Christianity in upholding the nation." The following July the government replaced the 1990 Religious Freedom Law with a more restrictive measure, withdrawing recognition from all but fourteen of Hungary's registered churches and religious associations. Yet the work of the country's larger historic denominations looks set to go on being contested. "Things would have been quite different if democratically elected MPs had been given longer to consider these crucial provisions," the Piarist order priest maintains. "But we didn't, in retrospect, make any serious preparations—the 40 years of communism were too long for us to have retained any kind of hope. Today, we're in much the same position as the countries of Western Europe. The social and economic changes have been so deep that it's difficult to place the churches in the new situation."[18]

In Romania interchurch ties have been tense since 1989 over the predominant Orthodox Church's refusal to return properties belonging to the Greek Catholic minority, which were seized by the state and handed over for Orthodox use when the Church was outlawed in 1948. The Greek Catholic Church, which is loyal to Rome but practices the Eastern rite, was forced to surrender 2,588 places of worship, 1,504 parish houses, and 2,362 schools and cultural centers, of which only 160 have been returned. Romania's governments have insisted property disputes should be settled by interchurch agreement rather than state intervention. But a Catholic-Orthodox commission, set up in 1998, one year before a visit by Pope John Paul II, has made little progress.

The Greek Catholic bishop of Oradea, Virgil Bercea, believes ecumenical ties have deteriorated rather than improved since the 2007 election of a new Orthodox patriarch, Daniel Ciobotea. In February 2009 Greek Catholic leaders protested a new draft law, which would confirm Orthodox ownership over still-disputed Catholic churches, warning in a letter to President Traian Basescu that they "reserved the right to use all the legal means, domestic and international," to obtain redress.[19] A case was duly taken to the European Court of Human Rights, and in a landmark January 2010 judgment, the Court ruled that the Romanian government had indeed violated articles of the 1950 European Convention on Human Rights by denying Greek Catholics access to courts, property rights, and religious freedom "without any objective or reasonable justification," and ordered it to pay compensation. During the same month, however, Romania's Orthodox Bucharest patriarchate dismissed Greek Catholic concerns as "artificial and exaggerated."[20]

The Orthodox Church nominally claims the loyalty of 87 percent of Romania's 23 million inhabitants, according to a 2002 census, but has itself had to defend the status of Orthodoxy as the predominant faith. In January 2007, following the country's EU accession, Church leaders protested a new religious law, which obliged church communities seeking registration to have at least 20,000 members and to have been in existence at least twenty years for full legal status. In June 2007 they vowed to resist a court ruling that endorsed calls for a ban on religious symbols at schools. Most Romanians wanted the crosses to stay, the Orthodox Patriarchate insisted. The proposed ban was also deplored as "abusive and discriminatory" by the Roman Catholic archbishop of Bucharest, Ioan Robu, who was waging an international campaign to prevent construction of a giant nineteen-floor tower block next to Bucharest's nineteenth-century St. Joseph's Cathedral.[21]

In summer 2009 Romanian church leaders urged the center-left government of Premier Emil Boc not to scrap the teaching of religion in state schools under a new education law that would have given secondary school pupils an alternative to religious classes and allowed students over sixteen to opt out altogether. Religious education was restored in January 1990, shortly after the collapse of communist rule, and made a requirement for all schools "in accordance with the specific requirements of each religious cult" under Article 32 of Romania's 1991 Constitution. Although subsequent laws gave parents the right to withdraw their children with a written request, some human rights groups claimed children were being pressured to attend classes run by Orthodox clergy. In an August 2009 open letter to President Basescu, however, Patriarch Daniel insisted religious education had always been fundamental to Romanian education and helped promote "spiritual and moral values at the heart of European and national culture." "Romania has declared itself a Christian country and the government listens carefully to the churches, who have more influence as a political force here than in secular Western Europe," agrees Otniel Bunaciu, president of the Baptist Union, which is Europe's second largest religion, numbering 129,000 in around 1,500 congregations in the 2002 census. "But I'm not sure whether this listening does much good. We also need a proactive and interactive dialogue, and this isn't taking place at a level in which churches could genuinely influence the life of our country."[22]

In much of the former Soviet Union, the influence of church-state provisions has been tangible. A 1997 Russian religious law distinguished "religious organizations" with full legal status from "religious groups," which can be registered but denied full rights, and "religious associations" of no recognized status. It stipulated that Russia was a "secular state" and rejected the idea of an official religion, but it gave the Orthodox Church special status, calling it an "inseparable element of Russia's historical, spiritual and cultural heritage." It also allowed Islam, Buddhism, and Judaism additional rights as "traditional faiths," while denying similar recognition to churches existing in Russia for less than half a century or that had not maintained places of worship in at least half the country's counties for fifteen years. This established the legislative framework for a rebuilt Russian Orthodox ascendancy, which has frequently served to disadvantage smaller churches, particularly under the authoritarian leadership of President (later Premier) Vladimir Putin.

In a July 2007 open letter, leading academics, journalists, and human rights activists accused the Orthodox Church of fostering a "new national and religious ideology" that risked negating democracy and "endorsing xenophobia and a cult of power." They added that Russia faced a "clericalism which attacks the constitution," citing plans for classes in "basic Orthodox culture" at state schools, for which 10,000 teachers were being trained by Moscow's Orthodox Spiritual Academy.[23] Such charges have since been denied by senior Orthodox figures. Metropolitan Hilarion Alfeyev, chairman of the Moscow Patriarchate's Department for External Church Relations, has insisted his Church has no wish to be an official state denomination, pointing to the shunning of political involvement enshrined in the "Social Doctrine Foundations" adopted by its Synod of Bishops in August 2000. The Orthodox Church's assertive role has found backers, however, even among minority churches and faiths, including the Vatican's nuncio, Archbishop Antonio Mennini. "The fact that the Russian constitution provides for separation between church and state ought not to exclude co-operation between the two for moral, social and spiritual growth," the Italian archbishop told Russia's Interfax news agency in August 2007. "Like other faiths here, the Orthodox church is regaining its place in Russian society after decades of atheism and repression, when millions of believers were denied any real opportunity to seek the Gospel's spiritual foundations and the moral values brought by the Good News."[24]

Moscow and the Vatican established ties in 1990, following a historic visit to Rome by Gorbachev, but continued to maintain only temporary representatives after the formation of an independent Russian state. Closer ties were believed impeded by repeated Orthodox complaints of Catholic proselytism, as well as by Orthodox objections to the February 2002 creation of four Catholic dioceses in Russia, which was followed by the expulsion of a Catholic bishop and denial of visas to four Catholic priests.

With just four dioceses, 225 parishes, and some 260 priests dispersed across the vast country, the Catholic minority should pose little trouble for Orthodox leaders, whose Church currently has 160 dioceses, 30,142 parishes, and 32,266 priests, according to data from January 2010, and has opened up to a hundred new places of worship each year in Moscow alone. The Catholic Church is represented, along with Baptists, Pentecostalists, and Adventists, on the Presidential Council for Co-operation with Religious Associations, established in 1995; in 2004 a Catholic-Orthodox working group was set up to discuss disagreements and find ways of working together. With ethnic Poles making up half of Russia's

1.5 million Catholics and two-thirds of its Catholic clergy, however, some Orthodox bishops have complained that the Catholic Church is too closely linked with Poland. In October 2007, when its long-serving ethnic Polish leader, Archbishop Tadeusz Kondrusiewicz, was replaced by an Italian, Archbishop Paolo Pezzi, the move was widely believed intended to play down the Polish connection in favor of a less emotional "Italian model" of Catholicism.

Some Catholics point to continued obstacles in obtaining visas for visiting clergy and to obstructive attitudes by local authorities and have urged the Holy See not to enter agreements without prior rights guarantees for local priests and parishes. The continuing problems were highlighted in September–October 2001, when charity premises belonging to Mother Teresa's Missionaries of Charity in Moscow were bulldozed for supposedly violating city planning regulations and a Roman Catholic parish in Pskov was barred from completing its church because of "legal technicalities," prompting complaints of "deliberate discrimination" by Archbishop Pezzi. The secretary-general of Russia's Bishops Conference, Father Igor Kovalevsky, thinks Catholic-Orthodox ties have improved, however, since the January 2009 election of a new patriarch, Kirill I. Most local problems, he insists, are caused by "burdensome Russian bureaucracy" rather than "bad attitudes" toward the Catholic Church. In March 2010, when Moscow-Vatican ties were finally upgraded to full ambassadorial level, the move was said to have been welcomed by the Orthodox Moscow Patriarchate. "Although we can't as yet say what it will mean in practice, a full relationship will clearly facilitate links at a time when both the Apostolic See and Russian Federation share common views on many international questions," Father Kovalevsky argues. "Our church's ties with state and society here are now significantly better, and we hope this process will develop further."[25]

Vatican and Russian Orthodox representatives intensified contacts after the election of Pope Benedict XVI and have since repeatedly pledged to work together to uphold religious faith and values in Europe, even hinting that the pope and patriarch could meet. The Orthodox precondition remains that points of dispute must first be settled, but Orthodox leaders have stated clearly that cooperation with Catholics must be given priority over ties with Protestants. "Our common activities and numerous encounters have confirmed that our positions coincide on many questions facing Christians in the modern world—including aggressive secularization, globalization and the erosion of traditional ethical principles," Patriarch Kirill I told a meeting of Orthodox bishops after marking his first year in office. "Benedict XVI has taken up positions very close to the Orthodox, as have high representatives of the Roman Catholic Church with whom we have contacts, particularly through our common vision for the protection of human dignity.... The Russian church has seen fewer Protestant communities co-operating in the cause of preserving the Christian legacy due to the Protestant world's relentless liberalization."[26]

Although the Russian Orthodox Church joined the Geneva-based World Council of Churches in 1961 and remains the largest of its 349 member denominations, it downgraded participation in 1998 amid complaints about liberal sexual attitudes among Protestant churches after Orthodox churches in Georgia and Bulgaria had withdrawn. It disbanded ties with the U.S. Episcopal Church and Sweden's official Lutheran Church over related issues and withdrew from the Conference of European Churches in October 2008 after disputes over Orthodox communities in Estonia. In late 2009 it came close to suspending relations with Germany's Evangelical Church after it elected a woman presiding bishop, Margot Kassmann, who soon resigned over a drunk-driving offense.

At the same time, the Orthodox Church rejoined a multilateral Catholic-Orthodox International Commission for Theological Dialogue, which is currently debating papal primacy using a "road map" to unity approved during the Commission's previous session at Ravenna in October 2007. In December 2009 it held its first meeting with a Brussels-based commission representing Europe's Roman Catholic bishops to prepare a common Catholic-Orthodox stance on the European Union. In March 2010 it inaugurated a separate commission with Poland's predominant Roman Catholic church to draw up a statement on mutual reconciliation and forgiveness.

Elsewhere in the region, the place of churches and religious groups varies widely, from the republics of Central Asia, where democracy has yet to take root, to the Baltic states of Lithuania, Latvia, and Estonia, which are now members of the European Union and NATO.

In Kazakhstan church leaders appealed in 2008 against a draft bill on freedom of conscience and religious associations, which would have imposed communist-style restrictions by requiring children to have written permission from both parents to attend church or catechism classes. The controversial bill was voted down, and in September 2009 a compulsory religious course was introduced to schools instead, in what the government of President Nursultan Nazabayev said would confirm Kazakhstan's reputation for religious freedom. In October 2001, however, the controversial Freedom of Conscience Law, reintroduced with government backing, was finally enacted, despite further complaints from local churches, the Organization for Security and Cooperation in Europe, and human rights groups. Kazakhstan's religious communities will now require at least five thousand adult members to register at the national level, while currently registered communities will be required to reregister after a "religious study examination" of their documents and teachings by state officials. Religious literature entering the country for public use will require government approval and be restricted to religious buildings and schools, while government consent will also be needed for new places of worship and for priests and ministers engaging in "missionary activities." Children will require consent from both parents to attend religious classes, and unregistered religious activity will be subject to tough penalties.

Throughout Central Asia governments have sought to reassert Muslim traditions since the 1991 collapse of Soviet rule, led by Turkmenistan, whose capital, Aschabad, is expected to host the world's largest mosque. Despite this, all five states—Kazakhstan, Turkmenistan, Uzbekistan, Tajikistan, and Kyrgyzstan—host significant Orthodox and Protestant minorities and also enjoy relations with the Vatican. In Kyrgyzstan, where ethnic tension and segregation spilled over into violence in summer 2010, religious leaders moved quickly to deny claims that the clashes had an anti-Christian theme.

Minority churches are denied legal status in Georgia, which is situated between Russia and Turkey and has Christian traditions dating back to the second century. In 2003 leaders of the country's minority Roman Catholic Church called it a "grave offense" when a treaty between Georgia and the Vatican, negotiated after a 1999 visit by Pope John Paul, was canceled under pressure from the Orthodox Church, which claims the loyalty of two-thirds of the 5.44 million inhabitants. Following the reelection of a pro-Western president, Mikheil Saakashvili, in the wake of opposition riots in early 2008, the government agreed to return Soviet-seized lands and properties to the Orthodox Church, including its former Tbilisi Seminary, and to rebuild 150 historic churches and monasteries. Minority Christian denominations have continued to cite harassment and discrimination at the hands of what one Roman Catholic priest described as "a local nationalism which supposes every Georgian should be Orthodox."[27]

Similar complaints have been heard in predominantly Orthodox Belarus under President Oleksandr Lukashenka, who was reelected in 2006 amid claims of ballot rigging and intimidation. In early 2009 the European Parliament warned that a "growing number" of Protestant and Catholic clergy had been denied the right to preach and teach in the country and said international cooperation would depend on the Lukashenka regime's respect for churches and ethnic minorities. In January 2010 four Roman Catholic priests and six nuns from neighboring Poland were refused visa extensions after coming to help in the country's 480 Catholic parishes, in the latest of several such actions by the Belarus authorities. The church's leader, Archbishop Kondrusiewicz, who was reassigned to Belarus after heading the church in Russia, nevertheless expressed optimism for church-state relations after holding talks in April 2010 with President Lukashenka in Minsk's Catholic cathedral. He was also hopeful that ties would improve with Belarus's Orthodox Church.[28] Negotiations are under way for a concordat between Belarus and the Vatican, which could also help codify and anchor the rights of Protestant associations.

Interchurch tensions have long simmered in neighboring Ukraine. Orthodox Christians make up around a third of the Ukrainian population of 50 million, but are divided between the Ukrainian Orthodox Church–Moscow Patriarchate, which is concentrated in the east with nine thousand parishes, and a smaller Orthodox Church–Kiev Patriarchate and Ukrainian Autocephalous Orthodox

Church, which are not recognized by other Orthodox hierarchies. Catholics make up a tenth of inhabitants but are also divided between a Latin rite Roman Catholic Church with four dioceses and a larger Greek Catholic Church with eleven. Both Catholic communities have faced property and jurisdictional disputes with Orthodox parishes since the country's 1991 independence from the Soviet Union. Numerous Catholic churches also remain in government hands, while Catholics have complained of being offered less state help than their Orthodox counterparts in renovating properties that have been given back.

There were fears that religious minorities could face hardship when a new president, Viktor Yanukovich, took office in February 2010, pledging to improve ties with Russia and reaffirm the country's links with the Orthodox world. The election of Yanukovich, five years after his previous disputed win was overturned by the Orange Revolution, was widely seen as a turning point in a country that has been pulled between rival Eastern and Western forces since independence from the Soviet Union in December 1991. The misgivings were heightened when Patriarch Kirill of Russia arrived in Kiev to give Yanukovich a special blessing and when Yanukovich failed to invite minority church leaders to a postinauguration service. In March bishops from the Greek Catholic Church, which was outlawed under Soviet rule, cautioned the president in an open letter that all faiths should be treated equally and recalled the cautionary note in St. Matthew's Gospel about the sad prospects of a "divided kingdom" (Matthew 12:25). "Unlike certain countries of the world, where one religious organization enjoys privileged status, Ukraine is a multi-confessional state," declared the bishops, whose followers are known pejoratively as "Uniates" by the Orthodox. "Any favoritism towards one faith at the cost of others can only deepen divisions between our state's citizens and harm the Ukrainian nation."[29]

As the heartland of ancient Kievan Christianity and a center for Orthodox monasticism and priestly vocations, Ukraine remains important for Russia's Orthodox Church, which may well use Yanukovich's presidency to strengthen its position. In May 2010, when the Catholic Bishops Conference president, Archbishop Mieczyslaw Mokrzycki, confirmed that the pope had accepted an invitation nine years after a previous Ukrainian pilgrimage by John Paul II, the plan was immediately criticized by the Moscow Patriarchate, which warned that a papal pilgrimage would set back interchurch relations. There have been calls for Ukraine's divided Orthodox churches to be reunited; in June 2010 President Yanukovich visited the ecumenical patriarch of Constantinople, Bartholomew I, to discuss moves in this direction. This has made the two smaller Orthodox churches anxious. In July 2010 the leader of the rival Kiev Patriarchate, Filaret Denisenko, accused Patriarch Kirill of "choking Ukraine in a brotherly embrace" while seeking to "destroy the independence and sovereignty" of local denominations.[30]

Some minority church leaders are determined to be optimistic. An All-Ukraine Council of Churches, set up in 1996, groups the two Catholic communities and three Orthodox churches, as well as Protestants, Muslims, and Jews. In the western capital of Lviv, which is home to Latin, Greek Catholic, Armenian Catholic, Orthodox, and Lutheran bishoprics and a variety of traditional and new Protestant denominations, the Ukrainian Catholic University regularly cooperates with Orthodox leaders and launched the world's first distance learning program in ecumenical studies in 2009, drawing on expertise from various confessions. "After eight decades of being barred from practising their faith, people here want to choose which church they belong to and the authorities are not really impeding them," explained Bishop Marian Buczek, secretary-general of Ukraine's Roman Catholic Bishops Conference. "Some public figures are talking up religious issues—and we need to react early to signs of trouble. But the rights of confessions are protected under the constitution; and after 19 years of statehood, Ukraine has its own governing structures. No sober person would think of handing it back to Russia or returning to the Soviet era of fighting the faith. If the Church doesn't get mixed up in politics, and if politics aren't imposed on the Church, everything will be OK."[31]

The fractious nature of interfaith relations in Ukraine contrasts markedly with the settled conditions for churches in the Baltic states. Yet here too the challenges are multiplying. In Lithuania, where Christians won universal praise for defending national identity and human rights under communist rule, the Roman Catholic Church now faces a severe shortage of priests, with only a handful ordained annually from its three surviving seminaries. Although Roman Catholics still make up 79 percent of Lithuania's population of 3.7 million, according to a 2001 census, only 15 percent practice their faith. Church leaders have criticized government failures to ensure a right to religious education in the former Soviet republic or to stem high divorce, corruption, and emigration rates. "Our church played its clearest role in Soviet times when it attracted people far from the faith," the Jesuit archbishop Sigitas Tamkevicius of Kaunas, a veteran of Soviet labor camps, who heads Lithuania's Bishops Conference, told the Catholic Information Agency in neighboring Poland. "Since independence, the situation has changed. Priests have withdrawn from political life at the request of their bishops. But some have gone too far, abandoning work for the social good. Although Lithuanian priests still have a strong link with the nation, we don't feel it in this pluralistic society."[32]

In neighboring Latvia and Estonia the predominant Lutheran Church has criticized moral and social attitudes since independence from the Soviet Union in 1991, as well as cooperating with minority denominations on issues ranging from religious education to social justice. Under Soviet rule, both republics were heavily settled by Russians, who still make up 33 percent of Latvia's 2.34 million inhabitants and over 80 percent in its second largest city, Daugavpils. The Lutheran Church, whose three hundred congregations make up 13 percent of the population, has worked with the smaller Orthodox Church to allay repeated tensions over Latvia's treatment of ethnic Russians, up to 100,000 of whom left in the 1990s, fueling an 11 percent decline in population. In May 2007, when Estonian government plans to remove Soviet military graves in Tallinn sparked ethnic Russian rioting in the capital and other towns, the country's Evangelical Lutheran archbishop, Andres Poder, sent a message to church congregations, similarly requesting members to avoid being drawn into breaches of the peace.

In all three Baltic states hopes of a mass religious revival were high in the first years after communist rule but faded as consumer lifestyles and materialistic outlooks diluted popular enthusiasm. Having overwhelmingly supported the postcommunist transition to democracy and the free market, local priests and ministers have had to face the consequences of Westernization and secularization. As in Russia, the infrastructural recovery and expansion that became a church priority over two decades face deep uncertainties. New places of worship have proliferated, along with church-run schools, charities, associations, and publications. How many will still be open and functioning, however, in another two decades? For now that question remains unanswerable.

The harassment and persecution suffered by Christians under communist rule brought a return to paradigms and archetypes born in the Early Church and could be seen as fulfilling the promises of republican, anticlerical, and secularist agitators from the French Revolution onward. They also changed over time, requiring Christian communities to change in their response by finding new forms of witness and self-expression to suit the evolving threats and challenges. In addition they taught crucial lessons about how religious faith could survive under hostile conditions, how religious communities could combine the demands of testimony with the needs of survival, and how religious believers could set moral and spiritual examples even in the most alien environments.

Yet the years since communism have taught lessons as well, about the necessary parameters of church-state cooperation, the respective roles of majority and minority denominations and faiths, and the desirable influence of religious communities over societies left confused and disorientated by traumatic past experiences. Would a chastened church learn from its past weaknesses and failures, reflect on its historical mistakes and misjudgments, and make efforts to avoid alienating public opinion and polarizing opposition? Or would it merely attempt, if given the chance, to regain the wealth and privilege it enjoyed before communist rule, to rebuild its power and resume its previous position? The multiple disputes that have characterized church-state and church-society relations since 1989—over religious education, abortion, property restitutions, and budget allocations—suggest a mixture of the two. Yet the growing problems facing the region's religious communities, from declining vocations and church attendance to media hostility and diminishing economic resources, also indicate a more complex picture, in which answers and solutions from past history will be of limited utility.

Krzysztof Zanussi, the Polish film director, thinks resistance to Christian pro-life values, even in his own country, is stronger now than under communism, when antichurch policies were implemented by hostile regimes but found little popular support. To make matters worse, he thinks church leaders have been divided and uncertain in their response. As the social capital gained by churches under communist rule diminishes, the key challenge for religious communities will be to confront the dangers but also use the opportunities presented by modern pluralistic societies and cultures. "We've been used to having strong spiritual leaders, and we don't seem to have maintained the high standards we set ourselves when times were hard," Zanussi points out. "Religious decline doesn't have to be the inevitable price of freedom and modernization—people are still strongly Christian in their thinking here. But we seem to have become more frivolous as we've become wealthier and more secure."[33]

In Hungary Father Lukacs agrees. When a definitive history is written of the forty years of communist rule, he points out, its permanent impact on church and faith may well turn out to have been less devastating than that of the years of freedom that followed. But these are normal challenges, for which the churches can draw on the wisdom and expertise of Christians in other democratic countries. The situation is still dynamic, the outcomes far from certain. "The mixed fortunes of the churches and religious communities have been something of a sideshow compared to the great overall political and social changes which have been occurring here," the Hungarian priest said. "What we know for certain now is that their future depends heavily on the broader situation. We are still waiting to see where it will all lead."[34]

Notes

1. George Lawson, *Negotiated Revolutions: The Prospects for Radical Change in Contemporary World Politics* (Aldershot, England: Ashgate, 2005), 72. See also Timothy Garton Ash, "Velvet Revolution: The Prospects," in *New York Review of Books* 56, no. 19 (2009).

2. Author's interview, Bucharest, January 3, 1990, published in Jonathan Luxmoore, *After the Fall: Church and State Rebuild 1990–1999* (Baltimore: Catholic International, 2000), 227–28.

3. Author's interview with Jaruzelski, Warsaw, February 8, 1991, and Gorbachev, March 19, 1997. See also Gorbachev's column in *La Stampa* (Milan), March 3, 1992. Vadim Zagladin, "Perestroika: A New Way of Thinking," *Catholic International* 2, no. 18 (1991): 866.

4. "Statement from the Meeting of Cardinals and Presidents of Bishops' Conferences of Central and Eastern Europe," Informativna Katolička Agencija, Zagreb, February 11, 2009.

5. Author's interview with Förner, *The Universe* (Manchester, England), September 27, 2009.

6. "Kard. Sterzinsky: Minęła euforia po upadku Muru Berlińskiego," Katolicka Agencja Informacyjna, Warsaw, November 10, 2009. German church figures in Katolische Nachrichten-Agentur, December 24, 2009.

7. "Najnowsze dane o polskiej religijności—Spadek o 3, 8 procent," Katolicka Agencja Informacyjna, Warsaw, April 7, 2009; "Instytut Statystyki Kościoła: Lekki wzrost liczby katolików na Mszach św," Katolicka Agencja Informacyjna, May 13, 2010. See also Jonathan Luxmoore, "More Catholics Staying Out of Pews in Poland," Ecumenical News International

(Geneva), May 27, 2010, and "Church in Poland Faces New Clergy Shortfall," Ecumenical News International, March 2, 2010.

8. *Rzeczpospolita* (Warsaw), June 14, 2010; The Universe, June 27, 2010; Jonathan Luxmoore, "The Poor Are Not the Priority," *The Tablet*, March 20, 2010.

9. Author's interview, Warsaw, December 15, 2009.

10. "Pastiersky list biskupov Slovenska na Prvú adventnú nedeľu 2007," Tlačová Kancelária Konferencie Biskupov Slovenska, December 2, 2007. The bishops also commented in "Pastiersky list biskupov Slovenska k Týždňu Cirkev pre mládež," Tlačová Kancelária Konferencie Biskupov Slovenska, November 11, 2007.

11. Jonathan Luxmoore, "Slovak Church Takes On U.S. Casino Tycoons to Block Gambling Complex," Catholic News Service, Washington DC, April 9, 2010.

12. *Katolický týdeník* (Prague), April 27, 2009.

13. "Prymas Czech dla KAI," Katolicka Agencja Informacyjna interview, June 7, 2010. See also *The Tablet*, June 19, 2010; Jonathan Luxmoore, "Prague Cathedral Deal Boosts Hopes of Minority Churches," Ecumenical News International, June 17, 2010.

14. Czech TV interview, April 8, 2010; "Prager Erzbischof: Aufarbeitung der Vergangenheit schwierig," Kathpress (Vienna), July 21, 2010.

15. "Chorwacja: Biskupi Europy Środkowej i Wschodniej uczcili pamięć," Katolicka Agencja Informacyjna, February 11, 2009; *The Tablet*, February 21, 2009.

16. "Message from the Bishops of the Croatian Conference of Bishops on the Upcoming Presidential Election in the Republic of Croatia," Informativna Katolička Agencija, November 23, 2009.

17. "Statement by the Croatian Conference of Bishops," Informativna Katolička Agencija, December 2, 2009; *The Tablet*, December 12, 2009.

18. Author's interview, Budapest, December 14, 2009.

19. Jonathan Luxmoore, "Romanians Protest Bill Threatening Ownership of Catholic Properties," Catholic News Service, February 23, 2009; author's interview with Bishop Bercea, February 19, 2009.

20. "Communicate de Presă: Atac nedrept şi Nedemn!," Press Office of the Romanian Patriarchate, Bucharest, January 4, 2010.

21. Jonathan Luxmoore, "Romanian Church Deplores Order to Remove Crosses from Schools," Ecumenical News International, June 27, 2007. See also "Church Leaders Urge Romania to Keep Religion Classes in Schools," Catholic News Service, September 22, 2009.

22. Author's interview, Bucharest, May 27, 2010.

23. *The Tablet*, August 25, 2007.

24. Interfax interview, Moscow, August 24, 2007; Jonathan Luxmoore, "Russian Orthodox Leader Says Church Will Not Interfere in Politics," Ecumenical News International, April 30, 2010.

25. Author's interview, Moscow, July 14, 2009; Jonathan Luxmoore, "Russian Catholics Condemn Demolition," Catholic News Service, September 29, 2011.

26. *The Tablet*, February 13, 2010.

27. Father Maciej Mamaj quoted in Jonathan Luxmoore, "Georgian Catholics Cite 'Growing Hardship' from Orthodox Pressure," Catholic News Service, June 27, 2008.

28. "Białoruś: Abp Kondrusiewicz ma nadzieję na pomyślny rozwój relacji Kościoła z państwem," Katolicka Agencja Informacyjna, April 7, 2010.

29. Ukrainian-language text in Religious Information Service of Ukraine, March 29, 2010.

30. Remarks at Kiev press conference, in RISU bulletin, July 1, 2010.

31. Author's interview, Kharkov, July 2, 2010.

32. "Arcybiskup Kowna zaprasza Polaków na uroczystości jubileuszowe do Szydłowa," Katolicka Agencja Informacyjna, September 1, 2008; Jonathan Luxmoore, "Lithuanian Archbishop Says Western Ideas Have Affected Catholicism," Catholic News Service, September 3, 2008.

33. Author's interview, December 15, 2009.

34. Author's interview, December 14, 2009.

8

Models of State-Religion Relations in Western Europe

SILVIO FERRARI

After a period of relative stability, the relations between state and religion in Europe have entered a phase of transition. In the past ten years new concordats and agreements have been concluded with the Catholic Church and other religious communities (in Albania, Italy, Portugal, Slovenia, and other countries), new laws on religious liberty have been enacted (Hungary, Kosovo, Portugal, Romania, and Slovenia), church-state systems have been changed (Sweden), important reforms have affected the teaching of religion at school (Russia), the religious dress codes (France), and other central features of church-state relations. These changes are too many and too close in time to be explained as simple coincidences; one has the impression that the national legal systems have finally understood the need to adjust to the socioreligious transformations of Europe and to adapt their content to the new situation.

This process must be carefully monitored. This chapter starts from an analysis of the present situation and then moves to a description of three different models of state-religion relations, those of England, France, and Italy,[1] that are taking shape in Europe. The final pages are devoted to a short assessment of their capacity to provide a sound legal framework for these relations. These three models are most well-developed in Western Europe but can, in some form, have applications to emergent states of Eastern Europe. Because chapter 7 in this volume analyzes the context of postcommunist nations, this chapter focuses primarily on the older democracies of Western Europe.

A European Model of Relations between States and Religions

At first glance the national systems of relations between states and religions give the impression of being extremely diverse. There are few similarities between Denmark, with a state church, and a separatist and secular France, or between the system of recognized religions that has been adopted in Belgium and that current in Greece, based on the predominance of a single religion.

In reality this first impression is superficial and stops at the superstructures of the legal system. We only have to go a little deeper to see that there are some shared principles that describe a common model of relationships between states and religions.[2]

The first of these principles is the religious freedom and equality of individuals, that is, the right to have, not to have, to change, and to practice one's own religion publicly. This is a principle with ancient roots, but in its present form it has been affirmed in the philosophical reflections of the Enlightenment and the work of liberal nineteenth-century jurists. It therefore presents itself as a key principle of modernity: every human being, simply by virtue of being human, has the right to make, in absolute freedom, choices in keeping with conscience, without being subjected to any discrimination in relation to those choices. It would be excessive to say that this principle is respected all over Europe without exceptions; there are restrictions that limit more or less markedly the right to practice one's own religion publicly (for example, in Greece proselytism is forbidden, in many schools of Belgium students cannot wear religious symbols, and in France a Sikh taxi driver cannot obtain a license without submitting a photo bareheaded). However, it is a fact that today, in all European countries, Catholics, Protestants, and Orthodox, atheists, apostates, and members of a minority religion are not subjected to any limitation of the civil and political rights enjoyed by all citizens because of the convictions they have or the religion they profess.[3]

The principle that the state has no competence in religious questions is more complex, but its constituent elements are clear. There is a remarkable convergence of Christian thought and liberal thought on this point; for different reasons, both affirm that it is not the task of the state to legislate on matters of dogmas, rites, and religious doctrines. This assertion might seem to be contradicted by the existence in some European countries of state churches where the sovereign, who is also the head of the church, nominates the bishops and exercises functions relating to the government of religion. But these states—Denmark, England, Norway, and a few others—seem less and less inclined to intervene in questions of faith and worship, even when they have the possibility of doing so, and tend to reduce their own powers to a form of ratification of the decisions taken by ecclesiastical bodies. In 1993 the British Parliament approved the

ordination of women to the priesthood, which had been decided on by the
General Synod of the Church of England; it would have been very difficult for
Parliament to have introduced such a reform on its own initiative. In Western
Europe the autonomy of the churches on matters of doctrine and organization
was reinforced throughout the twentieth century, along with the consolidation
of the notion of the secularity of the state, which had already been affirmed
since the second half of the nineteenth century.

The third and last element that distinguishes relations between states and
religions is their cooperation. Throughout Europe, after the collapse of the
communist regimes, cooperation between states and religions is the rule; it
manifests itself in direct financing (as in Belgium, where the state pays the salaries of religious ministers) and in tax exemptions; in the provision of religious
assistance in hospitals, prisons, and the armed forces; in the teaching of religion
in state schools; in free access of the religious confessions to the public mass
media; and so on. Even secular and separatist France is no exception here: the
military chaplains are paid by the state, and the maintenance of many Catholic
churches is paid for with public funds. But everywhere in Europe this cooperation is selective. States do not collaborate in the same way with all religious communities: some receive more and others less, and yet others nothing at all. The
readiness of states to collaborate with religious groups is greater where there is
harmony between the values that regulate religious society and those that lie at
the basis of civil society; it is less where this harmony does not exist. That is the
reason why almost everywhere in Europe it is more complicated and expensive
to build a mosque than to build a church, and it explains why, in many countries,
the Christian congregation of Jehovah's Witnesses proportionately pays more
taxes than the Catholic Church. In other words, state support is mainly directed
toward those religious communities that, by virtue of the number of their members, the time they have been in a country, or the political weight they carry, are
better integrated into the cultural and social traditions of a people and are in
harmony with the rules and values that inspire it. This state attitude frequently
implies a different treatment of minority religions (and particularly the so-called
new religious movements) that can have a negative impact on their collective
religious liberty.

This model of relations between states and religions—characterized by religious freedom and equality at an individual level, by the autonomy of religious
organizations, and by selective collaboration between states and religions—has
been adopted by the countries that emerged from Catholic confessionalism
during the 1960s and 1970s (Portugal, Spain, and Italy) and those that have
more recently abandoned or reformed the state church system (Sweden, Finland, in the future Norway). Its basic features can be found in the legal systems
of many other countries of Western Europe (from Germany to Belgium, the
Netherlands, and France) and has provided the point of reference followed,

though with persistent delays and resistance, by many formerly communist countries. For these reasons the European system of relations between states and religions has appeared solid. Its main weak point seemed to be an excessive inequality between the religious confessions, in particular in the countries of Central and Eastern Europe; if they had succeeded in correcting this defect (as was vigorously requested by the United States and some international organizations after 1989), there was every indication that the system would be long term. But things have proved to be more complicated than had been foreseen.

A Model in Process of Transformation

The system of relationships between states and religions described in the previous section is now in the process of being subjected to growing tensions which threaten to unbalance its equilibrium.

Over the past thirty years Europe has been involved in enormous transformations: the fading of Marxist ideology and the collapse of the communist regimes; the growth of immigration and the emphasis on multiculturalism in many countries of Western Europe; the weakening of the welfare state and economic systems based on the stability of the workforce; and the decline of established styles of life and cultural models under the impact of globalization and immigration. These are only some of the changes.

The signs of this transformation are not unequivocal and cannot be put in a homogeneous framework; however, there is no doubt that they have brought a sense of disorientation and uncertainty to a large part of the European population, followed by a marked demand for identity, by a quest for symbols by which people can recognize themselves, and by a need for traditions that are shared and that will lead to sharing.[4] In this context religion has appeared to many people to be an important reservoir of values that can help them to respond to this demand.

In the case of Christianity this religious revival has expressed itself in two ways. First, for a narrow elite, this has constituted an intense experience of being "born again," often within church movements and communities that call for the total allegiance of their followers, in private and in public. However, for the majority of Europeans, Christianity has not in fact proven to be a point of reference for choices about the family, leisure time, political activity, or sexual life; sociological surveys confirm that the process of secularization of private life is proceeding apace and not slowing down in any significant way. Yet these same surveys register a growing appreciation of the value of Christianity for culture and identity; many Europeans show a significant attachment to Christian religious symbols even when they observe few, if any, of the precepts of the religion and do not consider themselves members of any church. In Germany and Italy, for example, the battle to keep the crucifix in schools has been waged by emphasizing the significance of the symbol in Western history and culture rather than its testimony to a specific religion; the value of the symbol for culture and identity counts more than its significance for faith. This makes it possible to gain support for the defense of a Christian symbol from more people than only those who believe or practice Christianity.

In Western Europe today the secularization of private choices is no longer keeping step with the secularization of public institutions, which is showing signs of slowing down. The split between the secularization of private life and the laicization of public life, which went hand in hand for the greater part of the past two centuries, seems to be a characteristic of postmodernity. Is this process destined to have an impact on the model of relationships between states and religions current in Europe?

The Juridical Scenario

If this process of desecularization of public life is confirmed, it is probable that in the next few years there will be an increased tendency to distinguish between the traditional religions—those that express the historical and cultural identity of a country—and all the others: Islam, new religious movements, religious minorities. Obviously traditional religions are to be identified country by country; for example, Catholicism is a traditional religion in Italy but not in Greece. However, some religions, in particular the so-called new religious movements and Islam (with the exception of some regions of the Balkans and Russia), are not traditional religions in any part of Europe. (The case is different for Judaism, which is a minority religion but has contributed toward shaping the identity of Europe through Christianity.)

The distance between the traditional and the nontraditional at the level of symbolic recognition and legal status will tend to increase. That will probably have no direct consequences on the religious freedom and equality of individuals (in other words, on the first characteristic of the model outlined at the beginning of this chapter), which are effectively protected by international law and by the constitutions of many countries. However, the autonomy of the religious confessions and above all cooperation between them and the state could become increasingly differentiated according to the social, cultural, and political roots that each religious group will be able to claim within a country.

In fact the traditional religions—even though their following of convinced and practicing believers is now small—have great importance for states in terms of social resources. In the area of culture, they serve to give a solid foundation to European identity in the face of or against another civilization. From an ethical point of view religion is used to control technological progress that seems to recognize no limit. Politically religions are helpful for reinforcing stability and social cohesion, which are put to hard tests by the process of immigration and terrorism. In principle this renewed attention to the social, cultural, and political dimensions includes all the religions; in reality, however, the Christian denominations and churches benefit from it because they are the only ones that can claim a central role in the definition of European identity and can therefore present themselves as guardians of the memory of Europe.

The strategy of liberalization of the European religious market supported by the United States does not fit well in this picture: it aims to apply the same legal framework to all religious communities, from the oldest and largest to the smallest and most recent, and this equalization is often seen as a deliberate attempt to erase differences rooted in history and culture. In Europe the social role the Christian churches can play encourages some forms of state protectionism, of the kind that is expressed by the preference given to religions and churches that are legally defined as traditional. The laboratory of church politics that is constituted by the formerly communist countries of Europe is already experimenting with this solution, giving explicit preference (in terms of registration, acquisition of legal personality, financing, and so on) to the majority religions firmly rooted in a country; the Law on the Right to Freedom of Conscience and Religion, and on Churches, Religions and Religious Community, adopted in Hungary on July 12, 2011, is a good example of this process. However, this system—in a rather more concealed way—is already in force in some countries of Western Europe.

Catholicism as a "Civil Religion" in Italy

Italy is a good example of this trend. The central core of the Italian experiment is the attempt to govern the ethical, cultural, and religious plurality of the country through the values of Catholicism, raised to the rank of civil religion.[5] More precisely, Catholicism supplies the cultural and ethical principles on which citizenship is based; provided they are prepared to accept this condition, non-Catholics can fully enjoy religious freedom rights (although not religious equality rights at the collective level). Governing diversity by stressing (Catholic) identity is the narrow and arduous path Italy is trying to follow.

The debate about the crucifix is the best example of the Italian way of dealing with the problems of social plurality and fragmentation. In Italian public schools a crucifix has to be hung on the walls of every classroom. Faced with requests to remove it, the Italian courts have stated that the crucifix is not only a religious symbol but also the symbol of Italian identity: it manifests the historical and cultural tradition of Italy and is a sign of a value system based on freedom, equality, human dignity, and religious tolerance. As citizenship is founded on these same values, which are to be respected by everybody, the presence of the crucifix in the classroom cannot be made dependent on the religious convictions of the students. These arguments are at the foundation of the appeal presented by the Italian government against the 2009 European Court of Human Rights decision in the case of *Lautsi v. Italy*.[6]

The Council of State went even further and declared that the crucifix is the symbol of the Italian model of secularity. According to the Council of State, in Italy the principles that are at the base of the idea of secularity cannot but have a religious origin; therefore the best way to manifest the secular character of the Italian school is the crucifix in the classroom. This conclusion does not mean that the crucifix is deprived of its religious significance. But according to the Council, it has a different meaning depending on the place where it is situated: when the crucifix is placed in a church or another place of worship, it is only a religious symbol; when it is placed in a school, it becomes a tool for educating students, independently from their religious beliefs, to the values of tolerance, mutual respect, dignity of the human being, human solidarity, nondiscrimination, and so on, that is, to the values that are at the core of the notion of secularity.[7]

According to other court decisions, the fact that Italian schools are attended by a growing number of non-Christian students does not affect the presence of the crucifix: on the contrary, this fact underlines its need, because the crucifix contributes to propagation of the principles of respect for diversity and rejection of radicalism (both religious and secular) that are at the foundation of the Italian legal system and that may not be familiar to students of other cultures and religions.[8] These judgments express in legal terms the idea, supported by large part of the Catholic hierarchy, the governing political coalition, and public opinion, that only the Catholic tradition can perform the role of civil religion in Italy and can provide the set of fundamental principles and values on which social cohesion is founded.

The accent placed on Catholicism as the civil religion of Italy is not without consequences for the way the relations between state and religion are shaped. Three examples confirm this. First, in the Italian public schools, the teaching of the Catholic religion is compulsory, in the sense that the state has the obligation to provide it, although the students can decide whether or not to attend Catholic religion classes; other religions can be taught, but only at the request of the students, and those teachers are not paid by the state (while the teachers of the Catholic religion are).[9] Second, in Italy there is no specific law concerning new religious movements, and no official institution is in charge of controlling or combating them. But these movements are far from enjoying the same legal status other religious communities have, and up to now only Judeo-Christian religions have been able to conclude agreements with the Italian state. (An agreement was signed with the Buddhist community in 2000, but Parliament never enacted the law required for its application.)[10] Third, the symbols of minority religions—such as the Islamic headscarf, the Jewish kippah, and the Sikh turban—are not a matter of concern in Italian schools. The public debate instead has focused on a symbol of the majority religion: when the Catholic crucifix was threatened almost everybody, from the president of the republic to the mayor of the smallest Italian village, felt compelled to join the public outcry in their defense.[11]

Up to a certain point minority religions have benefited from the dominant position of Catholicism in Italian society. The agreements concluded by the state with some non-Catholic religions replicate on a smaller scale the structure and content of the concordat signed with the Catholic Church and extend to the former some of the advantages reserved to the latter. But there is a price to pay for that: the integration of non-Catholic religious communities in Italian society passes through the acceptance of the dominant position of Catholicism as the civil religion of the country. As some scholars have underlined, "The cross in Italy's state school is the main defender of the headscarves of Muslim pupils." As there are so many Christian symbols in the public space, it is difficult to object to the presence of symbols of other religions.[12] But non-Catholic religions have to accept the Catholic Church's role of gatekeeper of the Italian identity

Laïcité as the Civil Religion in France

Not all European countries are ready to follow the Italian path; for example, in France *laïcité* is conceived as the general principle that can include and reconcile the particular values of the religious, racial, ethnic, cultural, and political communities living in the country. In this perspective *laïcité* is seen as a cluster of universal and abstract values—among them, liberty, equality, and tolerance— that every citizen must embrace independently from his or her origins, preferences, and belonging. Citizenship is built around these values, which are, as described by the former president Jacques Chirac, "at the heart of our republican identity."[13] Consistent with this approach, the contract of *accueil et integration* that each immigrant has to sign when entering France lists *laïcité*, together with democracy and equality, among the nonnegotiable values on which the French republic is founded.[14]

If we now take into consideration the examples of the Italian pattern, the impact on the religion-state system of the two different paths to social cohesion becomes evident. In the field of education, the French curricula (with the exception of Alsace and Moselle) include neither the teaching of religions nor the teaching about religion. This is an exceptional case, as all EU states and almost all European countries include either denominational or nondenominational religious instruction as a compulsory or optional subject.[15] In addition

France is spearheading the fight against the so-called new religious movements in Europe; it has enacted a law and created a governmental body to combat nontraditional sects and the *derives sectaires*. According to this law, "sectarian movements which undermine human rights and fundamental freedoms" can be dissolved once they or their managers have been the subject of definitive convictions for a number of crimes (e.g., endangering the life, the physical or psychological integrity, the freedom, dignity, or identity of a person; placing minors at risk; illegally practicing medicine).[16] On the question of religious symbols, France has taken a very clear position by passing a law that prohibits the wearing at school of religious symbols that are too conspicuous and, more recently, a law that forbids wearing the burqa in public spaces. Once more, no other EU country (with the partial exception of Belgium) has followed this path.[17]

The difference with Italy is striking, and in my opinion there is a link between the secular conception of national identity prevailing in France and these legal and political choices. If national identity has to be built around the notion of *laïcité*, "it is the role of the state to create laïque citizens" by educating them to the values of *laïcité* and shielding them from the competing values upheld by religions.[18] This attitude explains the exclusion of the teaching of religion from the school curriculum, the prohibition of wearing religious symbols in school, and the need to protect citizens from the threat to freedom posed by the new religious movements.

"Unity from Diversity" in England

Both the French and the Italian models are based on the presupposition that social cohesion requires a homogeneous set of values, be they secular or religious, shared by the majority of the citizens. In contrast, the English pattern is inspired by the conviction that this type of homogeneity is an outdated legacy of the past. In a multicultural and multireligious society, social cohesion can be founded only on different and even competing sets of values, accepting as part of the bargain some degree of dissociation between the national state, seen as the place of loyalty, and the different cultural, ethnic, and religious communities that live within it and that are conceived by their members as the place of identity.[19]

At least to a certain extent the English pattern is based on the state's recognition of its inability to forge the identity of its citizens. Consequently it gives up this claim, limiting itself to providing the legal framework necessary for the peaceful coexistence of different individuals and groups in a plural society. The debate in England about "what it means to be English" and the weakness of "Englishness" is a symptom of this transformation.[20] The task to create commitment, solidarity, and responsibility—that is, the ingredients that constitute a collective identity—is largely left to the particular communities, where it is still possible to experience the feeling of belonging that once was provided by the nation. A good measure of legal pluralism, without which such communities cannot develop and maintain their collective identity, is an integral part of the pattern. It is symptomatic that the debate on legal pluralism made the headlines in England, after the speech of the archbishop of Canterbury in 2008. Archbishop Rowan Williams advocated a system of "transformative accommodation...in which individuals retain the liberty to choose the jurisdiction under which they will seek to resolve certain carefully specified matters," including "aspects of marital law, the regulation of financial transactions and authorized structures of mediation and conflict resolution." This speech was interpreted as the endorsement of a system of "overlapping jurisdictions," where Islamic law and other religious laws could be recognized within the English legal system, and ignited a lively debate.[21] To some extent this model is reminiscent of premodern times, when a number of tasks that later became prerogatives of the state were performed by different social communities, equality of citizens had not acquired the all-encompassing significance it has now, and religious tolerance was more important than religious freedom.

As in the case of France and Italy, the English system of relations between church and state reflects this background. It is no coincidence that in English state schools religious education is prevalent in the form of teaching about religions,[22] which is different both from the Italian teaching of religion and from the French teaching of no religion. The focus is primarily placed on religious plurality; students are taught to know and understand the different religions practiced in the country. It is also significant that the presence of various religious symbols in the public space, such as the Sikh turban and the Muslim headscarf, has raised less conflict than in France. While in France a law that prohibits wearing a burqa in public spaces has been enacted, in the United Kingdom the University of Cambridge has decided to allow Muslim students to wear burqas at graduation.[23] And the new religious movements have been accepted in the United Kingdom much more readily than in Italy and especially in France.[24]

However, there is a point that needs to be clarified: Why did religious plurality not seriously question the existence of an established church? How can the multireligious composition of England be reconciled with a sovereign who is the head of the Church of England, whose bishops are seated in the House of Lords? This state of affairs—which would be inconceivable not only in France but also in Italy—has many explanations. One is the wise policy of the Church of England to use its privileged position to speak on behalf of all religious groups in the country. Another is the fact that the denominational connotation of the state can be accepted more easily because its citizens are not required to identify with the state and recognize it as the main provider of their identity.

Conclusion

Before drawing conclusions from the models described, it should be underlined that no model exists in pure form. Rather these three models are ideal types helpful for analyzing social phenomena. Each model has its own weaknesses and strong points.

The Italian pattern is based on the gamble that citizenship and social cohesion can be built around a particular religious and cultural tradition. In the short term this strategy may work, but nobody knows how long it will be able to face the challenge of the growing numbers of non-Christian immigrants. The public reaffirmation of the Catholic identity of Italy can contribute to reassure its citizens and help them to come to terms with changes that are of unusual speed and magnitude. It can make the whole process of integration more sustainable. But sooner or later Italy will have a large number of Muslim citizens, and they will demand their say in defining the cultural profile of Italy, that is, of their own country.

How much the French model can cope with the two driving forces that are changing the European religious landscape—the increasing plurality of religions and their growing public character[25]—is open to discussion. The weakest point of the French pattern is the assumption that not only the state and its institutions but also society and politics have to be independent from particular traditions and conceptions of life.[26] Both historic religions and immigrant communities are increasingly challenging this privatization of religion.

Finally, it is still too early to assess the chances of success of the English experiment. Its most interesting feature is the attempt to distinguish between social cohesion and cultural homogeneity. In a multicultural society, the foundation of social cohesion has to be found less in a shared set of values and more in the common interest for a legal framework within which different ethnic, religious, and cultural groups can live and develop. But the strength of such a framework, and its capacity to resist the centrifugal forces generated by the growing plurality, is a question that has yet to be answered.

Taking into account the cultural and social diversity of the European countries and the different impact that immigration and religious pluralism have on each of them, it is possible that these patterns and their regional variations will coexist for quite a long time. It is likely that none of them will become *the* European pattern without including components derived from the other two.

Notes

1. This chapter aims at identifying three different patterns of church-state relations. Therefore I will not give a detailed description of these systems: only their main features will be taken into account.

2. I have developed the observations in this paragraph at greater length in "The Legal Dimension," in *Muslims in the Enlarged Europe: Religion and Society,* ed. Brigitte Maréchal, Stefano Allievi, Felice Dassetto and Jørgen Nielsen (Leiden: Brill, 2003), 219–54.

3. One qualification concerns countries (e.g., England, Denmark, and Norway) where some state authorities are held to profess a particular religion; however, these are norms that, although they have a very great symbolic significance, interest a quite limited number of people.

4. For the observation that follows, see Grace Davie, *Religion in Modern Europe: A Memory Mutates* (Oxford: Oxford University Press, 2000); Grace Davie, *Europe: The Exceptional Case. Parameters of Faith in the Modern World* (London: Darton, Longman & Todd, 2002); Danièle Hervieu-Léger, "Les tendances du religieux en Europe," in *Croyances religieuses, morales et éthiques dans le processus de construction européenne,* ed. Commissariat Général du Plan (Paris: La Documentation française, 2002).

5. This program was explicitly supported by the president of the Italian Bishops Conference, Camillo Ruini, on February 11, 2005; see his address at http://chiesa.espresso.repubblica.it/articolo/23170.

6. See Mémoire du Gouvernement Italien pour l'Audience devant la Grande Chambre de la Cour Européenne des Droits de l'Homme (Lautsi c. Italie), http://www.strasbourgconsortium.org/document.php?DocumentID=5450.

7. Council of State, decision of February 13, 2006, n. 556, http://www.olir.it/ricerca/index.php?Form_Document=3517.

8. Administrative Court of Veneto, decision of March 17, 2005, n. 1110, http://www.olir.it/ricerca/index.php?Form_Document=2075.

9. See Silvio Ferrari, "State and Church in Italy," in *State and Church in the European Union,* ed. Gerhard Robbers (Baden-Baden: Nomos, 2005), 218–20.

10. See ibid., 214–17.

11. See "Human Rights Ruling against Classroom Crucifixes Angers Italy," *Guardian,* November 3, 2009; "European Court Bans Crucifix in Italy's Classrooms," *Telegraph,* November 3, 2009.

12. Alessandro Ferrari, "Religious Education in a Globalized Europe," in *Religion and Democracy in Contemporary Europe,* ed. Gabriel Motzkin and Yochi Fisher (London: Alliance, 2008), 119.

13. This passage of a speech given by Chirac in 2003 is quoted by Blandine Chélini Pont and Jeremy Gunn, *Dieu en France et aux Etats-Unis: Quand les mythes font la loi* (Paris: Berg, 2005), 15.

14. See www.legifrance.gouv.fr/affichCode.do?cidTexte=LEGITEXT000006070158&dateTexte=vig.

15. On the teaching of religion in French schools, see Jean-Paul Willaime, "Teaching Religious Issues in French Public Schools: From Abstentionist Laïcité to a Return of Religion to Public Education," in *Religion and Education in Europe: Developments, Contexts and Debates,* ed. Robert Jackson, Siebren Miedema, Wolfgang Weisse, and Jean-Paul Willaime (Münster: Waxmann, 2007), 87–102. About Europe, see Elza Kuyk, Roger Jensen, David Lankshear, Elizabeth Löh Manna, and Peter Schreiner, eds., *Religious Education in Europe* (Oslo: Iko-ICCS, 2007), 71–75; Luce Pépin, *Teaching about Religions in European School Systems: Policy Issues and Trends* (London: Alliance, 2009).

16. Loi n. 2001–504 du 12 Juin 2001, *Journal Officiel,* n. 135 du 13 Juin 2001. On this topic, see Susan Palmer, *The New Heretics of France: Minority Religions, la Republique, and the Government-Sponsored "War on Sects"* (Oxford: Oxford University Press, 2011).

17. On these issues, see John R. Bowen, *Why the French Don't Like Headscarves: Islam, the State, and Public Space* (Princeton, N.J.: Princeton University Press, 2006); Christian Joppke, "Limits of Restricting Islam: The French Burqa Law of 2010," available at http://www.unige.ch/ses/socio/rechetpub/dejeuner/dejeuner2010-2011/chapter.burka2010.pdf.

18. Peter Berger, Grace Davie, and Effie Fokas, *Religious America, Secular Europe? A Theme and Variations* (Aldershot, England: Ashgate, 2008), 76.

19. The distinction between loyalty and identity is made by Hanne Petersen, *Beyond National Majority/Minority Dichotomies: Towards Legal Traditions and Religions of World Society,* in *Law and Religion in the 21st Century. Nordic Perspectives,* ed. Lisbet Christoffersen, Kjell Å. Modéer, Svend Andersen (Copenhagen: DIØF, 2010), 321–44, speaking of the situation in the Nordic countries before the nineteenth century, when "*loyalty* was probably more important than *identity*. Ordinary people would *identify* with neither God nor King, but

they might seek privilege and protection from these sources of authority by showing obedience, loyalty and faith."

20. On this debate, see Krishan Kumar, *The Making of English National Identity* (Cambridge: Cambridge University Press, 2003); Robert Colls, *Identity of England* (New York: Oxford University Press, 2002).

21. See Rowan Williams, "Civil and Religious Law in England," *Ecclesiastical Law Journal* 10, no. 3 (2008): 262–82. On the debate about legal pluralism in the United Kingdom, see Rubya Mehdi, Hanne Petersen, Erik Reenberg Sand, and Gordon R. Woodman, eds., *Law and Religion in Multicultural Societies* (Copenhagen: DIØF, 2008), in particular the contributions of Werner Menski, "Law, Religion and Culture in Multicultural Britain" (43–62); Prakash Shah, "Religion in a Super-Diverse Legal Environment: Thoughts on the British Scene" (63–82).

22. See Pépin, *Teaching about Religions*, 63–67.

23. See http://islamineurope.blogspot.com/2009/10/cambridge-burkas-allowed-in-graduation.html.

24. See Eileen Barker, "General Overview of the 'Cult Scene' in Great Britain," in *New Religious Movements in the 21st Century*, ed. Phillip Charles Lucas and Thomas Robbins (New York: Routledge, 2004), 22–28; Anthony Bradney, "New Religious Movements: The Legal Dimension," in *New Religious Movements: Challenge and Response*, ed. Bryan Wilson and Jamie Cresswell (Abingdon, England: Routledge, 1999), 81–100.

25. On these transformations, see Silvio Ferrari, "State Regulation of Religion in the European Democracies: The Decline of the Old Pattern,' in Motzkin and Fischer, *Religion and Democracy in contemporary Europe*, 103–12.

26. This assumption emerges clearly in the "Déclaration sur la *laïcité*" prepared by Jean Bauberot, Roberto Blancarte, and Micheline Milot and made public on December 9, 2005 (see Articles 4 and 9). The text is published in Jean Bauberot, *L'intégrisme républicain contre la laïcité* (Paris: Aube, 2006).

9

Emerging Challenges to Religious Freedom in America and Other English-Speaking Countries

GERARD V. BRADLEY

The gravest challenges to religious freedom in most parts of the world bear little resemblance to those in the United States. The most dramatic threat in Nigeria, Sudan, India, and Egypt (among other countries) is the unwillingness of their governments to curtail private violence against religious minorities. This impunity is often aggravated by the government's unwillingness to bring offenders before the bar of justice.

American public authorities face no such challenges. They do sometimes face the challenge of what to do about pressure, and even coercion, by religious communities in the recruitment or retention of members and, occasionally, as retaliation against those who have left the fold. This challenge calls for a creative and supple but (as need be) decisive response by the state. Any suitable response must be animated by the demands of justice and of genuine religious freedom, just as it must be shaped by a realistic appreciation of the limited good that legal intervention into a religious community can do.[1] The problem elsewhere is much simpler: it is about delivering equal protection of laws against violence and intimidation.

Antiproselytizing laws are an emerging challenge to religious freedom in many countries, but not in America. Likewise laws against blasphemy, apostasy, or the vilification of others' religious beliefs are not issues in the United States. From the American founding up to the Civil War there were occasional prosecutions of a blasphemer or contemnor of religion. In the most famous of these cases, one Ruggles opined loudly that "Jesus Christ was a bastard, and his mother must have been a whore."[2] The purpose of these infrequent prosecutions was not the spiritual reform of the speaker, nor was it to buttress the people's belief in the Christian religion as *true*. The point of these proceedings was well expressed by the Delaware Supreme Court, when it upheld a conviction for utterances indistinguishable from Mr. Ruggles's. The court in *State v. Chandler* said that "it is the open, public vilification of the religion of the country that is punished...to preserve the peace [by enforcing] outward respect" for the socially prevalent religion.[3]

By around 1950 the last traces of this older American tradition, which was somewhat hospitable to the conceptualizations of religious freedom and social harmony upon which restrictive laws abroad today depend, were finally eliminated by constitutional decision.[4] Since then and *notwithstanding* the growing view that religious belief is subrational, and *notwithstanding* gains made by an "identity politics" in which disagreement with another's defining beliefs is tantamount to denying equal respect, and *notwithstanding* confusion in law and culture about the foundations of religious liberty, there is nonetheless no support in America for antiproselytizing or religious libel laws.

There really never was. Antiproselytizing laws are a corollary of anticonversion strictures. Together they form a coherent matrix, even where they are supplemented by laws against blasphemy and apostasy. This matrix is often justified elsewhere as protecting "religious liberty," in the special sense of vindicating a "community's right to be left alone to its traditions,"[5] where a "stance on noninterference is central to those traditions."[6]

This sort of claim has never had much traction on American thought or practice. The early blasphemy prosecutions were meant to vindicate public order and public morality; they were not justified as protections of religious liberty. And these sorts of claims have *zero* traction now. The reasons are many, and they are related in complex ways. Americans have always understood their religious commitments to be more tentative and subject to revision than those tempted to support antiproselytizing laws believe religion to be. A deeper commitment here to *individual* freedom of religion further explains Americans' disinterest in restrictive laws. Overarching constitutional commitments to freedom of expression, including religious expression, have contributed to a culture of robust theological disputation, a milieu incompatible with such restrictions. America's critical culture owes most, however, to the traditions of inquiry, argument, and evidence internal to the Christianity that has been paramount in the American religious experience. Transcending all these contributory factors is an important and unbreakable connection between the nature of religious freedom and the pursuit of religious *truth*. This pursuit of truth tames any temptation to leave believers in the undisturbed possession of whatever their traditions happen to be.

French *laïcité* and Turkish *laiklik* are readily distinguishable from American separation of church and state. There is, to be sure, a large and lively jurisprudence in America about religious expression by the government and about its display of religious symbols. Constitutional litigation over Ten Commandments plaques and "under God" in the Pledge of Allegiance are illustrative of the genre. The case results are mixed, and these do reveal a minority opinion in America, call it "strict separationism," which favors a secularism scarcely distinguishable from, for example, *laïcité*.

But the American public mostly supports such noncoercive government affirmations as those recently litigated. Public officials routinely speak in religious tones and terms that are unimaginable in, say, France. While President Obama is more secular-minded than any of his predecessors (save, perhaps, for Thomas Jefferson), he is still no exception to the prevailing norms of rhetorical indulgence. The whole political culture of the United States is much more religious, in content and in language, than is the politics in laicized countries.

The burqa and the veil are not issues in America. Although the day might come to America when security and identity concerns clash with the niqab, for example, there is no chance that an assimilationist impulse would produce any such conflict. Uniform dress policies abound today, not just for military and police personnel but for many other classes of government employees. A growing number of public elementary and secondary schools are turning to student uniforms. Often enough religious liberty claimants petition public authorities for exemption from these policies, and they do so with occasional success. The policies themselves originate, though, not in any aversion to public display of religion-distinctive clothing or symbols. The policies are rooted in nonreligious considerations about grooming and uniformity of appearance. In the case of student uniforms, school authorities are moved by considerations of modesty, expense to parents, and ghoulish or outlandish—and thus distracting—dress. Any state-sponsored uniform dress policy that originated in distaste for a specific religion or that targeted religious dress in particular would be patently unconstitutional.[7]

There is little in the American tradition that resonates with the overseas secularism that is intolerant of religious dress. In the late nineteenth century and early twentieth, some American states enacted laws restricting what public school teachers could wear to work. The meaning and transparent aim of these laws were to prevent Catholic nuns from taking such jobs. The deeper objective was to stymie maneuvers whereby municipalities with heavily Catholic populations blurred the line between public and parochial schools altogether, through various shared cost and facility plans. (Today's charter schools bear some resemblance to these experiments.) If the nuns could not teach in them, there was little incentive, given the circumstances of the time, for Catholic authorities to seek control of "public" schools. In any event, the teacher garb laws have fallen into desuetude.

The most urgent challenges to religious freedom in the United States today involve *conscience protection*. There are two contexts in which the issue is today especially serious. One is health care. In years past it was typically a religiously scrupulous patient or parent of a patient—a Christian Scientist or a Jehovah's Witness, perhaps—who sought legal immunity from the administration of unremarkable and all but universally accepted medical procedures. In years past too there was a flourishing legal culture of granting generous relief to persons and institutions that, because of religious or moral convictions, could not conscientiously undertake certain duties.

The recent passage of the comprehensive Patient Protection and Affordable Care Act (PPACA) has dramatically changed this picture, in both of the foregoing respects. Now the conscientious objectors include large institutional providers sponsored by mainstream religions. The largest of these is the Catholic network of more than six hundred facilities. The objectors seek relief too from complicity in morally controversial medical treatments, chiefly abortion. PPACA does not provide these claimants the generous relief they avidly sought during the health care reform debate. Later I critically examine this set of challenges to religious freedom.

The second *conscience-protection* context pivots on the remarkable, and remarkably swift, turnaround in legal attitudes toward homosexual and lesbian behavior. Not just in America but in other English-speaking jurisdictions such as Canada, Australia, and the United Kingdom, legal norms mandating nondiscrimination in employment and social services have been applied to religious schools, universities, and charities, notwithstanding their claims that religious freedom principles (properly understood) require their exemption from these laws.

This challenge is heightened where same-sex couples can legally marry. Otherwise at least some religious institutions might not violate the nondiscrimination stricture by dint of their treating *all* unmarried persons (gay or straight) the same. The recent abandonment of charitable ministries by Catholic authorities in two American jurisdictions, Boston and Washington, D.C., indicates the high stakes involved and probably the pattern of the future. Later I look at how public authorities—judicial and legislative—in overseas English-speaking jurisdictions as well as in the United States have navigated the issue. In a brief conclusion I trace the possible and perhaps probable future trajectory of the twin challenges herein examined.

I

Conscience protection in American law is as old as the American republic. The Constitution itself protects those scrupulous of swearing an oath, providing (in Article VI, clause 3) that government officers "shall be bound by oath *or affirmation,* to support the Constitution" (my emphasis). Relief for those conscientiously opposed to bearing arms was already commonplace at the founding, at least for adherents of "peace churches" like the Quakers. Exemption for Saturday Sabbatarians from conflicting civic obligations (such as giving court testimony) was more patchy. But the *question* was surely a legitimate one: almost everyone agreed that, if conditions permitted, Jews (for example) ought not to be disturbed in their Sabbath observance.

Conscience protections of various sorts are strewn about the federal legal corpus, so many bits of evidence of a long-standing, healthy tradition of respect for religious freedom. The most famous of the exemptions declared by the Supreme Court are those secured by Jehovah's Witnesses plaintiffs in 1943 (against compelled participation in flag salute ceremonies)[8] and by the Old Order Amish in 1972 (releasing secondary school-age children from compulsory education requirements).[9]

Statutory conscience protections are plentiful, at both the state and the national level. Included among them is a federal statute that provides an exemption regarding capital punishment. No employee of *any* governmental unit (national, state, or local) may be required to "attend" or "participate in... any prosecution or execution" if doing so "is contrary to the moral or religious convictions of the employee." The protective shield around the objecting employee is large. "'Participation in executions' includes personal preparation of the condemned individual and the apparatus used for execution and supervision of the activities of other personnel in carrying out such activities."[10]

Federal law exempts religious health plans from certain contraceptive coverage mandates, that is, from laws that require any health insurance plan that covers prescription drugs to include prescription contraceptives. Federal law also protects individuals who refuse to prescribe or provide contraceptives due to "religious beliefs or moral convictions."[11] Congress has approved every year since 2000, for example, a resolution expressing its "intent" that District of Columbia officials include a "conscience clause" in any law that they should enact mandating that health insurance plans cover the cost of prescription contraceptives.[12]

The 1973 Church Amendment (named for its sponsor, Senator Frank Church of Idaho, and not for its contemplated beneficiaries) stipulates that hospitals and individuals who receive federal funds may not be required to participate in abortion and sterilization procedures, so long as their objection to doing so is based on moral or religious convictions. This law also forbids hospitals receiving federal funds from making anyone's unwillingness or willingness to perform these procedures a condition of employment. Another provision prohibits entities that receive public health service funds from discriminating against applicants who decline to participate in abortions or sterilizations on account of religious beliefs or moral convictions.

The 2004 Hyde-Weldon Conscience Protection Amendment protects physicians and nurses, hospitals, health insurance companies, and other health care entities from being forced by state or federal government to perform, pay for, provide coverage of, or refer for abortions. Congress has approved it every year since 2004.

This tradition of solicitude for religious freedom in the health care field is the framework within which to evaluate the conscience protections contained in PPACA, the Obama administration's comprehensive reform of America's leading industry. The Act repeals none of the protections just described, nor does it roll back any others not here mentioned. It also contains some important positive developments for the sake of conscience. Under Section 1553 of the Act governments at all levels are forbidden to discriminate against conscientious objectors with respect to assisted suicide, mercy killing, and euthanasia. So far so good, one might observe. The great worry about PPACA, however, is that it generates *new* threats to religious freedom, especially by creating distinctive funding streams and new categories of services to which *existing* protections do not apply, without including any protection comparable to, for example, Church or Hyde-Weldon.

This deficiency cannot be attributed to oversight. Many affected health care providers, including most notably the leaders of the Catholic Church in America, and many members of Congress, including most notably Representative Bart Stupak and Senator Tom Coburn, issued repeated, urgent calls to bring PPACA into line with the existing framework of conscience protection. Some early versions of the bill did as much; their deletion from the enacted version was certainly not inadvertent. This is especially certain given that President Obama implicitly recognized the problem when he promised to issue an executive order that would supply "adequate conscience protection," a phrase he had elsewhere used to describe his own determination to align health care reform with religious freedom.[13]

The promised executive order unfortunately delivered far less than promised. The president declared that the Church and the Hyde-Weldon Amendments "remain intact." Indeed they do. But neither provides any relief from the new conscience challenges engendered by PPACA. That Act does contain some valuable but limited conscience protections, and the executive order highlighted them. But it also contains some gaping holes in its conscience protection, and nowhere did the president *supplement* them (even where he possessed discretion to do so) in his executive order.

The text of the PPACA focuses on conscience protection for health care providers, both individuals and institutions. However, *patients* are put in an unprecedented predicament by PPACA. This new burden arises, ironically, from the law's attempt to avoid using federal funds to finance abortion, in keeping with the long-standing tradition of sparing taxpayers who oppose abortion from paying for other people's abortions. The PPACA segregates abortion funding so that anyone who enrolls in an abortion-covering health insurance plan must make two premium payments, one of which goes *exclusively* for abortion coverage. Because some people conscientiously opposed to abortion may have very strong reasons for choosing such a plan (the only non-abortion-covering plan available may be vastly inferior in some other respects), they are faced with the prospect of paying into a fund that does nothing but pay for abortions.[14]

The importance for conscience protection is manifold. First, recent comprehensive health reform is a sharp departure downward from the established level of conscience protection. Second, this departure was taken in the face of assertions by spokesmen for such large providers as the huge Catholic hospital network that the PPACA might cause them to withdraw from some fields of treatment—and possibly even to close—in order not to compromise their integrity. Third, the downward departure reflects a conscious value judgment on the part of those who favored it. The American Civil Liberties Union said that those seeking conscience protection would "take patients out of the equation." The National Women's Law Center said that it opposed conscience protection even for pharmacists, regardless of whether a particular service (such as chemical abortion) could be readily obtained elsewhere. A substantial portion of the rhetoric opposing conscience protection makes it sound like those seeking it are aggressors of some sort, that their desire to opt out would somehow impose the morality of those seeking exemption on clients or patients. This proposed way of viewing the question is remarkable and new. But the position of those *seeking* conscience protection would be better described as seeking to avoid immoral complicity in an injustice, namely, the killing of an unborn human being. Fourth, these high valuations of countervailing rights have not been presented as sufficient to *defeat* a well-pleaded and appealing religious freedom claim, as if a meritorious claim was regrettably unavailing. Instead it is more commonly said that the measure of conscience protection provided in PPACA is desirable or "adequate"; the defeated claim is thus construed as unworthy. And so the PPACA episode may be evidence of a shift in the *meaning* of religious freedom as opposed to a development about its extrinsic limits.

This pattern is further evidenced by the adoption by many states over the past decade or so of laws imposing "contraceptive mandates." (The federal provisions discussed earlier pertain only to the national government.) A statute litigated in New York is identical to many and similar to almost all of these new statutes. Its most controversial provision amended the state's insurance laws and required that any employer health plan "which provides coverage for prescription drugs shall include coverage for the cost of contraceptive drugs or devices."

Plaintiffs in *Catholic Charities of Diocese of Albany v. Serio* were ten "faith-based social service organizations," eight of which were affiliated in some way with the Roman Catholic Church and two affiliated with the Baptist Bible Fellowship.[15] All had purchased health insurance for their employees. These plans included prescription drug coverage. The problem, as the New York Court of Appeals described it, was that "[p]laintiffs believe contraception to be sinful, and assert that the challenged provisions of the law compel them to violate their religious tenets by financing conduct that they condemn."[16] Plaintiffs raised the possibility that they could not remain in business without relief from the mandate. "At the heart of this case," the court wrote, is the statutory definition of a "religious employer." Such an employer may request an insurance contract "without coverage for . . . contraceptive methods that are contrary to the religious employer's religious tenets." Wherever such a request is granted, the insurance carrier must "offer coverage for contraception to individual employees, who may purchase it at their own expense at the prevailing small group community rate."[17]

The test for this exemption, however, severely narrowed conscience protection. In order to qualify, an organization would have to have as its purpose the "inculcation of religious values." It would also have to employ as well as *serve* "primarily" members of the sponsoring organization's faith.[18] In effect the only "religious employers" who qualified for this exemption were religious congregations themselves: churches, synagogues, and the like. No religious school, hospital, or charitable institution could be exempted. The only justification offered for so excluding these religious institutional works was the legislators' determination to make prescription contraceptives widely available and thus (it was said) to promote women's equality.[19] This value judgment was later incorporated into the Obama Administration's contraceptive mandate, creating a firestorm of controversy and a flood of lawsuits by religious institutions and businesses.

II

Over the course of a generation ending at the millennium, same-sex sexual conduct was practically decriminalized in the United States and in other English-speaking jurisdictions as well. Over the past decade, the law in these countries has moved rapidly from a stance of respect for sexual privacy toward a place where the political community affirms a favorable moral evaluation of same-sex acts and the orientation they express. Most if not almost all discrimination by the state—in employment, housing, services—against homosexuals and lesbians has been made unlawful. Nondiscrimination laws stretching into the private sector now often include "sexual orientation" alongside race, ethnicity, and gender as prohibited bases for decisions and actions. Legal recognition of same-sex relationships as marriages or as "civil unions" is common and increasing.

The British legal scholar Ian Leigh describes the "new orthodoxy" as a "fascinating reversal" of the celebrated Hart-Devlin debate over the legal enforcement of sexual morality. The focal point of that debate in the late 1950s was the Wolfenden Commission's recommendation to decriminalize homosexual conduct. Hart famously championed liberal principles against Devlin's arguments that society could justly enforce its shared morality, even with regard to private sexual acts.[20] Leigh argues persuasively that today " 'homophobia' is the new homosexuality and sexual orientation equality is the new shared morality." Public authorities have begun to treat "dissent from the new orthodoxy...as offensive to public opinion."[21]

One illustration of the developing sea change was supplied by British Prime Minister Tony Blair. Defending an Equality Law that made ineffective provision for religious exemptions, Blair declared, "There is no place in our society for discrimination. That is why I support the right of gay couples to adopt like any other couple. And that way there can be no exemptions for faith-based adoption agencies offering publicly funded services from regulations that prevent discrimination."[22]

"By a strange irony," Leigh observes, "it is religious conservatives who are now out of step with the new morality and find themselves in need of the protection of liberal principles."[23] Religious freedom is chief among these principles. In this section of the chapter I offer, first, a brief survey of pertinent recent developments in the United States, United Kingdom, Canada, and Australia and, second, an analysis of the emerging challenge that the "new orthodoxy" presents to religious freedom.

Recent Developments

Same-sex marriage has been legally recognized across Canada since 2005. In the run-up to enactment, the Canadian Supreme Court opined (at Parliament's request) that compulsion of religious officials or conscription of "sacred places" for same-sex weddings would violate the Charter of Rights.[24] Parliament thereafter included some express, but limited, conscience protections in the marriage law. Religious officials could lawfully refuse to perform same-sex marriages. Any religious group that upheld traditional marriage in its teaching was to be free of discrimination by any other Act of Parliament.[25]

The extent of this protected space was almost immediately tested by a lesbian couple who sought to use a Knights of Columbus (i.e., Catholic) hall for their wedding celebration. The provincial human rights tribunal upheld the Knights. This tribunal's opinion was nonetheless very critical of the Knights' decision, and the question of how much space dissenters may safely occupy without legal penalty remains unsettled.[26] The most perceptive analyst of religious freedom issues in Canada is close to the mark, in any event, when he says that when the state decides in favor of same-sex marriage, religious groups upholding traditional marriage assume the status of "tolerated discriminator." To many of the dissenting groups, this looked like "pretty thin ice."[27]

In the spring of 2010 an independent Catholic school in Vancouver effectively dismissed an openly lesbian teacher named Lisa Reimer. The school authorities did not cite the integrity of their mission or the truths of Catholic faith as reasons for their action. They instead pointed the finger at outraged parents, saying that they responded to parental complaints about the incompatibility of Reimer's example with the school's Catholic identity.[28] Reimer declined to lodge a complaint with the provincial Human Rights Commission, even though the Human Rights Code applies to all publicly funded schools (which, in Canada, includes Catholic schools).[29] For that reason her case supplies no binding legal precedent, even if it does indicate the substance of future challenges by other aggrieved parties.

Australia famously possesses no national charter or bill of rights. A sizable movement to enact one crested in early 2010, short of the needed critical mass. For the foreseeable future, then, the several Australian states will be the theaters of conflict between the "new orthodoxy" about sexual orientation and religious freedom.

The earliest such conflict appears to be that of Jacqui Griffin. Sometime around 1995 she applied to the Sydney Catholic Education Office (CEO) for a teaching position. Griffin appears to have been academically qualified for the post. She was also a well-known lesbian activist; in fact she was a co-convener of the Gay and Lesbian Teachers and Students Association. The CEO rejected Griffin's application, stating (according to the hearing record) that she promoted views and causes "contrary to the teachings and values of the Catholic Church."[30] New South Wales law prohibited discrimination in employment on grounds of "sexual preference." (Religious schools in Australia, including those of the Catholic Church, are heavily subsidized by the government.) Section 3 of the law granted an exception for religious organizations "conducted in accordance with the doctrines, tenets, beliefs or teachings of a particular religion or creed," if the discrimination was made in "good faith in order to avoid injury to the religious susceptibilities of adherents of that religion or that creed."

The Human Rights and Equal Opportunity Commission hearing officer held in favor of Griffin. He found that, notwithstanding contrary claims by the Church's representatives, the "known or public stance of Ms. Griffin in relation to homosexuality does not conflict with the official teachings of the Catholic Church." Nor was her exclusion from employment "necessary to avoid injury to the susceptibilities of adherents of the [Church's] official teachings."[31] The CEO's action was therefore "not protected by the religious institutions exception" of the Act.[32]

The Wesley Mission case arose under the same New South Wales Anti-Discrimination Act. The Wesley Mission arranged foster care placements as an agent of the state. A homosexual couple applied to be foster parents; they were turned down because their relationship was contrary to the religious doctrines to which the Mission professed devotion. The hearing board upheld the couple's complaint in April 2008. The main basis for the holding seems to have been the tribunal's decision to treat the relevant "religion" not as anything distinctively Wesleyan but as Christianity writ very large, within which there were (according to the Tribunal) several streams of theological opinion about homosexuality. Thus there was no (one) "doctrine" of "that religion" on which the Mission could rely for the statutory exception. Late in 2009, however, an appeals panel reversed this ruling and remanded the case for new proceedings. The appellate ruling cited deficient interpretations of the terms *religion, religious doctrine,* and *religious adherents.*[33]

In 1988 the British Parliament prohibited local governments in England from doing anything to "intentionally promote homosexuality" or to "promote the teaching in any [government-]maintained school of the acceptability of homosexuality as a pretended family relationship." This law was repealed in 2000. The Sexual Orientation Regulations of 2003 prohibited employment discrimination on grounds of "sexual orientation." The Equality Act of 2007 made it unlawful to discriminate on those grounds in the provision of goods or services, including family services such as adoptions. The 2010 parliamentary extension of employment nondiscrimination norms occasioned a lively debate about whether Catholic bishops risk prosecution if they do not ordain women and sexually active gays to the priesthood.[34]

The Sexual Orientation Regulation of 2003 included an exception for "employment for purposes of an organized religion." The exception applied where the employer uses sexual orientation as a criterion "to comply with the doctrines of the religion" or "because of the nature of the employment and the context in which it is carried out, so as to avoid conflicting with the strongly held religious convictions of a significant number of the religion's followers." The exception was immediately attacked as invalid in court proceedings brought by some teachers' unions. The judgment of the High Court upheld the validity of the exception.

It was a hollow victory for religious freedom. The unions secured from the government in the course of litigation, and then from the Court itself, a limiting interpretation of the statutory exception: it had no application to schools or to almost all other religious employers. The High Court determined that "[e]mployment for the purposes of organized religion clearly [is limited to] a job, such as a minister of religion, involving work for a church, synagogue, or mosque."[35] Even work for a synagogue or church or mosque itself was exempted only if either the faith's doctrines or the strongly held convictions of its members *required* that the position be limited to, say, heterosexuals. The effective scope of this exemption tracks very closely that found in the many American state laws mandating prescription contraceptive coverage.[36]

In the United States criminal laws against same-sex sexual acts were very rarely enforced after around 1980. Not until 2003, in *Lawrence v. Texas,*[37] did the U.S. Supreme Court declare that such laws violated the Constitution. The *Lawrence* opinion was partly motivated by the Court's wider belief that different treatment of homosexuals and lesbians in *any* context was unjust: "When homo-sexual conduct is made criminal by the law of the State that declaration in and of itself is an invitation to subject homosexual persons to discrimination in the public and the private spheres."[38] Within months Massachusetts' highest court relied on *Lawrence* to make that state the first to recognize same-sex marriage.[39] Massachusetts legislators subsequently legalized same-sex marriage in 2004, but only as a result of judicial compulsion. Since then Connecticut and Iowa have recognized same-sex marriages by dint of judicial ruling, and Vermont and New Jersey did so (like Massachusetts) under judicial constraint. New Hampshire is the only state so far that has legally recognized same-sex marriage without pres-sure from its courts. A case now making its way through the federal courts in California portends the nationalization of same-sex marriage as a requirement of the constitutional guarantee of equality.[40]

Two telling American illustrations of the tension between the "new ortho-doxy" and religious freedom involve Catholic social services. The cases are from Boston and the nation's capital. The Washington City Council in late 2009 decided to legally recognize same-sex relationships as marriages. After fruit-lessly seeking an accommodation with the city, the Catholic Archdiocese of Washington announced that its local social service organization, Catholic Chari-ties, would no longer facilitate foster care. The archdiocese also limited employee health care benefits to avoid coverage of same-sex "spouses."

In Boston the conflict centered on Massachusetts' requirement—again, with no concession in favor of religious freedom—that state-licensed adoption agen-cies treat same-sex married couples like any other married couple when it comes to adoption services.[41] In 2004 Massachusetts famously became the first state to legally recognize same-sex relationships as marriages. But even before then it had permitted same-sex couples to adopt children; marriage was not a predicate to the legal formation of families in same-sex households. Boston Catholic Charities had arranged its first "gay" adoption in 1997, in response to an earlier state administrative rule against discrimination on the basis of sexual orienta-tion. By 2005 Catholic Charities had placed thirteen children with *unmarried* gay couples. Charities President J. Bryan Hehir, S.J., said, "[I]f we could design the system ourselves we would not participate in adoptions to gay couples, but we can't.... We have to balance various goods."

The Massachusetts Catholic bishops had final authority over the conduct of Catholic social services. They issued a statement on February 28, 2006, rejecting any "balancing" analysis. Absent an exemption from the legal requirement not to discriminate against gay couples, they concluded, Catholic Charities would have to withdraw from the adoption business. The state did not relent. Catholic Charities then abandoned adoptions after more than a century in the field, a field they entered in 1903 from concern that the state was consciously placing orphaned Catholic children in Protestant homes.

The Values at Stake

"An important tenet within the Church is a belief in the sanctity of marriage, together with the belief that the model for family life is provided by the Holy Family of Nazareth." Because of that belief, according to Justice Briggs in the *Catholic Care of Leeds* decision of March 17, 2010, Catholic Care's trustees refused to place children with same-sex couples.[42]

The *truth* of such theological matters as marriage's sanctity and the unique merits of the Holy Family is beyond the competence of the state to judge. Public officials therefore cannot intelligibly weigh the importance of protecting these beliefs (just as such) over against the conviction that sexual-orientation discrimination in adoption is unjust. That latter belief might, of course, be mistaken. But the truth or falsity of it is not beyond the state's ken. Public authorities can nonetheless intelligently value assertions about, for example, the Holy Family. They can do so by treating them as members of a class of beliefs to which respect is owed because a member of the community possesses the belief. Coupled with the assumed fact that some state action has placed a wedge between the belief and its possessor, public authority can rightly try to promote the good of harmony among any person's beliefs, choices, and conduct by relieving that person of the state-imposed burden.

This good we might call *personal integrity*. Its value can be enhanced by connection between a belief possessed and a greater-than-human source of meaning and value. The good of personal integrity then acquires the added value of harmony with God, the gods, or some other divine principle. When this connection is made, public authority can promote *two* goods by making it easier rather than harder for persons in the community to be religious: a person's inner harmony and that same person's harmony with the higher power.

Thus there are two important values more or less constantly on hand and available to be promoted by public authority: personal integrity and the good of religion itself. We might say that together they make a prima facie case for "conscience protection." Over against many state justifications (such as administrative convenience or uniformity for its own sake) they might well be sufficient to justify conscience protection.

So far belief in the Holy Family is indistinguishable from other member beliefs of the same class. The weakness of the prima facie or standing case is that any of these beliefs might be deeply mistaken, antisocial, or even pathological. The prima facie case can be pretty easily defeated by good extrinsic reasons, such as protecting an important component of public morality or forestalling injustice to specific individuals. For example, nothing in the Leeds defense implies or even suggests that Tony Blair was wrong about the gross injustice of sexual-orientation discrimination. The prima facie case by its own force has no tendency to belie assertions of that sort.

Interestingly Catholic Care's lawyer "abjured" (the court's word) any such basis as "respect [for] the beliefs of the Roman Catholic Church." "Wisely" so, said the court. Counsel argued that Leeds Catholic Care was an indispensable performer: it was uniquely successful placing "hard to place" children. For the children's sake, the court ought to grant the charity's prayer for relief.

This move is understandable enough. But its vulnerability is easy to see: the performance argument dissipates as soon as any competitor adoption agency catches up. This move also leaves untouched the claim that Catholic Care would do a serious injustice to same-sex couples. The performance standard's advantage lies elsewhere, in defeating that claim by claiming even greater injury to the kids.

In fact the value of organizational ministries such as Leeds Catholic Care transcends the scientifically measurable results of their activities: the number of children placed in foster or adoptive homes, the number of homeless persons fed a decent meal, the gross output of a hospital's surgical rooms, or the standardized test scores of parochial school pupils. Religious providers are not generic institutions that happen to employ some people with peculiar private motivations for doing what they do. There is a great *public* good—that is, an invaluable service to the common good of the political society—precisely in the conspicuous presence of religion integrated into the ordinary affairs of society.

Boston's Catholic authorities did a better job articulating the grounds for an exemption than did their counterparts in Leeds. Like Leeds, Boston Catholic Charities was successful in placing difficult kids. Boston defenders also referred to the good of religious witness (in effect, the twin pillars of the standing case). On several occasions they also said that a Catholic institution could not "promote an agenda that it views as morally wrong."[43] But often enough Boston defenders pointed to the proper "moral development" and thus the genuine "best interests" of the adopted child. In the words of one authoritative Church teaching, the absence of "sexual complementarity" between the parents "creates obstacles to the normal [moral] development of children."

The main thought here is that a child placed with a gay couple can scarcely be expected to receive from his or her parents sound example and moral advice about marriage as the union of male and female. When the child is later exposed to the proposal that the truth about marriage and sexual morality is deeply at odds with the parents' life together, that child is placed in an awful position. He or she is then faced with a choice between accepting the proposal and a profound repudiation of those who have loved and nurtured him or her. This raises the possibility that the Boston authorities sought to avoid complicity in injustice more or rather than seeking conscientious exemption, as is often the case with abortion-related exemptions.

This richer line of argument appeals mainly to morality, as it can be known to unaided human reason. This does not make the Boston Catholic Charities' claims true. If they are false, though, they are mistaken about what is reasonable and not only about what Catholic faith discloses. The advantage of this line of argument is that it engages Tony Blair's position. The point would be that no same-sex couple is wrongfully discriminated against if the only way to avoid that putative wrong is to do wrong to another person—here, the child. Even in a state that recognized same-sex marriage, the common good may be enriched by a plurality of social service providers. It does not have to be one-size-fits-all. There can be state-supported works that do not, for various good reasons, mimic the moral stance of the state.

Someone might object that this is the Boston defense's great weakness. This objector might say that this line of argument (about the moral hazard to children placed in same-sex households) runs headlong into a conclusive, contrary moral judgment by the state, namely, that marriage is *not* necessarily heterosexual. Same-sex marriage is good. The objection is misplaced. No doubt Massachusetts law establishes that civil marriage is available to same-sex couples. Boston Catholic Charities does not dispute that fact. Their argument appealed rather to the truth about marriage and about sexual morality and to what is genuinely in a child's "best interests." These claims are not necessarily incompatible with Massachusetts law. The grounds for legally recognizing same-sex marriage in American jurisdictions have in fact been political norms about equality and autonomy for the adults involved. The deciding authorities in these jurisdictions have eschewed reliance on claims about the nature or meaning of marriage itself. So nothing in the legal recognition of same-sex marriage as such contradicts the proposition that Catholic Charities contributes to the common good of political society precisely by taking the stand that it would take on sexual morality, chastity, and marriage while placing difficult children in loving heterosexual households.

Another objector might say that the case studies in this section show how unfortunately individualistic the prevailing conception of freedom of religion has become. This objector would mount claims on behalf of the group or the institution or the collective and try to craft a synthetic new meaning for "religious freedom."

This objection contains an important element of truth. But that element may be obscured by introducing the concept of group. The operations of Catholic Charities or the Wesley Mission are best viewed, in my judgment, as a collaboration of so many individuals for a set purpose, a mission, or (if you like) a specific organizational common good. Whether they collaborate in health care, education, or social services, these individuals are united by their dedication not only to providing competent service but to doing so with additional shared purposes, namely, to promote or otherwise witness to the truth (value, soundness) of the religion that animates their shared work.

Once we see thus far it becomes apparent that when any member's conduct is reasonably judged by those in charge to be *contrary* to that set of purposes—like that of Lisa Reimer or Jacqui Griffin—then that person frustrates the collaboration. In doing so she treats the others involved in the work unfairly; she (in effect, even if not by design) undermines their project and takes away from them the opportunity to do as they have covenanted to do.

Conclusion

The central emerging challenge to religious freedom in the United States is the threat to conscience protection. The formidable novelty today is that the threat stems not from administrative convenience or collective interests but from claims about public morality, the demands of justice, and the rights of others. The high valuation of abortion access and sexual-orientation equality among powerful segments of American society is the critical force. For religious freedom to flourish, this force would have to be stymied somewhere short of Leigh's "new orthodoxy." Anyone can see that resistance to sexual-orientation equality (less so abortion) is already treated by many as if it were morally indistinguishable from racism. Insofar as that comparison flourishes, adequate conscience protection will be lost. Indeed we can already see two arcs of development in the law of conscience protection under this sort of pressure. One is captured in Tony Blair's comments: there is a "public realm" whose precise boundaries may be disputed but which includes at least any act or institution that receives public funds. In that realm there is one set of norms for all comers, all players, without exception. (No discrimination whatsoever by anybody. Full stop.) The second arc is found in the American contraceptive mandates and in some of the foreign laws examined herein, where the subject matter of religious freedom is limited to belief and to acts within the church (or synagogue or mosque), mainly the community's worship. These arcs seem to converge upon the same point: the privatization of religion.

Notes

1. For an illuminating discussion of these issues, see K. Greenawalt, "Coercion and Religious Exercises", in G. Bradley, ed., *Challenges to Religious Liberty in the Twenty-First Century*, 49–70 (Cambridge 2012).
2. *People v. Ruggles*, 8 Johns. 290 (NY Sup. Ct. 1811).
3. *State v. Chandler*, 2 Del. 553, 577–578 (1837).
4. *Burstyn v. Wilson*, 343 U.S. 495 (1952).
5. John Witte. "Soul Wars: New Battles, New Norms," *Review of Faith & International Affairs* 5, no. 1 (2007): 13–19.
6. Rosalind Hackett, ed., *Proselytization Revisited* (London: Equinox, 2010), 68.
7. *Church of Lukumi v. Hialeah*, 508 U.S. 520 (1993).
8. *Barnette v. West Virginia*, 319 U.S. 624 (1943).

9. *Wisconsin v. Yoder*, 406 U.S. 205 (1972).

10. 18 U.S.C. 3597(b) 1994.

11. Sec. 728 of Title VII of Division C (Financial Services and General Government Appropriations Act) of the Consolidated Appropriations Act, 2010, Pub. L. No. 111–117.

12. Sec. 811 of Title VIII of Division C (Financial Services and General Government Appropriations Act) of the Consolidated Appropriations Act, 2010, Pub. L. No. 111–117.

13. "Obama's Commencement Address at Notre Dame," *New York Times*, May 17, 2009, http://www.nytimes.com/2009/05/17/us/politics/17text-obama.html.

14. I am grateful to Christopher Tollefsen for pointing out this conscience challenge.

15. *Catholic Charities of Diocese of Albany v. Serio*, 859 N.E.2d 459, 462–463 (NY Ct. App. 2006).

16. Ibid., 463.

17. Ibid., 462.

18. Ibid.

19. Ibid., 468.

20. Robert George, *Making Men Moral: Civil Liberties and Public Morality* (New York: Oxford University Press, 1993), 48–82.

21. Ian Leigh, "Homophobic Speech, Equality Denial, and Religious Expression," in *Extreme Speech and Democracy*, ed. Ivan Hare and James Weinstein (New York: Oxford University Press, 2009), 375–76.

22. "No Exemption from Gay Rights Law," BBC.uk.com, January 29, 2007, http://news.bbc.co.uk/2/hi/uk_news/politics/6311097.stm.

23. Leigh, "Homophobic Speech," 375–76.

24. Reference re: Same-Sex Marriage (2004) 3 S.C.R. 698 (Can.).

25. Civil Marriage Act, SC 2005, ch. 33 §§ 3, 3.1.

26. *Smith and Chymyshyn v. Knights of Columbus*, 2005 BCHRT 544.

27. Iain Benson, "The Freedom of Conscience and Religion in Canada: Challenges and Opportunities," *Emory International Law Review* 21, no. 2 (2007): 146.

28. Robert Matas, "Catholic School Denies Firing Lesbian Teacher," *Globe and Mail* (Toronto), April 29, 2010.

29. Jeff Lee, "Sexual Orientation Led to Firing, Teacher Claims," *Vancouver Sun*, April 29, 2010.

30. Human Rights and Equal Opportunity Commission, *Report of Inquiry into a Complaint of Discrimination in Employment and Occupation*, HRC Report No. 6, 1998.

31. *Catholic Care (Diocese of Leeds) v. Charity Commission for England and Wales & Anor* [2010] EWHC 520 (Ch) (March 17, 2010), para. 16.

32. Ibid.

33. See CNS press release (copy in author's possession).

34. Simon Caldwell, "English, Welsh Bishops Say Equality Bill Redefines Who Can Be Priest," *Catholic News Service*, December 9, 2009, http://www.catholicnews.com/data/stories/cns/0905419.htm.

35. *R. (Amicus) v. Secretary of State for Trade and Industry* [2004] EWHC 860 (Queen's Bench Division) (Administrative Court) para. 104.

36. Notes 25–29 and accompanying text.

37. *Lawrence v. Texas*, 539 U.S. 558 (2003).

38. Ibid., 575.

39. *Goodridge v. Department of Public Health*, 798 N.E. 2d 941 (2003).

40. "Plaintiffs' Notice of Motion and Motion for a Preliminary Injunction, and Memorandum of Points and Authorities in Support of Motion for a Preliminary Injunction," scotusblog.com, May 27, 2009, http://www.scotusblog.com/wp-content/uploads/2009/05/prop-8-injujnx-motion-5-27-09.pdf.

41. Daniel Avila, "Same-Sex Adoption in Massachusetts, the Catholic Church, and the Good of Children," *Children's Legal Rights Journal* 27, no. 3 (2007): 1–47.

42. *Catholic Care (Diocese of Leeds) v Charity Commission for England and Wales & Anor* [2010] EWHC 520 (Ch) (March 17, 2010), para. 4.

43. Avila, "Same-Sex Adoption in Massachusetts," 13.

PART FOUR

CONSTITUTIONAL MODELS, LAW, AND THE ISLAMIC EXPERIENCE

10

Assertive and Passive Secularism

State Neutrality, Religious Demography, and the Muslim Minority in the United States

AHMET T. KURU

Introduction

In November 2004 I presented a summary of my book project on assertive and passive secularism at a panel in Paris.[1] Several French graduate students in the audience seemed to be uncomfortable by my depiction of assertive secularism in France as exclusionary toward religion in the public sphere, in opposition to the passive secularism in the United States, which tolerates public religions. One student reflected that discontent in her question about restrictive state policies toward Muslims in America in the aftermath of 9/11. Beyond being a critique of overromanticizing religious liberty in the United States, that question was referring to a major challenge to the United States: the integration of Muslims. In this chapter I argue that the problems American Muslims faced following 9/11 are not because of but despite passive secularism in the United States.

I define the United States as a secular state because its Congress and courts are free from institutional religious control and it is constitutionally neutral toward religions, as reflected in its lack of an officially established religion. I do not include the "separation of the state and religion" into the definition of secularism because the state and religion always have certain levels of interactions even in well-known examples of secular states, such as the United States, France, and Turkey.[2] "Religious liberty" is not part of my definition either, because it is neither a necessary nor a sufficient condition of being a secular state. By having a secular legal system and constitutional neutrality toward religions, *secular states* diverge from *religious states* (such as Iran, Saudi Arabia, and the Vatican) that embrace religious laws and have official religions; *states with established religions* (such as England, Greece, and Denmark) that have secular legal systems but also established religions; and *antireligious states*

(China, North Korea, and Cuba) that combine legal secular systems with a certain level of hostility toward religions.

Despite their shared characteristics as secular states, there is a sharp policy distinction between the United States, which allows students to display religious symbols; France, which bans such symbols in public schools; and Turkey, which prohibits them in all educational institutions. This difference can be explained by the dominance of two distinct types of secularism in these cases. Assertive secularism, which requires the state to play an assertive role in excluding religion from the public sphere, is dominant in France and Turkey. The dominant ideology in the United States, however, is passive secularism, which demands the state to play a passive role by allowing public visibility of religion.[3]

The constitutions of these three states indicate the dominance of the two types of secularism. The French and Turkish Constitutions similarly identify their states as secular: "France is an indivisible, secular, democratic, and social Republic" (Article 2), and "The Republic of Turkey is a democratic, secular and social State" (Article 2). They both refer to secularism as an identifier of the state without delineating the limits of state intervention in the religious realm. The U.S. Constitution, in contrast, does not explicitly use the term *secular*. Instead the First Amendment prohibits the state from establishing or prohibiting a religion: "Congress shall make no law respecting an establishment of religion, or prohibiting the free exercise thereof." The First Amendment is part of what is known as the Bill of Rights. This implies that secularism in the United States is primarily an issue of individual rights rather than an established comprehensive doctrine that defines the good life.

In general these three states have opposite attitudes toward religion in their public spheres. In the United States there is officially sanctioned public visibility of monotheism. The Pledge of Allegiance daily recited in public schools includes the phrase "one nation under God."[4] "In God We Trust" appears on all U.S. currency. Several official oaths, including the presidential oath of office, customarily contain the statement "so help me God" and are often made by placing the left hand on a Bible. Sessions of the U.S. Congress begin with a prayer by a publicly funded chaplain, and the sessions of the U.S. Supreme Court start with the invocation "God save the United States and this Honorable Court." Such official religious discourses are unthinkable in France or Turkey.

The dominance of a secular ideology always faces resistance. Therefore states are not monolithically assertive or passive secularist. Ideological struggles result in changes, inconsistencies, and exceptions in state policies toward religion. In France the supporters of assertive secularism (*laïcité de combat*) have been dominant, while those of passive secularism (*laïcité plurielle*) have been in opposition. Similarly in Turkey there has been a conflict between the dominant assertive secularists (the Kemalists) and the resisting passive secularists (the pro-Islamic conservatives and liberals).

Passive secularism has been dominant in the United States, but there has been a struggle between its two opposite interpretations: accommodationism and separationism. The accommodationists regard close state-religion entanglements, including official monotheistic references, organized school prayer, and public funding of religious schools through vouchers, compatible with secularism as long as the state does not favor one particular religion at the expense of others. The separationists, however, see close relations between the state and religion as contrary to secularism. The ideal principle of relationship for them is absolute separation symbolized by the metaphorical "wall of separation." According to data collected by Kenneth Wald and Joseph Kobylka, from 1943 to 1980 the U.S. Supreme Court made thirteen separationist decisions (59 percent), eight accommodationist decisions (36 percent), and one mixed decision on significant state-religion cases. From 1981 to 2002, however, the numbers are almost reversed: fifteen separationist decisions (35 percent), twenty-six accommodationist decisions (60 percent), and two mixed decisions.[5]

Accommodationists and separationists represent moderate groups within the conservative and liberal blocs in the United States. The extremists on the conservative side are the members of the Christian Right who seek to establish cultural dominance of Christianity. On the liberal side, the extremists are the assertive secularists, who aim to exclude religion from the American public sphere. The Christian Right and the assertive secularists have played secondary roles in shaping U.S. policies toward religion, which have been largely shaped by nonextremist accommodationists and separationists. Despite their opposite policy preferences, these two mainstream groups jointly oppose both a cultural establishment of Christianity and an assertive secularist exclusion of religion from the public sphere. That is why I define them as defenders of two different interpretations of passive secularism.

Muslims under Assertive and Passive Secularism

The overwhelming majority (98 percent) of Turkish society is Muslim. Due to the assertive secularist dominance in the military and judiciary, however, the Turkish state has imposed sharply restrictive policies toward Islam in the public sphere, as reflected in the ban on headscarves for all students, civil servants, and elected politicians; discrimination against the graduates of Islamic public (Imam-Hatip) schools in university enrollment; and the prohibition against teaching the Qur'an to children under fifteen (and to those under twelve in summer). Seventy-five percent of people in Turkey oppose the headscarf ban, and 85 percent are against the discrimination against the Imam-Hatip graduates.[6] Thus the passive secularist (i.e., conservative and liberal) parties have generally received 75 percent of votes in elections, yet they could not lift the restrictions on public

Islamic expression in Turkey because the generals and judges have adamantly defended assertive secularism.

In France Muslims constitutes the biggest minority (8 percent), with a population of 4.5 million.[7] As the Council of State—the highest administrative court—stresses in a report, Muslims in France have experienced trouble in constructing mosques and opening schools due to historical and financial reasons, as well as bureaucratic restrictions.[8] In terms of political debates, right-wing parties have generally supported conservative Catholic views against the assertive secularist leftist politicians. Public funding of Catholic schools was a key controversial issue between these two groups. With regard to the Muslim headscarf question, however, right-wing Islamophobes allied with left-wing assertive secularists. On the other hand, multiculturalists among both rightists and leftists opposed the headscarf ban and defended passive secularism. Eventually the alliance of Islamophobes and assertive secularists dominated public opinion and imposed the ban on wearing headscarves in public schools.[9]

Although accommodationists and separationists in the United States disagree on their particular understandings of passive secularism, they agree on defending students' right to display religious symbols, such as headscarves, crosses, and kippahs. It is unconstitutional in the American legal system to prohibit some religious practices by singling them out. Therefore the prohibition of students' religious symbols in France and the headscarf ban in Turkey are unthinkable in the United States.[10] Moreover some federal and state laws in the United States provide exemptions for religious practices even from generally applicable prohibitions. In this regard, Muslim headscarves rarely became a controversial issue in America. In 2004 an elementary school in Oklahoma attempted to ban a sixth-grade Muslim student from wearing her headscarf due to the school dress code policy. During the judicial process, the U.S. Justice Department supported the student, who eventually won the case against the school.[11]

In 2007 the Pew Survey reported that there were 2.5 million Muslims in the United States, thus constituting slightly less than 1 percent of the population.[12] According to the U.S. Census Bureau, in 2000 there were 1.6 million immigrants in the United States from Muslim-majority countries.[13] Given the population increase during the past decade and the fact that a third of American Muslims are native-born,[14] it would be reasonable to calculate the number of American Muslims today as more than 3 million. Muslim sources generally cite estimates of 3 to 7 million American Muslims.[15]

Due to dominant passive secularism, Muslims have enjoyed religious freedom in the United States in terms of wearing religious dress, constructing mosques, opening Islamic schools, and founding associations.[16] American Muslims' main concerns concentrate on the spread of Islamophobia in the media and the religious profiling after the 9/11 terrorist attacks. This focus can be observed in the activities of nationwide Muslim organizations, such as the Council on American-Islamic Relations and the Islamic Society of North America.[17] Since 2001, as a result of religious and ethnic profiling, about 100,000 Muslims have experienced "FBI home and work visits, wiretapping, seizures of property, removals of aliens with technical visa violations,... and mandatory special registration" as well as "mass arrests" and "indefinite detentions."[18] Beyond individuals, investigations also targeted Muslim foundations and charitable organizations.[19]

Some televangelists and media pundits have contributed to the spread of Islamophobia in the United States.[20] Yet because passive secularism is dominant in the country, the Islamophobes failed to impose nationwide bans on Muslims' activities. If the assertive secularists had been dominant in the United States, they would have allied with Islamophobes to impose oppressive public policies on Muslims, as they did in France.

The Transformation of State Neutrality: Patterns of Change and Continuity

A contention of this chapter is that current problems Muslims face in the United States are not unique; instead they are very similar to the negative public attitudes that Catholics, Jews, Mormons, and the unaffiliated have experienced throughout American history. Both religious liberty and discrimination have followed certain historical trajectories. Analyzing such historical patterns can help us see the possibility of Muslims' integration into the United States.

In the United States the meaning of state neutrality toward religions has been constantly challenged and transformed. Throughout these transformations, changes in religious demography played crucial roles because religious affiliations are significant carriers of specific religious and ideological views. Multiple Protestant denominations in the founding period, Catholic and Jewish immigration in the late nineteenth century and early twentieth, and the growing unaffiliated, Mormon, and Muslim populations in the late twentieth century all deeply affected passive secularism, particularly the meaning of state neutrality toward religions.

I will first analyze the semi-establishment of Protestantism during which the state was supposed to be neutral toward only Protestant denominations. Then I will explore the integration of Catholics and Jews to the conceptions of passive secularism and state neutrality. The final section surveys the process in which the unaffiliated, Mormons, and Muslims have tried to become part of mainstream America and demanded a new conceptualization of state neutrality.

Passive Secularism as State Neutrality toward Protestant Denominations

The United States lacked a federally established religion from the beginning. The disestablishment of several state churches began in 1776 with the Declaration of Independence and ended in 1833, the year of disestablishment in Massachusetts. Yet the lack of established churches did not mean absolute state neutrality toward religion. Until the early twentieth century, state neutrality basically implied impartiality toward various Protestant denominations. Protestant activism, especially during the Second Great Awakening, led to the semi-establishment of nondenominational Protestantism. The evangelical mobilization against Sunday mail service in 1810–30 shows that Protestant activism was both social and political.[21] The Protestant influence "encompassed the entire public realm of education and religious instruction, and it extended to the mass media and to societies and movements for moral and social reform."[22] Christianity was taken as "a part of the common law,"[23] and public schools were acculturating students to nondenominational Protestantism. The federal government was supporting Protestant missionaries, particularly in their attempt to convert Native Americans and southern slaves, as well as in their activities abroad.[24]

According to Sydney Ahlstrom, the heyday of Protestant "quasi-establishment" was the period between 1815 and 1860.[25] During the Civil War (1861–65), this semi-establishment was shaken by the division among Protestants and the use of religion for bloody conflicts. The Civil War era included "a vociferous battle of words debating the sinfulness or godliness of slavery, a retributive, bloody, fratricidal war in which both sides claimed God's favor, and a widespread belief that out of carnage would come the fulfillment of Christ's millennial promise."[26]

In the words of Robert Handy, "[B]etween 1870 and 1920 especially the state courts were moving away from a perception of America as a Christian nation toward a secular-based perspective."[27] The evangelical forces were still fighting back. In the 1910s eleven states made obligatory either or both morning prayer and Bible reading in public schools. That was something only one state, Massachusetts, had been enforcing. In response, courts in five other states banned Bible reading in public schools. As a result, "the America of 1920" was different from "what it had been in 1880" because "the informal hegemony that the Protestant movement had long held over American religious and cultural life by its numerical pluralities and the power of its organizational networks was weakened."[28]

In the late nineteenth century and early twentieth, two factors led to the demise of Protestant semi-establishment. The first was the growing influence of Catholic and Jewish immigrants. In 1789 Catholics numbered only 35,000 among 4 million Americans. The Catholic population reached 1.7 million by

1850 and 3 million by 1860; that led to the anti-Catholic nativist movement.[29] Protestants sought to maintain their dominance in the public schools, which taught the Protestant King James version of the Bible[30] and the Protestant version of the Ten Commandments, which prohibits idolatry.[31] The public schools' curricula were "rife with material that Catholics and Jews found offensive."[32] For that reason, Catholics opened their own schools. In 1910 the Catholic population reached 16 million out of 92 million Americans.[33] Between 1880 and 1920 the Jewish population also increased, from around 250,000 to 3.5 million, mainly due to immigration from Eastern Europe and Russia.[34] The Jews also became better organized and pushed for further state-religion separation.[35] In 1913 the Anti-Defamation League was founded to defend Jews' rights and interests and criticize any state favoring of Protestantism.

The second factor that weakened the Protestant domination was the spread of secularist ideas, including those based on European scientific perspectives, among the American elite. Jose Casanova associates "the secularization of American higher education" with "the loss of Protestant cultural hegemony."[36] Some scholars explain the disestablishment of Protestantism through modernization theory, arguing that American public life, especially education, "was secularized not as the result of direct attacks by militant secularists. Instead, as with the modern civilization generally, secular values and ways of thinking gradually (and for the most part unobtrusively) acquired power in the hearts and minds of people."[37] Christian Smith and his colleagues rightly criticize this perspective in *The Secular Revolution*.[38] They attach importance to human agency and ideological struggles in the disestablishment of Protestantism. Smith writes, "[H]istorical secularization of the institutions of American public life was not a natural, inevitable, and abstract by-product of modernization; rather it was the outcome of a struggle between contending groups with conflicting interests seeking to control social knowledge and institutions."[39]

The secularists who challenged Protestant domination formed two major groups. One group included those who held secularism as a personal ideology and were generally members of associations like Freemasons and Freethinkers.[40] The other group was made up of new professionals, such as teachers, journalists, writers, artists, and businesspeople, who regarded Protestant principles and prohibitions as a barrier to their professionalism and social mobility.[41] These groups secularized American schools and universities by founding new institutions, secularizing old ones, and taking over the National Education Association.[42] They also influenced the U.S. Supreme Court to adopt new separationist legal perspectives by lobbying for the appointment of liberal justices and writing *amicus curiae* briefs.[43] In sum, the semi-establishment of Protestantism was weakened by the early twentieth century as a result of both secularist and religious (Catholic and Jewish) challenges.

Passive Secularism as State Neutrality toward Catholics and Jews

In 1928 Al Smith, the four-time governor of New York, became the first Catholic to run for president as a major party nominee. Smith, the candidate of the Democratic Party, received 41 percent of the vote, while his Republican rival, Herbert Hoover, won the election with 58 percent. Smith's experience had dual meanings. On the one hand, his nomination showed that Catholics were perceived as an integrated part of American sociopolitical life. On the other hand, anti-Catholic prejudices, which played a major role in his electoral failure, indicated that negative perceptions toward Catholics still persisted and that full integration of Catholics would take more time.

According to some observers, Smith was defeated mainly because of "Prohibition, Prejudice[,] and Prosperity."[44] The United States was a prosperous country at that time, which helped Hoover as the nominee of the incumbent Republican Party. Prejudice mainly refers to anti-Catholic sentiments among the Protestant majority. Prohibition was a related factor because it was primarily supported by Protestant activists.[45] Since the ratification of the Eighteenth Amendment in 1919, there had been a nationwide prohibition of the manufacture, sale, and transportation of alcohol. Smith was largely perceived as being against Prohibition, which limited his chance to receive votes from Prohibition's supporters. According to Joseph Gusfield, "Prohibition had become a symbol of cultural domination or loss. If the Prohibitionists won, it was also a victory of the rural, Protestant American over the secular, urban, and non-Protestant immigrant."[46] In 1933 the Twenty-first Amendment abolished federal Prohibition and left the issue to the states and local administrations. The failure of Prohibition damaged the prestige of Protestant social activism and undercut its effort to defend morality through legal restrictions.

During and immediately after World War II, the Jewish population increased to around 5 million,[47] while its sociopolitical impact reached deeper. Having waged a war against Nazi Germany and reacting to human rights violations during the Holocaust, the United States became more eager to eliminate anti-Semitic discrimination at home.

In addition to the constantly growing Catholic and Jewish influences, court activism for church-state separation further weakened Protestant domination in the United States. In *Everson v. Board of Education* in 1947, the U.S. Supreme Court reinterpreted the First Amendment in a sharply separationist way:

> Neither a state nor the Federal Government can set up a church. Neither can pass laws which aid one religion, aid all religions, or prefer one religion over another.... No tax in any amount, large or small, can be levied to support any religious activities or institutions, whatever they may be

called, or whatever form they may adopt to teach or practice religion. Neither a state nor the Federal Government can, openly or secretly, participate in the affairs of any religious organizations or groups and vice versa. In the words of Jefferson, the clause against establishment of religion by law was intended to erect "a wall of separation between Church and State."[48]

Protestants reacted to *Everson* in different ways: Evangelicals generally criticized the decision, while mainline Protestants largely supported it. The latter founded the Protestants and Other Americans United for Separation of Church and State in 1947 to support separationism.[49]

In the 1950s a monotheistic perspective emerged with a discourse shared by many Protestants, Catholics, and Jews. That discourse was in line with U.S. policy against the "godless" communists at home and abroad, particularly during the McCarthy era (1950–54). In 1952 Congress passed legislation to declare that each year there would be a National Day of Prayer, which was signed into law by President Harry Truman. Three subsequent legislations were signed by Dwight Eisenhower. In 1954 Congress added the phrase "under God" to the Pledge of Allegiance, which had existed since 1892 without such a reference.[50] In 1955 Congress passed a law that made it mandatory for all coinage and paper currency to display the motto "In God We Trust."[51] Since 1864 this motto had been used in a limited way, appearing on only some coins. In 1956 another law was enacted to declare "In God We Trust" the national motto of the United States, replacing "E Pluribus Unum" (Out of Many, One), which had been used since the founding period.[52] Eisenhower's famous statement summarizes the official mood of this period: "Our government makes no sense unless it is founded on a deeply held religious belief—and I don't care what it is."[53]

Beyond these official discourses, the monotheistic mood also became dominant in American public institutions, including the armed forces and hospitals.[54] Even the U.S. Supreme Court followed the zeitgeist of the 1950s and took a more accommodationist stand toward state-religion relations. An important case of that period was *Zorach v. Clauson* (1952). The Court upheld a "released time" program in which public schools allowed students to be dismissed from classroom activities in order to take religious instruction in religious institutions; no public facilities or sources were used, and students were attending based on parental requests. Justice Douglas wrote the majority opinion with an accommodationist perspective: "We are a religious people whose institutions presuppose a Supreme Being."[55]

During the 1950s accommodationism emerged as the dominant perspective that reinterpreted passive secularism as state neutrality toward three monotheistic religions (Protestantism, Catholicism, and Judaism). In the 1960s, however, it faced a strong challenge from the separationists, who primarily asked for state neutrality toward the unaffiliated, as explained below.

Passive Secularism as State Neutrality toward the Unaffiliated, Mormons, and Muslims

According to the Pew Forum's 2007 data, the same proportion of Americans expressed a favorable view of Mormons (53 percent) as American Muslims (53 percent), which is a higher proportion than those favorable toward atheists (35 percent) but lower than favorability ratings for Evangelical Protestants (60), Catholics (76), or Jews (76). The survey was conducted at a time when a Mormon politician, Mitt Romney, was running for the Republican presidential nomination. Therefore it also included a question about presidential candidates and their religion. Higher ratios of Americans were unlikely to vote for an atheist (61 percent), a Muslim (45), or a Mormon (25) than those with reservations toward an Evangelical Protestant (16), a Jew (11), or a Catholic (7).[56] Obviously public opinion toward certain groups of people and state neutrality toward them are two different phenomena, but they are still strongly connected to each other, especially in the United States. This section analyzes three groups that have yet to be fully integrated into the American sociopolitical system: the unaffiliated, Mormons, and Muslims.

The Unaffiliated

The proportion of the unaffiliated in American society (16 percent) has doubled since 1990.[57] They include atheists (4 percent) and those without a religion (agnostics or believers in God but who profess no religion; 12 percent). Percentages of those with a religious affiliation are Evangelical Protestants (26 percent), mainline Protestants (18), black Protestants (7), Catholics (24), Mormons (2), Jews (2), Muslims (1), and others (4).[58]

The unaffiliated have been strong supporters of separationism. Their impact on state policies toward religion in the United States has been greater than their sheer number would suggest because the unaffiliated are disproportionately elite members of American society. Several plaintiffs in crucial Supreme Court decisions, such as those on religious instruction, Bible reading, organized prayer, and the Pledge of Allegiance in public schools, were unaffiliated, including atheists.[59]

Since the 1960s the Supreme Court has played a leading role in weakening the monotheist domination and expansion of state neutrality toward the unaffiliated. In 1962, in *Engel v. Vitale*, the Court decided that it was unconstitutional for public schools to officially compose particular school prayers and to require their recitation. The prayer tried in the Court was "Almighty God, we acknowledge our dependence upon Thee, and we beg Thy blessing upon us, our parents, our teachers and our Country." The Court banned this prayer by stressing that "[n]either the fact that the prayer may be denominationally neutral nor the fact that its observance on the part of the students is voluntary" could make prayer in public schools constitutional.[60] A year later, in *Abington v. Schempp*, the Court ruled against the voluntary recitation of Bible verses and the Lord's Prayer in public schools.[61] Since that time the Court has declared unconstitutional several related issues, such as a state law on "a moment of silence" and a public school's student-led prayer at a football game.[62]

The *Engel* and *Abington* decisions took place during the presidency of John F. Kennedy, who "in both his personal style and his political philosophy, was arguably the most secularist American president since Jefferson."[63] Kennedy particularly emphasized church-state separation to respond to criticisms that as a Catholic, he would mix the two.[64] According to public surveys from 1963 to 1994, opponents outnumbered supporters of the Supreme Court's prohibition of school prayer by an average of 60 to 35 percent.[65] Conservative Protestants and Catholics initiated several school prayer amendment proposals to overturn Court decisions.[66] Despite mass support, these proposals were unsuccessful, mainly due to elite backing of the Supreme Court's decisions, especially by separationist civic associations such as the American Civil Liberties Union and elite religious groups such as liberal Protestants and Jews. Elite support for the decisions "was demonstrated when Leo Pfeffer, Counsel for the American Jewish Congress, rounded up 110 law school deans and professors of law and political science to sign a letter to the Senate Judiciary Committee supporting *Engel* and opposing school-prayer amendments."[67]

Secularization of public school system was an important step toward state neutrality toward the unaffiliated. Yet the debate about this issue is still going on, as seen in the controversy over the phrase "one nation under God" in the Pledge of Allegiance.[68] Even the Supreme Court judges disagree on the meaning of state neutrality. In a recent case, the accommodationist Justice Scalia, joined by Justices Rehnquist and Thomas, argued that the public honoring of God and the Ten Commandments is constitutional, because "[t]he three most popular religions in the United States, Christianity, Judaism, and Islam—which combined account for 97.7% of all believers—are monotheistic. All of them, moreover (Islam included), believe that the Ten Commandments were given by God to Moses, and are divine prescriptions for a virtuous life." He added that "it is entirely clear from our Nation's historical practices that the Establishment Clause permits this disregard of polytheists and believers in unconcerned deities, just as it permits the disregard of devout atheists."[69] Liberal Justice Stevens, joined by Justice Ginsburg, criticized Scalia's conception of neutrality as an "evil of discriminating" against polytheists and atheists, which was forbidden by the Establishment Clause.[70]

Mormons

Like Catholics and Jews, the followers of the Church of Jesus Christ of Latter-day Saints (Mormons) faced official and societal discrimination in the nineteenth and twentieth century. Mormons are still objects of stereotypes and prejudices, like the unaffiliated and Muslims. Mormons' impact on the transformation of passive secularism and state neutrality in America was relatively marginal due to their limited population and geographical isolation. Seventy-two percent of all American Mormons live in Utah.[71]

The first Free Exercise Clause case that the U.S. Supreme Court heard was on Mormon polygamy. In *Reynolds v. U.S.* (1878), which is still a frequently cited precedent in cases on Free Exercise and even the Establishment Clause, the Court upheld the Morrill Anti-Bigamy Act that prohibited the Mormon practice of polygamy. The Court compared polygamy to human sacrifice as religious worship and defined it as "odious," "an offence against society," and "almost exclusively a feature of the life of Asiatic and African people."[72] A decade later the Court made two other decisions with clearly anti-Mormon language. In *Davis v. Beason*, it criticized polygamy for being a crime "by the laws of all civilized and Christian countries."[73] In *Mormon Church v. United States*, the Court depicted polygamy as a "nefarious doctrine," a "barbarous practice," and a "plot on our civilization." The Court also targeted the Mormon Church by defining it as an "organization of a community for the spread and practice of polygamy" and therefore "a return to barbarism."[74]

The official attitude toward Mormons became less discriminatory with the above-mentioned expansion of state neutrality toward non-Protestant religions. Mormons have also actively endeavored to integrate themselves into mainstream America. Theologically they abolished polygamy (in 1890–1904) and ended antiblack racial discrimination (in 1978). They have also attached importance to defining Mormonism as a local, American religion. Politically Mormons have the highest tendency among religions in the United States of being conservative and supporting the Republican Party.[75]

Romney's run for the Republican presidential nomination in 2008 was similar to the experience of the Catholic Al Smith in 1928. On the one hand, it revealed Mormons' integration into the American sociopolitical system; on the other hand, the pubic debate around Romney's religious identity showed the persistence of anti-Mormon attitudes in certain segments of American society. Nevertheless, in 2012 elections, Romney succeeded to become the first Mormon nominee for U.S. president from a major party (GOP).

Muslims

U.S. policies toward Muslims, unlike those toward the unaffiliated and Mormons, have always had some international dimensions. For the separationists, one of the strongest historical documents suggesting that the United States was not founded as a Christian state was the Treaty of Peace and Friendship signed with the ruler of Tripoli, a semi-independent province of the Ottoman Empire. It was signed in 1796, unanimously approved by the Senate a year later, and signed by President John Adams. Its most important part is Article 11:

> As the government of the United States of America is not in any sense founded on the Christian religion,—as it has in itself no character of enmity against the laws, religion, or tranquility of Musselmen,—and, as the said States never entered into any war or act of hostility against any Mehomitan nation, it is declared by the parties that no pretext arising from religious opinions shall ever produce an interruption of the harmony existing between the two countries.[76]

More than a century later, Muslims became visible in the American public sphere during the civil rights movement of the 1960s with figures such as Malcolm X and Muhammad Ali. The expansion of the American Muslim population was associated with the 1965 immigration reform law, which eliminated discrimination against non-European immigrants. Following this legal reform, the total number of people in the United States who were immigrants from Muslim-majority countries increased from 142,202 in 1960 to 185,953 in 1970, 487,654 in 1980, 858,243 in 1990, and 1,582,746 in 2000.[77]

The habit of equating Arabs and Muslims in the United States is deeply misleading. Among Arab Americans "an estimated two-thirds are Christian."[78] Among American Muslims, Arabs constitute only 26 percent.[79] The United States, apart from the Hajj, "is the only place in the world in which every ethnic Muslim group in the *ummah* and every Muslim school of thought currently in the world are found."[80]

Starting with Bill Clinton, U.S. presidents have made regular gestures toward Muslims at home and abroad, such as celebrating Muslim holidays with public messages and organizing official *iftaar* dinners in the White House during the month of Ramadan. Since 2001 the U.S. Postal Service has issued a stamp with Arabic calligraphy to commemorate Islamic holidays.[81] In 2007 Keith Ellison of the Democratic Party was elected to the U.S. Congress as the first Muslim representative. A year later another Muslim congressperson, André Carson, was elected.

During the 2008 presidential campaign, some opponents falsely portrayed Democratic nominee Barack Hussein Obama as a secret Muslim. When he endorsed Obama, the former secretary of state Colin Powell, a Republican, responded to such rumors: "Well, the correct answer is, he is not a Muslim, he's a Christian.... But the really right answer is: What if he is? Is there something wrong with being a Muslim in this country? The answer's no, that's not America.... Yet I have heard senior members of my own party drop the suggestion, 'He's a Muslim and he might be associated with terrorists'."[82]

The first female president of the Islamic Association of North America, Ingrid Mattson, was among several religious leaders who delivered the inaugural prayer for Obama in the National Cathedral.[83] Since his election President Obama has attached particular importance to reshaping the public perception of the United States in Muslim societies. Following 9/11, anti-Americanism in Muslim-majority countries increased due to the U.S. invasion of Iraq and Afghanistan, while Islamophobic discourse also increased in the United States. To stop the vicious cycle of anti-Americanism and Islamophobia, Obama gave a speech in Ankara, Turkey, within the first hundred days of his presidency, stressing, "[T]he United States is not and will never be at war with Islam." A few months later he gave a speech in Cairo, Egypt, in which he presented freedoms Muslims enjoy in and their contribution to the United States as proof that the country is not against Islam:

> The dream of opportunity for all people has not come true for everyone in America, but its promise exists for all who come to our shores—and that includes nearly 7 million American Muslims in our country today who, by the way, enjoy incomes and educational levels that are higher than the American average. Moreover, freedom in America is indivisible from the freedom to practice one's religion. That is why there is a mosque in every state of our union, and over 1,200 mosques within our borders. That is why the U.S. government has gone to court to protect the right of women and girls to wear the hijab, and to punish those who would deny it. So let there be no doubt: Islam is a part of America.[84]

Despite these official efforts, negative views toward American Muslims still persist. This is largely due to two trends that feed each other: Islamophobic propaganda and isolated incidents of terrorist activities among American Muslims. These two factors were effective in the controversy on the planned Islamic center near Ground Zero. According to *Time* magazine, 61 percent of Americans opposed the project, while just 26 percent supported it.[85]

The contention of this chapter is that in the future American Muslims will express deeper willingness to integrate into American society, which will be facilitated by expansion of state neutrality and societal toleration toward them. This process is similar to the integration of and state neutrality toward other religious minorities in the United States.

In sum, state neutrality and societal toleration toward the unaffiliated, Mormons, and Muslims have taken important steps forward but have yet to be fully achieved. Two different public discourses have come forward in the United States, both of which promise the incorporation of certain minority groups. A secularist discourse, which emphasizes the wall of separation between the state and religions, has offered more state neutrality toward the unaffiliated (including atheists) and nonmonotheists (including Buddhists and Hindus). Meanwhile religious discourse has become more inclusionary; it had already transformed from "Protestant" to "Judeo-Christian" and has recently become "Abrahamic" (incorporating Muslims).[86]

Conclusion

State policies toward religions are not monolithic in any country. States treat diverse religions differently regarding such factors as their majority or minority status, demographic proportion, and historical legacy, as well as the state's own ideology. The dominant type of secular ideology plays a key role in shaping state policies toward religion. Assertive secularism, which aims to exclude religion from the public sphere, has been the dominant ideology in France and Turkey. It has led to exclusionary policies toward religion in general and Islam in particular in both of these countries, although Muslims are a minority in France and the majority in Turkey. In the United States the dominant ideology has been passive secularism, which requires the state to play a passive role that allows public visibility of religion. State-religion controversies in the United States have focused on two interpretations of passive secularism: accommodationism and separationism. In spite of their disagreements on such issues as organized prayer in public schools, state funding of private religious schools, and monotheistic official discourses, both groups defend individuals' religious freedoms, including those of Muslims.

Despite religious-friendly passive secularism, Muslims have faced religious profiling and other legal restrictions in the aftermath of 9/11, owing to security concerns and rising Islamophobia in the United States. That is not a uniquely Muslim experience, but rather is part of the general transformation process of state neutrality in the United States. From the founding period to the early twentieth century, state neutrality basically implied impartiality toward all Protestant denominations. Later years of the century brought the decline of official and societal discrimination against Catholics and Jews and thus included them in the expanding definition of state neutrality. Currently the U.S. Supreme Court includes six Catholics, three Jews, and not a single Protestant justice, which reveals how integrated into the American sociopolitical system these groups have become. Starting in the 1960s, the challenge has been the political and social integration of the unaffiliated, Mormons, and Muslims, which has led to a reconceptualization of the meaning of state neutrality and passive secularism. This transformation has included dynamic interactions between the changing religious demography and ideological struggles.

Among several minority groups discussed in this chapter, Catholics hold a special position because they have the largest population and anti-Catholic agitation had the biggest impact on the transformation of state neutrality in the United States. Casanova emphasizes that there are "striking similarities between today's discourse on Islam as a fundamentalist, anti-modern religion incompatible with democracy, and yesterday's discourse on Catholicism."[87] Beyond their similarly nativist characteristics, anti-Catholic and Islamophobic sentiments also have different aspects. A major feature of anti-Catholicism was the claim that Catholics owed allegiance to a foreign authority (the Vatican), and thus their loyalty to the United States was suspicious. Thus Kennedy, in his famous address on faith and politics, stressed, "I believe in an America . . . where no public official either requests or accepts instructions on public policy from the Pope."[88] The distrust toward Muslim Americans does not focus on their alleged loyalty to an authority abroad (there is no longer a caliph); instead anti-Muslim perceptions concentrate on their loyalties to a different set of laws (Islamic law) and political perspectives (on the U.S. policy toward the Middle East).[89] Orthodox Jews, for example, are also loyal to their own religious laws, but their policy preferences about the Middle East are largely compatible with official U.S. policies toward the region.

Religion-friendly passive secularism provides a more effective route for the integration of unconventional religious groups, including Muslims, than assertive secularism, which is intolerant toward public religions. Facing the challenge of integrating Muslim, French rulers have tried to create an "Islam of France." Yet they have not sufficiently endeavored to rethink their own understanding and practice of secularism to facilitate Muslims' integration. Achieving integration requires dual actions: Muslims' adaptation to the local conditions in terms of both thought and behavior, and Western states' transformation of their theory and practice of state neutrality. Assertive secularism finds it hard to achieve such a transformation due to its ideological stiffness and its inability to recognize religious communities in the public sphere. Passive secularism, on the other hand, is ideologically much more flexible and respects the public existence of multiple religious communities. Passive secularism and state neutrality experienced significant transformations in U.S. history, and they have the potential to evolve further for integrating Muslims.

Notes

1. I would like to thank Allen Hertzke, Andrew Koppelman, and Kambiz GhaneaBassiri for their helpful comments on an earlier draft of this chapter. Some portions of the chapter are adapted from my book, Ahmet T. Kuru, *Secularism and State Policies toward Religion: The United States, France, and Turkey* (New York: Cambridge University Press. 2009); they are used with permission.

2. Analyzing particular state regulations of religion, Jonathan Fox concludes that the United States is the only example of absolute state-religion separation in the world. Jonathan Fox, *A World Survey of Religion and the State* (New York: Cambridge University Press, 2008), 108. Yet there are constant state-religion interactions in the United States at symbolic and discursive levels. State-religion entanglements are also visible in American political campaigns and religious lobby groups. See Allen D. Hertzke, *Representing God in Washington: The Role of Religious Lobbies in the American Polity* (Knoxville: University of Tennessee Press, 1998).

3. For various types of secularism, see Charles Taylor, "Modes of Secularism," in *Secularism and Its Critics*, ed. Rajeev Bhargava (Delhi: Oxford University Press, 1999); Wilfred M. McClay, "Two Concepts of Secularism," in *Religion Returns to the Public Square: Faith and Policy in America*, ed. Hugh Heclo and Wilfred M. McClay (Baltimore: Johns Hopkins University Press, 2002); Alfred Stepan, "The Multiple Secularisms of Modern Democracies and Autocracies," in *Rethinking Secularism*, ed. Craig Calhoun, Mark Juergensmeyer, and Jonathan VanAntwerpen (New York: Oxford University Press, 2010).

4. According to a survey in 2002, nine out of ten Americans think that the phrase "under God" should remain in the pledge. "Vast Majority in U.S. Support 'under God,'" June 30, 2002, http://archives.cnn.com/2002/US/06/29/poll.pledge/.

5. Kenneth D. Wald, *Religion and Politics in the United States* (New York: Rowman & Littlefield, 2003), 85–87; Joseph F. Kobylka, "The Mysterious Case of Establishment Clause Litigation: How Organized Litigants Foiled Legal Change," in *Contemplating Courts*, ed. Lee Epstein (Washington, D.C.: CQ Press, 1995), 96, 102–3.

6. Ali Çarkoğlu and Binnaz Toprak, *Değişen Türkiye'de Din, Toplum ve Siyaset* (Istanbul: TESEV, 2006), 71, 55.

7. Farhad Khosrokhavar, "La Laïcité française à l'épreuve de l'islam," in *La Laïcité à l'épreuve: Religions et libertés dans le monde*, ed. Jean Baubérot (N.p.: Universalis, 2004), 43.

8. Conseil d'Etat, "Rapport public 2004: Réflexions sur la laïcité," La Documentation Française, 2004, 318–19, http://www.ladocumentationfrancaise.fr/rapports-publics/044000121/index.shtml, accessed on March 20, 2012. For Islamic schools in France, see John R. Bowen, *Can Islam Be French? Pluralism and Pragmatism in a Secularist State* (Princeton, N.J.: Princeton University Press, 2009), 110–132.

9. Islamophobia, according to the European Monitoring Centre on Racism and Xenophobia, has several components, including the following: "1. Islam is seen as a monolithic bloc, static and unresponsive to change. 2. Islam is seen as separate and 'other.' It does not have values in common with other cultures, is not affected by them and does not influence them. 3. Islam is seen as inferior to the West. It is seen as barbaric, irrational, primitive, and sexist. 4. Islam is seen as violent, aggressive, threatening, supportive of terrorism, and engaged in a clash of civilizations." European Monitoring Centre on Racism and Xenophobia, "Muslims in the European Union: Discrimination and Islamophobia," 2006, 61, http://fra.europa.eu/fraWebsite/research/publications/publications_per_year/previous_publications/pub_tr_islamophobia_en.htm, accessed on May 25, 2012.

10. Derek H. Davis, "Reacting to France's Ban: Headscarves and Other Religious Attire in American Public Schools," *Journal of Church and State* 46, no. 2 (2004): 232–33.

11. Brian Knowlton, "U.S. Takes Opposite Tack from France," *International Herald Tribune*, April 3, 2004.

12. Pew Research Center, "Muslim Americans: Middle Class and Mostly Mainstream," 2007, 3, 13, http://pewresearch.org/assets/pdf/muslim-americans.pdf, accessed on May 27, 2010.

13. I calculated the data on immigrants from thirty-five Muslim-majority countries using U.S. Census Bureau, "Table 3. World Region and Country or Area of Birth of the Foreign-Born Population: 1960 to 2000," www.census.gov/population/www/documentation/twps0081/ tables/tab03.xls, accessed in December 2010. For a detailed explanation, see Ahmet T. Kuru, "Muslims in France and the United States: Comparing Secular State Policies," in *The Challenge of Integration: Muslims in the United States and France*, ed. Ousmane Kane (New York: Columbia University Press, forthcoming).

14. Pew Research Center, "Muslim Americans," 1.

15. Zahid H. Bukhari, "Demography, Identity, Space: Defining American Muslims," in *Muslims in the United States,* ed. Phillippa Strum and Danielle Tarantolo (Washington, D.C.: Woodrow Wilson International Center for Scholars, 2003), 7.

16. Mücahit Bilici, "Finding Mecca in America: American Muslims and Cultural Citizenship," PhD dissertation, University of Michigan, 2008, 1; Jocelyne Cesari, "Islam, Secularism and Multiculturalism after 9/11: A Transatlantic Comparison," in *European Muslims and the Secular State*, ed. Jocelyne Cesari (Burlington, Vt.: Ashgate, 2006), 83.

17. Ibid., 154–79.

18. Louise A. Cainkar, *Homeland Insecurity: The Arab American and Muslim American Experience after 9/11* (New York: Russell Sage Foundation, 2009), 119.

19. Cesari, "Islam, Secularism and Multiculturalism," 38–40; Agha Saeed, "Muslim-American Politics: Developments, Debates and Directions," in Strum and Tarantolo, *Muslims in the United States*, 41–44.

20. Allen D. Hertzke, "The United States of America—American Muslim Exceptionalism," in *The Borders of Islam: Exploring Huntington's Faultlines, from Al-Andalus to the Virtual Ummah*, ed. Stig Jarle Hansen, Atle Mesoy, and Tuncay Kardaş (New York: Columbia University Press, 2009), 282–83; Laurie A. Brand, "Middle East Studies and Academic Freedom: Challenges at Home and Abroad," *International Studies Perspectives* 8, no. 4 (2007): 384–95; Juan Cole, "Islamophobia as a Social Problem," *MESA Bulletin* 41, no. 1 (2007): 3–7. For the historical roots of American Orientalism and Islamophobia, see Timothy Marr, *The Cultural Roots of American Islamicism* (New York: Cambridge University Press, 2006).

21. Noah Feldman, *Divided by God: America's Church-State Problem and What We Should Do about It* (New York: Farrar, Straus and Giroux, 2005), 54–56; Isaac Kramnick and R. Laurence Moore, *The Godless Constitution: A Moral Defense of the Secular State* (New York: Norton, 2005), 131–49.

22. Jose Casanova, *Public Religions in the Modern World* (Chicago: University of Chicago Press, 1994), 137.

23. John Witte Jr. and M. Christian Green, "American Constitutional Experiment in Religious Human Rights: The Perennial Search for Principles," in *Religious Human Rights in Global Perspective: Legal Perspectives*, ed. Johan D. van der Vyver and Jr. John Witte (The Hague: Martinus Nijhoff, 1996), 533.

24. James W. Fraser, *Between Church and State: Religion and Public Education in a Multicultural America* (New York: St. Martin's Griffin, 1999), 43, 83–103. For Supreme Court decisions favoring Christianity, see *Vidal v. Girard's Executors*, 43 U.S. 127 (1844) and *Holy Trinity Church v. U.S.*, 143 U.S. 457 (1892).

25. Sydney E. Ahlstrom, *A Religious History of the American People* (New Haven, Conn.: Yale University Press, 1972), 556.

26. William F. Deverell, "Church-State Issues in the Period of the Civil War," in *Church and State in America: A Bibliographical Guide. The Civil War to the Present Day*, ed. John F. Wilson (New York: Greenwood Press, 1987), 1.

27. Robert T. Handy, *Undermined Establishment: Church-State Relations in America 1880–1920* (Princeton, N.J.: Princeton University Press, 1991), 160.

28. Ibid., 189. See also John F. Wilson and Donald L. Drakeman, *Church and State in American History: Key Documents, Decisions, and Commentary from the Past Three Centuries* (Boulder, Colo.: Westview, 2003), 30.

29. Ahlstrom, *A Religious History of the American People*, 555–68.

30. Philip Hamburger, *Separation of Church and State* (Cambridge, Mass.: Harvard University Press, 2004), 220. In 1844 a school board in Philadelphia responded positively to the "request by the local bishop that Catholic children not be required to read from King James Bible." That led to a Protestant riot, as a result of which fifty-eight people were killed and more than a hundred were wounded. Frank S. Ravitch, *School Prayer and Discrimination: The Civil Rights of Religious Minorities and Dissenters* (Boston: Northeastern University Press, 1999), 5–6. For another "Bible conflict," in 1872 in New York, see Feldman, *Divided by God*, 72.

31. Denis Lacorne, *De la Religion en Amérique: Essai d'histoire politique* (N.p.: Gallimard, 2007), 106–12.

32. Jonathan D. Sarna and David G. Dalin, *Religion and State in the American Jewish Experience* (Notre Dame, Ind.: University of Notre Dame Press, 1997), 16.

33. Casanova, *Public Religions in the Modern World*, 168; Stephen Macedo, *Diversity and Distrust: Civic Education in a Multicultural Democracy* (Cambridge, Mass.: Harvard University Press, 2000), 60.

34. American Jewish Historical Society, *American Jewish Desk Reference* (New York: Random House, 1999), 35.

35. Sarna and Dalin, *Religion and State in the American Jewish Experience*, 13; Handy, *Undermined Establishment*, 69–70.

36. Casanova, *Public Religions in the Modern World*, 137.

37. Warren A. Nord, *Religion and American Education: Rethinking a National Dilemma* (Chapel Hill: University of North Carolina Press, 1994), 96.

38. Christian Smith, ed., *The Secular Revolution: Power, Interests, and Conflict in the Secularization of American Public Life* (Berkeley: University of California Press, 2003).

39. Christian Smith, Preface, in ibid., vii.

40. Robert Wuthnow, *The Struggle for America's Soul: Evangelicals, Liberals, and Secularism* (Grand Rapids, Mich.: William B. Eerdmans, 1990), 26–27; Hamburger, *Separation of Church and State*, 360–75, 391–99, 451.

41. Christian Smith, "Introduction," in *The Secular Revolution*, 36–37, 48–53; P. C. Kemeny, "Power, Ridicule, and Destruction of Religious Moral Reform Politics in the 1920s," in Smith, *The Secular Revolution*; Richard W. Flory, "Promoting a Secular Standard: Secularization and Modern Journalism, 1870–1930," in Smith, *The Secular Revolution*.

42. Kraig Beyerlein, "Educational Elites and the Movement to Secularize Public Education: The Case of the National Education Association," in Smith, *The Secular Revolution*.

43. David Sikkink, "From Christian Civilization to Individual Civil Liberties: Framing Religion in the Legal Field," in Smith, *The Secular Revolution*; Macedo, *Diversity and Distrust*, 139–45.

44. John A. Ryan, *Questions of the Day* (1931; New York: Books for Libraries Press, 1967), 91.

45. Robert Booth Fowler, Allen D. Hertzke, Laura R. Olson, and Kevin R. Den Dulk, *Religion and Politics in America: Faith, Culture, and Strategic Choices* (Boulder, Colo.: Westview, 2004), 19–21.

46. Joseph R. Gusfield, *Symbolic Crusade: Status Politics and the American Temperance Movement* (Urbana: University of Illinois Press, 1986), 110.

47. American Jewish Historical Society, *American Jewish Desk Reference*, 35.

48. *Everson v. Board of Education* 330 U.S. 1 (1947).

49. Later this association changed its name to Americans United for Separation of Church and State.

50. 36 U.S.C. 172.

51. 36 U.S.C. 186.

52. 31 U.S.C. 5112(d)(1).

53. Quoted in N. J. Demerath and H. Williams, "A Mythical Past and Uncertain Future," in *Church-State Relations: Tensions and Transitions*, ed. Thomas Robbins and Ronald Robertson (New Brunswick, N.J.: Transaction Books, 1987), 78. See also Jon Meacham, *American Gospel: God, the Founding Fathers, and the Making of a Nation* (New York: Random House, 2007), 176–79.

54. Dean M. Kelley, "Beyond Separation of Church and State," *Journal of Church & State* 5, no. 2 (1963): 181–98.

55. *Zorach v. Clauson*, 343 U.S. 306 (1952).

56. Pew Research Center, "Public Opinion about Mormons," December 6, 2007, http://pewresearch.org/pubs/648/romney-mormon.

57. Susan Jacoby, *Freethinkers: A History of American Secularism* (New York: Metropolitan Books, 2004), 6–7.

58. The Pew Forum on Religion and Public Life, "U.S. Religious Landscape Survey," March 30, 2008, http://religions.pewforum.org/reports; Andrew Kohut, John C. Green, Scott Keeter, and Robert C. Toth, *The Diminishing Divide: Religions' Changing Role in American Politics* (Washington, DC: Brookings Institution Press, 2000), 18; Barry A. Kosmin, Egon Mayer, and Ariela Keysar, "American Religious Identification Survey 2001," 2001, http://www.gc.cuny.edu/faculty/research_studies/aris.pdf, accessed on June 13, 2008., 12–13.

59. See, for examples, *McCollum v. Board of Education* 333 U.S. 203 (1948) and *Elk Grove Unified School District v. Newdow*, 542 U.S. 1 (2004).

60. *Engel v. Vitale*, 370 U.S. 421 (1962).

61. *Abington v. Schempp*, 374 U.S. 203 (1963). The Court combined this case with *Murray v. Curlett*, where the appellant was Madalyn Murray, who later founded the American Atheists.

62. The U.S. Department of Education, under the Clinton and George W. Bush administrations, issued guidelines to clarify the prayer issue regarding Court decisions. The guidelines stressed that students in public schools were allowed to pray and read religious texts, individually or jointly, as an extracurricular activity, as long as these activities were not endorsed by teachers or administrators. They even noted that students could preach to each other without coercion. "Guidance on Constitutionally Protected Prayer in Public Elementary and Secondary Schools," February 7, 2003, http://www.ed.gov/policy/gen/guid/religionandschools/prayer_guidance.html. See also John Dilulio, *Godly Republic: A Centrist Blueprint for America's Faith-Based Future* (Berkeley: University of California Press, 2007). 2007, 64–65.

63. Jacoby, *Freethinkers*, 319. See also Kramnick and Moore, *The Godless Constitution*, 179–80.

64. Randall Balmer, *God in the White House: A History* (New York: Harper One, 2008), 6–46.

65. Samuel Kernell and Gary C. Jacobson, *The Logic of American Politics* (Washington, D.C.: CQ Press, 1999): 145.

66. John G. West Jr., "The Changing Battle over Religion in the Public Schools," *Wake Forest Law Review* 26, no. 2 (1991): 361–63.

67. John C. Jeffries Jr. and James E. Ryan, "A Political History of the Establishment Clause," *Michigan Law Review* 100, no. 2 (2001): 322.

68. T. Jeremy Gunn, "Religious Freedom and Laïcité: A Comparison of the United States and France," *Brigham Young University Law Review* 24, no. 2 (2004): 419–506.

69. Justice Scalia's dissenting opinion, *McCreary County v. ACLU*, 545 U.S. (2005) (I removed the citations).

70. Justice Stevens's dissenting opinion, *Van Orden v. Perry*, 545 U.S. 677 (2005).

71. "U.S. Membership Statistics," http://www.mormonwiki.com/Membership_Statistics_U.S., accessed on March 4, 2010.

72. *Reynolds v. U.S.*, 98 U.S. 145 (1878).

73. *Davis v. Beason*, 133 U.S. 333 (1890).

74. *Mormon Church v. United States*, 136 U.S. 1 (1890).

75. The majority of fourteen Mormon members of the Congress are Republican. James M. Penning, "Americans' Views of Muslims and Mormons: A Social Identity Theory Approach," *Politics and Religion* 2 (2009): 281.

76. Quoted in Marr, *The Cultural Roots of American Islamicism*, 59; Rob Boston, "Joel Barlow and the Treaty with Tripoli: A Tangled Tale of Pirates, a Poet and the True Meaning of the First Amendment," *Church & State* 50, no. 6 (1997): 11–4.

77. U.S. Census Bureau, "Table 3. World Region and Country or Area of Birth of the Foreign-Born Population: 1960 to 2000." For slightly different numbers, see Kambiz GhaneaBassiri, *A History of Islam in America* (New York: Cambridge University Press, 2010), 294.

78. Jen'nan Ghazal Read, "Discrimination and Identity Formation in a Post-9/11 Era: A Comparison of Muslim and Christian Arab Americans," in *Race and Arab Americans before and after 9/11: From Invisible Citizens to Visible Subjects*, ed. Amaney Jamal and Nadine Naber (Syracuse, N.Y.: Syracuse University Press, 2008), 305.

79. Zahid H. Bukhari, "Demography, Identity, Space: Defining American Muslims," in Strum and Tarantolo, *Muslims in the United States*, 10.

80. Osman Bakar, "The Intellectual Impact of American Muslim Scholars on the Muslim World, with Special Reference to Southeast Asia," in Strum and Tarantolo, *Muslims in the United States*, 151.

81. "The Eid Stamp," http://georgewbush-whitehouse.archives.gov/infocus/ramadan/eidstamp .html, accessed on May 20, 2012.

82. "It's official: Colin Powell Endorses Barack Obama," *Los Angeles Times*, October 19, 2008.

83. Muslim imams have also been invited to deliver the opening prayer before Congress. A recent example is the prayer by Abdullah Antepli on March 3, 2010.

84. "Remarks by the President on a New Beginning," Cairo University, Egypt, June 4, 2009, http://www.whitehouse.gov/the_press_office/Remarks-by-the-President-at-Cairo-University-6-04-09/.

85. "Is America Islamophobic?," *Time*, August 30, 2010.

86. Jose Casanova, "Immigration and the New Religious Pluralism: A European Union–United States Comparison," in *Secularism, Religion and Multicultural Citizenship*, ed. Geoffrey Brahm Levey and Tariq Modood (New York: Cambridge University Press, 2008), 161.

87. Ibid., 160.

88. John F. Kennedy's Address to the Houston Ministerial Association, Rice Hotel, Houston, Texas, September 12, 1960.

89. See Hertzke, "The United States of America," 275, 278.

11

Identity, Social Repression, and Public Policy

A Case Study of Anatolian Towns

BINNAZ TOPRAK

This chapter, based on original research,[1] somewhat diverges from the major theme of the volume in that my main argument is not primarily about restrictions and threats to religious liberty. Rather my emphasis is on social repression and governmental discrimination in Turkey against people with different identities or lifestyles stemming from small-town conservatism, religious orthodoxy, or both. Nevertheless the chapter reflects the theme of religious liberty as not only the liberty of people to practice their faith but also their liberty to live a life of their choice that is free from religious definitions of what is moral, proper, or acceptable. As such, freedom of and freedom from religion are two sides of the same coin.

Freedom from religion is at the center of the modern transformation from community to society that social scientists have long talked about. Community is a form of social organization in which social relationships are face-to-face rather than contractual, personal lives are subject to the scrutiny of the community, and religion and traditions rather than a system of rights and responsibilities shape the lives of individuals. One could easily read the historic struggle for freedom as a struggle to free the individual from the repression and control of the community. Indeed the passage from community to modern society has meant that the individual is now under the protection of law from religious, communal, or traditional restrictions to his or her freedom of choice. This, I think, is an important issue that not only has implications for rights and liberties but is equally important for the construction of a multicultural society where all identities—religious, ethnic, sexual, or otherwise—have legal guarantees and social respect.

From the point of view of liberal theory, the issue of freedom from religious definitions of moral life and the issue of religious liberty are equally problematic.

This is especially pertinent in Muslim-majority countries where understandings of moral behavior are generally collective and based on religion rather than left to individual choice, whether that be according to one's faith or belief in a secular ethic. There are ample examples, both historical and contemporary, of nonsecular Islamic states that have criminalized a wide range of individual choices, such as converting to another religion; for women, marrying someone of a different faith; questioning the belief system in speech, writing, or art; deciding on one's sexual preference and conduct; publishing material that authorities consider to be "amoral"; for women, the refusal to cover; consuming alcohol; even using drugs that help with sexual performance.

Quantitative studies show that the overall question of morality, as it manifests itself through values concerning gender and sexuality, is one of the most problematic areas in Muslim societies. The World Values Surveys, conducted over the years and covering around 80 percent of the world's population, reveal that gender and sexuality are the two indicators that distinguish the values of Muslims from the values of people of all other faiths, with Muslims displaying the most conservative opinions on these two questions. As the authors put it, what distinguishes Muslims from the West is not "about demos but rather about eros."[2]

Although this might come as a relief to Westerners who are worried about the lack of democracy in the Muslim world, its implications are serious for women living under Muslim law or subject to social repression. Take the famous case of a couple in Egypt, a country that is not an Islamic state but nevertheless subscribes to the sharia in family law. The husband writes a book interpreting the Qur'an which the ulema of Al Azhar find heretical. Although there is no excommunication in Islamic theology, Al Azhar clerics nevertheless declare that the man can no longer be considered a Muslim and open a divorce suit against the couple on the grounds that a Muslim woman cannot stay married to a man who is not Muslim.

As this example shows, the interpretation of religious doctrine and practice by conservative clerics or patriarchal authorities in Muslim-majority countries touches on several layers of personal choice and freedom, especially for women. A host of examples shows the difficulty of reconciling religious conservatism with pluralist democracy unless the state has a secular legal system and, most important, secular civil law, which protects individual rights and liberties. Even then secular states may not find it easy to fight off social conservatism that emanates from local practice and/or conservative understandings of religion. A case in point is the honor killings in Turkey, although the country has a secular legal system.

In the Muslim geography, Turkey has a unique position as the only secular and democratic state. However, surveys conducted in Turkey show that people who define themselves as "very religious" display more conservative or discriminatory attitudes toward people of different faiths and different lifestyles. For example, a study conducted in 2006 based on survey research found that whereas those who placed themselves on the "secularist" side on a scale showed a high level of tolerance toward people with different identities, those who placed themselves on the "Islamist" side had a lower level of tolerance than the country average.[3] As I will argue below, the study on which this chapter is based, conducted through in-depth interviews, revealed the depth of this conservatism and the precarious balance between secularism and political Islam.

This issue of secularism versus Islamism has a long history in Turkey. The debate started in the mid-nineteenth century when the Ottoman Empire engaged in a series of Westernizing reforms to halt its apparent decline in the face of Western industrial and technological superiority. Toward the end of the century, two schools of thought had emerged: the Islamists versus the Westernists. Whereas both agreed that Western technology and industry should be adopted, they disagreed about what else to take from the West. For members of the Westernist school, industrial and technological change had to be supplemented by institutions and cultural forms taken from the West. For the Islamists, on the other hand, the decline of the empire had as much to do with this "aping" of Western institutions and culture as its failure to industrialize.[4]

The republic signified the victory of the Westernists. For the founding fathers, the new Turkish republic would henceforth take its place among what they considered to be the only "civilized nations," those of the West. In this conception, Islam could have a role solely as an individualistic faith. Henceforth religion would be kept out of the public sphere. The series of reforms during the formative years of the republic were devoted to secularizing all public institutions and erasing outward symbols of Islamic civilization. Abolishing the office of the caliphate, changing the Islamic calendar to the Gregorian, substituting Sunday for Friday as the weekly day of rest, changing the Arabic alphabet to the Latin, Turkifying the language by getting rid of Arabic and Persian words, adopting Roman numerals and the metric system, introducing Western painting and music, and the like, were all symbolic attempts to turn the country's vision for the future toward the West.

Along with the adoption of a secular legal system and secular education, the emancipation of women especially struck at the heart of Islamic society. Women were given equal legal status with men, including the right to vote and be elected; the veil was outlawed for civil service women and discouraged for use by urban dwellers; and unprecedented opportunities in professional and working life were opened up for educated women. As early as the 1930s there were large numbers of women in highly prestigious jobs as judges, lawyers, doctors, and professors. To this day, for example, the percentage of women in academia (35 percent) is the highest of all European countries.

The original response of the Islamist "camp" to these reforms was a series of rebellions. But once these were suppressed, the Islamist opposition went underground, to reemerge after the transition to democratic politics in 1946. When it did so, it had lost much of its original radicalism and chose to function as an important depot of votes for center-right parties that did not have the same kind of vigilance about secularism as the Republican People's Party, which had dominated as the only political organization that was permitted to exist. It was not until the 1970s that the Islamists were able to establish their own party, the National Salvation Party, under Necmettin Erbakan's leadership. His *Milli Görüş* movement was quite successful at the polls during the 1970s and turned the party into a major player in politics and a partner in the coalition governments of the decade.

When the National Salvation Party was closed down after the 1980 coup, it reemerged under a different name, Refah, which gradually gained in electoral strength until, in the 1990s, votes cast for the party carried Erbakan to the office of the prime minister in a coalition government. When Refah too was closed down by the constitutional court on charges that the party had violated the secular principles of the republic, the movement split up, and a group of younger MPs, known as the "reformists," founded the Justice and Development Party (AKP). The AKP won the 2002 elections with a sizable percentage of votes and was able to form a single-party government, a victory that no party had enjoyed for decades. Since then the AKP has been the ruling party.

Although the AKP did engage in a series of important reforms, such as its attempts to curtail the power of the military and to civilianize Turkish politics, it was unable to quell the suspicions of the secularist bloc that the party's aim was to eventually Islamize the country. These suspicions became all the more pronounced when one after another important post was filled with party men and the party leadership seemed determined to capture all power centers within the bureaucracy. The country gradually plunged into what the *Wall Street Journal* recently called "a civil war without bloodshed."

In recent years many observers have pointed out that there are "two Turkeys"; each has a lifestyle and a vision of its place in the world that differentiates it from the other. Indeed a survey in 2006 clearly delineated a one-third of the population who are urban, better educated, have more income and wealth, and define their place closer to the "secular" side of the spectrum and a two-thirds who are rural or small town, are less educated, have less income and wealth, and define their place closer to the "Islamist" side. Crosstabulations of the data showed that, overall, these two groups have different attitudes on questions concerning social and political issues. Contrary to perceptions of Islamists and some intellectuals, it was consistently the one-third that gave the most liberal and tolerant answers to a variety of questions concerning political and social life.[5] The current polarization of politics stems from the inability of these two camps to reach a consensus on fundamentals of social and political life.

Since the founding of the republic in 1923, Islamists have been complaining about discrimination and social repression by republican or secular elites and state authorities. Islamist intellectuals and politicians have coined a term to describe this discrimination: they call themselves the "Blacks of Turkey," juxtaposed against what they term the "White Turks." Indeed the Islamists were left out of political power centers, social status groups, and intellectual prestige circles for many years. Articles in various republican constitutions, laws on political parties, labor unions, and associations, as well as the criminal code have severely limited the political space for Islamist parties and organizations. It was on the bases of this legislation that various Islamist parties were closed down in the past. Although this type of marginalization of Islamic groups is no longer the case since the ascendancy to power of the AKP in 2002, the AKP too has been under threat of closure and has faced a court case against it as well as a letter of warning by the military.

Because there is a wealth of literature on Islamist parties and movements in Turkey, the aim of the research carried out in 2008 under my direction was to "look at the other side," that is, those who are not part of Sunni Islamic networks. Other members of the team were İrfan Bozan of the NTV network, the freelance reporter and writer Tan Morgül, and Nedim Şener of the daily *Milliyet*. Twelve Anatolian towns and two districts of Istanbul were designated as sites of observation. These towns were chosen with an eye to include different levels of economic development so as not to bias the results by observing only either the less or the more developed parts of the country. At least one town was included from each geographic area. At the same time, we included towns where voter turnout in the last elections of 2007 overwhelmingly favored the ruling AKP, with roots in the Islamic movement, and others where the staunchly secular Republican People's Party received higher votes than its national average.

Thus the twelve towns that were chosen were located in different parts of the country, had different economic development levels, and were different in terms of voter preferences. The two Istanbul districts, distinguished for their migrant populations from Anatolia, were added for comparative purposes, to see whether migration to a metropolis made a difference in attitudes.

We visited these sites over a one-year period, for three to four days each, and carried out in-depth interviews with 401 men and women whom we thought might be the subjects of social repression because of their identity. These included the Alevi (a minority religious sect within Islam); the few Christians we could find in these towns; the Roma; Kurdish and leftist university students; women who are uncovered; young men and women who do not conform to the dress codes of the towns in which they live; people who do not fast during Ramadan or who do not attend Friday prayers; as well as teachers in public schools, doctors and nurses in state hospitals, employees of government bureaus, small businessmen, artisans, and traders, CEOs of big companies, and professionals—all of whom either defined their identity as "secular" or were not part of the AKP or *tarikat* network.

Thus individuals who were included in the research varied in terms of their backgrounds and attitudes toward secularism but converged on one point: except for the Alevi, none of them defined their identity in religious terms. For the Alevi, religion was at the heart of their identity, but that was only because of their status as a minority group who had been persecuted in history by the Sunni majority. In other words, religion figured in their definition of identity vis-à-vis their minority status. For the Alevi, the question of religion was a question of community solidarity against a Sunni public that ostracized them and, as we found out, against government authorities who discriminated against them. Like all the other groups we interviewed, they too faced discrimination because they were not part of the Sunni coalition of groups for whom Islam is a reference point in their personal, public, and political relations.

That does not mean, however, that the others in the study are unbelievers or are all strict secularists. Undoubtedly, for some, the term *secular* is important for self-definition. However, for most, it is not an issue that had central importance in their lives. To put it differently, not all of the individuals whom we interviewed were necessarily diehard secularists who had biased attitudes toward Islamist groups. In fact most were not.

It was against this political background that we carried out the research. Our aim was to find out whether the complaints of secularists against the AKP had any real grounds. Originally we wanted to investigate instances of social repression and ostracism, if any, toward people with a nonmajority identity. We chose Anatolian towns rather than metropolises where lives are relatively free from social constraint. Although some neighborhoods in big cities might be more conservative than others, overall the big city allows quite a bit of breathing space for people who are different from the majority by birth or who choose to live nonconformist lives.

The fact that we left out the complaints of the Islamist groups was one of the major criticisms against the research. However, because so much has been written and researched about the Islamists, we excluded them and aimed to look at the other side of the picture. There have been no studies by social scientists that attempt to understand the secularists or people with a nonmajority identity and/or choose to live differently from conservative Sunni Muslims. Our research aimed to fill this lacuna.

At the start of our journey, however, we soon realized that we could not restrict the topic to social repression alone since the government employees whom we talked to complained about discrimination from those in higher positions within their respective bureaucracies and workplaces because of their secular lifestyle and identity. A similar complaint was voiced by the Alevi and the Roma, who claimed that under the AKP government, it was impossible for them to find jobs in the government bureaucracy or in municipal governments. The Roma, for example, said that they could not even find jobs as construction workers on municipal projects. When asked how it was that the authorities recognized them as Alevi or Roma, their unanimous answer, in one town after another, was that they were recognized on the bases of home addresses that they had to declare in applications, referring to the fact that they lived in neighborhoods populated solely by the the Alevi or the Roma.

At the same time, professionals, traders, and businessmen complained about a new religious network, the Fethullah Gülen movement, and the difficulties of conducting business unless one is part of, as they put it, the "AKP-Gülen coalition." University students told us about the dormitories and houses which members of this movement own and the life of the students there. Hence the final report went beyond social repression and included complaints about government authorities as well as the Gülen movement.

We reported our findings in a 183-page document in Turkish, which was originally disseminated to the public at a meeting with academics and journalists as well as published online.[6] It was subsequently published as a book.[7] Our conclusion following the completion of the field research was that to be different in most Anatolian towns is to pay a price. Many of the people we interviewed had been subjected to social pressure, discrimination, and at times violence by neighbors as well as strangers. These included insults in public, ostracism by neighbors, boycotts of businesses, and assaults.

The research raised a major controversy in Turkey, carried out in the press and the media. Within two weeks the number of debates and programs on various television networks and comments and op-eds in newspapers and journals exceeded seven hundred. The networks were bombarded by email comments from citizens during these debates, and we received additional emails. The reaction itself could be the topic of new sociological research. No doubt a major reason for this reception was that the study had touched on an extremely sensitive issue in Turkey, namely, the relationship between Islam, secularism, and modernity, a political issue that has divided this country since the founding of the republic in 1923. The debate over the report indicated the continuation, and perhaps even intensification, of this division within Turkish society. What was most interesting was the reaction of the Gülen community to the report, which took the form of a campaign—carried out in their networks, newspapers, and journals—against its findings as well as against the authors, a reaction that cast serious doubt about the movement's claims of tolerance and dialogue.[8]

In a short chapter for this volume, it is of course not possible to include all of the problematic areas that were covered by the research. The following is a brief summary of the most important issues that our respondents singled out during the interviews. These are all based on incidents that they personally experienced rather than on impressions or political views. In other words, we excluded from the report political opinions and only recorded conversations that were based on personal situations.

The Alevi seemed to be the most affected as a minority group. Sunni prejudices against the Alevi cover all sorts of urban myths: that they are unclean because they do not observe the Muslim ablutions; hence it is religiously forbidden to eat anything they offer; or that one cannot trust their morality because they engage in incestuous relationships. Many such myths stem from the different forms of ritual, and hence lifestyles, that the Alevi follow. As followers of Ali but differentiated from both the Arab Alewites and the Shia, the Alevi faith is singularly to be found in the Anatolian geography and is associated with Anatolian folk culture. They do not perform the *namaz* and do not go to the mosque or fast during Ramadan. The Alevi have no qualms about drinking alcohol; urban Alevi women generally do not cover; and gender segregation is not among their traditions. Their places of worship are called *cemevi,* and rituals are performed with mixed gender groups and involve music and dance. Instead of Ramadan they have a one-week fast called Muharrem to mourn the death of Ali's son, Hüseyin, at Kerbela.

Because the Alevi have been persecuted by Sunni Turks since Yavuz Sultan Selim's massacre of the Alevi in early sixteenth century, members of the community have generally tended to hide their religious beliefs. As public opinion surveys show, only a minority of the Alevi reveal their religious affiliation; estimates are between 15 million and 20 million. Given that there have been several incidents in recent years involving violence against the Alevi—especially the notorious case in Sivas where thirty-five people died in a hotel fire set by a mob during a literary meeting organized by Alevi intellectuals—and given prevalent social ostracism, it was no surprise to find out that the Alevis we interviewed indicated that most of them hide their identity. We even came across Alevi who had known each other for years but learned that both were Alevi only during our joint conversation.

Many of the Alevi told stories of how their neighbors would not touch any food they offered, how they often heard insinuations about their loose morals or incestuous relations, how the derogatory term *Kızılbaş* was indiscriminately used by their Sunni neighbors and acquaintances, how their children were objects of ridicule by classmates, how Alevi students would sometimes be insulted even by teachers at school, how Sunni clients who did business with the Alevi would be reproached by other Sunni, and the like.

At the same time, a major problem of the Alevi was the difficulties they faced building *cemevi* because of the resistance of AKP mayors to give construction permits. Many Alevi pointed out that they too are taxpayers and hence should receive the same kind of financial help for their places of worship that is given to mosques, such as free water and electricity that the mosques enjoy as well as payment of Sunni imams, the upkeep of the mosques, and the building of new mosques paid for by the state budget. They complained that when they apply for similar privileges, they are told that if they are Muslims they should use mosques, although authorities well know that the Alevi do not go to the mosque.[9] In one of the two districts we visited in Istanbul, the former AKP mayor had even gone as far as naming the Alevi neighborhood "Yavuz Sultan Selim neighborhood," a name that had almost wiped the Alevi from the Anatolian geography. When they applied to the municipality to change the name, carrying a petition with 11,000 signatures, the mayor told them that nobody in Turkey could talk against Sultan Selim and that he did not want to hear any such complaints.[10]

Besides the Alevi, the Kurds and the Roma face similar discrimination. The complaints of the Roma basically centered on unemployment as well as the reluctance of municipal authorities to provide services to their neighborhood. We heard the same complaint from the Alevi that no roads were built to connect their villages with the towns, or if they lived in an urban district, their neighborhoods received no help from municipal governments to modernize the district's infrastructure. In Sultanbeyli, for example, a district of Istanbul where rural migrants live, the Alevi neighborhood had muddy roads, whereas all the adjacent roads were paved. When we asked about this, the residents told us that they had sent several petitions to the municipality and that although each time municipal authorities (controlled by the AKP) promised to take care of the problem, nothing was ever done. The poorest Alevi and Roma neighborhoods we visited in some of these towns received no help from either municipal budgets for the poor or from various Sunni groups, such as the Gülen community, which is known for its philanthropic activities. These apparently target only the Sunni poor who are, or pretend to be, religious. An Alevi in an Istanbul district, for example, had heard a conversation between a poor Alevi and the district's AKP mayor. When the poor man asked the mayor why the municipality did not help him, the answer was that philanthropic organizations want their money to go to people who perform their religious duties.

We tried unsuccessfully to start a conversation with the few Christians left in these cities, but they seemed unwilling to talk to strangers about questions of social discrimination. Consequently the report has only a few observations about them, most involving eyewitness accounts of the reaction to the murder of Christian missionaries in one of the towns we visited and the assassination of a prominent Armenian journalist in Istanbul whose murderer came from a town on the Black Sea coast that was included in our sample. These eyewitness accounts revealed that many residents downplayed these incidents as provocation or were indifferent, including some who found fault with the victims.

We talked to a number of Kurdish students at various universities in Anatolia. All complained that they were either isolated or beaten up by fellow students with nationalist views for having spoken Kurdish or having listened to Kurdish music. Some even feared to talk to their parents in Kurdish on the phone and would regularly answer in Turkish even when their parents spoke no Turkish. They also had difficulty renting flats in the city since no owner would rent to them, a problem they tried to overcome either by hiding their identity or by using Turkish friends as go-betweens.

Similar problems were faced by students who dressed differently. For example, young men who wore earrings, colorful T-shirts, or Bermuda shorts or had long hair or a goatee would often be insulted by strangers in buses and city streets and sometimes be beaten up by ultranationalist youth groups. Young women who wore skirts or sleeves that were a bit too short would be warned by strangers to dress properly or even, in a few cases, insulted as "prostitutes" or assaulted. Most students complained that they could rent flats with the condition that no friend of the opposite sex would visit. Leftist students complained about violence against them by ultranationalist fellow students.

In almost all towns with AKP mayors, restaurants that served liquor were ordered to relocate outside of city limits. Government-owned recreational centers for state employees had AKP directors who banned liquor on these premises. New applications by markets and small stores to get licenses for selling alcohol were turned down by municipal governments. Young people complained that they could find no establishments in the city where they could dance or find an open place in the evenings where they could just hang out. At night the streets of most of these cities seemed to indicate that only men were residents. Students felt that they were under constant surveillance by city dwellers and university campuses were the only place where they felt comfortable.

Except for a few, almost all the men and women we interviewed said that their city was a much more relaxed and open place in the past. They all believed that a certain conservatism had gotten hold of the city, as a result of which most people felt the pressure to look as if they were religious. We were told that there is increasing sex segregation at weddings and other social gatherings; that wives of government employees have begun to cover; that people who used to drink now shy away from drinking in public places; that government employees who never went to Friday prayers now do so; that businesses and many government offices, including schools and some hospital units, close down for Friday noon prayers;[11] that shopkeepers close their shutters at noon on Fridays even if they do not go to the mosque for fear that they will be singled out as nonbelievers; that people who do business or who are government employees feel compelled to either fast or pretend to be fasting during Ramadan. We heard endless stories of people who were beaten in public because they dared to smoke or eat publicly during Ramadan. People who did not fast complained that it was impossible to find an open restaurant during lunch hour during Ramadan and that even universities, government offices, and big companies had stopped serving lunch for students and employees. In short, many residents with a secular identity in these towns felt that there was an overall pressure to look and act like a pious person.

The research also showed that part of this discrimination emanates from government and municipal officials against civil servants and workers in their bureaus who do not seem to lead a Muslim way of life. Teachers, nurses, and doctors with a secular identity who work in public schools and hospitals complained that their workplaces are constantly shifted, that many of their colleagues have been appointed to distant towns or villages, that these appointments often separate husband and wives, that night shifts or extra duties are given to them, and that they cannot get the necessary evaluations from their superiors for promotion. High school students talked about discriminatory comments by "pious" and/or "nationalist" teachers on the status of women in general and uncovered women in particular, as well as lectures against the Alevi and the Christians. We even heard stories from university students about similar behavior by some of their professors, such as the case of an unemployed young Alevi who had dropped out of the university in his town after an exchange with one of his professors who had insulted him in class. As we stated in the report, much of this is probably due to the behavior of local party members or supporters who feel encouraged to engage in discriminatory policies simply because their party is in power, without explicit orders or encouragement from the central AKP leadership.

Discrimination also included the refusal to give jobs to the minority Alevi or the Roma. Many complained that they could get jobs neither in the state bureaucracy nor in municipal governments. At the same time, we heard complaints about non-merit-based appointments to top positions within the government bureaucracy based on the person's affiliation with or sympathy for either the AKP or the Gülen community. Although the party leadership claims that appointments are based on merit, official statistics show that the membership of the pro-AKP union of state employees increased to 315,000 in 2008 from 42,000 in 2002, when the AKP first came to power, whereas membership figures for the leftist and nationalist unions remained more or less the same.[12] These statistics alone give some credibility to complaints of favoritism and patronage.

The Gülen movement's activities were another source of complaint. Owners of small businesses as well as big companies pointed out, in one town after another, that it is difficult to enlarge one's business or even to maintain it unless one belongs to the movement. Many small businessmen with a secular identity complained about the fact that their businesses were being boycotted. To give an example: although our report mentioned no names or even the name of the towns where people we talked to lived, for fear that they might be identified, we inadvertently gave the name of a town where a radio station owner had complained about a boycott that targeted his business because he had broadcast a program on the Gülen movement. After the broadcast he had suffered a great financial loss because business establishments had withdrawn their ads. When our report became public, the movement's major newspaper, Zaman, reported that we had fabricated the stories because they had found this man—whose name did not appear in our report—who apparently told them that he had said nothing of the kind. Although we had his voice on tape, we decided not to publicize it for fear that he might face further boycotts. This incident in itself shows not only the power of the movement but also the fear of those outside of it. Government employees have similar fears. Indeed some of them wrote to us later and asked us not to report anything they said. An associate professor who first agreed to talk to us, for example, later wrote that we should please excuse him.

That these fears are not based on paranoia was confirmed by later developments. One of the participants of this research, Nedim Şener, subsequently wrote a book on the assassination of the Armenian journalist Hrant Dink and the questionable role of the security forces in failing to prevent it. He was tried for it (the prosecutor asking for 37 years for him compared to the 28 years for the assassin), was acquitted, wrote a second book on the Gülen movement, and was then charged with claims of involvement in the so-called Ergenekon network that the authorities claim was plotting to overthrow the government by force. He spent a year in jail without a trial and was recently released although the case against him continues. Ahmet Şık, another journalist, was similarly taken into custody on the same charges a day before his book on the Gülen movement would come out for sale, although it never did because it was banned from distribution. He too spent a year in jail without a trial and was recently released, awaiting his next trial. A third person, Hanefi Avcı, who served for long years in the top echelons of the security forces, was taken into custody a few weeks after his book on the Gülen movement came out. The charge against him was the same, i.e., involvement in the Ergenekon network to overthrow the government. He is still in jail, awaiting trial. A fourth person, İlhan Cihaner, who is now an MP from the Republican People's Party, spent time in jail for similar charges after he decided to investigate the activities of the Gülen movement in Erzincan where he served at the time as the public prosecutor.

Owners of large companies claimed that they could not get government contracts or credits which, according to them, were being distributed to people who belonged to and/or supported the AKP or the Gülen movement. We were told about the social isolation of people who refused to attend meetings of the Gülen movement, separately held for men and women. We were also told about the means by which the Gülen community received donations, all of which were tax-exempt, and the financial empire that the community had thus built.

Students who knew about Gülen dorms or *Işık Evleri* (Light Houses) described how residents are restricted in a variety of ways, from the way they dress to what they read, which TV stations they watch, and the like. We were told that women students in these houses are advised to cover, that social life revolves around religious talk and prayers, and that young men and women are banned from forming friendships with each other.

Overall our conclusion at the end of our field research was that these towns at first sight appear modern. Many have tree-lined boulevards, five-star hotels, shopping centers, and new apartment buildings, which gives an impression of transformation and modernity. However, unlike expectations of social scientists that economic development leads to social change, this transformation is not reflected in the everyday life of the city. When you talk to residents with a non-majority identity, they will tell you stories of having been cornered into a life-style that leaves no room for individuality and difference. Townspeople who live differently from the way the Sunni Muslim majority live are indeed restricted, ridiculed, and ostracized in a variety of ways.

No doubt one cannot generalize about the Turkish population as a whole on the basis of the sample we used, which is not representative of the whole country. Nevertheless it would be equally erroneous to argue that no generalizations can be made and that these stories are unique and unrepresentative. On the contrary, they were repetitive. For example, in the first city we visited, we were told that men offer their seats on buses to covered women even when uncovered older women are standing up. This story was repeated to us by countless women in many towns we visited and, surprisingly, even in one of the districts of Istanbul where rural migrants live. Over and over again we heard similar stories from the Alevi, government employees, teachers and doctors, Kurdish students, young men and women who dress differently or who do not fast during Ramadan, businessmen and professionals with a secular identity. As for unique stories, we left them out of the final report. Hence although the study does not argue that the results show widespread intolerance, it nevertheless reveals serious problems in Turkish society that the government and opposition parties as well as intellectuals and the media have to address in order to create a more democratic and culturally plural society.

The report included a recommendations section where we suggested that an office should be established to look specifically into complaints against government officials who discriminate against people with a nonmajority identity or employ discriminatory employment procedures. We also recommended that a campaign be launched by the government to fight discrimination and that this campaign include education on rights and liberties from first grade on, as well as emphasizing the importance of equal treatment for all and politically correct behavior and language. Part of this educational effort, we suggested, should also use the media to teach good citizenship values to the Turkish population at large.

In the extremely polarized political atmosphere of Turkey, the report has unfortunately been used by both the secularists and the Islamists to argue their respective political agendas. As policy-oriented research, it remains to be seen how many of its warnings and recommendations will be taken seriously by the political establishment.

Notes

1. For the English translation of the report, see Binnaz Toprak, İrfan Bozan, Tan Morgül, and Nedim Şener, *Being Different in Turkey: Religion, Conservatism, and Otherization*, 2009, at www.aciktoplumvakfi.org.tr.
2. See Ronald Inglehart, ed., *Human Values and Social Change* (Leiden: E. J. Brill, 2003).
3. See Ali Çarkoğlu and Binnaz Toprak, *Religion, Society and Politics in a Changing Turkey*, trans. Çiğdem Aksoy Fromm (Istanbul: TESEV, 2006), 53.
4. For this controversy at the end of the nineteenth century and the beginning of the twentieth, see Tarık Zafer Tunaya, *İslamcılık Cereyanı* (Istanbul: Baha Matbaası, 1962).
5. Çarkoğlu and Toprak, *Religion, Society and Politics*, 104.
6. Binnaz Toprak, İrfan Bozan, Tan Morgül, and Nedim Şener, *Türkiye'de Farklı Olmak: Din ve Muhafazakarlık Ekseninde Ötekileştirilenler*, www.aciktoplumvakfi.com.tr.
7. Binnaz Toprak, İrfan Bozan, Tan Morgül, and Nedim Şener, *Türkiye'de Farklı Olmak: Din ve Muhafazakarlık Ekseninde Ötekileştirilenler* (Metis, 2009).
8. For my answers to these criticisms, see the postscript in Toprak et al., *Being Different in Turkey*.
9. The AKP government had a series of meetings with various Alevi organizations as well as journalists and academics who are knowledgeable on the issue to look into means of reform to alleviate some of these complaints. However, not much came out of these meetings. Some information on the Alevi faith was added to school textbooks on religion, disregarding Alevi demands that their children be exempt from the required religion courses that teach mostly about Sunni Islam. An Alevi father took his daughter's case to the European Court of Justice which decided in his favor. It was in response to the ECJ's decision that the AKP government made changes in textbooks, although these are far from satisfactory. On the other hand, the government continues to argue that the Alevi cemevi are not places of worship and hence can receive no financial help from the state budget.
10. My several attempts to change the name of the district, including pleas with the prime minister and the mayor of Sultanbeyli, have been unsuccessful. The name stands as is.
11. Friday is a workday in Turkey.
12. See *Resmi Gazete* (Official Gazette), July 7, 2002 and July 5, 2008.

Are Muslim Democrats a Threat to Secularism and Freedom of Religion?

The Turkish Case

TALIP KÜÇÜKCAN

Three events involving religious groups occurred in Turkey in the fall of 2010. The first was the Muslim fasting month of Ramadan, which started on August 11 and culminated with the end of Ramadan celebrations on September 9, which drew millions of participating Turks. There is nothing unusual in this annual event, so much a part of the social and cultural landscape of Turkey. The other two events indicate potential transformations in the rights of non-Muslims and unorthodox Muslims amid the shifting of powers between secular Kemalists and Muslim democrats who came to power in 2002. On September 14 thousands of Orthodox Greeks from around the world gathered at the Sumela Monastery for a liturgy after its closure eighty-eight years ago. On September 19 hundreds of Orthodox Armenians, some of whom traveled from Armenia, worshipped in the newly renovated Akdamar Orthodox Church.

The two events involving non-Muslims suggest growing acceptance of pluralism and religious freedom in a country where many issues once regarded as taboo are openly discussed, such as cultural rights for the Kurds, claims of the heterodox Alevi community, rights for the Roma people, the opening of Halki Seminary, belonging to the Greek Orthodox community, and changing the military-imposed constitution of 1980. Major developments are taking place to democratize Turkey under a conservative government whose religious identity was met with skepticism and suspicion at the beginning of their term. In contrast to claims that Muslim democrats have a hidden agenda of gradually Islamizing the country, Turkey's new direction is set for full membership in the European Union and institutionalization of its values, though there is resistance from Germany and France to Turkey's membership on predominantly cultural grounds. Turco-skeptics in Europe propose a "privileged partnership/membership" instead of full accession.[1] Although there is negotiation fatigue and slow progress, incidents such as those described earlier clearly illustrate Turkey's new direction and provide a powerful answer to the question of whether Muslim democrats in power are implementing religious policies to establish an Islamic state or consolidating liberal and secular democracy.

On May 19, 2007, the Akdamar Church (the Armenian Cathedral of the Holy Cross), a 1,100-year-old place of worship on Akdamar Island on Lake Van in eastern Anatolia, was opened as a museum after being renovated by the Turkish government, which is led by the Justice and Development Party (AK Party). Senior officials attended the opening ceremony following its $1.5 million restoration, which saved the neglected building and its intricate wall carvings depicting biblical scenes.[2] Calls were made by several figures, including Patriarch Mesrob II, spiritual leader of the Armenian Orthodox community in Turkey, that the AK Party government should open up the restored church for worship at least once a year. The government responded positively to this call, and the worship service was held in the fall of 2010.

Reception of this extraordinary event by the local people, which contradicts old habits of the state, is a clear indication of where Turkish society is heading. Because the hotels were fully booked, a campaign was launched in Van to host Armenian visitors who wanted to witness the historical ceremony at the Akdamar Church. A large number of local Muslim families volunteered to host Armenians, which seems unthinkable to many people given the supposedly deeply rooted hostility between the Turks and the Armenians. People in Van deconstructed such images by opening their homes to Armenians, who accepted the invitations. An optimist might read the restoration of the Akdamar Church as a museum and its opening for a religious ceremony even once a year by the Turkish government as an act of goodwill. The beginning of people-to-people relations on such occasions can be regarded as the first step in reconciliation, which should be expanded and consolidated by the Turks and the Armenians on state and civil levels.

Sumela Monastery, on the Black Sea in northeastern Turkey, was founded in 386 and went through ups and downs throughout the centuries. When it fell into the hands of Muslim Turks following the conquest of Istanbul, it remained untouched and continued its educational and spiritual activities uninterrupted. With the collapse of the Ottoman Empire, the last religious ceremony was probably held in 1923, before a large-scale population exchange took place between Turkey and Greece.

As the Sumela and Akdamar events indicate, there are hopeful signs of an increasing toleration and acceptance of minority religions and the recognition of other identities and lifestyles, in the form of the Kurdish and Alevi initiatives, launched by the AK Party. No other political parties since the establishment of modern Turkey were able to take such bold steps to democratize the country and publicly recognize the grievances of its marginalized and neglected minorities.

In contrast to claims that the AK Party is consolidating conservatism and preparing grounds for social pressure on groups who don't share its ideology, by looking at the reforms since 2002 one can strongly argue that the AK Party is bringing Turkey closer to Western standards of democracy, rule of law, human rights, and equal citizenship. Moreover by opening itself to the world through trade and active foreign policy, Turkey is becoming a more engaged actor in international affairs and integrated into the Western system, which motivates Turkey for further democratization and transparency. Therefore the debate on Turkey should focus on who the agents of democratization and transformation are and the role that the AK Party government played in this process, not on the outdated cliché that Islam and democracy are incompatible and that Muslims fail to recognize the rights of laicists, Kemalists, unorthodox communities, and non-Muslim minorities.

Contextualizing the Debate in Turkey

The two events described earlier took place in a political environment dominated by the AK Party, which is constantly accused by its adversaries of having a secret agenda of establishing an Islamic state, despite categorical denials by party leadership. A fear circulated in Turkey is that under the AK Party government, religious conservatism is on the rise and is transforming Turkish society, creating social pressure on people to conform to Islamic ideals in such matters as alcohol consumption, clothing, and religious observance. Although these claims are frequently repeated, there are no legal regulations, court decisions, large-scale sociological evidence, or a record of complaints that might indicate this strong move in a conservative direction. However, there is discussion of what Şerif Mardin termed "neighborhood pressure."[3] It is argued that the ideology of the governing AK Party encourages like-minded people to force others to conform to conservative lifestyles.

Binnaz Toprak, who is one of the leading proponents of this view, bases her claims on field research results involving a sample of over four hundred people in thirteen cities in Turkey.[4] Toprak's report indicates that "neighborhood pressure" is manifold, and many people with a different view, appearance, faith, and lifestyle from that of the majority faced some degree of discrimination either from government bureaucrats or from the majority group. She argues that since the AK Party came to power, there has been an increase in conservative pressure, especially in rural Turkey.

However, contrary evidence points to the "cultural mosaic" of Turkish society that appreciates and accepts diversity. Hakan Yılmaz found in his 2006 survey involving a sample of 1,644 that 75 percent of participants are not disturbed by unveiled women, and 93 percent do not feel uncomfortable by veiled women, a result indicating that there is large-scale acceptance of the practice of veiling. The same research also found that 79 percent of the survey participants do not agree with the view that others should be forced to accept the religious beliefs and lifestyles of a particular group.[5] A recent survey of nearly 2,200 individuals indicates that 80 percent of the respondents do not face discrimination or pressure by other sectors of society because of the way they describe themselves. However, the same research does show that "otherness" is a common denominator when it comes to discrimination and social pressure. When asked which group is discriminated against the most, 37.5 percent said veiled women, 18 percent said the Kurds, 5.5 percent said Alevis, 4.5 percent said women wearing all-black attire (chador), 3.5 percent said secularists, and 7 percent said all these groups, including atheists, face discrimination. Each social, ethnic, or faith group claims that its political and cultural identity faces discrimination more than others.[6]

Although social pressure and discrimination are often attributed to religious conservatism in Turkey, there is almost no mention of how secular elites, who see themselves as the bearers of republican values, can contribute to discrimination. Indeed the secular Kemalist state discriminates against Alevis and Roma, not to mention Muslims, while ultranationalists have denied Kurdish rights and identity. Recent research on "elites and social distance" indicates that respondents who were educated in prestigious schools and enjoy higher-status jobs have less proximity than Muslims to the Kurds, which makes them more indifferent to the Kurdish problem. The same research demonstrates that secular elites believe that the AK Party has a hidden agenda of turning Turkey into a more conservative country. Muslim newcomers to power are seen as "occupiers" against republican secular values. Thus many secular elites favor closure of the AK Party, though in principle they affirm democratic values. As far the headscarf is concerned, veiled women are regarded as "others" by elite respondents and seen as a threat. Moreover the elite social environment is largely closed to veiled women, an isolation that produces "essentialist" views toward such others.[7]

Although one should acknowledge the presence of various forms of discrimination in the workplace, in state institutions, and in society, these are neither the product of the AK Party government nor can all be attributed to Muslim democrats. Moreover there is no evidence that Muslim democrats advocate such attitudes and practices. On the contrary, it was Muslim democrats in the current government who initiated direct talks with the Kurds, the Alevis, and the Roma people for the first time as state representatives in republican history. Therefore Toprak's findings should be interpreted within the context of the historical trajectory of state building and concomitant modernization in Turkey, which largely aimed at forming a homogeneous identity. Given democratization trends, new entrepreneurs, rising middle classes, civil society participation, wide access to education, and plurality in the media, the Kemalist state can no longer exercise the same militant power to preserve the status quo. In this context, when various subidentities make public claims they are perceived as a threat by Kemalists.

A recent survey of over 1,800 respondents on identity perceptions of self and others confirms the observation that Kemalists are not immune to processes of "othering" those whose differences are seen as a threat to their own values or lifestyles.[8]

Modern Turkey was established on the ruins of the Ottoman Empire, which was predominantly a Muslim kingdom with multicultural, multireligious, and multilingual social structures. The Ottoman Empire managed to govern such a diverse territory through multiple agencies and mechanisms. The disintegration of the empire led to the establishment of more than thirty nation-states (including the Republic of Turkey) in the Balkans, the Middle East, and North Africa, where the Ottomans reigned for centuries. As new systems of political organization, nation-states, by their very nature, distance themselves from their immediate past, with the objective of creating homogeneous political communities and a sense of belonging formed on the basis of shared identity, culture, myths, and legacy. The formation of modern nation-states took place through a secular discourse rather than a religious one because such polities sought to liberate the community from religious alliances and build loyalty to the secular state rather than the religious establishment.

The Turkish model of the state-religion system has evolved over the years from that of having Islam as a state religion in the first constitution to a strongly secular state since then. The aim of this chapter is to first examine the development of state-religion relations and law in Turkey and then explore the ideological, religious, and legal trajectories in secular nations with predominantly Muslim populations. The case of Turkey provides an opportunity to see that countries with Muslim majorities took different paths in their management of religious affairs than their counterparts in Europe.

Secularism, State, and Religion in Modern Turkey

The establishment of a modern nation-state in Turkey crystallized the ideological orientation of the republican elite that aimed to reshape the state and its institutions on the basis of a secular model inspired by the West. Political, social, and religious developments in modern Turkey were influenced by the ideals of modernism and secularism. As Nilüfer Göle argued, "Since its foundation, Turkey's political elites voluntarily attempted the most radical secularization among the Muslim countries. The principle of democracy was secondary to that of state secularism."[9] This observation indicates that secularism was accepted as the state ideology above every other orientation at the expense of liberties as experienced especially during single-party rule in the country until 1950.

Inspired by the principles of modernization, sweeping changes were introduced in Turkish society. Secularization reforms, which were undertaken during the first decade of the new republic, aimed at minimizing the role of religion in every walk of Turkish society. The motive behind the secularization program was to reduce the societal significance of religious values and eventually disestablish cultural and political institutions marked by Islam. Reforms during the formative period of the republic were aimed at undermining the legacy of the Ottoman social, political, and cultural influence to establish a modern and secular framework to define the new Turkish nation. In an attempt "to eliminate every symbol that had a relationship with the Ottoman-Islamic heritage" and to radically "break from the Ottoman era,"[10] earlier reforms included abolition of the caliphate (1924), closure of religious shrines (*türbes*) and the dervish lodges (*tekkes*) (1925), abolition of the Ministry of Religious Affairs and Pious Foundations (1924), removing an article from the constitution that declared Islam as the state religion (1928), "Turkification" of the call to prayer (1932), and change of the alphabet from Arabic to Latin (1928), which meant a complete disconnection from cultural and literary products of the past.[11]

The state elite wished to purify the Turkish language and therefore cleansed it of its Arabic and Islamic influences deemed to counteract inculcation of a secular identity through literature, education, and the media. With the introduction of the Latin alphabet, books, magazines, newspapers, and official documents were placed in the archives for years to come. Other major reforms between 1924 and 1935 included the acceptance of the Western style of clothing, the adoption of the Gregorian calendar (1926), the introduction of Western music in schools, the change of the weekly holiday from Friday to Sunday, adoption of the Swiss civil and Italian penal codes, and the adoption of laws pertaining to the unification of education (1924),[12] which facilitated the emergence of secular myths, symbols, and rituals. Şerif Mardin, a leading sociologist, notes that "between 1918 and 1939 Turks embarked on a major identity switch. This involved a change in status, from subjects of a multi-ethnic, cosmopolitan empire to citizens of a republic that set down and affirmed its true Turkishness."[13]

Religion and Secularism in the Constitution

Constitution

As noted earlier, the Turkish system of state-religion relations evolved, gradually moving away from being a constitutionally Islamic state and anchoring in a strongly secular state. The Constitution of 1924 included the declaration "[T]he religion of the Turkish Republic is Islam."[14] In 1928, however, this declaration was removed from the Constitution, and secularism as a constitutional principle was added in 1937.[15] Although the Turkish state is defined as secular, it has incorporated religion in its bureaucracy with the establishment of the Directorate of Religious Affairs (the Diyanet İşleri Başkanlığı), which is a constitutional public body with a mandate to administer religious affairs for Muslims.[16] The Directorate was established in 1924, when the Ministry of Religion and Pious Foundations was abolished.

Directorate of Religious Affairs

The 1961 Constitution organized the Directorate of Religious Affairs as a constitutional institution and gave it a constitutional set of duties and responsibilities.[17] Thus it is sometimes argued that the republican elite inherited and preserved an Ottoman legacy, albeit in different forms and with different functions.[18] There is also a contrasting view that considers the Directorate as "an administrative tool to propagate official ideology regarding Islam" in the absence of an organized body of clergy and a central organization set up by Muslims.[19] The 1982 Constitution, which was accepted following the 1980 military coup, also recognized the constitutional status of the Directorate. Article 136 of the current Constitution states, "The Directorate of Religious Affairs, which is within the general administration, shall exercise its duties prescribed in its particular law, in accordance with the principles of secularism, removed from all political views and ideas, and aiming at national solidarity and integrity."[20] The particular law pertaining to the Directorate, which was passed in 1965, explains the Directorate's objectives and its scope of activities and responsibilities as follows: "to execute the works concerning the beliefs, worship, and ethics of Islam, enlighten the public about their religion, and administer the sacred worshipping places."[21]

Over the years constitutional mandates and duties have empowered the Directorate as a public institution that receives its entire operating budget from the state and employs approximately 80,000 people throughout Turkey. The Directorate administers all mosques in Turkey, trains imams, and organizes religious courses for young people and adults during the summer holidays. The fact of the Directorate's mere presence in the state system as well as its provision of services only to Turkey's Muslim population raises questions about Turkey's status as a secular state and whether the Directorate's presence is compatible with secularism. Another issue in Turkey is the dominantly orthodox Sunni interpretation of Islam, which informs the Directorate's main activities. This debate will continue in Turkey, whether or not the AK Party runs the government.

Religious Education

Compulsory religious education in primary and secondary schools, as required by the Constitution, is also a contested issue in Turkey. Until 1980 religious education was an elective course. In the 1982 Constitution, which was drafted after the 1980 military coup, instruction in religious culture and morality became compulsory for Muslim children regardless of their sectarian affiliation.[22] Non-Muslim children were, however, exempted from taking these courses. It is ironic to see that generals of the military coup, who were strictly committed to secular ideals and considered themselves guardians of the state, introduced compulsory religion education. Arguably the generals wanted to control the curriculum and observe religious inculcation closely instead of leaving it to independent religious groups or pushing religious education underground. Yet one might also argue that compulsory religious education was implemented to educate young people, as religion could play a unifying role following the period of political fragmentation that led to street fighting prior to the military coup. Turks generally approve compulsory education, excluding the Alevi community and liberal organizations. Yet when it comes to the nature of the curriculum and the content of the teaching material, a heated dispute emerges. Domestic and external factors, such as EU membership negotiations and decisions by the European Court of Human Rights, often lead to fierce debates and court cases, which resulted in amendments to the curriculum in 2008.[23]

Because the complete rejection of compulsory religious education is futile—because new regulations require a constitutional change, which is not possible in the current political configuration—the confessional content of the curricula became a target, especially for the Alevi community. The Alevis argue that the curriculum represents only Sunni Islam and does not incorporate any teachings of Alevi beliefs and doctrines.[24] They have challenged this policy as discrimination in the courts.[25] In fact about four thousand cases filed by members of the Alevi community are pending in the Turkish courts.[26] In an exemplary case, after the internal legal procedures had been exhausted, the parents of an Alevi student appealed to the European Court of Human Rights.[27] In October 2007 the Court ruled that the content of the curriculum dominantly represented Sunni Islam and urged the Turkish government to make necessary amendments to introduce a more diverse curriculum including the Alevi beliefs.[28] It is noteworthy that the Court did not rule against the compulsory status of religious education; rather its ruling pertained to the content of the course curriculum. The Court argued that Alevism is distinct from the Sunni interpretation of Islam and that the content of religious courses did not meet the European Convention on Human Rights criteria of objectivity and plurality.[29] Following this decision, the Ministry of National Education made several changes. Notably, in March 2009 a local court in Antalya, a southern city, ruled in favor of Alevi parents who demanded that their daughter be exempt from compulsory religious instruction.[30]

The Dress Code and the Headscarf Issue

There is no law that prohibits female students from wearing the headscarf in the universities, but there is a formal dress code that bans women veiling in public offices, such as in schools, hospitals, libraries, ministries, military establishments, and Parliament. Private companies such as banks, stores, shopping centers, restaurants, and large supermarkets predominantly follow a policy of banning the veil. Although empowerment of women through education and employment is frequently mentioned by state authorities and political parties, a significant number of women in Turkey face difficulties in accessing higher education and the job market because of the headscarf ban.

The headscarf ban at the universities started in the mid-1980s as a result of ad hoc decisions by some university administrators of not allowing veiled students to enter the university premises. When this practice was supported by the Council of State, the ruling Motherland Party passed a law (No. 3511) in 1988 to lift the ban. The first attempt to allow female students "to cover their hair and necks because of their religious convictions" was blocked by a Constitutional Court ruling in 1989.[31] The second attempt by the Motherland Party, which passed a law (No. 3670) to lift the ban in 1990 was again blocked by the Constitutional Court on April 9, 1991, on the application of the main opposition party.[32] Based on the rulings of the Constitutional Court, university administrators continued the headscarf ban. Those who supported the ban argued that it was in place to protect secular principles; its critics claimed that the ban was a violation of freedom of religion.

When the AK Party came to power in 2002, its leaders initially remained silent on the issue and didn't initiate a legal process to lift the ban. During the party's second term, with the support of the Nationalist Action Party, it pressed the Turkish Parliament to pass a constitutional amendment on February 9, 2008, by 411 to 103 votes, with the purpose of ending a long-running ban on Islamic headscarves at universities. On February 22 President Abdullah Gül approved the changes.

The changes to the Constitution were concerned with the principle of equality and the right to education by all; lifting the ban on headscarves was not explicitly mentioned in the law. Under heavy pressure from staunch secularist circles and the establishment, however, the Constitutional Court—described as "the stronghold of secularists"[33]—annulled the amendments that would lift the ban at the universities the same year. The court ruled on June 5, 2008, that the Turkish Parliament had violated the constitutionally enshrined principle of secularism by making amendments to lift the ban.[34] In particular the main opposition party, the Republican People's Party (RPP), maintained that the AK Party had a secret agenda to Islamize the country, which is why the party made such changes.[35] However, with the leadership change in the RRP, there has been a move toward acknowledging the headscarf question in Turkey. In contrast to previous policies supporting the ban, Kemal Kiliçdaroğlu, the new leader of the RPP, claimed that his party could solve the problem. A commission was established by the RPP to prepare a report to seek alternative options to resolve Turkey's headscarf controversy;[36] its findings and recommendations are awaited.

Kiliçdaroğlu's statement created an expectation but also caused in-party disputes about the RPP's traditional position toward secularism and religion. Although Kiliçdaroğlu offered no formula for the solution and took no initiative, he had to soften the tone of his promises based on "concerns" expressed by some RPP deputies.[37]

Debates on the headscarf focus largely on university students. However, it is likely that headscarf question will be discussed within a larger framework in the near future in a democratizing Turkey. Recent research indicates that the headscarf ban, or negative attitudes toward it, affect not only women in higher education but also women in the job market. The state does not employ women who wear a headscarf in public offices. The headscarf ban for working women has a chain effect, which is copied by the private sector. Veiled women face unfavorable treatment at the beginning of their employment, during work, and in the process of promotion.[38] Unless resolved by the participation of major political parties and actors, the headscarf ban will continue to be one of the main issues of controversy in Turkish politics and a polarizing question.

Unorthodox Muslims and Non-Muslim Communities
The Alevi Community

The Alevi community is the largest nonorthodox Muslim group in Turkey. "Although the meaning of Alevism is still disputed among the Alevi groups, their common claims revolve around public recognition of Alevi identity and institutions."[39] If we look at more specific demands, the following list covers most of the Alevi claims:

> Legalization of the status of cemevis as places of worship (ibadethane); Abolition of compulsory religious courses; abandonment of the policy of building mosques in Alevi villages; abolition of the Administration of Religious Affairs (Diyanet) or allocation of a budget to cemevis; recommendation of saz (lute) as a musical instrument in secondary school curriculum; handing over the administration and control of the historical Bektaşi shrines (dergahs) including the Hacı Bektaş Dergah, Şahkulu Dergah to Alevi-Bektaşi foundations and associations; removal of religion column from the national ID cards; broadcast of programs on Alevi culture and rituals at official TV and radio broadcasting company, TRT (Turkish Radio and Television); Positive discrimination for Alevi citizens in bureaucratic jobs; free water, electricity, and land for cemevis; financial compensation to Alevi dedes.[40]

For the Alevi community there are signs of positive developments. First, the deputy head of the Directorate of Religious Affairs has publicly declared that his institution had neglected the Alevis.[41] After this public declaration, representatives of some Alevi organizations met with officials of the Directorate to discuss their views and air their expectations. It is important to note that the Alevi community is very diverse and its definition of Alevism, as well as its connection with Islam, differs considerably among Alevi groups.[42] Some Alevi groups claim that Alevism represents a liberal and progressive interpretation of Islam; some argue that it is marked by humanism; while other Alevi groups reject any Islamic connections and argue that Alevism is a worldview with its own philosophy and rituals.[43] These groups believe that the existence of the Directorate undermines secularism, and they therefore refuse to cooperate with it. Yet Alevi groups that see Alevism under the umbrella of Islam are engaging in a dialogue with the state and the Directorate in an attempt to get full recognition and equal representation.[44] The current government started, for the first time, direct engagement with the Alevi community. Prime Minister Recep Tayyip Erdoğan appointed an Alevi member of Parliament from the AK Party as an envoy to bring both sides into a discussion.[45] Furthermore, in a gesture of recognition of Alevi claims, Prime Minister Erdoğan participated at dinners with the Alevi leaders, organized on ritually important days for the community.[46]

More recently the government initiated a special series of Alevi workshops to identify Alevi problems and claims and to prepare a road map to solutions.[47] As of this writing, seven workshops had been held in 2009 and 2010 under the auspices of Directorate of Religious Affairs. The first workshop brought together Alevi community leaders; the next five workshops invited intellectuals and opinion leaders from all backgrounds, including political scientists, historians, theologians, and representatives from civil society organizations and the media.[48] The final workshop brought together a mix of the participants in previous meetings to formulate recommendations to the government.[49]

Non-Muslims

Though reports indicate that over 98 percent of the population of Turkey is Muslim,[50] there are also several non-Muslim religious groups inherited from the Ottoman state, most of which are concentrated in Istanbul and other large cities. Because census results do not contain any data on the religious affiliation of Turkish citizens, the exact membership figures of non-Muslim communities are not available.[51] The 1923 Lausanne Peace Treaty, which formally established the Republic of Turkey, recognizes the existence of religious minorities and makes specific references to guarantees and protections for all non-Muslim minorities.[52] Article 39 of the Treaty guarantees equality among Turkish citizens regardless of their religious conviction: "Turkish nationals belonging to non-Moslem minorities will enjoy the same civil and political rights as Moslems. All the inhabitants of Turkey, without distinction of religion, shall be equal before the law." Article 40 of the Lausanne Treaty stipulates that "Turkish nationals belonging to non-Moslem minorities shall enjoy the same treatment and security in law and in fact as other Turkish nationals. In particular, they shall have an equal right to establish, manage and control at their own expense, any charitable, religious and social institutions, any schools and other establishments for instruction and education, with the right to use their own language and to exercise their own religion freely therein." Article 42 reaffirms that "[t]he Turkish Government undertakes to grant full protection to the churches, synagogues, cemeteries, and other religious establishments of the above-mentioned minorities. All facilities and authorization will be granted to the pious foundations, and to the religious and charitable institutions of the said minorities at present existing in Turkey, and the Turkish Government will not refuse, for the formation of new religious and charitable institutions, any of the necessary facilities which are guaranteed to other private institutions of that nature." Despite these articles, however, non-Muslim minorities in Turkey have faced problems since 1936 regarding property ownership, renovation, and expansion of their places of worship and other institutions.

The Office of Foundations (Vakiflar Genel Müdürlüğü) regulates some activities of non-Muslim religious groups and their affiliated churches, monasteries, religious schools, and related property. There are 160 "minority foundations" recognized by the Office of Foundations,[53] including Greek Orthodox (approximately seventy sites), Armenian Orthodox (approximately fifty), and Jewish (twenty), as well as Syrian Christian, Chaldean, Bulgarian Orthodox, Georgian, and Maroni foundations. On January 2, 2003, Parliament amended the law pertaining to the property of community (non-Muslim minority) foundations, lifting strict restrictions and enabling these foundations to have more freedom in keeping, maintaining, and purchasing new premises.[54] Under the 2003 law, community foundations became eligible to purchase new property for religious, social, cultural, and educational functions, as well as for providing health services under more flexible conditions with the permission of the Foundations Directorate.[55] Parliament also voted in favor of a new Foundation Law on February 2008 that expands freedoms for minority foundations in Turkey, which was approved by President Gül.[56]

Turkey's policy toward its non-Muslims subjects is moving in the right direction in terms of consolidating and expanding rights and liberties they were not able to fully enjoy under Kemalism, which tended to favor a nationalist and exclusivist interpretation of secularism. The performance of the current Turkish government under the AK Party offers positive signs for the future. New legal provisions in 2003 have granted "places of worship" status to existing churches and synagogues, and a new Protestant church opened in 2006. Following these developments Parliament passed an amendment that enables churches and synagogues to have the same right as mosques to use free water and electricity.[57] However, the question of reopening the Halki Seminary, which was established on Heybeli Island in 1844 and closed down in 1971, still remains unresolved, though government ministers and politicians have made positive statements.

It should be noted that the Halki Seminary was not closed down on religious grounds, and there is no court decision specifically aiming at closing this institution. Closure of the Halki Seminary should be viewed in the context of state intervention and centralization of education in Turkey. When Turkey was founded as a nation-state, the education system was centralized through the Unification of Education Law (No. 789, March 3, 1924, Tevhid-i Tedrisat Kanunu), which consolidated state control on all educational institutions in the name of establishing a single system for the inculcation of cultural conformity. Moreover in 1926 the Law Pertaining to Education Organization stipulated that "no school can be established without the permission of the state." These two laws formed the basis for direct state homogenization of institutions of education. A subsequent Constitutional Court decision in 1971 led to closure of private higher education institutions, including higher sections of Halki Seminary and the American Robert College.[58] The Court held the view that "Article 120 of the Constitution stipulates that higher education institutions can be established by the state only." With that decision, private higher education institutions faced two options: either become part of a state university by accepting its control and authority or close down their higher education sections. Robert College chose the first option and converted to a state university in 1971 under a new name, becoming a reputable and leading university in Turkey. The Halki Seminary did not accept the same option and therefore had to close down its higher education section.

Demands for the reopening of the Halki Seminary by the Greek Orthodox community in Turkey were met largely by silence by previous governments. Democratization moves by the AK Party government have involved consideration of the demands of the Greek Orthodox community. Although no concrete steps have been taken so far, moves toward democratization are indicated by the constitutional referendum on September 12, 2010, which changed twenty-six articles of the current Constitution. As noted earlier, the AK Party government initiated two major projects popularly known as the Kurdish Opening and the Alevi Opening. A further initiative for freedom of religion for all communities is expected to be undertaken by the AK Party government. AK Party leadership appears willing to expand religious liberty and lift bans for individual and institutional freedom. Following a meeting with his Greek counterpart, Yorgo Papandreu, Prime Minister Erdoğan said this: "A legal committee has been working on this issue. We hope to find a solution to the Halki Seminary question during our term in the government."[59]

There are two main obstacles preventing the AK Party government from taking radical steps to resolve religious freedom issues in the current political climate. The first is the perceived threat that the party would be banned if it takes on these issues. Charging that the AK Party was weakening the secular foundations of the state, the chief public prosecutor of the Court of Cassation opened a case in 2008 at the Constitutional Court to shut down the party and ban more than seventy politicians. Although the Court did not close the AK Party, the case has set the prosecutor's sword at the party's neck. The closure of twenty-six parties since 1954 largely on grounds of ethnic separatism or a focus of antisecular activities seems to have made the AK Party leadership more cautious and less willing to take any risks to avoid yet another closure case.[60]

The second reason seems to be concern for public opinion in the lead-up to general elections to be held in summer of 2011. Although the Directorate of Religious Affairs[61] and the Higher Education Council[62] see no problem with the opening of the Halki Seminary, public opinion seems to be divided; a recent survey reported that 28 percent of Turks support the opening, 41.5 percent are against it, and 31 percent are undecided.[63] The AK Party is not expected to take bold steps in case this might alienate some of its constituency. Moreover the AK Party government does not get any support from the main opposition party, the RPP, on eliminating limitations on religious liberty, particularly on the issue of reopening the Halki Seminary. If the RPP lends support to the AK Party to expand freedom of religion in Turkey, AK Party leadership will most probably feel more confident to take radical steps. The RPP seems to be undecided on resolving freedom of religion issues, which leaves the AK Party on its own and less willing to act, given the closure case it faced earlier and ambivalent public opinion. If the AK Party wins the 2011 elections with a clear majority, it is expected that concrete steps will be taken to resolve this question since the party leadership will have a consolidated mandate for the third term in office and feel less vulnerable in removing obstacles to religious liberty. The reopening the Halki Seminary will be one of the major test cases for Muslim democrats in Turkey.

Turkish Foreign Policy Orientation

Turkey's changing relations with the EU, the United States, Israel, Iran, and the Arab world are increasingly analyzed through the prism of identity shift, of a tilt toward the Middle East in general and the Muslim world in particular. Diverse international initiatives since 2002 have raised questions about the direction of Turkey's foreign policy. As the October 2010 cover page of *The Economist* asked, Is Turkey turning its back on the West?[64] This is a legitimate question given Turkey's relations with Iran and Syria, its rift with Israel over the Gaza issue, and strained relations aggravated by the *Mavi Marmara* flotilla crisis.

If one looks at Turkey's new foreign dynamism and its diverse directions from a Eurocentric or U.S.-centric position, one gets the impression that the republic is anchoring itself in the Muslim Middle East. This shortsighted view fails to capture the complexities and multidimensional nature of foreign policies pursued by a country stretching between East and West, neighboring Iraq, Syria, Iran, and Armenia—a crisis-ridden and unstable region. From a realistic perspective, it is neither in the interest of Turkey nor in the interest of Europe and the United States to turn their back on this volatile region. Since coming to power, the AK Party has been pursuing a zero-problem policy with neighboring countries, leading to closer relations and better economic and security cooperation. As a result of the zero-problem policy, Turkey established close working relations with Syria, with which it was on the brink of war over Syria's hosting of Abdullah Öcalan, leader of the PKK terror organization.

Turkey's improved relations in the Middle East paid off well, to the extent that Turkey has played a mediating role between Israel and Syria, convinced various parties to take part in general elections in Iraq, facilitated Turkish business investments in northern Iraq, and bilaterally lifted visas with Syria, Lebanon, and Jordan. Turkey's closer relations with the Arab world and its possible membership in the EU should be seen as strategic assets for the democratization of the region rather than as leaving the West. Turkey has established better relations not only with the Middle Eastern Muslim countries but also with Russia and Greece. Turkey and Russia bilaterally lifted visas, and Russia became the largest trade partner of Turkey. Moreover the AK Party tried to close the rift with Armenia, despite significant resistance from the opposition parties. All these developments require us to reconsider the Eurocentric or U.S.-centric perspective on Turkish foreign policy and acknowledge that Turkey's soft power has a potential to consolidate peace and stability in the region.

It is time to recognize that the cold war is over and foreign policy options are more diverse for countries like Turkey. The cold war framework was shaped predominantly by security concerns. The United States still seems to hold on to this view and expects its allies to pursue their foreign policy on this principle. However, this view is no longer compatible with the realities of Asia, the Middle East, Africa, and South America. New power centers have emerged, with different priorities and interests than those of the West, though not necessarily contradictory. India, China, Russia, and Brazil are described as emerging powers, a development that transforms the parameters of international relations. These emerging powers have economic growth, military strength, energy sources, and demographic capital. From this perspective, Turkey can be described as an emerging power in the region, with its hard and soft power. It should be remembered in this context that Turkey has the second largest military power in NATO after the United States. It is the seventeenth largest economy globally and the fifth in Europe. As far as the region is concerned, Turkey also has deep cultural relations as well as an increasing trade volume where it can capitalize on soft power to pursue a constructive and stabilizing role, especially in Iraq and

Afghanistan, major areas of concern for the United States and Europe. As pointed out by a longtime observer of Turkey, the AK Party's foreign "policies remain essentially nationalist, Turkey-centered and commercially opportunistic; it is a misconception to think of them as Islamist, or even ideological. Whatever the country's problems, Turkey's primary principal relationships remain those with Europe and the United States."[65] Turkey's record-breaking increase in trade with neighboring countries and its attraction of significant foreign investment from the Middle East and Europe confirm that the AK Party is driven by rational and pragmatic concerns, not ideological motives.[66]

The end of the cold war ushered in several "changes in geopolitics, economy, energy, and human mobility in Turkey's neighborhood and have presented the country with complex challenges, as well as opportunities. In response, over the last decade Turkey has defined a new foreign policy doctrine."[67] The new dynamism in Turkish engagement in the Middle East, the Balkans, and the Caucasus and its closer relations with Muslim countries should be viewed in the context of post–cold war realities and opportunities as well as requirements to adapt and respond to the new challenges.

Conclusions

Turkey's state system is strongly secular, though it is a Muslim-majority country by population. There is a strict wall of separation between the state and religion. Therefore religion, religious institutions, and religious groups have no influence on legislation, which is solely based on secular procedures. Religion is not a source of law in the country, which aspires to become a full member of the European Union. To achieve this objective, Turkey has introduced several harmonization packages to bring its legal system in line with that of the EU. These reforms positively contributed to expand freedom of religion both for the majority Muslim population and nonorthodox communities and non-Muslim minorities.

The rise of the AK Party in 2002 was a source of concern for the secular elite, including the military, judiciary, high-level bureaucracy, and the main opposition Republican People's Party, which feared that the AK Party would undermine democracy, destroy the secular foundations of the republic, and establish an Islamic state. The AK Party is governing Turkey for a third term after winning the 2011 elections. Records of the AK Party policies since 2002 and research findings, as analyzed in this chapter, demonstrate that these fears and suspicions are not persuasive. In fact the AK Party initiated a "silent revolution";[68] "instead of undermining democracy, it ha[s] done more to widen civil liberties than any preceding government since 1960s."[69] The political attitude of the current AK Party government has also paved the way for the emergence of more progressive and libertarian views, with the objective of lifting prohibitions on religion and establishing liberties and legal entitlements for religious communities. As the September 12, 2010, constitutional referendum indicates (58 percent approved), there is an expectation for further democratization, liberalization, and transparency in the changing domestic and foreign policy environment in Turkey.

Despite promising developments in reconciling with the universal standards of freedom of religion and granting rights to believers of all kinds, there are still issues that need to be addressed by the AK Party. Two of these issues are lifting the headscarf ban for university students and allowing formal religious education for children at an early age rather than waiting until they finish eight years (average age fifteen) of compulsory primary education.[70] Moreover the headscarf ban for staff in public offices should be lifted since it prevents veiled women from entering the public workforce and makes them vulnerable citizens. A system granting legal personality to both Muslim-majority and non-Muslim minority religious groups is still waiting to be addressed. As the Venice Commission notes, the Turkish legal system does not have any instrument whereby "religious communities can register and obtain legal personality."[71] Additionally the government should endeavor to meet some of the demands of Alevi communities on the basis of consensus and common understanding. Open discussions on the question of the Halki Seminary should take place, and the Greek Orthodox community should be engaged in the debate. The AK Party took courageous steps to resolve the Kurdish question, first recognizing the presence of such a question and then introducing a Kurdish TV channel. It should take similar bold steps for the opening of the Halki Seminary and should also reach out to the Armenian Orthodox community to resolve their claim to equal citizenship.

Notes

1. William Hale and Ergun Ozbudun, *Islamism, Democracy and Liberalism in Turkey: The case of the AKP* (London: Routledge, 2010), 122; Ali Resul Usul, "The Justice and Development Party and the European Union: From Euro-skepticism to Euro-enthusiasms and Euro-fatigue," in *Secular and Islamic Politics in Turkey: The Making of the Justice and Development Party*, ed. Umit Cizre (London: Routledge, 2008), 185.

2. "Ankara Restores Armenian Church," BBC News, March 29, 2007, http://news.bbc.co.uk/2/hi/europe/6505927.stm.

3. Ruşen Çakır, *Mahalle Baskısı: Prof. Şerif Mardin'in Tezlerinden Hareketle Türkiye'de İslam, Cumhuriyet, Laiklik ve Demokrasi* (Istanbul: Doğan Yayıncılık, 2008).

4. Binnaz Toprak et. al, *Türkiye'de Farklı Olmak, Din ve Muhafazakarlık Ekseninde Ötekileştirilenler* (Being Different in Turkey: Alienation on the Axis of Religion and Conservatism) (Istanbul: Boğaziçi Üniversitesi Matbaası, 2008).

5. Hakan Yılmaz, *Türkiye'de Muhafazakarlık, Aile, Din ve Batı* (Conservatism in Turkey: Family, Religion and the West) (Istanbul: Boğaziçi University and the Open Society, 2006).

6. Yasin Aktay et al., *Türkiye'de Ortak Bir Kimlik Olarak Ötekilik Araştırması*, (Research on Otherness as a Shared Identity in Turkey), Egitim Bir-Sen Strategic Araştırmalar Merkezi, EBSAM, Ankara, 2010. The full text in Turkish is available at http://www.egitimbirsen.org.tr/dokuman/otekilik.pdf.

7. Füsun Üstel and Birol Caymaz, *Elitler ve Sosyal Mesafe* (Elites and Social Distance)(Istanbul: Bilgi University and Open Society Foundation, April 2010), 38, 39, 52.

8. Hakan Yılmaz, *Türkiye'de 'Biz'lik, 'Öteki'lik, Ötekileştirme ve Ayrımcılık: Kamuoyundaki Algılar ve Eğilimler*, ("We," "Others," "Othering" and "Discrimination" in Turkey: Perceptions and Trends in the Public Opinion) (Istanbul: Open Society Foundation and Bogazici University, 2010).

9. Nilüfer Göle, "Authoritarian Secularism and Islamist Politics: The Case of Turkey," in *Civil Society in the Middle East*, ed. Augustus Richards Norton (Leiden: E. J. Brill, 1995), 17, 19.

10. Sena Karasipahi, *Muslims in Modern Turkey* (London: I. B. Tauris, 2009), 10.

11. Şerif Mardin, *Religion, Society, and Modernity in Turkey* (Syracuse, N.Y.: Syracuse University Press, 2006), 234.

12. Ahmet Kuru, *Secularism and State Policies toward Religion: The United States, France and Turkey* (Cambridge: Cambridge University Press, 2009), 222; Umit Cizre-Sakallioglu, "Kemalism, Hyper-Nationalism and Islam in Turkey," *History of European Ideas* 18, no. 12 (1994): 258.

13. Şerif Mardin, "Playing Games with Names," in *Fragments of Culture: The Everyday of Modern Turkey*, ed. Deniz Kandiyoti and Ayse Saktanber (London: I. B. Tauris, 2002), 115.

14. The Constitution of Republic of Turkey, 1924.

15. Kuru, *Secularism and State Policies toward Religion*, 217.

16. The Constitution of Republic of Turkey, 1982, Article 136, "The Law about the Presidency of Religious Affairs, Its Establishment and Obligations," 633, dated June 22, 1965; http://www.diyanet.gov.tr/turkish/dy/default.aspx.

17. The Constitution of Republic of Turkey, 1961.

18. Gazi Erdem, "Religious Services in Turkey: From the Office of Şeyhülislam to the Diyanet," *Muslim World* 98 (April–July 2008): 207.

19. İştar B. Gözaydın "Diyanet and Politics," *Muslim World* 98 (April–July 2008): 221.

20. The Constitution of Republic of Turkey, 1982, Article 136.

21. "The Law about the Presidency of Religious Affairs, Its Establishment and Obligations," 633.

22. The Constitution of the Republic of Turkey, 1982, Article 24/c.

23. *Annual Report of the United States Commission on International Religious Freedom* (Washington, D.C., 2009), 204, 205; Hadi Adanalı, "The Many Dimensions of Religious Instruction in Turkey," http://www.iarf.net/REBooklet/Turkey.htm.

24. John Shindeldecker, "Turkish Alevis Today," http://www.alevi.dk/ENGELSK/Turkish_Alevis_Today.pdf accessed on June 6, 2012.

25. Commission of the European Communities, *Turkey* 2009 *Progress Report*, October 14, 2009, 21.

26. U.S. Bureau of Democracy, Human Rights, and Labor, *International Religious Freedom Report* 2008.

27. ECHR Decision No 1448/04.

28. Ibid.

29. Ibid.

30. Shindeldecker, "Turkish Alevis Today"; Saban Kardaş, "Religious Freedom Still Tenuous in Turkey," February 26, 2009, http://www.jamestown.org/single/?no_cache=1&tx_ttnews%5Btt_news%5D=34559.

31. The Turkish Constitutional Court Decision No. 1989/12.

32. Hale and Ozbudun, *Islamism, Democracy and Liberalism in Turkey*, 71, 72.

33. Suna Erdem, "Judges Defy Government to Uphold Turkey Headscarf Ban," *Times Online*, June 8, 2008, http://www.timesonline.co.uk/tol/news/world/europe/article4076180.ece.

34. The Turkish Constitutional Court Decision No. 2008/116.

35. "CHP Türbanda Gerekçeli Karardan Ne Kadar Memnun?," http://www.cnnturk.com/2008/turkiye/10/22/chp.turbanda.gerekceli.karardan.memnun/497824.0/index.html.

36. "Turkish Opposition's Headscarf Move Seen as Political by Some Groups," *Daily News* (Turkey), August 25, 2010, http://www.hurriyetdailynews.com/n.php?n=chps-headscarf-move-draws-diverse-reaction-2010-08-25.

37. "CHP Chief Moves to Transform Turkey's Oldest Party," *Daily News* (Turkey), October 10, 2010, http://www.hurriyetdailynews.com/n.php?n=chp-chief-presses-button-to-transform-the-party-2010-10-10.

38. Dilen Cindoglu, *Başörtüsü Yasağı ve Ayrımcılık: Uzman Meslek Sahibi Başörtülü Kadınlar* (Headscarf Ban and Discrimination: Professional Women with Headscarf) (Istanbul: TESEV, October 2010), 8.

39. Talha Köse, *Alevi Opening and the Democratization Initiative in Turkey*, Seta Policy Report, March 2010, 7.

40. Ibid., 22.

41. "Diyanetten Özeleştiri: Bugüne Kadar Aleviliği Ihmal Ettik," *Zaman*, http://www.zaman .com.tr/haber.do?haberno=515066.

42. Tahire Erman and Emrah Göker, "Alevi Politics in Contemporary Turkey," *Middle Eastern Studies* 36, no. 4 (October 2000): 100–112: David Schankland, *Alevis in Turkey: The Emergence of a Secular Islamic Tradition* (London: Routledge Curzon, 2003), 21–22; Karin Vorhoff, "'Let's Reclaim Our History and Culture!' Imagining Alevi Community in Contemporary Turkey," *Die Welt des Islams* 38, no. 2 (July 1998): 240.

43. İştar Gözaydın, *Diyanet* (Istanbul: İletişim yayıncılık, 2009), 290; Vorhoff, "Let's Reclaim Our History and Culture!," 220–52.

44. Gözaydın, *Diyanet*, 290; Vorhoff, "Let's Reclaim Our History and Culture!," 235.

45. "AK Party to Expand Dialogue with Alevis," *Today's Zaman*, January 15, 2008, http://www .todayszaman.com/tz-web/news-131698-ak-party-to-expand-dialogue-with-alevis.html.

46. "PM Erdoğan: Alevi-Bektaşi Tradition at the Core of Our Identities," *Today's Zaman*, January 12, 2008, http://www.todayszaman.com/tz-web/news-131514-pm-erdogan-alevi-bektasi-tradition-at-the-core-of-our-identities.html.

47. "Political Authority Taking First Serious Steps to Solve Alevis' Problems," *Today's Zaman*, November 11, 2009, http://www.todayszaman.com/tz-web/news-192572-political-author-ity-taking-first-serious-steps-to-solve-alevis-problems.html; "Alevi Workshop Submits Roadmap to Government," *Today's Zaman*, February 1, 2010, http://www.todayszaman.com/tz-web/news-200249-alevi-workshop-submits-roadmap-to-government.html.

48. "Gov't steps on Alevi issue 'historic,' says Çelik," http://www.todayszaman.com/tz-web/news-192670-govt-steps-on-alevi-issue-historic-says-celik.html; "Government Consults Religious Scholars on Alevi Problem," *Daily News* (Turkey), August 19, 2009, http://www.hurriyetdaily-news.com/h.php?news=government-hears-religious-scholars-for-alevi-problem-2009-08-19.

49. "Alevi Workshop Submits Roadmap to Government."

50. CIA, "The World Factbook," https://www.cia.gov/library/publications/the-world-factbook/ geos/tu.html.

51. There are approximately 65,000 Armenian Orthodox in Turkey, 23,000 Jews, and 2,500 Greek Orthodox. *Annual Report of the United States Commission on International Religious Freedom*, 205.

52. Treaty of Peace with Turkey Signed at Lausanne, July 24, 1923, Articles 38–45.

53. For recent debates on the status of non-Muslims foundations, see Istanbul Bar Association, Human Rights Center, Minority Rights Working Group, *Cemaat Vakıfları* (Community Foundations), 2002.

54. Law No. 4778 (2003).

55. Ibid.

56. "Gül Gives Consent to Minority Foundations Law," *Today's Zaman*, February 28, 2008; http: //www.todayszaman.com/tz-web/detaylar.do?load=detay&link=135111:VakıflarKanunu,Kanun No. 5737.

57. Kerem Karaosmanoğlu, "Reimagining Minorities in Turkey: Before and After the AKP," *Insight Turkey* 12, no. 12 (2010): 203.

58. Constitutional Court Decision, No. 1971/3, January 12, 1971, http://www.anayasa.gov .tr/index.php?l=manage_karar&ref=show&action=karar&id=328&content=özel yüksek okulların.

59. "'Heybeliada'yı çözeceğiz' sözü," *Taraf Daily Newspaper*, October 23, 2010, http://www.taraf .com.tr/haber/heybeliada-yi-cozecegiz-sozu.htm.

60. Birce Albayrak Coşkun, "Türkiye'de Siyasi Parti Kapatma ve Avrupa Örnekleri," *Memleket, Siyaset Yönetim* 3, no. 7 (2008): 184.

61. "Bartholomeos'a yanıt," *Vatan*, January 2, 2010, http://www9.gazetevatan.com/haberdetay .asp?Categoryid=1&Newsid=279566.

62. "YÖK: 'Ruhban okuluna olumlu bakıyoruz,'" CNN Turkey, July 9, 2009, http://www.cnnturk.com/2009/turkiye/07/09/yok.ruhban.okuluna.olumlu.bakiyoruz/534319.0/index.html.

63. Aktay et al., *Türkiye'de Ortak Bir Kimlik Olarak Ötekilik Araştırması*, 205.

64. "A Special Report on Turkey," *Economist*, October 24–29, 2010.

65. Hugh Pope, "Pax Ottomans," *Foreign Affairs* 89, no. 6 (2010): 162.

66. Ziya Meral and Jonathan Paris, "Decoding Turkish Foreign Policy Hyperactivity," *Washington Quarterly* 33, no. 4 (2010): 85.

67. Ahmet Evin et al., *Turkey, Its Neighbors and the West* (Washington D.C., Transatlantic Academy Report, 2010), 12.

68. Sultan Tepe, "A Pro-Islamic Party? Promises and Limits of Turkey's Justice and Development Party," in *The Emergence of a New Turkey, Democracy and the AK Party*, ed. M. Hakan Yavuz (Salt Lake City: University of Utah Press, 2006), 129.

69. Hale and Ozbudun, *Islamism, Democracy and Liberalism in Turkey*, 151.

70. Diyanet İşleri Başkanlığı Kur'an Kursları Yönergesi (Diyanet Directive on Qur'an Courses), published in the Official Gazette, no. 23982, March 3, 2000, http://www.diyanet.gov.tr/turkish/mevzuat/mevzuaticerik.asp?id=2301.

71. Ergun Özbudun, "Democratic Opening: The Legal Status of Non-Muslim Religious Communities and the Venice Commission," *Insight Turkey* 12, no. 12 (2010): 218.

13

Human Rights in Islamic Jurisprudence

Why Should All Human Beings Be Inviolable?

RECEP ŞENTÜRK

In the diversity of their religious communities, Muslim cities of the Middle Ages, such as Istanbul, Jerusalem, Baghdad, Samarkand, Bukhara, and Cairo, looked like the modern New York, San Francisco, Berlin, Paris, and London. In contrast, European cities during the Middle Ages were quite homogeneous, usually encompassing one predominant Christian denomination. This continued more or less until the second half of the nineteenth century. Since then Western cities have clearly turned into cosmopolitan metropolitan centers housing diverse faith and ethnic groups.

What made Muslim cities during the Middle Ages similar to modern cosmopolitan centers? I contend that it was because they operated under norms of Islamic jurisprudence regarding universal human rights, particularly freedom of religion. This finding is surprising given the lagging status of religious freedom in many Muslim-majority nations today, and it suggests that recovering that classical Islamic tradition could have enormous global significance.

In previous research I demonstrated that the inviolability of human beings (*ismah al-âdamiyyîn*) has been one of the most fundamental principles of Islamic law and morality.[1] In this chapter I would like to explore the reason that this was so, or, more plainly put, how universal human rights were grounded in Islamic jurisprudence. Paradoxically the ages-old tradition of advocating universal human rights in Islamic jurisprudence has been almost completely forgotten today as the Muslim world suffers from human rights dependency on the West.

I will try to answer the following question: Why should all human beings be inviolable according to Islamic jurisprudence? As I demonstrated in previous work, Muslim jurists are divided on the issue of human rights. One group, led by the Shafii School, advocates for civil rights only, that is, the rights of citizens specifically accorded by the state. Another group, led by the Hanafi School of law, advances rights for all human beings regardless of innate, inherited, or acquired qualities such as sex, race, religion, and citizenship. My focus here is on these "universalist" Muslim jurists who ground human rights in classic Islamic jurisprudence. By surveying selected works from Abu Hanifa (d. 767) to Huseyin Kazım Kadri (d. 1934), I will demonstrate the continuity of a universal human rights tradition in Islamic jurisprudence from the eighth century until the era of legal secularization in the Muslim world during the early twentieth century. After legal secularization severed intellectual ties with the Islamic legal tradition, the Muslim world became dependent on Western human rights discourse, if not opposing it. I will conclude by offering an explanation for this fateful discontinuity.

Classical Islamic jurisprudence accepted the right of the inviolability of human beings from the time of Prophet Muhammad (d. 632) fifteen centuries ago. However, classical Muslim jurists never claimed that they were the fathers of the idea of universal human rights. On the contrary, they claimed that human inviolability is accepted by all religions since the time of Adam. Thus it is a universal rule that constitutes the foundation of all legal systems past and present. Consequently they called the rights that are covered by inviolability axiomatic rights (*daruriyyat*), foundations or fundamental principles (*usul*), and universal rights (*kulliyyat*), which include the right of the inviolability of life, property, mind, religion, family, and honor. These rules, which constitute a special set of laws in Islamic law, constitute the common ground between Islamic and non-Islamic legal systems. According to Islamic jurisprudence, the rules in this category do not get abrogated (*naskh*) since they are universal and transcend time and space, unlike other legal rules, which may change from religion to religion depending on time and geography. This approach provides a way to justify universal human rights based on eternal precedence. At the same time, it demonstrates that classical Muslim jurists produced a nonexceptionalist jurisprudence and legal philosophy.

Such a claim to Islamic exceptionalism would be against Islam's self-perception, the way it presents itself in the Qur'an and the sayings of Prophet Muhammad. Islam sees itself as the restoration of the eternal religion of God since the beginning of time rather than a new religion. All the prophets who came earlier are mentioned in the Qur'an with great respect, including Adam, Noah, Moses, and Jesus. Muslims are required to believe in all the prophets, and they venerate the Virgin Mary as well, after whom a chapter is named in the Qur'an. Therefore Islam presents itself as the authentic continuation of the previous heavenly religions rather than their replacement. For this reason, claiming that Islamic law is the first law that granted universal human rights would contradict this concept of religion and law in Islam. This approach is diametrically opposed to Eurocentric exceptionalism, with its claim that universal human rights emerged for the first time in the European secular legal culture. Classical Islam gives priority to emphasizing the common ground and continuity among religions rather than religious innovation.

I divide civilizations into two groups: open civilizations and closed civilizations. An open civilization does not see itself as the only civilization. It respects other civilizations and supports a world order where multiple civilizations can coexist. In contrast, a closed civilization sees itself as the only true civilization and tries to eliminate all other cultures to establish a world order with a single dominant civilization. Classical Islam belongs to the first category, as it established an open civilization extending from Andalusia to India, where Muslims, Christians, Jews, Buddhists, Hindus, and Zoroastrians lived together. Consequently one can say that Muslims experienced in the Middle Ages what the West came to experience only recently. This historical phenomenon brings to mind the following question: Why did Muslims establish an open civilization during the Middle Ages while most of the other religious groups established closed civilizations? How could Muslims accommodate members of diverse civilizations under a polity? In other words, what was the legal and political infrastructure on which civilizational pluralism was founded?

My answer to these questions comes from Islamic jurisprudence, which provided human rights to people regardless of their religion and civilization. It is commonly known that Islam provides human rights to the People of the Book. What is less commonly known is that the universalist Islamic legal tradition provides the same rights to all human beings regardless of their religion. The concrete historical evidence for this is the case of India, where Buddhists and Hindus enjoyed the same rights Christians and Jews enjoyed in Andalusia. If Islamic law had given human rights only to the People of the Book, the Buddhists and Hindus would not have been given these rights, which they enjoyed under Islamic rule for centuries.

Islamic law thus granted human rights by allowing legal pluralism, which may be seen as an extension of freedom of religion, whereby different religious communities can practice their traditional laws if they prefer to do so. This is what is commonly known as the Ottoman *millet* system. Prior to secularization, religious law was an important part of religion. Depriving people of the practice of the law of their religion would have been a source of discontent among the subjects whose behavior was guided by the norms of religious laws. Consequently Islamic law is an "open law" in the sense that it allows not only multiple Islamic schools of law (*madhahib*) to coexist but also non-Islamic legal systems to be implemented at the same time in the same society.

At this point I should mention another important characteristic of Islamic law: it belongs to the Western legal tradition because Islam belongs to the Western Abrahamic religious tradition, along with Judaism and Christianity. It is commonly known that historians of religion group Islam under the category of Western religions vis-à-vis Eastern religions. Therefore it would be inconsistent not to consider Islamic law as part of the Western legal tradition. In addition to their common historical roots, Islamic law reflects many commonalities

with the Jewish, Christian, and Roman laws, and with modern Western jurisprudence as well. This is not to deny the significant differences from Jewish, Christian, Roman, and modern secular jurisprudence. But one of the important areas
where classical Islamic law reflects significant commonalities with the modern
Western legal tradition is the area of universal human rights. This may be attributed to the fact that they all originate from the same Abrahamic legal tradition.

To understand the Islamic cosmopolitan tradition we must explore the roots
of universal human rights and fundamental freedoms in the teaching of Prophet
Muhammad and how later generations of Muslim jurists built on his legacy and
systematized it. This survey will demonstrate the continuity in the universalist
tradition in Islamic jurisprudence until the twentieth century.

Prophet Muhammad's Farewell Sermon: Universalizing Human Rights

The Farewell Sermon of Prophet Muhammad[2] vividly illustrates his contribution to
the development of human rights and how he laid the foundations of the idea of
universal human rights in a world previously dominated by tribalism.[3] He gave this
sermon to a large group during his last pilgrimage to the Holy Ka'ba in the square
of Arafat a few months prior to his death. Hence the title Farewell Sermon.

In his Farewell Sermon Prophet Muhammad said,[4] "O people! Your lives and
your property, until the very day you meet your Lord, are as inviolable to each
other as the inviolability of this holy day you are now in, this holy month you are
now in, and this holy city you are now in. Have I conveyed the divine message?—
O Allah, be my witness!"[5]

This instruction is about the inviolability of life and property. In the original
Arabic the term *haram* is used to indicate inviolability and sanctity. It was used even
during the pre-Islamic period and was attributed to human beings, times (months,
days), places (Mecca), and objects (idols in the Ka'ba). For instance, *al-shahr al-haram*
means "the inviolable month"; *al-masjid al-haram* means "inviolable temple." Prior
to Islam, Arabs considered four months sacred and thus inviolable: Muharram,
Dhi'l-Qa'da, Dhi'l-Hijjah, and Rajab.[6] During these months people were inviolable
according to the Arabic custom. Likewise according to the Arabic custom, the Ka'ba
was a sacred place in which human beings were inviolable.

Therefore human inviolability during the pre-Islamic period was limited in
time and space. This limitation was a deviation from the laws set by Abraham,
the architect of the Ka'ba. For Arabs, such a limited rule of law, security, and
peace was needed to make Hajj and commerce possible in Mecca, which they
needed to generate income. People were inviolable only in the Ka'ba (Masjid
al-Haram) and during the four haram months. This allowed for the powerful
Arab tribes to exercise their will in a legally and morally unbound manner during

the rest of the year. However, because total anarchy would have caused the collapse of the economy, they maintained four holy months during which commercial and religious activities could be carried on in peace.

With his statement Prophet Muhammad abolished these time and place limitations, thus universalizing human inviolability in all times and places. This was a revolution against the Arab custom and could easily have been rejected by the community. Prophet Muhammad emphasized his injunction in his wording, as well as the time and place where he uttered it. The sermon was given during Hajj, which took place at a sacred time and in a sacred place, and he repeated his injunction several times on several occasions. He also made it explicit that this injunction was from God and that God was the witness when Prophet Muhammad conveyed it to the people.

What did Prophet Muhammad do by uttering these words? And what did the narrative do after his death? There are two conflicting answers from Muslim jurists which shows the mediating role of agency between narrative and its meaning in the ensuing practices.

Simply put, the question that divided the Muslim jurists is as follows: What did Prophet Muhammad mean when he said "O People"? Did he mean Muslims alone or all human beings? Did he completely abolish all the boundaries among human beings, or did he draw a boundary between Muslims and non-Muslims? Put in a more technical way, did he want to found *universal human rights* or *civil rights*?

Subsequent Muslim generations, in particular jurists, differed in their interpretation of what Prophet Muhammad intended by his Farewell Sermon. Two major answers emerged: one by "universalist" Muslim jurists and one by "communalist" Muslim jurists.

Humanity as a whole is inviolable, argued the universalist jurists. They argued that when Prophet Muhammad said "O People!" ("*Yâ ayyuha al-nâs*") he meant all human beings around the world regardless of religion, sex, color, or race. From this perspective, Prophet Muhammad set up the foundations of universalism. This view was adopted by universalist jurists, in particular those from the Hanafi School of law, who argued for the universal inviolability of human beings. For them, the life, property, and honor of all human beings are sacred and inviolable because that is the law given by the Lawgiver (*shâri*), Prophet Muhammad.

However, not all jurists agreed; some argued that when Prophet Muhammad said "O People!" he meant only the Muslim community. From this perspective, what Prophet Muhammad did was justify communalism. In other words, his vision of Islamic law was based on the concept of civil rights, which grants rights only to a nation's citizens. Consequently communalist Muslims translate the statement of Prophet Muhammad as follows: "O People! Just as you regard this month, this day, this city as sacred, so regard the life and property of every Muslim as a sacred trust."[7] One can easily see how this interpretation is used to justify the communalist argument because the audience is all Muslims.

Nevertheless the Farewell Sermon has been rediscovered and put to a new use by Muslims in support of the 1948 United Nations Universal Declaration of Human Rights.[8] From this modern perspective, what Prophet Muhammad did was present the first human rights document. Among the first who advanced this view was Muhammad Hamidullah.[9] This view is very popular today among Muslims. For instance, "The Islamic Charter of Humanity" is the subtitle Nuh Ha Mim Keller uses in his translation of "The Farewell Address of the Holy Prophet Muhammad p.b.u.h." Tahir Mahmood, an Indian Muslim professor of Islamic law, also interprets the Farewell Sermon in the modern context. His universalistic approach is reflected in the translation of "*Yâ Ayyuhâ al-Nâs!*" as "O mankind!": "O mankind! The Arab is not superior to non-Arab, nor vice versa; the white has no superiority over the black, nor vice versa; and the rich has no superiority over the poor. All of you are Adam's descendants and Adam was made of earth."[10] Tahir Mahmood calls the Farewell Sermon "a Declaration of the Equality of Mankind."

This view is advanced to serve both as an apology for Islam and as a justification to enhance human rights compliance by Muslim societies. In any case, this is a new usage to which many Muslims have put the Farewell Sermon. A multitude of examples can be found, published in many languages and on the Internet. My goal here is not to provide an exhaustive list of those who use the Farewell Sermon as the first human rights declaration but to provide a few examples to demonstrate the openness of hadith to new usages and interpretations as the context changes.

Down through the generations, the teachings and practice of Prophet Muhammad have been interpreted by universalist jurists to ground universal human rights in Islamic law, in contrast to communalist jurists, who used the same teachings to ground civil rights. This demonstrates that his legacy, like the legacy of all great masters, allows different interpretations. However, because the focus of this chapter is on the grounding of universal human rights, I will survey the works of leading Hanafi jurists—without any claim to be exhaustive—mostly from the formative period when universal human rights were grounded in an Islamic philosophical and conceptual framework.

Dabusi (d. 1039): The Rights of God Cannot Be Fulfilled without Human Rights

Dabusi is one of the first who theorized on the universality of human rights. We should see him as a link in the chain beginning with Abu Hanifa and his students because he was affiliated with the Hanafi School of law. Dabusi's views on universal human rights are best illustrated by the following citation:

> A human being [*âdamî*] is created only and only with this covenant (with God) and the right to personality [*dhimmah*]; it is impossible to

think that he may be created otherwise. A human being is created only and only with a capability to be accorded with legal/public rights [huquq al-shar']: It is impossible to think that he may be created otherwise. Likewise, a human being is created free and with his rights; it cannot be thought that he may be created otherwise. The reason why these honoring gifts [karâmât] and legal personality [dhimmah] are given to human beings is because he is responsible to fulfill the "rights of God" [huqûq Allah].[11]

This excerpt demonstrates, first of all, that Dabusi accepts the existence of two fundamental rights, which are universally granted to all human beings: freedom and legal personality. However, Dabusi talks about other rights as well without specifically naming them. He emphasizes the importance of these rights to such an extent that, for him, the creation of human beings without them would be unimaginable. For Dabusi, the right to legal personality is a prerequisite for human beings to have other legal rights and duties.

His approach to fundamental rights clearly reflects the idea of "inherent rights" and "God-given rights." This is significant because it demonstrates that Dabusi does not recognize the state authority as the source of basic rights. Instead, for him, basic human rights are born rights, which emanate from God. The consequence of this approach is that the state cannot take these rights away from individuals because the state is not the one that granted them. Nor are the rights based on a contract between the state and the citizens, which is the case in the Shafii School of law.

It is explicit that this excerpt provides a distinct way of grounding universal human rights. For Dabusi, fundamental universal human rights are given to human beings so that they can fulfill the "rights of God." God's right is to be worshipped and obeyed. The term *rights of God* is the opposite of the term *rights of human beings* (huquq al-'ibad). Public rights are also considered rights of God, as the victim is not allowed to forgive the violator.

According to Dabusi, God's rights on human beings cannot be fulfilled without basic human rights. We may translate this view into modern terminology as follows: human rights are a prerequisite for freedom of religion. More explicitly, human beings should have freedom and legal personality so that they can fulfill their duties, God's rights on them.

Sarakhsi (d. 1090): God Granted the Right to Inviolability, Freedom, and Property

Abi Bakr Muhammad b. Ahmad b. Abi Sahl al-Sarakhsi (d. 490 AH) is among the first scholars who systematically discussed the philosophy and methodology of Hanafi jurisprudence. He is the author of the well-respected *Usul al-Sarakhsi* (literally translated, The Methodology of al-Sarakhsi) and *al-Mabsut* (literally, The Detailed Book). Sarakhsi is known as the one who systemized the works of scholars from previous generations, such as the work of Muhammad Hasan al-Shaibani, Dabusi, and Bazdawi.

According to Sarakhsi, as he explains in great detail in his *Usul*, all people are addressed and held responsible by God, including non-Muslims, because Prophet Muhammad was sent to humanity as a whole. God calls everyone to be faithful (*al-iman*) and to carry the burden of the responsibility of being a human and enjoying the rights stemming from it. That means God considers everyone equal before Islamic law. In the Qur'an, God commands Prophet Muhammad, "O Muhammad say: O people verily I am God's Messenger to you all." This call beyond doubt includes all human beings, even non-Muslims,[12]

Sarakhsi argues that the divine call has important implications. Being addressed by God gives a special status to human beings. It gives them the right to legal personhood (*al-ahliyyah*) at the universal level. Since God called upon them all, each human being is qualified for equal rights and duties by birth.

According to Sarakhsi, the divine call comprises three fields: faith, criminal law, and transactions and rituals. Refusing faith in the content of the divine message, although it is the most important part of the divine call, does not disqualify one from having rights and responsibilities in other areas. As a result of receiving the divine call (*hukm al-khitab*), even if they do not acknowledge that it is a divine message, the criminal law of Islam is applicable to non-Muslims who live under Islamic rule. Likewise the laws concerning transactions are also applicable to them. As to the other rules, the scholars of Islamic law unanimously accept that non-Muslims will be questioned in the Hereafter for not complying with them. Hasan al-Shaibani said in his *Siyar al-Kabir*, "[W]hoever denies a rule from the rules of Islamic law he has refused the meaning of the statement that 'There is no god but God.'"[13]

The purpose of God in calling humans is to try them (*ibtila*), which can be actualized only if those who are called have free will (*ikhtiyar*) and the freedom (*hurriyyah*) to exercise it. Sarakhsi writes: "The prohibition requires abstention from the prohibited through an action which is attributed to the earning [*kasb*] of the human being and his free will because the prohibition is a trial similar to the obligation. The trial can only be achieved if the human being has a choice in the matter." He emphasizes the issue of freedom by saying that even if people perform what they are commanded and refrain from what they are prohibited, without having the right to chose otherwise this is not what God intends because it is not a trial (*ibtila*).[14] Freedom to choose the opposite is what makes compliance with the divine commands virtuous. The action must be the choice of the person out of his free will.

Related to this issue is the damage caused by animals to human beings. Since animals are not addressed by the divine call and are not free actors, a legal judgment cannot be attributed to their actions. Muhammad al-Shaibani said that the action of an animal does not incur a legal punishment (*heder*). This is unlike a slave, whose actions can be legally attributed.[15] Consequently if a camel harms someone, the owner is not punishable for it. The fact that he has the right to the inviolability of his property (*'ismah*) and the right to property does not make him punishable for the actions of his animal.[16]

Sarakhsi dedicated a special chapter to the legal personhood of all human beings, which makes humans qualified to acquire rights and duties[17] and also shoulders them with responsibility.[18] It is a discussion about why every human being (*al-adami*) is qualified for legal personhood (*al-ahliyyah*) for legally required rights and duties. These rights and duties are related to the divine purpose for which human beings are created. Human beings carry the burden of the divine mission, which they took as a trust from God (*al-amanah*).

There are two types of qualifications: qualification for prescribing the laws (*ahliyyat al-wujub*) and qualification for performing the laws (*ahliyyat al-ada'*). The source of these qualifications is responsibility (*dhimmah*) to which legal and moral judgments are attributed. Human beings alone have responsibility.[19] The Arabic word *dhimmah*, which stands for "responsibility" also means "covenant" (*al-'ahd*). The term *ahl al-dhimmah*, which is used for non-Muslims who sign a compact with the Islamic state, is derived from the same origin; it means "those who make a covenant with Muslims." The *dimmah* in this context is used for the covenant of human beings with God before coming to this world. The embryo has only rights but no duties. Therefore he can receive a legacy, he has the right to lineage and family, and he receives what is given to him in a will. Birth makes him qualified for all rights and duties at the level of prescription.[20] He is gradually required to perform them as he grows, until he reaches puberty, which is when he is fully required to perform all his duties. God says, "We attached the responsibility of every one to his neck."[21] At birth one's rights and duties (*mahall*) and their cause (*sabab*) come into existence. Since the child is not able to perform his duties for a while, he is not required to perform them until he can do so. For this reason his qualification is incomplete.

The following passage is an excellent summary of Sarakhsi's views on human rights:

> Upon creating human beings, God graciously bestowed upon them intelligence and the capability to carry responsibilities and rights (personhood). This was to make them ready for duties and rights determined by God. Then He granted them the right to inviolability, freedom and property to let them continue their lives so that they can perform the duties they have shouldered. Then these rights to carry responsibility and enjoy rights, freedom and property exist with a human being when he is born. The insane/child and the sane/adult are the same concerning

these rights. This is how the proper personhood is given to him when he is born for God to charge him with the rights and duties when he is born. In this regard, the insane/child and sane/adult are equal.[22]

This passage demonstrates that Sarakhsi, like Dabusi, accepts born rights and links basic human rights to the responsibilities of human beings toward God. He also emphasizes the equality of all human beings vis-à-vis these rights.

Kasani (d. 1191): No External Justification Is Needed for Human Inviolability

The well-known Hanafi jurist Kasani argues that the inviolability of a human being is due to an innate quality (*hurmah li 'aynih*).[23] In other words, humans are inviolable in themselves; their very existence is sufficient for them to have the right to inviolability. That means the right to inviolability does not require an external reason other than being human.

However, Kasani argues, the right to the inviolability of property is for external reasons (*hurmah li ghayrih*). That means property is not inviolable in itself. This is because inviolability is not intrinsic to property right; instead it is justified as serving a goal external to its own existence. This line of thought is also maintained, as we will see, by Ibn 'Abidin, who argues that inviolability of property was legislated due to necessity (*darurah*) because God created property in the beginning not for individuals but for humanity as a whole. In other words, personal property came later in human history as a result of social and economic necessity.

Kasani's distinction between life as intrinsically inviolable and property as inviolable for external reasons brings another dimension to the discussion of human rights. His claim that life is essentially inviolable and requires no other justification is a distinct way of grounding the right to the inviolability of life.

Other inviolable rights, in particular property rights, are grounded on the right to life for serving human life. Property is not intrinsically sacred or inviolable, but because human life requires it to be so. From this perspective, the right to life is inviolable in itself, and all other rights are inviolable because they are prerequisites for the right to life.

Marghinani (d. 1197): The Right to Inviolability Is Due to Humanity

Burhan al-Din al-Marghinani[24] is the author of *al-Hidayah*, which is the most frequently used and referenced canonical textbook of the Hanafi School of law. Due to its common usage, this book was translated into English after the British invasion of India. Unlike the other books I analyze in this chapter, *al-Hidayah* focuses on practical issues (*furu' al-fiqh*) instead of doctrinal and philosophical issues (*usul al-fiqh*). However, it explores the ways the legal rules are grounded through rational and traditional or scriptural arguments. Marghinani deals with the issue of human inviolability primarily in the chapter on international law (*kitab al-siyar*), yet it is possible to find references to it in other chapters as well.

According to Marghinani, who follows the traditional Hanafi line of thinking, "the right to inviolability is due to humanity [*al-'ismah bi al-âdamiyyah*]."[25] Marghinani takes "human" as the subject of law to which rights and duties are accorded, which reflects the Hanafi opinion. His concept of inviolability has three important characteristics:

1. The only source for the right to inviolability is being a human.
2. The right to inviolability is granted to all human beings without exception.
3. The right to inviolability is enforced by the state, and violators are punished by predetermined penalties according to Islamic penal law.

These characteristics demonstrate that the principle of the inviolability of human beings in Islamic jurisprudence protects the rights of all human beings, not only Muslims or the citizens of the Islamic state. It also makes explicit that the right to inviolability is not only a moral right but is also a legal right enforced by state power. The penalties for the violation of the right to life, property, freedom of religion, family, and honor are predetermined in Islamic law, some of which are stated clearly in the Qur'an and Hadith. This approach sets Islam apart from other ancient religious teachings, where the inviolability of human beings is accepted as a moral right without predetermined legal enforcement.

The issue of enforcing the right to inviolability plays a significant role in Marghinani's theory of universal human rights. Marghinani discusses the distinction between two types of right to inviolability regarding the consequence of its violation: (1) that which causes sin (*'ismah al-muaththimah*) and (2) that which causes penalty (*'ismah al-muqawwimah*). Consequently he divides the right to inviolability into two categories from the perspective of legal enforcement:

1. *Al-'ismah al-muqawwimah*: the measurable and enforceable right to inviolability whose violators are punished by predetermined penalties. The right to the inviolability of property is the best example of measurable and enforceable inviolability.
2. *Al-'ismah al-muaththimah*: the kind of right to inviolability that cannot be enforced by the state and whose violators cannot be legally punished. Minor violations such as backbiting are impossible to legally enforce.

Also violations outside the territory of the Islamic state are difficult to en-force, particularly given the conditions of the Middle Ages, when there was no international collaboration to fight crimes. However, violators who escape punishment by the authorities, because of the impediments in the realization of this worldly justice, cannot escape from divine justice in the Hereafter.

Marghinani argues that the *'ismah al-muathtimah* is the right of all human beings despite the fact that the state has no power to legally enforce it. Without this right it would be impossible for human beings to carry out the legal and moral responsibilities God gave them. Marghinani argues that human beings can real-ize the purpose for which God created them only if they enjoy the protection of inviolability (*hurmah al-ta'arrud*).

However, according to Marghinani, measurable and enforceable inviolability (*al-'ismah al-muqawwimah*) is a more developed form of the *'ismah al-muatthimah* because it is accepted not only as a sin but also as a legally punishable crime. For him, the fact that the *'ismah al-mu'aththimah* remains only a moral and reli-gious rule is a shortcoming. He claims that an enforced right is more developed compared to a moral right that is not enforced.

The inviolable rights are hierarchically ordered. The right to the inviolability of life has the highest priority compared to other rights. This is because if life were not inviolable other rights would have no meaning. The right to the invio-lability of property comes after the right to the inviolability of life because it is required (*darurah*) to serve the continuity of human life and progeny. Conse-quently, in case of a conflict between the two, life is given precedence over property.

Marghinani argues that the *'ismah al-muaththimah* is more suitable for the right to the inviolability of life, whereas the *'ismah al-muqawwimah* is more suit-able for the right to the inviolability of property. This is because the loss of prop-erty is measurable and can be compensated through legal punishment. However, the loss of life is not measurable and cannot be compensated through legal pun-ishment. Even if we impose a punishment for the violation of life, life cannot be brought back. Assessing and determining the amount of the damage requires measurement (*taqawwum*) and commensurability (*tamathul*), which is possible for property but not life.[26]

On the other hand, the *'ismah al-muqawwimah* is applied only in an Islamic state (Dar al-Islam). Presence in the Dar al-Islam (*al-ihraz bi al-dar*) is necessary for the Islamic state to be able to enforce those rights and produce remedies. Territory is not an obstacle for having human rights, but it poses an obstacle for their enforcement. The legitimacy of political authority comes, according to Islamic law, from its protection of the citizenry. An authority that fails to protect the inviolable rights of the citizenry loses its legitimacy.

Marghinani criticizes the Shafii approach to human rights, according to which the right to inviolability is gained by accepting Islam or by becoming a citizen of an Islamic state:

> With respect to the arguments of *Shafii*, we reply that his assertion, that *"the sin-creating* protection is attached to *Islam,"* is not admitted; for, the *sin-creating* protection is attached, *not* to *Islam*, but to the *person*; because man is created with an intent that he should bear the burdens imposed by the LAW, which men would be unable to do unless the molestation or slaying of them were prohibited, since if the slaying of a person were not illegal, he would be incapable of performing the duties required of him. The person therefore is the original subject of protection, and property follows as the dependant thereof, since property is, in its original state, neutral, and created for the use of mankind, and is protected only on account of the right of the proprietor, to the end that each may be enabled to enjoy that which is his own.[27]

Marghinani refuses the Shafii claim that the *'ismah al-muaththimah* is accorded only to the Muslims. This is because for Marghinani, the *'ismah al-muaththimah* is associated with being a human but not being a Muslim, on the grounds that human beings are created for carrying religious and legal responsibilities. However human beings cannot fulfill these duties unless they are protected against violations. If the murder of a human being is not prohibited, he cannot perform the duties expected of him. Consequently a human being is the primordial subject of inviolability. In connection to this, property also becomes a primary subject of inviolability because, although property in itself is neutral, it is created for the use of humanity. Here again we see the primacy of the right to life and its use to justify the right to property.

Abdulaziz Bukhari (d. 1330): Human Rights Are a Prerequisite for Human Beings to Carry the Divine Trust

Abdulaziz Bukhari is known for his highly detailed commentary on the book of the famous jurist Fakhr al-Islam Bazdawi (d. 1089), whose views on the inviolability of human beings were discussed earlier. In his commentary, Bukhari devoted a considerable amount of space to the philosophical foundations of human inviolability because a human being is, from the perspective of Islamic jurisprudence, the subject of law (*mahkum alayh*) to whom rights and duties are accorded.

Bukhari explains Bazdawi's text sentence by sentence. Bazdawi states that "all Muslim jurists reached a consensus among themselves that every child of

Adam is born with legal personality [*dhimmah*]." In explaining this sentence, Bukhari demonstrates that legal personality is a prerequisite for human beings to carry the divine trust.[28] For him, having divine trust means having rights and duties. It requires human beings to have liability for their actions and license to perform acts (*ahliyyah*), which means being equipped with all the required qualities for God to charge them with duties and to fulfill these duties. God talks about divine trust in the Qur'an: "Human beings shouldered the trust" (Ahzab 72). Bukhari states that all human beings have *ahliyyah* but the children use it through their parents. The term *ahliyyah* is related in his thinking with another term: *'uhdah*. The term *'uhdah* can be understood as the quality of a person to have duties or the human quality to which duties are attached.

According to Bukhari, the foundation of liability is legal personality (*dhimmah*). For him, the fact that all human beings, unique among the creatures, are born with liability is the evidence that they all have legal personality. If human beings are born with legal personality, that means they are born ready to have rights and duties. Similar to Bazdawi, Bukhari also argues that the fact that there is consensus among jurists on the existence of legal personality is sufficient evidence to prove its existence. Showing the continuity in the Hanafi School, Bukhari also confirms that human beings have the right to inviolability (*'ismah*), freedom (*hurriyyah*), and property (*malikiyyah*).[29]

Bukhari explains in detail the meaning of divine trust (*amanah*) and how human beings are given that trust. He also talks about the two types of inviolability: (1) the inviolability whose violation causes sin (*al-'ismah al-mu'atthimah*), which is enforced by social and religious means, and (2) the inviolability whose violation causes legally determined punishment (*al-'ismah al-muqawwimah*), which is enforced by legal measures.

According to Bukhari, for inviolability to be a right, it must be enforced. Otherwise such a right remains only a religious and moral preaching. Muslim jurists accept the principle of human inviolability as a universal rule, yet they are aware that not every violation of inviolability can be legally enforced in practice. For instance, backbiting and slandering are violations of the inviolability of human beings. However, in practice it is impossible for the state to punish all instances of backbiting and slander. Likewise violations of inviolability that cannot be proved by evidence or witness escape legal punishment. Another example is the violations that take place outside the territory of the Islamic state, which are beyond its jurisdiction.

Consequently Bukhari concludes that only those human rights violations that take place within the territory of an Islamic state (*al-ihraz bi al-dar*) can be legally enforced. However, this limitation does not disprove the rule that inviolability is a universal human right. Those who escape legal punishment, for the reasons mentioned above, will face religious and moral punishment. If a criminal who violated the inviolability of a human being succeeded in escaping from this worldly punishment (either because it took place outside the territory of the state or because there was not enough evidence to prove it) cannot possibly escape divine justice because he is a sinner in God's eyes.

As a matter of fact, all violations of human inviolability are sins. For this reason, the category of al-'ismah al-muaththimah is broader than the category of al-'ismah al-muqawwimah. This is because the former encompasses the latter. Bukhari emphasizes that there is no exception to the inviolability of human beings. He states that even the lives of slaves are inviolable because "slavery does not affect the right to inviolability of human beings."[30]

Bukhari provides an excellent example of how inviolability of religion is grounded in Islamic jurisprudence. For him all religions are inviolable because they are all from God. However, if the rulers in a particular religion inserted a rule that is against human rights, that rule is not acceptable. Thus it falls outside the domains of freedom of religion, such as sati practice in India. God could not possibly set these rules. This is because the inviolability of human beings is an eternal and universal rule and is the foundation of all religions and legal systems. Therefore it must be the same in all religions. However, other rules and practices may change from religion to religion. They are all respected and inviolable even if they contradict Islamic principles and practices.

For Bukhari, this is a result of lack of knowledge, which leads to a defect in liability of people from those religions. These people continue practicing ancient religions because they do not know that Prophet Muhammad is the last Messenger of God. Consequently their religions are inviolable. There is only one single duty for the people in this category: knowing Prophet Muhammad and believing in him. *However, this is a religious duty but not a legal duty.* More plainly put, they are required to know Prophet Muhammad and believe in him out of religious conviction, but this cannot be imposed on them by the state through legal measures. If non-Muslims do not believe in Prophet Muhammad, they will be punished in the Hereafter by God, but not in this world. However, if they voluntarily choose to believe in Islam, they will be required to fulfill all the duties Islam imposes on its followers. Non-Muslims cannot be required to fulfill Islamic commandments before knowing Prophet Muhammad as the last Messenger of God and believing in him. In sum, for Bukhari, religion protects a person from violation (*mani' al-ta'arruz*).[31]

Ibn Humam (d. 1457): Human Inviolability Is a Rational Argument

Ibn Humam is well-known for his commentary on the canonical work of al-Marghinani, *al-Hidayah* (literally, Right Guidance).[32] As I mentioned earlier, he disagrees with Marghinani on the relationship between the two types of inviolability. For him, the moral right to inviolability is not a primitive form of the legal right to inviolability because these are two separate principles.

Ibn Humam argues that the *'ismah al-muqawwimah* is primarily applicable to the violation of property rights because property is measurable and replaceable. In contrast, the *'ismah al-muaththimah* is primarily applicable to the violation of the right to life because life cannot be monetarily measured, compensated, or replaced. However, in practice, although the primary use and application of these two concepts are in different areas, they are used in both cases in jurisprudence and law. This is because in practice measurable penalties are needed to be imposed in cases of violation of life or property.

He argues that the right to inviolability is based on a rational argument rather than a scriptural argument from the Qur'an or the Sunnah: "The idea that human beings have the right to inviolability because of their humanity is a rational argument [*dalil ma'qûl*]."[33] This statement is extremely significant in demonstrating that Hanafi jurists employed reason in grounding human rights.

Ibn 'Abidin (d. 1836): Human Rights Are a Prerequisite for Prosperity and Peace

Ibn 'Abidin is considered one of the greatest Hanafi jurists of the nineteenth century. His voluminous commentary *Hashiya ibn 'Abidin* (Commentary by Ibn 'Abidin) is still being used as a major reference worldwide by followers of the Hanafi School. He wrote his book at a time when Muslims faced modernity and Western expansion for the first time.

For Ibn 'Abidin, human rights constitute a prerequisite for human beings to lead a peaceful and prosperous life. Social and economic life requires that basic human rights are given to all human beings; without fulfilling this prerequisite (*daruri*), social and economic life is impossible.

Ibn 'Abidin argues that the inviolability of property (*ismah al-mal*) was legislated as a result of necessity. Initially human beings had no personal property. Yet without recognizing personal property as an inviolable right, economic and social life is impossible. Therefore all human beings are allowed to have property. However, the right to property expanded beyond the limits of necessity (*darurah*).[34]

Ibn 'Abidin postulated that "a child of Adam, even if he is an infidel, has the right to dignity according to Islamic law [*al-adamiy mukarram shar'an wa law kafiran*]."[35] The fact that even an infidel is protected by Islamic law demonstrates Ibn 'Abidin's universalism of human rights. Of course, this view is not peculiar to Ibn 'Abidin. His writing reflects the traditional universalist Hanafi doctrine on human rights.

The Paradox of Apostasy and Freedom of Religion

At the close of this survey of authorities from the Hanafi School of Islamic jurisprudence, I want to present their views on apostasy. Outsiders may find it quite paradoxical that Islamic law pioneered in giving freedom of religion to non-Muslims, prohibited forcing people to convert to Islam, and grounded religious liberty on a sophisticated jurisprudential thinking—yet still prohibited apostasy. More plainly, once a person accepts Islam out of his free will he is not allowed to leave it. One should keep in mind that only the male apostate is punished by death. This is what seems paradoxical: if one chooses to remain outside of Islam, one is granted complete freedom of religion. However, if one enters Islam and wants to leave it, one has no freedom to do so. Why is this so? I will try to explain how this issue is viewed by the classical Muslim jurists.

According to traditional Islamic law, when a person leaves Islam and declares it in public he is considered an apostate. Islamic law requires that the apostate should be questioned about his reasons and motives for leaving Islam and Muslim scholars should be brought to clear his doubts and expose the weakness of his arguments—if he has any—against Islam. Once it is demonstrated to him in a convincing manner that his doubts and arguments are not grounded, which may take days or weeks, if he still insists on his apostasy, and involves in a war against Muslims as a combatant (harbi), he is punished by death.

I think it is exactly because Islam granted total freedom to non-Muslims in not choosing Islam that it limited freedom to leave Islam. One is completely free in not accepting Islam, but not so in leaving Islam after accepting it. That means one has to make a firm commitment and decision before entering Islam and should not become a Muslim unless one is completely convinced in an unshakable manner.

Yet an apostate who is not proven to be a combatant (harbi) against Islam and Muslims cannot be punished by death because his life remains inviolable. Punishing apostasy by death is, according to the Hanafi jurists, due only through involvement in a war against Islam but not because of the apostasy. This is because the universalist Hanafi jurists do not accept apostasy as a reason for taking away the right to inviolability of a human being. In their view, a human being loses his right to inviolability only when he becomes a combatant (harbi) against Islam, akin to a traitor in modern law. Therefore according to the Hanafi jurists, an apostate can be punished only when he is involved in a war against Islam, which may take the form of making propaganda against Islam or collaborating with the enemies of Islam (dar al-harb).

However, for the Shafii jurists, apostasy itself constitutes the legitimate ground for capital punishment because it is the greatest sin and should not be tolerated. For them, the right to inviolability is gained either due to faith in

Islam or, if one is non-Muslim, due to citizenship in the Islamic state (*dhimmi*). Consequently if a person loses his citizenship status as a Muslim or *dhimmi*, he loses his right to inviolability. An apostate who abandons Islam loses his citizenship. Therefore he loses his right to inviolability also.

This jurisprudential discussion between the Hanafi and Shafii jurists demonstrates explicitly that religion at the time of the Prophet meant something more than what it means today: it was the ground for citizenship and political allegiance to a nation. In the modern age, on the other hand, when political citizenship has little tie to religion, apostasy laws lost their ground.

The Forgotten Universalist Tradition

Fatefully, modern human rights discourse in the Muslim world represents a break from the universalist tradition in Islamic jurisprudence. The chain of memory through which the universal human rights tradition had been transferred from generation to generation was severed with the collapse of the Ottoman Empire, the last state to adopt the human rights doctrine of the Hanafi School.

The Ottoman Empire had made significant reforms in Islamic law during the second half of the nineteenth century. These reforms are known as Tanzimat (declared with a royal edict by Sultan Mahmud II in 1839), which required reorganization and reregulation of the Ottoman legal and political system without severing ties with the Islamic tradition. Tanzimat as a reform project was based on combining modern Western and traditional Islamic ideas and institutions. In this reform period, Ottomans introduced universal citizenship and abolished the different statuses between Muslim citizens and non-Muslim citizens (*dhimmis*). In accordance with this, they abolished the special poll tax (*jizya*) collected from non-Muslim citizens. They adopted the constitutional parliamentary system with multiparty elections by which non-Muslims could enter the Ottoman Parliament.[36]

The significance of these reforms comes from the fact that they gained the approval of the caliph, the leader of Muslims worldwide, and the sheikhulislam, head of the religious scholars, Ulema. Therefore their Islamicity cannot be disputed. This is unlike other reform projects by academics or intellectuals, which can easily be disputed by their colleagues because they lack the approval of the highest traditional religious and political authorities.

These reform efforts were brought to an end in 1918 by the British invasion of Istanbul, which closed the Ottoman Parliament and sent the representatives into exile. This terminated an effort to establish a democratic system with universal human rights grounded in Islamic jurisprudence. The new Turkish Republic shifted to a new paradigm to Westernize the state and totally secularize the legal system. It should be noted in passing that Turkey did not adopt Western models of secularism but the Soviet model and put religion under the strict control of the state rather than separating state and religion. This model was more restrictive and authoritarian than French laicism, wherein the church has autonomy and religious education is not given by the state. In contrast, in the Turkish secular system religious education can be given only by the secular state, which is unheard of in the West. This meant ending all the reform efforts in Islamic law to give universalist Islam a modern voice.

Beyond Turkey, the Muslim world was almost completely colonized. Nation-states with secular ideologies were set up by the colonizers to rule Muslim populations. In the postcolonial era, the reaction against the West provoked a majority of Muslim intellectuals to depict the human rights project after World War II as yet another imperialist project to strengthen Western hegemony. Key Turkish Muslim scholars, however, supported the UN Universal Declaration of Human Rights in 1948.[37]

Another important development took place. As secular ideologies such as nationalism and socialism lost public appeal because of their failure to deliver what they promised, Islamists gained popularity. The regimes they established, unfortunately, were divorced from the universalist Islamic legal tradition; instead they adopted reactionary practices that cannot be justified from the perspective of Islamic law as understood and practiced by universalist jurists for centuries. In particular these regimes gave strikingly disproportionate emphasis to penal law, to the extent that they almost equated Islam with the penal law of sharia.

Currently universalist Islamic jurisprudence and its doctrine of human rights are not implemented anywhere in the world by a state nor clearly represented by an intellectual community. Secularism, on the one hand, and radicalism, on the other, pushed aside the universalist Islamic tradition and cut the chain of memory. Therefore I can describe the present legal and human rights practice in the Muslim world as a deviation from the Islamic universalistic tradition.

Consequently confusion about universal human rights prevails in the Muslim world. We saw a lack of consensus among Muslim countries in their approach to the Universal Declaration of Human Rights: some approved all of it, and some objected to various articles. If Muslims recover a clear idea about their human rights tradition, we will not have these disagreements about whether or not an article is compatible with Islamic law.

I term this state of the Muslim world "human rights dependency on the West," by which I mean positioning oneself as the receiver or the opponent of the human rights discourse without making any contribution or offering an alternative to it. In their approach to human rights there are two groups of Muslim intellectuals. One group accepts and employs the present human rights discourse yet without contributing to it. The other group rejects the present human rights discourse but without formulating a viable alternative to it.

I think it is high time for Muslims to make a dialogical contribution to the current human rights discourse in the world instead of simply accepting or rejecting it. In my opinion, the only way for Muslims to critique and contribute to the present human rights discourse is to firmly ground their approach in the universalist legal tradition in Islam and its practice over centuries and extending from eastern Turkistan to India, the Balkans, and Andalusia.

Conclusion

Although the foregoing survey is not exhaustive, it clearly demonstrates how classical Muslim jurists grounded the right to human inviolability over centuries. Drawing on the work of these jurists, and my own experience, I conclude that all human beings are inviolable because inviolability is a prerequisite to fulfill the divine purpose for which the universe and humanity were created. God created this universe to try and test human beings. Yet a fair test cannot be achieved if people are not granted the right to inviolability. People who act without choice cannot be punished or rewarded for their actions.

If true freedom of religion does not prevail in the world, the very purpose of the creation, and of Paradise and Hellfire, cannot be achieved. This is because action under pressure cannot be rewarded or punished by God, either in this world or in the Hereafter. Therefore universal human rights and freedom of religion are prerequisites to achieve the purpose and meaning of Creation.

The foregoing study does not make the claim that Islam fathered universal human rights because Islamic law is a nonexceptionalist law. It does not present itself as the only true religion and the Prophet Muhammad as the only Messenger of God. Instead it presents Islam as the last manifestation of the same religion God sent to humanity over and over through countless Messengers. Muslims are required to believe in the message of Jesus, Moses, Abraham, and all the other previous prophets mentioned in the Qur'an and the Bible. From an Islamic perspective, God is one and He has only one religion, though its expressions over time may vary, especially in the field of law.

This self-perception has implications for Islam's view on human rights. It accepts that basic principles of all religions and legal systems are the same because they come from the same God. These are called "axiomatic rights" (*daruriyyat*).[38] They involve six basic rights: the right to the inviolability of life, property, religion, mind, honor, and family. That means Islam has no claim to being exceptional in granting these rights for the first time. This is what I call the nonexceptionalism of Islam. In contrast, the claim that these rights had always been recognized, even before Islam, provides legitimacy for their existence in Islamic law also. This view grounds universal human rights on primordial precedence and universal consensus.

Notes

1. Recep Şentürk, "Sociology of Rights: Inviolability of the Other in Islam between Communalism and Universalism," in *Contemporary Islam,* ed. Abdul Aziz Said, Mohammed Abu-Nimer, and Meena Sharify-Funk (New York: Routledge, 2006), 24–49; Recep Şentürk, "Sociology of Rights: *I Am Therefore I Have Rights.* Human Rights in Islam between Universalistic and Communalistic Perspectives," in *Islam and Human Rights: Advocacy for Social Change in Local Contexts,* ed. Mashood A. Baderin, Lynn Welchman, Mahmood Monshipouri, and Shadi Mokhtari (New Delhi: Global Media Publications 2006); Recep Şentürk, "Minority Rights in Islam: From *Dhimmi* to Citizen," in *Islam and Human Rights,* ed. Shireen T. Hunter and Huma Malik (Washington, D.C.: Center for Strategic & International Studies, 2005), 67–99; Recep Şentürk, "Sociology of Rights: Human Rights in Islam between Communal and Universal Perspectives," *Muslim World Journal of Human Rights* 2, no. 1 (2005): 1–30; Recep Sentürk, "*Adamiyyah and 'Ismah*: The Contested Relationship between Humanity and Human Rights in the Classical Islamic Law," *Turkish Journal of Islamic Studies* 8 (2002): 39–70. See also my book in Turkish, *İslam ve İnsan Hakları: Fıkhi ve Sosyolojik Yaklaşımlar* (İstanbul: Etkilesim yayıncılık, 2007).

2. It is commonly known in Arabic as the *khutbah al-wadâ'*. It is cited in almost all books of Hadīth. Following Ahadīth in *Sahih Al-Bukhari* refer to the sermon and quote part of it. See Al-Bukhari, Hadīth 1623, 1626, 6361. Sahih of Imam Muslim also refers to this sermon in Hadīth 98. Imam al-Tirmidhi has mentioned this sermon in Hadīth 1628, 2046, 2085. Imam Ahmed bin Hanbal has given us the longest and perhaps the most complete version of this sermon in his Musnad, Hadīth 19774.

3. Another important document that should be remembered in this context is the Wathiqa, the Constitution of Medina under the rule of Prophet Muhammad, which is considered to be the first written constitution in the world based on a consensus by the followers of different religions to constitute a pluralist state.

4. Bukhârî, Hajj, 132; Maghâzî, 77, 78; Muslim, Hajj, 132, 147, 283; Qasâme, 26; Jihâd, 20; Abû Dâwûd, Manâsik, 56, 77; Talaq, 40; Tirmidhî, Juma, 80; Radâ', 11; Tafsîr, 10; Manâqib, 32; Ibn-i Mâjah, Manâsik, 63, 76, 84; Sadaqa, 9; Dârimî, Muqaddima, 24; Manâsik, 34, 84; Ahmad ibn Hanbal, V, 30; Ibn Hishâm, IV, 275–76; Yâ'qubî, II, 109–10; Hamîdullâh, al-Wathâiq, pp. 360–68.

5. For a complete translation in English by Nuh Ha Mim Keller, see http://muslimcanada.org/farewell.htm (last visited on May 26, 2012).

6. The Qur'an says that at times powerful Arab tribes changed the established order to get around the prohibition of war during these months. This practice was called *nasî'* (Tawba 37).

7. "The Last Sermon of the Prophet," http://www.soundvision.com/info/hajj/lastsermon.asp.

8. For the uses of the Farewell Sermon as the first Islamic human rights document, see the following sources: Ahmed Akgündüz, *İslâm'da İnsan Hakları Beyannamesi* (İstanbul: OSAV, 1997); Haydar Baş, *Veda Hutbesinde İnsan Hakları* (İstanbul: İcmal yayınları, 1994); M. Emin Demirçin, "Hz. Peygamberin Getirdiği İnsan Hakları," in *Doğu'da ve Batı'da İnsan Hakları* (Ankara: TDV, 1996), 155–61; Osman Eskicioğlu, "Veda Hutbe'sinin İnsan Hakları Yönünden Kısaca Tahlili," in *Doğu'da ve Batı'da İnsan Hakları* (Ankara: TDV, 1996), 125–30; Osman Eskicioğlu, *İnsan Hakları Alanında Temel Belgeler* (İstanbul: Nun Yayıncılık, 1996); Muhammed Hamidullah, "İslam'da İnsan Hakları," in *İslam ve İnsan Hakları,* trans. Tahir Yücel and Şennur Karakurt (İstanbul: Endülüs Yayınları, 1995), 147–52; Hayreddin Karaman, *İslâm'da İnsan Hakları* (İstanbul: Ensar Neşriyat, 2004).

9. Hamidullah, "İslam'da İnsan Hakları," 147–52.

10. See, Tahir Mahmood, "Human Rights in Islamic Law" (New Delhi: Genuine Publications, 1993).

11. Abu Zaid Abdullah ibn Umar ibn Isa al-Dabusi, *Taqwîm al-Adillah fî Usûl al-Fiqh*, 1421 (Beirut: Dar al-Kutub al-'Ilmiyyah, 2001), 417.

12. Abi Bakr Muhammad b. Ahmad b. Abi Sahl al-Sarakhsi (d. 490 ah), *Usul al-Sarakhsi,* ed. Abu al-Wafa al-Afghani (Istanbul: Kahraman yay, 1984).

13. Ibid., 73.

14. Ibid., 86–88.

15. Ibid., 326.

16. Ibid., 327.

17. The term Sarakhsi uses is *wujub al-huquq lahu wa alaihi*, which literally means "the necessary requirement of the rights for him and the rights upon him." He is following the terminology used earlier by the founder of the Hanafi School, Abu Hanifa, who defined al-Fiqh, the science of law, as "the knowledge of the self about the rights for him and upon him [al-Fiqh ma'rifat al-nafs ma laha wa ma 'alayha]." Ibid., 332.

18. Bab ahliyyat al-adami li vujub al-huquq lahu wa 'alayhi wa fi al-amanati allati hamalaha al-insan.

19. Wa li hadha ikhtassa bihi al-adami duna sair al-hayawanat allati laysat laha dhimmah salihah.

20. Sarakhsi writes, "Za'ama ba'd mashayikhuna [he is al-Qadi Abu Zayd] enne bi'tibar salahiyyat al-dhimmah yathbut wujub huququllah ta'ala fi haqqih min hinin yuledu wa innema ma yasqut ma yasqut ba'd dhalik bi udhr al-saba li daf' al-haraj."

21. An'am 17/13. "Wa kull insanin alzamnahu tairahu fi unuqih."

22. Sarakhsi, *Usul*, 333–34. "Li anna Allah ta'ala lemma khalaqa al-insan li haml amanatih akramahu bi al-'aql wa al-dhimmah li yakuna biha ahlan li wujub huquqillah ta'alah alayhi. Thumma athbata lahu al-'ismah wa al-hurriyyah wa al-malikiyyah li yabqa fa yatamakkana min ada'i ma hummila min al-amanati. Thumma hazihi al-amanah wa al-hurriyyah wa al-malikiyyah thabitah li al-mar'i min hinin yuladu, al-mumayyiz wa ghayr al-mumayyiz fihi sawaun. Fakazalika al-dhimmah al-saliha li wujub al-huquq fiha thabit lahu min hinin yulad yastawi fihi al-mumayyiz wa ghayr al-mumayyiz."

23. Kasani, *Badayi' al-Sanayi'*, 1417 (Beirut: Dar al-Fikr, 1996), VII, 349. There is a detailed discussion on this issue in Kitab al-Siyar (international law).

24. Burhan al-Din ibn Abi Bakr al-Marghinani (d. 593 ah/1197 ce) was born in Marghinan, which is located in Farghana, presently in Uzbekistan. He was martyred by the soldiers of Cengiz Khan during the massacre in Bukhara. His Islamic law book, *al-Hidayah*, has been used as the highest level textbook in the Hanafi madrassas in Central Asia, India, and the Ottoman Empire as well as other parts of the Muslim world until today. The book was translated into English twice and Turkish.

25. Abu al-Hasan Burhanaddin Ali ibn Abi Bakr Marghinani, *al-Hidayah Sharh Bidayah al-Mubtadi*, 1420, ed. Muhammad Muhammad Tamir and Hafiz Ashur Hafiz (Cairo: Dar al-Salaam, 2000).

26. Bkz. Abd al-'aziz al-Bukhari (d. 730), *Kashf al-Asrar 'an Usul-i Fakhri'l-Islam al-Bazdawi*, 1418, ed. Muhammad Mu'tasim Billah al-Baghdadi (Beirut: Dar al-Kitab al-'Arabi, 1997), I, 378–79.

27. Marghinani, *The Hedaya or Guide: A Commentary on the Musulman Laws*, trans. Charles Hamilton (Karachi: Daru'l-Ishaat, 1989), II, 201–02.

28. Ala al-Din Abdulaziz ibn Ahmad al-Bukhari, *Kashf al-Asrar 'an Usul-I Fakhr al-Islam al-Bazdawi*, 1417, ed. Muhammad al-Mu'tasım billah al-Baghdadi (Beirut: Dar al-Kitab al-Arabi, 1997), IV, 393–94.

29. Ibid., IV, 322.

30. Ibid., IV, 488–90.

31. Ibid.

32. Kamal al-Din Muhammad ibn Abd al-Wahhab ibn Abd al-Hamid ibn Humam, *Sharh-u Fath al-Qadir* (Bulaq: al-Matba'ah al-Kubra al-Amiriyyah, 1315), IV, 356.

33. Ibid.

34. Ibn 'Abidin, *Radd al-Mukhtar 'ala al-Durr al-Mukhtar Sharh Tanwir al-Absar*, 1415 (Beirut: Dar al-Kitab al-'Ilmiyyah, 1994), IV, 159–65.

35. Ibid., V, 58.

36. For details, see my article "Minority Rights in Islam: From Dhimmi to Citizen," 67–99.

37. See, for instance, Huseyin Kazım Kadri, *İnsan Hakları Beyannamesinin İslam Hukukuna Göre İzahı*, ed. Osman Ergin (İstanbul: Sinan Matbaası, 1949). In this book, which was written before the UDHR was officially declared, the author defended the UDHR project and tried to convince Muslims to support it by providing an explanation for each item in it from the perspective of Islamic law.

38. These rights are referred to in classical Islamic jurisprudence as *daruriyyat, kulliyyat, ismah, hurmah* or *huquq al-adamiyyin*. The terms *daruriyyat* and *kulliyyat* imply that these rights are axiomatic and universal in the sense that all legal systems are founded on them.

PART FIVE

RELIGIOUS FREEDOM, GLOBAL SECURITY, AND DIPLOMACY

14

Religious Freedom and Global Security

CHRIS SEIPLE AND DENNIS R. HOOVER

In the early 1990s a few scholars of international relations began to dissent from the foreign policy establishment's long-standing habit of ignoring the role of religion. But they diverged sharply on what the role of religion has been and what it could or should be. On one end of the spectrum was Samuel Huntington, who in 1993 published his famous *Foreign Affairs* article, "The Clash of Civilizations?" Catalyzed by the end of the cold war and the ensuing search for new paradigms to understand international relations, this article argued that religion would henceforth be a primary source of global conflict:

> World politics is entering a new phase, in which the great divisions among humankind and the dominating source of international conflict will be cultural. Civilizations—the highest cultural groupings of people— are differentiated from each other by religion, history, language and tradition. These divisions are deep and increasing in importance. From Yugoslavia to the Middle East to Central Asia, the fault lines of civiliza- tions are the battle lines of the future.[1]

On the other end of the spectrum, at about the same time that Huntington was developing this bold if oversimplified and ominous thesis, Douglas Johnston was working on his Religion and Conflict Resolution Project at the Center for Strategic & International Studies, which culminated in the much-cited 1994 volume (coed- ited with Cynthia Sampson), *Religion, the Missing Dimension of Statecraft*. The book argued that religion should be brought back into the study and praxis of interna- tional diplomacy and policy not just because religion is a causal factor in many international conflicts but also because it can play and has played a key part in fostering positive change nonviolently and in preventing or resolving conflict.[2]

The Huntingtonian and Johnstonian perspectives generated vigorous discussion, yet the international relations field still did not truly mainstream the study and engagement of religious forces. Then came 9/11. Nearly three thousand people—citizens of ninety countries and every major faith group, including 2,752 Americans[3]—lost their lives in horrific fashion because a small group of educated Muslim suicidals was determined to fight what was, in their minds, a religious war with the United States. Consequently in most U.S. foreign policy circles a rapid consensus formed that religion, especially Islam, should be a high-priority topic in national security. While some took the event as confirmation of the clash-of-civilizations paradigm, many have resisted that interpretation. Ambiguities and disagreements about the role of religion and the foreign policy implications thereof have persisted. What's changed is that now most recognize that religion is, at least, a legitimate analytical factor in understanding realpolitik, if not in the social sciences.[4]

One area that has been particularly complex and contested is the relationship between *religious freedom* and security. For some observers, the lesson to be learned from episodes like 9/11 follows a fairly straightforward logic: religion (at least in "fundamentalist" or "radical" forms) is a big part of the problem; hence restricting religion must be accepted as a necessary part of the solution. Authoritarian governments, which generally have no sincere commitment to religious freedom in the first place, have been particularly eager to use real and imagined threats of religiously motivated terrorism as justification for crackdowns against religious groups of all kinds. But even among some governments that genuinely value the principle of religious freedom, 9/11 fostered a zero-sum attitude: because security is the top priority, promotion of religious freedom and other human rights must be lower priority.

However, others—and we count ourselves among them—have put forward a counterargument, namely, that religious freedom, properly conceived and implemented, is foundational to sustainable security. This chapter discusses why, concluding with a brief summary of implications and recommendations for various governmental and nongovernmental actors in contemporary world affairs.

Religious Freedom: From Human Rights to Security Interests

In the mid-1990s, in response to rising awareness of religious persecution and mounting frustration over the relative neglect of religious freedom in U.S. foreign policy, a grassroots campaign formed to enact legislation mandating and institutionalizing U.S. attention to the issue. The result was the International Religious Freedom Act of 1998. IRFA created the position of ambassador-at-large for international religious freedom and a new State Department office focused on the issue. Among other things, this office is charged with producing an annual report on the status of religious freedom in every foreign country in the world. In addition IRFA created the independent U.S. Commission on

International Religious Freedom, which monitors religious freedom and makes its own policy recommendations.

IRFA was a major achievement and went some way toward at least partially correcting what had been a major blind spot of the foreign policy establishment. Yet the primary argument used to justify the campaign was to frame international religious freedom as a *human rights* issue that had been underprioritized relative to other human rights issues. The idea that religious freedom is also a *security* issue simply was not discussed. It is perhaps not surprising, therefore, that most of what IRFA created is housed (some say buried) within the State Department's Bureau of Democracy, Human Rights, and Labor. International religious freedom was not integrated into the mainstream of national security institutions and policymaking at any level because it was not understood as such.

Our organization, the Institute for Global Engagement (IGE), is a "think-and-do tank" that studies the role of religion in public life and seeks practical methods to build religious freedom worldwide through local partners. Drawing from its own diplomatic experiences and international partnerships, as well as from its own research and the work of other scholars, IGE has long argued that responsible religious liberty is a necessary condition for sustainable security.[5] An early example of IGE's involvement was a national conference it convened in 2003 on religious freedom and security, which led to publication of *Religion & Security: The New Nexus in International Relations* (Rowman & Littlefield, 2004). As the book noted, the nexus is "new" only in the sense that it had not yet penetrated national security and foreign policy circles. Especially in the wake of 9/11, the notion that greater freedom for religion enhances security was not necessarily intuitive. But in fact there is long historical precedent for this positive linkage. *Religion & Security* underscored this point in part by reference to American history. Indeed the epigraph of the book was taken from the Rhode Island Colonial Charter of 1663: "They have ffreely declared, that it is a much on their hearts...to hold forth a livlie experiment, that a most flourishing civill state may stand and best bee maintained...with a full libertie in religious concernements."[6] Many of the first Europeans to migrate to America were minorities fleeing persecution for their beliefs.[7] Yet some of these same people established colonies wherein they persecuted anyone who did not believe as they did. Fortunately this pattern was recognized and broken early on, when Roger Williams fled Massachusetts (which maintained various forms of religious restriction and privilege) to establish the colony of Rhode Island. There liberty was defined not as the opposite of religious fundamentalism, namely secularist fundamentalism, but rather as *religious pluralism*. (Unlike its neighbor, Rhode Island never had any witch trials or hanged anyone of a minority faith.) This robust form of religious freedom was later institutionalized through the leadership of other Founders, such as William Penn, James Madison, and Thomas Jefferson.

This is not to suggest that, in the contemporary context, security will always be enhanced by simply granting any and all religious groups carte blanche.

There are times when giving certain already radicalized religious groups too much freedom can create serious security risks. One need only recall the case of Aum Shinryko in Japan, where, because of its religious status, it was constitutionally protected from investigation before its March 20, 1995, saran gas attack on the Tokyo subway. A similar phenomenon took place with the 7/7 bombers in London, among whom was a former disciple of the Islamist group Hizb ut-Tahrir, which was banned in Germany, where they have historic experience with hate speech, but not banned in the United Kingdom.

The perennial problem, however, is that governments respond in simplistic ways to the risk of religious radicalism. It is not enough for a government to grant a measure of freedom to those religious groups it deems nonthreatening and to suppress those it deems threatening. Religious groups are not static entities that can be assigned permanently to "good" and "bad" categories. Instead a state's security interests will be served best by cultivating a cultural and legal environment of responsible religious liberty for its citizens, one characterized by mutual respect between different religious groups and between all religions and the government.

The case for this integral connection between religious freedom and security is now more mainstream, having been made in a variety of ways by a variety of scholars and practitioners, especially in the past few years.[8] The arguments generally point to two underlying dynamics: a negative cycle (in which religious repression leads to insecurity) and a positive cycle (in which religious freedom supports social stability and well-being, and hence security over the long term).

The Negative Cycle

When governments establish religiously repressive regimes, over time they create the conditions in which religion can easily become a major security problem. Recall that fifteen of the nineteen hijackers who perpetrated the 9/11 attacks on the United States were nationals of Saudi Arabia. That Saudi Arabia promotes a particular form of Islam while maintaining a repressive policy against other forms of Islam (not to mention other faiths) is at least suggestive of a systemic connection between state intolerance and the growth of violent religious extremism.[9]

The root of the negative cycle is human nature itself. Mircea Eliade famously described human beings as "homo religiosus";[10] that is, all people have a natural drive to seek their own answers about the divine and about transcendence. States that trample on these natural impulses play with fire when, for example, they try to enforce atheism or some prescribed state religion. Religious yearning is elemental, and religious identity (or lack thereof) cannot be forced without a high risk of fomenting violent push-back and religious radicalization in one form or another. "Religion," a Soviet minister of education once said, "is like a nail; the harder you hit it, the deeper it goes."[11]

The negative cycle of religious repression and insecurity is also fostered by a number of social realities. Although there are indeed some historical examples of campaigns of religious repression so draconian that they virtually eliminated the targeted religious groups,[12] in most cases persecution just drives a religious group underground; the group remains a part of society but now in "illegal" and clandestine forms. And ironically sometimes persecution seems to result in the religious group's growing in size. In China, for example, the communists' attempt to eradicate religion did not stop the growth of Christianity. Indeed even though Western missionaries were expelled in 1949, conservative estimates put the total number of Christians in that country today at 70 million[13] (which is now more than the membership of the Communist Party). The period of Marxist rule in Ethiopia provides another example, as persecuted churches there went underground, adopted a secret cell structure, and grew explosively.[14] These examples also illustrate that underground religious groups will not necessarily turn violent. But there are several ways in which the experience of living under constant threat does sharply increase the risk of conflict, subversion, instability, or even outright rebellion.

First, strict control or repression of religion segregates the population, which can increase tension between religious groups and spark interreligious violence. Under religious repression, an opaque, rumor-based atmosphere emerges that poisons society, undermining interpersonal and community relationships. Where there is no trust, there is less opportunity for shared values to develop.[15] When groups are cloistered off from one another, they have no channels of information exchange, no inroads by which to communicate. Faith communities build rigid walls around themselves and hunker down in a defensive stance. Ashutosh Varshney's case studies of two cities in India, Calicut and Aligarh, illustrate this point. In Calicut, Varshney noticed that Hindus and Muslims were "interlocked" in many relationships, both formal and informal, due in part to shared media resources. Consequently violence was rare. Conversely, in Aligarh, a city where Muslims and Hindus had few common associations or shared information pools, anger and communal violence was more common: "In Aligarh . . . the average Hindu and Muslim do not meet in those civic settings—economic, social, educational—where mutual trust can be forged. Lacking the support of such networks, even competent police and civil administrators look on helplessly, as riots unfold."[16]

Another natural response to religious oppression is to strike back. While some religious groups go underground and isolate themselves, others are radicalized and adopt some form of militancy. As Philip Jenkins wrote in his chapter in *Religion & Security*:

> [P]ersecuted groups often become highly effective warriors, and some of the world's toughest fighters owe their origins to the need to defend

religious dissidence. Examples are quite numerous. We may think of the Sikhs, originally founded in sixteenth century India as a tolerant and peaceful order pledged to achieve reconciliation between Islam and Hinduism. Over time they were persecuted more and more savagely by India's Mughal rulers, until by the eighteenth century, extinction seemed imminent. The solution was found in transformation into a military brotherhood, the *khalsa*, in which every man was a lion, a *singh*. The Sikhs survived and flourished in independence, and their fighting qualities deeply impressed the British Raj. Wise governments of India have respected the Sikhs' right to be left alone, a principle violated in the 1980s by Prime Minister Indira Gandhi, who attacked their Golden Temple. She of course perished soon afterwards at the hands of her Sikh bodyguards.[17]

Another vivid illustration of this dynamic can be seen in Miriam Lanskoy's work on Daghestan, where the government demonized alleged Wahhabis as criminals and dissidents—a tactic that turned into a self-fulfilling prophecy. Until 1997 the religious conflict in Daghestan had been primarily theological in nature between the Wahhabis and the Sufis. But out of a feeling of insecurity, the long unpopular local government got involved and exaggerated the Wahhabi threat in order to draw funding from Moscow. Ironically this only served to destabilize the entire region. Daghestani Wahhabis fled to Chechnya and joined dissident Chechnyan Wahhabi groups. Then they came back and challenged the authority of the Daghestani government. A previously theological debate became politicized.[18]

The Daghestani example also illustrates a third reason why denying people their religious freedom can be dangerous to the government and counterproductive in terms of security. While some people in oppressed groups insulate and isolate themselves (building tension between groups) and others are radicalized against the state, still others flee the country. Having fled, they continue to maintain their ties from a position of diaspora. Those outside the country can sometimes be even more ideological than those on the ground (as exiles no longer have to personally face the constraints of local realpolitik). Even if the efforts of the government to suppress a religious minority are seemingly having the desired effects within the country, the diaspora is less likely to cooperate and will at times feed the instability from abroad.[19]

Where religion is perceived as the reason for persecution, transnational political activism extends even beyond the diaspora. Foreign believers who have no ethnic or national ties to the oppressed group often become activists as well, which can be threatening to the local government's sense of national sovereignty. Consider the Saudi role—sometimes governmental, sometimes individual—in supporting Wahhabism throughout the world (including Daghestan, as previously noted), destabilizing one country after another.[20] Or consider the Iranian role in supporting radical Shi'a political movements in Lebanon and elsewhere.

Especially in our contemporary context of globalization, the persecution of a religious minority carries serious risks of transforming that religious minority into a fifth column.

Moreover religious persecution can breed fascination with apocalyptic speculation and a cult of blood and martyrdom among the persecuted. In their most severe form these tendencies can lead to suicide attacks, which are extraordinarily difficult to defend against. But even short of this worst-case scenario, a religious group that has been persecuted to the point of sacralizing its persecution will often be, understandably, highly uncooperative with governmental aims. As Jenkins points out, "A persecuted people is hard to govern—an obvious point, but one that is often neglected. It is easy for activists to manipulate that kind of sentiment, to manipulate the idea of the blood of the martyrs, in order to generate opposition to the state."[21]

Finally, it's important to note that evidence of the negative cycle of religious persecution and insecurity is not just anecdotal. There are contemporary empirical data verifying the linkage. The sociologists Brian J. Grim and Roger Finke have conducted rigorous analysis of data on religious freedom and conflict in 143 countries. Grim summarizes their findings: "[S]ocial restrictions on religious freedom lead to government restrictions on religious freedom and the two act in tandem to increase the level of violence related to religion—which in turn cycles back and leads to even higher social and government restrictions on religion. This creates what we call the *religious violence cycle*."[22] Roger Finke and Jaime D. Harris recently expanded on that line of research, looking specifically at how social and governmental restrictions on religion affect religiously motivated violence. They found that societal restrictions on religion were the strongest and most consistent statistical predictors of this violence and that government restrictions also correlated with violence and were a strong predictor of isolation and societal restriction of religious groups, which in turn feeds religious violence.[23]

The Positive Cycle

Religious persecution and security threats can all too easily become locked into a self-reinforcing downward spiral. Real or imagined security threats emanating from religion inspire overzealous repression of religion, which ironically creates the conditions that genuine religious radicals are seeking: an atmosphere in which the radicals are the only opposition to the state, which builds sympathy for them among those who would otherwise be religious moderates, therefore decreasing the legitimacy of the state. A regime of responsible religious liberty helps avoid this destructive downward spiral. But not only that; it can also foster a constructive upward spiral that enhances the legitimacy and therefore the stability of the state.

Where religion is permitted to thrive on a level playing field of justice, fairness, and nonviolent competition in a battle of ideas, history tells us that there is a greater likelihood that it will provide a state with positive social capital. Religious freedom that is actively promoted will function as an impetus for respect, charity, forgiveness, and humility—both within and between nations. Hard-nosed security-minded realists simply cannot afford to subvert or ignore the "soft power" of religious freedom and its pro-social, stabilizing effects.

None of this is to deny, of course, the blood-soaked history of religion when it links perversely with radical nationalism, militant fundamentalism, and other dangerous "isms." But we should also bear in mind that "religious extremists" are not as numerous or as popular as is generally supposed. Akbar Ahmed and J. Douglas Holladay point to the critical role the media has played in unduly amplifying the voices of religious radicalism today, giving the impression that they reflect a much larger trend than they really do.[24]

Some secular moderns insist that the only sure way to prevent violence associated with the mix of religion and politics is to radically privatize religion. But this is counterproductive; it merely replaces one problem with another. The safe path to modernity does not necessitate radical secularization. Rather it necessitates greater pluralism—*principled* pluralism, not relativism—if international stability is going to be sustained.

A person who lives in a society and under a rule of law that respects his or her freedom of religious conscience will be likely to maintain feelings of loyalty to the state and to be motivated to live out religious ethics in socially responsible and constructive ways (as Roger Williams foresaw in the 1663 Colonial Charter of Rhode Island). Again, the individual's religious conscience is basic to human nature, and consequently religious persecution sparks rebellion because it goes against the grain of human nature. But the flip side of the coin is also true: religious freedom goes with the grain of human nature, and consequently it facilitates social stability and well-being. As Kevin J. Hasson has observed, "[I]t is natural to human beings to wonder about and search out the possibility that there is a God.... Thus a healthy state will neither suffocate nor forcefully intubate their citizens on matters religious. A state that accommodates the religious aspirations of its citizenry promotes stability and security for a very simple reason: such a state accurately recognizes who its citizens are."[25]

Beyond this basic anthropological dimension, the positive cycle of religious freedom and security has a complex sociological dimension. The crux is the relationship between freely practiced religion and civil society.[26] Civil society has become a popular buzzword among scholars and policymakers. Adam B. Seligman describes civil society as a sector of society wherein "free, self-determining individuality sets forth its claims for satisfaction of its wants and personal autonomy."[27] Another leading expert, Larry Diamond, defines civil society as the "realm of organized social life that is voluntary, self-generating, (largely) self-supporting, autonomous from the state, and bound by a legal order or set of shared rules." According to Diamond, civil society is at its best when "it is dense, affording individual opportunities to participate in multiple associations and informal networks at multiple levels of society."[28]

However, especially at the international level of analysis it is important not to romanticize civil society as a cure-all, nor to conceptually impose secular Western individualism on the civil society of cultures that may be much more religious and communal. Since the end of the cold war the civil society discussion has become deeply intertwined with the discussion of democratization. Yet it would be misleading to say that one necessarily denotes the other. In a 1999 *Foreign Policy* article titled "Think Again: Civil Society," Thomas Carothers points out that a seemingly strong civil society can actually have dangerous political weaknesses.[29] Carothers draws on Sheri Berman's example of Nazi Germany to illustrate his point: "In the 1920s and 1930s, Germany was unusually rich in associational life, with many people belonging to the sorts of professional and cultural organizations that are the mainstays of prodemocratic civil society. Berman argues, however, that not only did Germany's democratic civil society fail to solidify democracy and liberal values, it subverted them."[30] Only a civil society that is suffused with positive values has the potential to be a bulwark of decent governance, let alone an impetus to the creation of stable liberal democracy. The creation of a healthy civil society cannot be divorced from the discussion of values, and values do not arise out of a vacuum—they arise from the complex mosaic that is culture, communities, and religion. Thus we cannot avoid the question of moral fortitude in civil society.

While the values in a "values-based" civil society will vary from culture to continent, we do know the content of values conducive to a healthy civil society and to security, attributes such as respect, nonrelativistic pluralism, civic loyalty, self-control, responsibility, charity, and moderation. Put simply, the true test of whether a civil society is really civil is whether that society promotes the common value of respecting another's freedom of conscience to believe or not (i.e., if that society fully embraces religious freedom).

Although Western-based development organizations have sometimes chosen foolishly to ignore religious associations and networks,[31] religion is a pervasive presence in civil society worldwide. Fortunately in recent years the religious dimension of civil society has begun to be taken seriously in scholarship and public discussion. This research, discussed below, shows that religious freedom leads to religious pluralism and vitality, and in all but the most extreme cases the end result is an enhancement of social capital, that is, habits of civic participation and norms of trust and neighborliness among different religious groups, as well as between the majority and minority cultures.

Some scholars use the phrase *spiritual capital* to refer to the ways that freely practiced religion can help foster a healthy civil society. Spiritual capital, as defined by Peter L. Berger and Robert W. Hefner, is "a subspecies of social capital, referring to the influence, knowledge, and dispositions created by participation in a particular religious tradition."[32] Recent research shows that religion has had a positive influence on a variety of social conditions, such as health, rule of law, volunteerism, and education—all factors that influence the vibrancy of civil society, not to mention the health of the economy.[33] For example, the most well-known scholar of social capital, Harvard's Robert Putnam, has conducted large-scale empirical studies and concluded that religion is a leading source of social capital.[34] Sydney Verba and colleagues have also demonstrated that church involvement is "an important incubator for civic skills" because active church participants learn to run meetings, discuss proposals, handle disputes, mobilize people, and more.[35] Importantly, these civic skills are imparted regardless of socioeconomic standing, so that people who might not otherwise feel civically empowered become so as a byproduct of congregational involvement. Likewise contributors to Corwin Smidt's 2003 volume, *Religion as Social Capital: Producing the Common Good*, document many positive linkages between religion and community involvement, volunteering, charitable giving, and political participation.[36]

The significance of all this for religious freedom should be obvious. Repression of and discrimination against religion severely limit the social capital benefits that would otherwise likely emerge from vibrant religious pluralism. Religious associations and networks that produce positive social capital thrive in contexts where religious freedom is well established, and in particular where there is an open educational environment that allows and encourages religious leaders to receive advanced education in their own tradition's theology and social ethics.[37]

In such a context, religious communities and institutions become constructive contributors to a pluralistic and independent civil society. The vast majority of religious institutions inculcate morality and help create responsible citizens who serve their neighbors at the local level, often alleviating the financial burdens of the state by providing services to orphans, widows, the destitute, and others. In developing countries a moral citizenry is a bulwark against the corruption that comes with the transition to a market economy. Taken together, these dynamics create a synergistic stability wherein government understands the (ethno)religious group as critical to the well-being of the state.

There is, moreover, an essential and mutually reinforcing relationship between religious freedom and all the other individual and communal freedoms that characterize a mature liberal democracy. With the introduction of religious freedom into a society, religious institutions, communities, and individuals are permitted to grow openly in a healthy and constructive manner, which reinforces popular engagement with governance and the legitimacy of the state. In other words, there is a link between religious freedom and the degree of broader political liberalization and stability within a nation. As Timothy Samuel Shah has argued, "Religious freedom can be the thin end of the wedge of broader liberalization and democratization."[38] And liberal democracy in turn enhances security, as liberal democracies tend to avoid violent conflict with each other. To quote Jack Miles: "It is an oft-repeated truism that democratic capitalist states do not make war on other democratic capitalist states in the pursuit of political or economic power. This can be expanded to include religion: societies in which there is freedom of religion do not make religious war on other religiously free societies."[39]

Recent cross-national empirical research has also directly tested the relationship between religious freedom and a wide array of indicators of social well-being and security. The findings are compelling. For example, a large study by the Hudson Institute's Center for Religious Freedom found positive correlations between religious freedom and higher levels of civil and political liberty, press freedom, economic freedom, health outcomes, earned income, better educational opportunities for women, and scores on the human development index. Moreover religious freedom also correlated with fewer incidents of armed conflict.[40] Using more advanced statistical analysis and a larger dataset, Brian Grim and Rodney Stark have confirmed that religious freedom makes a significant contribution to positive social outcomes. As Grim summarizes:

> The empirical data are clear on two points. First, religious freedom is part of the "bundled commodity" of human freedoms that energize broader productive participation in civil society by all religious groups, which is conducive to the consolidation of democracy and to socio-economic progress. Secondly, religious freedom reduces conflict and increases security by, among other things, removing grievances religious groups have toward governments and their fellow citizens.[41]

What Is to Be Done?

So, to borrow from Lenin, "what is to be done?"[42] How might we practically address the conceptual framing and actual implementation of policies that take into account the negative and positive possibilities of religion in any given situation?

There are no quick fixes to this problem, but there are several near-, mid-, and long-term steps that can be taken. In the near term what is most needed is a comprehensive mapping that identifies the gaps in a government's ability to engage this issue. For example, in the United States the White House's Office of Faith-based and Neighborhood Partnerships recently completed

(July 2010) an initial survey of what U.S. governmental agencies are (or are not) doing to engage religion and faith-based actors. This mapping exercise might serve as an example for other governments to consider. More of such efforts worldwide would strengthen overall awareness among societal and state actors alike, while disseminating lessons learned and identifying areas for continued development.

There is also a near-term need for official guidance on religious freedom and religious engagement for governmental agencies (and related nongovernmental organizations) whose work is international in scope. At least within the U.S. government, the U.S. military is leading the way here on two key fronts. The military has had a vigorous conversation about the role of religion in joint operations and has recently published a new doctrine on it, "Religious Affairs in Joint Operations."[43] Beyond accepting such affairs as normal objects of analysis and strategy (which is itself a major step forward), this publication mandates that military chaplains not only provide for the spiritual care of troops (the traditional role of chaplains), but that they also be capable of assessing, analyzing, and advising on the social-cultural-religious environments to which they are assigned. In need of more study, it will be fascinating to see if other countries follow suit, prescribing new roles for their military chaplains or for other personnel from whom expertise on religion is expected. Meanwhile American Combatant Commanders (e.g., Central Command, which is responsible for the Middle East, Afghanistan-Pakistan, and Central Asia) are beginning to explore how social-cultural-religious engagement might be done more intentionally in their theater of operations. This trend calls for careful preparation of personnel, as religious affairs are obviously complex and often sensitive.

In fact the near term and midterm require practical training courses (designed to be accessible, relevant, and realistic for busy professionals) that teach participants at least basic understandings and tools necessary to engage the nexus between religion and security in a meaningful manner. Fortunately a few examples of this kind of training are beginning to emerge. For instance, the military chaplaincy has begun offering short courses on this topic.[44] Another example is the U.S. Agency for International Development, which has already created a toolkit for religious peacemaking;[45] as with the military, the global implications are enormous as sister agencies and departments in governments worldwide consider how they will (prepare to) interface with the United States on these issues. Still another example is the U.S. State Department, which has begun to consider how it might equip its foreign service officers to better engage religious communities overseas.[46] Indeed the secretary of state's "Strategic Dialogue with Civil Society" includes a working group on religion and foreign policy. This working group will establish the processes through which civil society actors worldwide can make recommendations to the U.S. State Department about foreign policy.[47]

In the long term, however, not just training but *education* is needed for entry-, mid-, and senior-level personnel serving in the governmental sector and related nongovernmental sectors.[48] In the American example, it is once again the military that is out in front. The military has a well-established educational system through which the relationship between security and religion and religious freedom can be readily studied and addressed. Such systems are not well-established among other governmental agencies or the private sector. As the world increasingly globalizes, it is in the best interest of the U.S. government—as well as other governments—to require future leaders to take educational courses on the role of religion and religious freedom and security, making them prerequisites for promotion. Meanwhile those courses should be made available to select professionals outside of government (e.g., journalists, NGO leaders, and business leaders).

Finally, our times call for the long-term development of a discourse within the academy—especially within the international relations graduate schools—that normalizes the study of religion in public life worldwide, particularly the relationship between religious freedom and security. This approach has begun, with notable funding efforts from the Luce Foundation, John Templeton Foundation, and others, to reintroduce religion to international affairs, but much more is needed. In particular much more research is needed, if only to ensure that the right questions are being asked in every discipline. It is our great hope that the comprehensive nature of this book inspires more of this kind of thinking, research, and curriculum development.

Conclusion

According to Gallup, 82 percent of the world's population says "religion is important in their daily lives."[49] Yet 70 percent of the globe's population is restricted in some form from living out their faith.[50] It is inconceivable that these two interrelated dynamics will not impact the security and stability of a state.

It should also be inconceivable that policymakers and practitioners would fail to account for the local manifestation of these two basic facts in the formation and implementation of foreign and national security policy. Unfortunately we in the West have generally not allowed for these two basic facts. Indeed in the name of the good governance that results from church-state separation, we have too often separated religion from analysis and therefore prevented its potential inclusion in any solution. Since the end of the cold war, however, reality has been intervening in ways that no one can ignore. In short, it took the death of the cold war paradigm to finally focus on the reality that had always existed: religion matters.

Notes

1. Samuel Huntington, "The Clash of Civilizations?," *Foreign Affairs,* Summer 2003, article summary at http://www.foreignaffairs.com/articles/48950/samuel-p-huntington/the-clash-of-civilizations.

2. Douglas Johnston and Cynthia Sampson, eds., *Religion, the Missing Dimension of Statecraft* (Oxford: Oxford University Press, 1994).

3. See Alex McVeigh, "President Remembers 9/11 Victims at Pentagon," Defense Department Documents and Publications, September 11, 2009; Carolee Walker, "Five-Year 9/11 Remembrance Honors Victims from 90 Countries," U.S. Department of State, Bureau of International Information Programs, September 11, 2006, http://www.america.gov/st/washfile-english/2006/September/20060911141954bcreklaw0.9791071.html#ixzz0t7WaXPf8 (accessed July 8, 2010).

4. For example, please see the Social Science Research Council's blog, The Immanent Frame, created in 2007: http://www.ssrc.org/programs/the-immanent-frame-blog/.

5. For extensive lists of IGE's online resources on this topic, see the links at "IGE on Engaging Islam," http://www.globalengage.org/pressroom/ftp/1158-ige-on-engaging-islam.html, and "IGE President Chris Seiple Addresses National Security Agency," http://www.globalengage.org/pressroom/releases/1129-ige-president-chris-seiple-addresses-national-security-agency-.html. See especially Chris Seiple, "Toward a World Safe for Religion and Politics," February 21, 2003, http://www.globalengage.org/issues/articles/freedom/564-toward-a-world-safe-for-religion-and-politics.html.

6. Charter of Rhode Island and Providence Plantations, July 15, 1663, http://www.beliefnet.com/resourcelib/docs/146/Charter_of_Rhode_Island_and_Providence_Plantations_1.html.

7. Portions of this section draw from Seiple, "Toward a World Safe for Religion and Politics."

8. See works cited throughout this article. Additional sources include, for example, Dennis R. Hoover and Douglas M. Johnston, eds., *Religion and Foreign Affairs: Essential Readings* (Waco, Texas: Baylor University Press, 2012); Chris Seiple, Dennis R. Hoover, and Pauletta Otis, eds., *Routledge Handbook of Religion and Security* (Oxford: Routledge, 2013); the summer 2008 issue of *The Review of Faith & International Affairs,* which was a special issue on U.S. international religious freedom policy (see http://www.tandfonline.com/toc/rfia20/6/2); Robert A. Seiple, "Security, Stability, and Religious Freedom," testimony before House Committee on International Relations, February 13, 2004, http://www.globalengage.org/issues/articles/freedom/607-security-stability-and-religious-freedom.html; Chris Seiple, "Memo to the State: Religion and Security," *The Review of Faith & International Affairs* 5, no. 1 (2007): 39–42; Thomas F. Farr, "Diplomacy in an Age of Faith" *Foreign Affairs* 87, no. 2 (2008): 110–24; Thomas F. Farr, *World of Faith and Freedom: Why International Religious Liberty Is Vital to American National Security* (Oxford: Oxford University Press, 2008);Chris Seiple, review of *World of Faith and Freedom, Journal of Church and State* 51, no. 3 (2009): 535–36; Thomas F. Farr and Dennis R. Hoover, *The Future of U.S. International Religious Freedom Policy: Recommendations for the Obama Administration* (Washington, D.C.: Berkley Center for Religion, Peace, and World Affairs at Georgetown University and the Center on Faith & International Affairs at the Institute for Global Engagement, 2008), http://www.globalengage.org/research/reports.html; Task Force on Religion and the Making of U.S. Foreign Policy, *Engaging Religious Communities Abroad: A New Imperative for U.S. Foreign Policy* (Chicago: Chicago Council on Global Affairs, 2010).

9. See the U.S. Commission on International Religious Freedom's Policy Focus on Saudi Arabia, http://www.uscirf.gov/briefings/13May04/saudiPolicyBrief.pdf. It should be noted that Saudi Arabia has taken some positive steps since 9/11. See Chris Seiple, "Interrogating Islam…and Ourselves," Institute for Global Engagement, February 3, 2004, http://www.globalengage.org/pressroom/ftp/451-from-the-president-interrogating-islam-ourselves.html. See also the "Council of Senior Ulema Fatwa on terror-financing," May 7, 2010, http://www.saudiembassy.net/announcement/announcement05071001.aspx.

10. Eliade Mircea, *The Sacred and the Profane: The Nature of Religion* (New York: Harcourt, 1959).

11. See David Powell, "Storming the Heavens: The Soviet League of the Militant Godless (review)," *Journal of Cold War Studies* 3, no. 2 (2001): 113–16.

12. Consider, for example, the seventeenth-century church in Japan or the seventh-century church in North Africa, both of which virtually disappeared after being subjected to extremely severe persecution.

13. Brian J. Grim, "Religion in China on the Eve of the 2008 Beijing Olympics," Pew Forum on Religion & Public Life, May 7, 2008, http://pewresearch.org/pubs/827/china-religion-olympics (accessed July 8, 2010).

14. Tibebe Eshete, "Evangelical Christians and Indirect Resistance to Religious Persecution in Ethiopia," *The Review of Faith & International Affairs* 8, no. 1 (2010): 13–22.

15. Seiple, "Toward a World Safe for Religion and Politics."

16. Ashutosh Varshney, "Ethnic Conflict and Civil Society: India and Beyond," *World Politics* 53 (April 2001): 362–98.

17. Philip Jenkins, "The Politics of Persecuted Religious Minorities," in *Religion & Security: The New Nexus in International Relations*, ed. Robert A. Seiple and Dennis R. Hoover (Lanham, Md.: Rowman & Littlefield, 2004), 28.

18. Miriam Lanskoy, "Daghestan and Chechnya: The Wahhabi Challenge to the State," *SAIS Review* 22, no. 2 (2002): 167–92.

19. Yossi Shain, "The Role of Diasporas in Conflict Perpetuation or Resolution." *SAIS Review* 22, no. 2 (2002): 115–44.

20. See Nina Shea, "Tread Softly," *National Review*, December 11, 2008; Alex Alexiev, "Wahhabism: State Sponsored Extremism Worldwide," Senate Testimony, U.S. Senate Subcommittee on Terrorism, Technology and Homeland Security, June 26, 2003, http://kyl.senate.gov/legis_center/subdocs/sc062603_alexiev.pdf (accessed July 8, 2010); Helene Cooper, "Saudis' Role in Iraq Frustrates U.S. Officials," *New York Times*, July 27, 2007, http://www.nytimes.com/2007/07/27/world/middleeast/27saudi.html?pagewanted = all (accessed July 8, 2010).

21. Jenkins, "The Politics of Persecuted Religious Minorities," 31.

22. Brian J. Grim, "Religious Freedom: Good for What Ails Us?," *The Review of Faith & International Affairs* 6, no. 2 (2008): 5. See also Brian J. Grim and Roger Finke, "Religious Persecution in Cross-National Context: Clashing Civilizations or Regulated Religious Economies?," *American Sociological Review* 72, no. 4 (2007): 633–58.

23. Roger Finke and Jaime D. Harris, "Wars and Rumors of Wars: Explaining Religiously Motivated Violence," paper prepared for the Argov Center Conference Religion, Politics, Society and the State: Israel in Comparative Perspective, Bar-Ilan University, Israel, January 8, 2009. On state religious exclusivity and conflict, see Jonathan Fox, Patrick James, and Yitan Li, "State Religion and Discrimination against Ethnic Minorities," *Nationalism and Ethnic Politics* 15, no. 2 (2009): 189–210.

24. Akbar Ahmed and J. Douglas Holliday, "Dialogue of Civilizations," presentations at the conference Enhancing Cross-Cultural Effectiveness: Strategies and Skills for International Business, Education, Training, and Development Professionals, International Management Institute, Washington, D.C., March 11, 2005.

25. Kevin J. Hasson, "Neither Sacred nor Secular: A Public Anthropology of Human Dignity, Religious Freedom, and Security," in Seiple and Hoover, *Religion & Security*, 153, 160.

26. The discussion of civil society herein draws in part from Chris Seiple, "Revisiting the Geo-Political Thinking of Sir Halford John Mackinder: United States-Uzbekistan Relations 1991–2005" (Ph.D. dissertation, Fletcher School of Law & Diplomacy, Tufts University, 2006).

27. Adam B. Seligman, *The Idea of Civil Society* (Princeton, N.J.: Princeton University Press, 1992), 3.

28. Larry Diamond, "Rethinking Civil Society toward Democratic Consolidation," *Journal of Democracy* 5, no. 3 (1994): 5, 14–15.

29. Thomas Carothers, "Think Again: Civil Society," *Foreign Policy,* Winter 1999–2000, 3. See also chapter 3 of Seiple, "Revisiting the Geo-Political Thinking of Sir Halford John Mackinder," for an ample discussion of America's inability to engage the three critical dimensions to Uzbek civil society: religion, clans, and elites.

30. Carothers, "Think Again," 3.

31. Scott M. Thomas. "Building Communities of Character: Foreign Aid Policy and Faith Based Organizations" *SAIS Review* 24, no. 2 (2004): 133–48.

32. Peter L. Berger and Robert W. Hefner, "Spiritual Capital in Comparative Perspective," Spiritual Capital Research Program, Metanexus Institute, http://www.metanexus.net/archive/spiritualcapitalresearchprogram/pdf/Berger.pdf.

33. Robert D. Woodberry, "Researching Spiritual Capital: Promises and Pitfalls," Spiritual Capital Research Program, Metanexus Institute, http://www.metanexus.net/archive/spiritualcapitalresearchprogram/pdf/woodberry.pdf.

34. Robert Putnam, *Bowling Alone: The Collapse and Revival of American Community* (New York: Simon and Schuster, 2000), 66.

35. Sydney Verba et al., *Voice and Equality: Civic Voluntarism in American Politics* (Cambridge, Mass.: Harvard University Press, 1995).

36. Corwin Smidt, *Religion as Social Capital: Producing the Common Good* (Waco, Texas: Baylor University Press, 2003).

37. On linkages between seminary and security, see Chris Seiple, "Engaging Conservative Islam," Institute for Global Engagement, February 4, 2010, http://www.globalengage.org/pressroom/ftp/1128-from-the-president-engaging-conservative-islam.html.

38. See Timothy S. Shah's testimony before the House International Relations Committee concerning the 2004 Annual Report on Religious Freedom, http://wwwc.house.gov/international_relations/108/sha100604.htm.

39. Jack Miles, "Religion and American Foreign Policy," *Survival* 46, no. 1 (2004): 32–33.

40. Brian J. Grim, "God's Economy: Religious Freedom and Socio-Economic Well-being," in *Religious Freedom in the World*, ed. Paul Marshall (Lanham, Md.: Rowman & Littlefield, 2008), 42–47.

41. Grim, "Religious Freedom: Good for What Ails Us?," 6. The large-scale "Prosperity Index" studies produced by the Legatum Institute also support the conclusion that there is a close interrelationship between religious freedom and other dimensions of human flourishing. See http://www.prosperity.com/.

42. This was the 1902 title of Lenin's treatise on why the "vanguard of the proletariat" was needed to catalyze the masses.

43. Joint Chiefs of Staff, "Religious Affairs in Joint Operations," http://www.fas.org/irp/doddir/dod/jp1_05.pdf.

44. See the winter 2009 edition of *The Review of Faith & International Affairs* for a comprehensive review of the chaplaincy's past and possible future roles, http://www.tandfonline.com/toc/rfia20/7/4.

45. The authors have taught chaplaincy courses together. For the USAID toolkit, see http://pdf.usaid.gov/pdf_docs/PNADR501.pdf.

46. Chris Seiple keynoted the first Religion & Foreign Policy course at the Foreign Service Institute, where the U.S. trains its diplomats, in June 2011; this three-day course was offered as an elective. In 2012, it was offered twice as an elective four-day course, with Seiple keynoting both times.

47. Chris Seiple is a senior advisor to the "Strategic Dialogue with Civil Society" and, as such, a member of the federal advisory committee to Secretary Clinton, and one of two civil society co-chairs of the Religion & Foreign Policy Working Group (along with the Undersecretary of State for Civilian Security, Democracy, and Human Rights, the Ambassador-at-Large for International Religious Freedom, and the executive director of the White House Office of Faith-based and Neighborhood Partnerships). For more information, see https://globalengage.org/pressroom/releases/1236-video-now-available-from-the-working-group-on-religion-and-foreignpolicy.html.

48. In an ideal world, education would come before training, but the need is so urgent and the challenge so generational that this approach is the only practical one there is.

49. Steve Crabtree and Brett Pelham, "What Alabamians and Iranians Have in Common," Gallup.com, February 9, 2009, http://www.gallup.com/poll/114211/Alabamians-Iranians-Common.aspx.

50. See the 2009 report of the Pew Forum on Religion and Public Life, "Global Restrictions on Religion," http://pewforum.org/Government/Global-Restrictions-on-Religion.aspx.

15

Religious Freedom and International Diplomacy

THOMAS F. FARR

Religious freedom raises hackles. It is today a highly contested human right and is staunchly resisted by a wide variety of governments, individuals, and groups worldwide. To some extent this opposition has been present since the very advent of the modern regime of human rights. During the debates over what became the 1948 UN Universal Declaration of Human Rights, the passages guaranteeing religious freedom were among the most disputed and occasioned in the final vote one of the rare abstentions to the Declaration itself.[1]

It is true that, in the aftermath of World War II, a vigorous *concept* of religious freedom emerged in international covenants, declarations, and constitutions. The Universal Declaration's guarantees of religious liberty were codified in 1966 with the passage of the International Covenant on Civil and Political Rights. In 1965 a significant doctrinal and political development occurred within Roman Catholicism with the promulgation of its Declaration on Religious Freedom.[2] Many of the national constitutions drafted after the war contained guarantees of religious liberty.[3]

But in the ensuing decades even this conceptual advance of religious freedom has gradually weakened. More than any other human right recognized in the multilateral and national documents as universal, religious freedom has yielded far more homage in word than it has in deed. To cite but one example, during the debate over the Universal Declaration in the 1948 UN General Assembly, Pakistani Foreign Minister Muhammad Zafrulla Khan enthusiastically endorsed the Declaration's article on religious freedom on behalf of what was at the time the world's largest Muslim country. Citing the Qur'an, Zafrulla Khan said that protecting religious freedom was necessary to "the honor of Islam."[4] Unfortunately, notwithstanding this potentially powerful evocation of Islam's most sacred text, Pakistan has in the years since its creation failed to protect religious freedom. Ironically Zafrulla Khan himself was an Ahmadi, an Islamic minority that has been treated with particular contempt and cruelty in Pakistan. Because its adherents are not regarded as Muslims, articles of the Pakistani penal code are designed to punish them with prison, or even execution, for identifying themselves as such.[5] More broadly Pakistan has placed significant restrictions on the religious liberty of most of its citizens.[6]

Pakistan is not, of course, the only nation to fail in its responsibilities under international law to guarantee religious freedom for all its citizens. The deficit in protections for religious freedom is so widespread that it ought to be a source of deep concern for governments that advocate for human rights and democracy around the world. An exhaustive study by the Pew Forum on Religion and Public Life recently demonstrated that nearly 70 percent of the world's population lives in countries where their religious freedom is subject to severe restriction by governments, social pressures, or both.[7] Many of these countries have Muslim majorities, but the two largest—China and India—account proportionately for the greatest number of people subject to harsh restrictions. Both have large Muslim minorities, themselves vulnerable to persecution along with Christians, Buddhists, and others. Perhaps most surprisingly, there is among Western societies (where religious liberty was first conceptualized) an increasing indifference to religious freedom as a fundamental human right and growing skepticism about religious ideas and actors in the public sphere.[8]

All of this is alarming at a moral and humanitarian level. It is simply unacceptable that, in the twenty-first century, so many human beings live in regimes where their religious beliefs and practices are at risk of unjust restriction or where they may be subject to torture and abuse because of their beliefs and practices (or those of their tormentors). Religious freedom is a necessary and constituent element of human dignity, flourishing, and justice.[9]

But as serious as these depredations are, the problem implicates far more than a moral crisis. The achievement and the maintenance of religious freedom, however difficult it may be, is crucial to international peace, development, and ordered liberty. As we shall see, religious liberty is a necessary part of the "bundled commodity of freedoms" that are required if democracy is to endure and to yield its social, economic, political, intellectual, and religious benefits equally to all its citizens and communities.[10] Moreover religious liberty can be a critical tool in the quest to contain or eliminate religion-based violence, extremism, and terrorism.[11]

If these propositions are true—if the advancement of religious freedom would be morally and practically advantageous to all societies—it is reasonable to expect that Western democratic nations would emphasize religious liberty in their respective foreign policies. It is reasonable to expect that at least some members of the United Nations, whose Universal Declaration trumpeted the importance of religious liberty, would give it priority. But do they? Among those nations seeking to advance human rights in their bilateral and multilateral relations, where does religious freedom fit? What role does international religious liberty play in multilateral human rights organizations such as the European Court of Human Rights?

This chapter will seek to explore these questions in three parts. First, we will survey the evidence that religious ideas and actors are a distinct and growing public phenomenon around the world and that religious freedom is the most appropriate mechanism to nourish and regulate this growth. Second, we will examine the performance of the only nation with a formally declared policy of advancing international religious freedom: the United States. While it might be assumed that America's historic championing of religious freedom provides an exception to growing international indifference, U.S. foreign policy is in some respects surprisingly reflective of world trends. Third, we will sample views of religious freedom among Western European nations and institutions in order to draw some conclusions about where that freedom stands in their human rights diplomacy.

The Return of God and What to Do about It

The evidence is overwhelming: religious actors and ideas have returned to the world stage, and, for better or worse, they are having an enormous impact on matters of public policy such as justice and governance, economic growth, women's rights, war and peace, and terrorism. The "revenge of God," as one scholar has labeled it, has placed great pressure on international affairs scholars and policymakers to cast aside their secularist assumptions and develop a framework within which they can understand the resurgence of religion.[12] More to the point, they must design policies that accommodate the religious impulses of men and are liberal, humane, and effective.

A key aspect of religion's resurgence is what scholars call the "desecularization" of the world. One need only peruse the polls to see the consistency of the findings:[13] with the exception of certain populations in Western Europe, the old British Empire, and a broad, thin layer of Western educated leaders outside the West,[14] people the world over are consistently, and apparently irretrievably, religious.

Of course, "being religious" can have several meanings, and faith need not necessarily lead religious adherents, their leaders, or their ideas into the public square. Some religious teachings encourage the privatization of religion, that is, foreswearing political involvement or proselytism. Bahai's, for example, discourage involvement in partisan politics.[15] Chinese Daoism has little history of political involvement, at least in the modern age.[16] Other religions, such as Judaism and Hinduism, are not typically proselytizing traditions and are often resistant when other communities seek conversions from their respective flocks.[17]

The privatization tendency is also prominent among some religious believers in the West for whom religion is less a matter of adhering to a body of teachings than it is belonging to a cultural or ethnic heritage, such as, in the United States, "Irish Catholicism" or "midwestern Lutheranism." Still others have constructed their own internal, highly individuated form of spirituality, in which any objective doctrinal content is minimal or nonexistent. Atheists and other skeptics of religion are naturally opposed to religious actors and ideas in public life.

But as the sociologist Jose Casanova and others have demonstrated, global desecularization has generally been accompanied by deprivatization.[18] Being religious usually means that people are born into or join a religious community and accept its truth claims, such as evangelical forms of Christianity, Roman Catholic social and moral teachings, or Islamic revivalism. Sometimes it means that the religious community is a source of identity much like ethnicity or nationality. Many Russian Orthodox, for example, associate their religious beliefs with being Russian. Many Indian Hindus associate their beliefs with being Indian. And, of course, both Christianity and Islam have historically been, and continue to be, proselytizing religions. All of these developments have had the effect of thrusting religion onto the world stage and into issues of public policy.

The data show that the vast majority of the world's people belong to religious communities.[19] Most embrace a set of teachings and doctrines that have some bearing on the way they live their lives and on the way they wish their society to be organized. We might call this set of beliefs a "political theology," or the application of belief to issues of public policy. Some political theologies are wicked, such as bin Ladenism. Others are humane and productive, such as the Protestant emphasis on freedom of conscience and the laws necessary to protect it.[20]

The reappearance of public religion on the world stage has complex implications. Religion has both bolstered and undermined stable self-government. It has advanced political reform and human rights but also induced irrationalism, persecution, and terrorism. In China a significant growth of religious devotion deeply worries communist officials, and periodically they respond with religious persecution. Religious ideas and actors affect relations between the nuclear powers India and Pakistan and in the consolidation of democracy in Latin America. Religion is influencing the fate of sub-Saharan African peoples, including whether they will be able to achieve economic growth and political stability or defeat the scourge of HIV/AIDS. Even in Western Europe—which has seen itself as a laboratory for secularization—religion, in the form of Islam and pockets of Christian revival, simply will not go away.[21]

Perhaps the most significant dimension of the worldwide resurgence of religion—and the one with the greatest impact on world peace—is the persistence of Islamist terrorism. While it may be fed by a number of historical factors or economic and social pathologies, this form of terrorism is energized by radical interpretations of Islam. In particular the pernicious political theology of Wahhabism, which has provided much of the theological oxygen for al Qaeda, is still dominant in Saudi Arabia and has been exported to Sunni communities internationally.[22] This particular interpretation of Islam has for decades been an intellectual force among Muslims in Western Europe and the United States.[23]

But Wahhabism is not the only example of Islamist extremism that has major implications for world peace. In Egypt the Muslim Brotherhood represents a strain of Islamism that has spawned or nourished radicals from Sayyid Qutb to Ayman al-Zawahiri and Osama bin Laden, although it now operates as a democratic political party. An offshoot of the Brotherhood, Hamas, has put Islamist extremism at the center of the Israeli-Palestinian conflict. Hezbollah has emerged as a major player in Lebanese democracy, even as it is funded from Tehran and continues to threaten Israel. And there is, of course, Iran itself, where the revolutionary Shi'ism bequeathed by Ayatollah Ruhollah Khomeini has combined with Iranian nationalism to present a potentially lethal policy combination: Islamic millenarianism, support for Islamist terrorism, and the capacity to build and deliver nuclear weapons.[24]

More broadly religion has had a bivalent effect on the growth of democracy around the world. Some majority religious communities have retarded democracy by employing the state to maintain a religious monopoly. This has been true at times of the Russian Orthodox Church, certain strains of puritanical Hindu nationalism, and Islamic communities in countries as various as Iran and Saudi Arabia or Afghanistan and Iraq.[25]

On the other hand, some religious communities have made the rooting of democracy more likely. The Protestant emphases on the individual's relationship with God, the critical need for literacy in order to read sacred scripture, the importance of hard work and self-discipline, and the call to faithfulness in marriage have provided political, economic, and social pillars of democratic development in Latin America, Africa, and Asia.[26] The development of doctrine represented by the Catholic Second Vatican Council, in particular its *Declaration on Religious Liberty*, as well as the pontificate of John Paul II, have provided the impetus to much of what Samuel Huntington labeled the third wave of democratization and what George Weigel called "the Catholic human rights revolution."[27]

There are encouraging democratic developments in the Muslim world as well. The ruling party in Turkey since 2002, the Justice and Development Party (AKP), is posing an interesting experiment in whether an Islam-based political party will over the course of time veer into fanaticism. Concerns about the AKP have recently emerged because of its courting of the radical government in Iran and because of talk in Ankara about an "Ottoman alternative."[28] However, the AKP achieved political success not with Islamist radicalism but with good governance, good economic policies, and what appeared to be a governing philosophy with significant liberal elements. Likewise in Indonesia Islamic communities are resisting extremism and making major contributions to civil society and democratic governance. However, while Freedom House ranks Turkey and Indonesia high on political freedom and civil liberties in general, both remain weak on religious freedom.[29] Consolidation of democracy in each will require progress on that front. It remains to be seen whether Islamic democracy will take root and remain stable in either nation, affording equality to all their citizens.

This brief overview demonstrates that, for better or worse, the world is rife with religious ideas, actors, communities, and movements—with very public consequences. And there is little reason to believe that this state of affairs will change any time soon. Two leading demographers of religion, Todd Johnson and David Barrett, have concluded that "over 80 percent of the world's population will continue to be affiliated to religions 200 years into the future."[30]

This "return of God" to the international stage raises important intellectual and policy questions. In the field of international relations, scholars have begun to grapple with the phenomenon, in particular its significance for the once highly prized but now highly questionable concept of secularization. For our purposes, the key questions are these: What is the most fruitful policy framework for understanding and addressing the religious ideas and actors that impact public matters, both within nations and in international affairs? To what extent might a broad understanding of religious freedom provide such a framework, and how might governments conceptualize religious freedom as an aspect of their respective foreign policies? Should religious freedom have a distinct or significant role in the foreign policies of states seeking to advance human rights in general? Emerging scholarship in the fields of political theory, international relations, and empirical sociology provides some interesting answers to these questions.

The work of the political theorist Alfred Stepan is a good place to begin. In an analysis of past and prospective transitions to democracy Stepan concludes that the best way to conceptualize a productive democratic role for powerful religious communities is not secularism as understood in modern liberal parlance, nor the separation of religion and politics, but the achievement of what he calls the "twin tolerations," that is, "the minimal boundaries of freedom of action that must somehow be crafted for political institutions vis-a-vis religious authorities, and for religious individuals and groups vis-a-vis political institutions."[31] Democracy, he writes, "is a system of conflict regulation that allows open competition over the values and goals that citizens want to advance." The critical challenge for religious societies is negotiating the democratic boundaries within which this competition can take place.[32]

Achieving the "twin tolerations," in other words, requires the acceptance of a democratic covenant between civil and religious authorities. For its part, government must permit both private and public religious activity, including activity designed to influence public policy, within very broad, equally applied limits. For their part, religious individuals and communities must agree to avoid actions that "impinge negatively on the liberties of other citizens or violate democracy and the law."[33] Stepan's analysis of contemporary Confucianism, Islam, and Eastern Orthodoxy suggests that each of these religious traditions, like Christianity, is not "univocal," and that each is capable of achieving the twin tolerations. That achievement, he writes, "normally requires debate within the major religious communities. And proponents of the democratic bargain are often able to win over their fellow believers only by employing arguments that are not conceptually freestanding but deeply embedded in their own religious community's comprehensive doctrine."[34]

Stepan's work provides a useful framework for understanding how religious actors might be encouraged to adopt a constructive public role within societies that are struggling to make their democracies stable and secure (e.g., Iraq, Afghanistan, Pakistan) or to consolidate and mature (e.g., Turkey, Indonesia, Russia, Chile, Mexico). In countries with large or growing religious communities, as we have seen, deprivatization is the norm. There are bound to be areas where religion and politics mix. Given the opportunity, those communities will inevitably attempt to influence the societies in which they are situated, the political arrangements under which they live, and the laws and policies of their states.

To expect otherwise—to believe that religious believers can or should be indifferent to the public rules and norms that shape their lives—is no more realistic than applying the same expectation to any other group within civil society. Indeed the very nature of religious conviction can *require* believers to engage in public policy debates. Bound in conscience to religious and moral truths, such believers do not have the freedom simply to pretend those truths are relevant only to them or that they have no public implications. It is also clear, of course, that religious actors can be antidemocratic or even theocratic if they enter the political realm without accepting limits on their authority (as we see in theocratic states such as Iran, Sudan, and Saudi Arabia and in nascent democracies such as Egypt, Iraq, and Afghanistan). Stepan's concept of the twin tolerations helps us to understand what those limits must be.

As such, the twin tolerations also provide a conceptual roadmap for national and multilateral foreign policies that seek to encourage stability, justice, and human rights. Such policies might attempt to encourage both civil and religious authorities in the pursuit of something like the twin tolerations, a stable politicoreligious relationship that can support the emergence of and the benefits of democracy.

Stepan's approach has been expanded by the international relations scholar Daniel Philpott. In a 2007 *American Political Science Review* essay, Philpott asks the following question: What combination of religious views about politics (political theology) and levels of differentiation between religion and state typically yields the most legitimacy and stability? His analysis of religion-state relationships, and their influence on the emergence of democracy and the frequency of terrorism, supports Stepan's conclusions. According to Philpott, a society in which religious actors possess, or are capable of possessing, liberal democratic political theologies is most likely to achieve what he calls "consensual differentiation" and religious freedom:

> Consensual differentiation is likely to be the most normatively stable.... [I]t guarantees religious freedom, and so is less likely to provoke the revisionism of minorities. It is most likely to result when religious communities hold a liberal democratic political theology. They renounce institutional prerogatives, which they might otherwise regard as guarantees of their preferred politics, and permit minority religions to compete for followers and influence. But they do not abjure political influence, which they may now exert from a differentiated position. The state, for its part, agrees to respect the autonomy of religious groups and to allow their participation in politics, even when groups promote ends that some elites disfavor.[35]

In a paper presented at a 2009 Georgetown University conference, Philpott focused on the relationship between religious freedom and religion-based terrorism. He asked, "Might religious freedom, and more broadly democratic regimes based on religious freedom, turn out to be...an integral strategy in that very struggle [against terrorism]?" Drawing on his own research into the incidence and nature of terrorism, he answered as follows: "[A]uthoritarian regimes who suppress religious freedom...encourage terrorism. Their control of religious actors prevents the political participation and competition that fosters compromise and moderation.... The pattern is strongest in the Islamic world, from where 91% of religious terrorists originate." Further, "democratic regimes who allow religious freedoms moderate terrorism." Philpott concluded with a recommendation for U.S. foreign policy that could be adopted by any nation interested in encouraging stable democracy and human rights: "a policy of great pressure towards democratization, the inclusion of religious freedom in democratization, and the 'constructive engagement' of religious actors might well promote democracy, stability, and the reduction of terrorism better than an unreflective presumption for alliances with authoritarian regimes who suppress their religious citizens."[36]

Philpott's work tends to emphasize and elaborate what Stepan suggests—that the political, social, economic, and religious well-being of societies depends at least in part on their ability to achieve religious freedom. That hypothesis has also found support in the field of empirical sociology. In a 2007 *American Sociological Review* essay, Brian Grim and Roger Finke looked carefully at the relationship between government *regulation* of religion (i.e., the opposite of

Stepan's twin tolerations or Philpott's consensual differentiation) and religion-based violence. Their findings are consistent with Philpott's. Employing coded data from the U.S. Department of State's *Annual Reports on International Religious Freedom*, they demonstrate that social violence involving religion, including religious persecution and religion-based terrorism, is highly correlated with government regulation of religion.[37]

In a separate analysis published in 2009, Grim asks a related, and highly important, question: "Does religious freedom *lead* to socio-economic well being?" (emphasis added). Drawing on a study of 101 countries conducted by the Hudson Institute's Center for Religious Freedom, he concludes that "the presence of religious freedom in a country mathematically correlates with the presence of other fundamental, responsible freedoms (including civil and political liberty, press freedom, and economic freedom) and with the longevity of democracy." Further, "wherever religious freedom is high, there tends to be fewer incidents of armed conflict, better health outcomes, higher levels of earned income, and better educational opportunities for women. Moreover, religious freedom is associated with higher overall human development, as measured by the human development index."[38]

But correlations, Grim correctly notes, do not necessarily prove causation. He then addresses what the data indicate about the causal relationship between a society's achievement of religious freedom and other social, economic and political goods:

> More advanced statistical tests suggest that there is indeed a critical independent contribution that religious freedom is making. A growing body of research supports the proposition that the religious competition inherent in religious freedom results in increased religious participation; and religious participation in turn can lead to a wide range of positive social and political outcomes.... Furthermore, as religious groups make contributions to society and become an accepted part of the fabric of society, religious freedom is consolidated.[39]

Taken together, the work of Stepan, Philpott, Grim, Finke, and others strongly indicates that stable democracy requires a "bundled commodity" of fundamental freedoms that cannot function properly without religious liberty. Absent that right, societies are highly vulnerable to democracy-killing religious conflict, persecution, and extremism. However, societies that protect religious freedom for all their citizens are far more likely to succeed as stable democracies that afford women's rights, equality under the law, and economic opportunity and remain at peace with their neighbors.[40]

History provides further evidence for the hypothesis that religious freedom is necessary for a successful transition to stable democracy. To take one example, most Catholic nations did not become democratic until the Church sanctioned religious liberty. At the Second Vatican Council Church Fathers embraced the powerful democratic principle of equality under the law for all individuals and religious communities.[41] The Catholic Church did not abandon its claim to be the one true Church, established by Jesus Christ. But for the first time in its history it abandoned any claim to privileged access to civil authority in order to maintain its religious monopoly.[42] The result was what Huntington labeled "the third wave" of democratization.[43] Not all Catholic societies have internalized or adopted the notion of equality under the law, but many have. Today in Latin America, for example, Catholics are helping democracy to consolidate by competing vigorously but peacefully with Pentecostals and by resisting the old temptation to seek advantage through civil law and policy.[44]

To repeat, the evidence is overwhelming: religion has returned to the international stage in very public ways. It can retard democracy and human rights or become the very engine of a liberal and humane society. Moreover there is ample evidence that its most positive contributions can be nourished only within a national regime of religious freedom, grounded in something like Stepan's twin tolerations, and based on full equality under the law. Any nation, Western or otherwise, that seeks to encourage the spread of stable democracy and the benefits we associate with it—human rights, including women's rights, economic growth, political stability, social harmony, and peaceful behavior in international affairs—must also seek to encourage religious freedom.

The American Experiment

The most forward-leaning attempt to recognize and advance an understanding of religious liberty as a political, economic, and social good has occurred in the United States. In 1998 the U.S. Congress passed and President Bill Clinton signed the International Religious Freedom Act, mandating that American diplomacy oppose religious persecution and advance religious freedom around the world. The law was the result of a typically American lobbying campaign. It began in the mid-1990s and in the initial stages was led by Evangelicals and Jews. The conservative provenance of the campaign made the proposed legislation controversial and, to some, threatening.[45] As late as the summer of 1998, the religious freedom bill was languishing in the Senate and was declared dead by secular news outlets such as the *New York Times*.[46]

But by then public support for the legislation had broadened significantly. Not only had a number of liberal religious groups lined up behind it, but some secular human rights organizations had endorsed it as well. The Clinton administration, led by Secretary of State Madeleine Albright, had initially opposed the law on the grounds that it would create an illegitimate "hierarchy of human rights" in U.S. policy. But in the end Congress passed the IRF Act unanimously, and Clinton signed it into law.[47]

As passed, the law was designed to put the advancement of religious freedom at the center of U.S. foreign policy. It created an office in the State Department, headed by a very senior diplomatic official, an ambassador-at-large, to implement the new policy. The ambassador was styled "principal adviser to the President and Secretary of State" on IRF matters and given the authority to represent the United States abroad in both bilateral and multilateral forums and negotiations. The treatment of this official by three administrations has been a bellwether of the health and effectiveness of U.S. IRF policy.

The law also created a separate, bipartisan IRF commission to act as a watchdog agency and issue its own recommendations. Nine commissioners from a variety of American religious traditions are appointed by the White House and congressional leaders. A majority is appointed by the president's party (three by him and one each by his party's leaders in the House and Senate). The other four are appointed by congressional leaders from the nonpresidential party. The commission has made important recommendations and has overall had a positive influence on U.S. policy. But it has proven controversial as well. Among other sources of dissension has been presidential and congressional lassitude in appointing new commissioners when vacancies have occurred; the treatment of some appointments as sinecures or political payoffs; and the failure of the commission to hold the State Department accountable for its inertia in pursuing IRF policy.

Since 1998 U.S. IRF policy has achieved some modest but important successes. IRF ambassadors have headed off a few bad laws and achieved releases of religious prisoners. President Clinton's ambassador, Robert Seiple, managed against significant odds to put China on the first annual list of severe persecutors, the "countries of particular concern," where it has remained since.[48] Seiple also established the bona fides of the office, a development that was in great part due to the respect he was afforded within the State Department, especially by Secretary Albright.[49] President Bush's ambassador, John Hanford, negotiated creatively with a few governments, including Vietnam and Saudi Arabia. Assisted by other American diplomats and NGOs, he convinced Hanoi to ban forced renunciations of faith and to allow reconstruction of destroyed houses of worship.[50]

Overall, however, U.S. IRF policy cannot be said to have made significant progress, either in securing a place for religious freedom as an important element of U.S. foreign policy or in actually advancing religious freedom abroad. As noted, exhaustive studies have demonstrated that severe restrictions on religious freedom are pervasive in the early twenty-first century, notwithstanding the decline of communist totalitarianism and the dramatic spread of democracy during the last quarter of the previous century.[51] While U.S. diplomacy is not responsible for this deficit, it cannot be said to have had much of an impact.

If anything, levels of religious persecution have increased, and levels of religious freedom have decreased, since 1998.[52]

There are many possible explanations for the relative ineffectiveness of U.S. policy. First and foremost, it is inherently difficult for any nation, especially the most powerful nation in the world, to advance religious freedom in other societies. Religion is among the most sensitive of issues, and resistance to outside meddling is the norm. Such attitudes are intensified by the realization that U.S. power and influence are being employed in the IRF project. The phenomenon of resistance is hardly surprising. Religion often lies at the heart of an individual's sense of dignity and well-being. In many cases it lies at the core of a community's identity. This means that suspicion of American IRF policy will always be present. Even in periods when the United States was popular abroad—as it was, for example, in the immediate aftermath of the September 2001 terrorist attacks— no nation welcomed U.S. inquiries into its religious affairs, especially those where the deficits in religious liberty were greatest.

That said, citing levels of difficulty is no excuse for failure. The charge that the United States is meddling in the internal affairs of other nations has been an obstacle to the success of U.S. diplomacy for decades. During the cold war, U.S. attempts to promote human rights in the Soviet Union met with similar complaints. And yet the U.S. and other Western governments secured Soviet agreement to human rights standards in the 1975 Helsinki Accords. That success is today credited with a significant role in the decline of the Soviet empire and the end of the cold war. Even though Soviet assent to the Helsinki standards was largely rhetorical, Western leaders could, and did, cite them repeatedly in public forums, thereby empowering Soviet dissidents and weakening the resolve of the regime.[53]

The reality is that the U.S. failure to advance religious freedom is due as much to the anemic nature of the policy itself, and internal resistance to its full-scale adoption, as it is to the obstacles posed by a recalcitrant international order. While they almost universally acknowledge it as a human right, few diplomats or foreign policy thinkers believe religious liberty should play a distinctive role in U.S. foreign policy.

The reasons for internal skepticism vary widely, from a "realist" wariness of involvement in the internal affairs of other societies, to liberal internationalist concerns that the export of religious freedom represents American hegemonic behavior and cultural imperialism. Even the neoconservative thinkers who were behind the George W. Bush administration's foreign policy in the greater Middle East were largely secular thinkers who resisted incorporating religion into their planning, despite the highly religious nature of the societies that were the objects of their attention.[54] In short, skepticism about religion in U.S. foreign policy is not the exclusive preserve of either liberals or conservatives; it emerges from all points on the political spectrum. On the Left some fear that the U.S. IRF policy is a tool of the Christian Right and is designed to protect Christian proselytizing overseas. Some believe that spreading religious liberty could frustrate an international LGBT and abortion rights agenda.[55] On the Right neocon secularist skepticism about IRF policy is reinforced by Christian fears of Islamist extremism, which reduces support for religious freedom in Muslim societies.[56]

Partly because of such scruples, many State Department and other foreign affairs officials prefer to see religious freedom policy as an ad hoc reaction to persecution, with the goal of freeing religious prisoners (when it does not interfere with other priorities), rather than as a systematic policy of advancing religious freedom in a political and cultural sense. Antipersecution efforts, in turn, tend to be largely rhetorical, mirroring the annual public designation, required by the IRF Act, of those governments guilty of "particularly severe violations" of religious freedom. Such violations usually entail torture, unjust imprisonment, "disappearances," and the like. Once the violators are identified by the State Department, however, no significant U.S. policy action follows. In short, the denunciations are largely policy irrelevant.[57]

The net result of this annual process is that foreign governments do not see U.S. IRF policy as a serious, long-term U.S. concern. Foreign ministries have concluded, with some justification, that they can "manage" this aspect of U.S. foreign policy by releasing a few prisoners from time to time. Securing prisoner releases is a worthy enterprise, no matter how infrequently it occurs. But if the United States could induce foreign governments and religious communities to see religious freedom as necessary to their own interests, this would not only reduce persecution far more effectively than current policy, but it would also lead to more stable democracies, economic and social benefits, and the reduction of religion-based violence, extremism, and terrorism.

Consider the case of Afghanistan. In 2003 a coalition led by the United States overthrew the vicious and theocratic Taliban government. The Afghans elected a democratic government and adopted a democratic constitution. Religious persecution dropped dramatically. But the Afghan government continued then, and continues today, to bring charges against apostates and blasphemers, including officials and journalists seeking to debate the teachings of Islam. Instead of seeing such cases as serious obstacles to the consolidation of Afghan democracy, the State Department has treated them as humanitarian problems. It declared a victory for IRF when U.S. pressure freed a Christian convert, Abdul Rahman, from an apostasy trial (and from certain execution), permitting him to flee the country in fear for his life.

But the Rahman case was actually a defeat for U.S. IRF policy because it ignored the real problem: Afghan democracy is unlikely to endure unless it defends the right of all citizens to full religious liberty—including the rights of Muslims not only to leave Islam but to debate Islam and its views of freedom and the public good, the role of sharia, and the religion-state relationship. This kind of sustained discourse is vital to the success of any Islamic democracy and to overcoming Islamist radicalism. IRF policy should be confronting this problem in Afghanistan and elsewhere, but it lacks the resources, the bureaucratic clout, and the policy mandate to do so.[58]

Within the State Department, IRF policy has been functionally and bureaucratically quarantined. Both the Clinton and the Bush administration nested the IRF ambassador and his office in the human rights bureau, itself out of the mainstream of foreign policy. This meant that the ambassador was subordinate to a lower ranking official and, unlike other ambassadors-at-large, did not attend senior staff or policy meetings. When senior meetings were held on U.S. policy in China or Saudi Arabia—or even on engaging Islam—IRF policy was not considered relevant. This may seem trivial to those outside the State Department, but inside it communicated a deadly message: that IRF is not a mainstream foreign policy issue and could safely be ignored.[59]

All of these problems were in place when Barak Obama was elected president of the United States and took office in January 2009. While Obama was not known as a religious freedom advocate, he had said intriguing things about the subject that led some to express cautious optimism about the future of U.S. IRF policy.[60] When, during a Cairo speech the following June, the president included religious freedom as one of the seven issues requiring attention in Muslim-majority countries, the optimism increased substantially.[61]

In the ensuing months, however, the administration consistently signaled its indifference to IRF policy. After the Cairo address, interagency task forces and working groups were established to transform the ideas in the speech into policy. Yet despite having been named by the president as a discrete problem requiring attention, religious freedom was not identified as a post-Cairo issue by the interagency community or its working groups. Perhaps sensing that IRF policy was being sidelined, a host of bipartisan groups urged the administration to put it front and center, not only in U.S. human rights policies but in democracy promotion, counterterrorism strategies, and national security policy. Such groups included the Chicago Council on Global Affairs, Freedom House, the U.S. Commission on International Religious Freedom, and a bipartisan congressional caucus.[62]

And yet when the president unveiled his National Security Strategy in May 2009, religious freedom was simply omitted.[63] The sixty-page document contains an extensive discussion of how to advance American interests abroad. It ruminates on how to defeat al Qaeda and other religion-based terrorists, how to invest in civil society abroad, how to strengthen human capital, achieve sustainable economic growth and development, build cooperation with centers of influence, and sustain cooperation on key global challenges.[64]

In each of these areas the new strategy simply ignored growing evidence that, in most countries of the world, none of these objectives is achievable without a robust regime of religious liberty. Oddly the document contains a five-page section entitled "Values." It begins with the following statement: "The United States believes certain values are universal and will work to promote them world-wide." Those values include democracy, human rights, and human dignity but not religious freedom. The only hint of religious liberty comes in a single reference to "an individual's freedom . . . to worship as they please." This is thin (and ungrammatical) tokenism. Not only is the phrase a brief, almost throwaway aside in an extended analysis of ostensibly universal American values, but the very concept of "individual freedom of worship" represents an impoverished understanding of religious liberty.

Given this sidelining of IRF policy, it is not surprising that the Obama administration gave little priority to finding an IRF ambassador-at-large to lead the policy. The administration quickly put into place senior envoys on a host of favored projects, including outreach to Muslim communities, HIV/AIDS, disabilities, and and Guantánamo. Very early in her tenure, Secretary of State Hilary Clinton established a working group at the Department of State to determine how the United States might advance the cause of lesbian, gay, bisexual, and transgender rights around the world. All of these initiatives were deemed more important than international religious freedom.

Indeed the administration felt no urgency in nominating someone to become ambassador-at-large for international religious freedom, a position required by the IRF Act. In June 2010, eighteen months into his presidency, Obama finally nominated as his ambassador Suzan Johnson Cook, a Baptist pastor well connected in the administration but lacking any experience either in international religious freedom or diplomacy. She finally entered her job in May 2011, when the administration was more than half over.

In retrospect it is clear that all three administrations (Clinton, Bush, and Obama) have had difficulties in advancing religious liberty as an aspect of U.S. diplomacy. Each has had some modest victories—Clinton in signing the bill and laying the groundwork for progress, Bush in employing the law creatively, and Obama in at least raising the issue with the Muslim world. All have had some success in freeing religious prisoners. But these positive steps have thus far been ad hoc and underresourced. Some of the reasons for the larger shortcomings—which I have elsewhere called "diplomacy's religion deficit"[65]—are common to all the administrations. This is especially true of the widespread skepticism within the U.S. foreign policy establishment about addressing religion as a policy issue and the reluctance to advance religious freedom as a means of accommodating and regulating the religious actors and ideas that, for better and for worse, have returned to the international stage. But, as the Obama administration has demonstrated, there are ideological blinkers as well. It is fair to conclude that unless these obstacles are addressed and overcome, IRF policy will remain in the backwaters of U.S. diplomacy, having on occasion some positive result but in the main failing to advance international religious freedom.

Religious Freedom outside America

Notwithstanding the problems it has encountered overseas and within its own foreign policy establishment, the United States is still the only country in the world with an official policy of advancing international religious freedom.[66] While religious freedom activists from Western European countries have occasionally expressed interest in their own governments' adopting such a policy, and some political leaders have paid rhetorical homage to the idea,[67] Western governments have for the most part declined to do so. My experience in engaging Western diplomats and other officials suggests that, while they are perfectly willing to include religious persecution in discussions of human rights violations in the course of conducting their foreign affairs, they see nothing exceptional about religious freedom. Indeed in many cases they seemed inherently suspicious of religious actors and of the idea of empowering them in any sense through the advancement of religious freedom.

Clearly some of this has to do with resentment of the United States, its power, and its influence in the world, combined with a belief that when America acts unilaterally on religious freedom it acts illegitimately. When I raised the issue of religious freedom with French, Belgian, German, and Austrian officials, for example, it was not only to seek their cooperation in the U.S. IRF venture but also to query them about some troubling aspect of their own domestic policies. In the 1990s the French and Belgians had produced official lists of disfavored religious "sects," lists that included Mormons, Baptists, and Jehovah's Witnesses. The Germans had an abiding skepticism about Scientologists, and the Austrians about proselytizing sects in general. It is safe to say that none of them were happy with the prospect of being criticized by the United States in the new *Annual Report on International Religious Freedom*.

The phenomenon of resentment was perhaps best typified by the French. I recall a particularly rancorous meeting with French officials at the Quai d'Orsay in Paris toward the end of the Clinton administration. Robert Seiple, Clinton's ambassador-at-large for international religious freedom, and I were there to express our concern about the French practice of stigmatizing minority religions in official lists (a practice that led us to craft a special section of the IRF report dealing with stigmatization).[68] Joining us in the meeting were senior diplomatic and other officials, including the official responsible for "combating harmful sects" in France.

The meeting began courteously enough, but by the end we had been warned in no uncertain terms that our interference in French internal affairs was not appreciated. At one point the most senior official present indignantly—and somewhat incongruously, given the official French list of suspect sects we were there to discuss—asserted that people's religious beliefs were their own private affair. He said he was embarrassed that an ally of France would come to Paris and raise such matters in an official meeting. As I left the meeting, one French diplomatic colleague told me privately that he could not understand why we were employing U.S. IRF policy to "attack the French nation."

Clearly we had struck a chord. But resistance among Western nations to adopting vigorous international religious freedom policies cannot be explained, even among the French, exclusively by their resentment of U.S. meddling. Most of these nations are long-standing, mature democracies with constitutional and legal protections for religious liberty. Most engaged in the negotiation and ratification of international declarations and covenants in which the normative status of religious freedom is robust.

For example, both the Universal Declaration of Human Rights and the International Covenant on Civil and Political Rights treat religious liberty as a core human right.[69] The latter, which constitutes a binding treaty obligation for those nations party to it, identifies religious freedom as one of the "non-derogable" rights, that is, a right from which no government may detract without compelling cause.[70] These and similar international covenants, such as the European Convention on Human Rights, treat religious freedom as a right that is not created by governments but exists prior to the state and must be recognized and protected by the state. As John Finnis puts it, "[T]hese declarations of constitutional, legal rights all, in their context, assert that what they declare and establish as legal and constitutional was already, beforehand and foundationally, a moral right of essentially the same extent."[71]

Why, then, are these states not on the front lines of advancing religious freedom? Clearly one answer is that some of these nations no longer understand the supreme value of the right as they once did. A sense of the a priori nature of religious freedom identified by Finnis, a status it has traditionally enjoyed with other fundamental rights such as freedom of speech, is in precipitate decline within many Western countries. The disappearance of any belief in the *foundational* nature of religious liberty may help to explain why such countries have not seen fit to incorporate into their respective foreign policies a vigorous defense of that right.

Part of the problem is the trend toward "defining religious liberty down" to a purely private endeavor. But, as the language of the UDHR and ICCPR suggest, a robust conception of religious freedom includes public activities, such as the right peacefully to manifest one's beliefs to others and the right to make religious and religiously based moral arguments in public policy debates. If religion is understood as properly and exclusively a private activity, such as prayer and worship, then the warrant of religious liberty can safely be narrowed to a right of privacy. This understanding helps to explain why many Western diplomats limit their religious freedom interventions to opposing physical persecution of or by religious actors (an approach that, as we have seen, was quickly adopted by the U.S. State Department as the least controversial way to implement the 1998 IRF Act). Indeed a number of recent developments call into question the commitment of Western nations to a broad understanding of religious freedom that is consistent with international laws and norms. In particular there seems to be a growing rejection of the historic Western European public practice of religion identified by Stepan and a growing suspicion of religious ideas and actors in public life.

An important caveat is in order here. Fear of public religion has long been a staple of modern French politics. France has never accepted the American understanding of religious liberty—that it was invested in each person by a Creator-judge, who desired that every man carry out his natural duty of religious worship and practice free from coercion by the state or any other human agent.[72] Instead both the French Enlightenment and the French Revolution expressly intended to remove from public life what were thought to be the superstitious and antiliberal forces of religion.[73] In consequence the French have traditionally understood religious liberty as a right to worship, and to assemble for that purpose, but not as a right to influence public policy with religious or religion-based arguments. Religious freedom is seen as a very limited right, constructed by the state and not the gift of God (or otherwise inherent in every person), and therefore a privilege to be managed and, when appropriate, vigorously restricted by the state.

And yet while French history and practice are distinctive in their mistrust of public religion, other Western nations have clearly inherited some of this skepticism. Unlike the case of the United States, religious practice in most of these nations has long been in precipitate decline.[74] Where this is true, skepticism about religion in public life is perhaps not surprising. Theoretically even in societies where religious liberty was once seen as a fundamental, God-given or otherwise intrinsic right, reduced religious observance and the consequent absence of religious influences in public life are not *necessarily* signs of antidemocratic practice. So long as minority religious individuals and communities are afforded full religious liberty—including the right to make religious arguments in the public square—democracy can be said to be operating appropriately. In practice, however, the decline of religious observance in Western societies appears to be associated with a decline in respect for the rights of religious actors.

Prevailing currents in Western European, Canadian, and Australian law and political practice increasingly pit religion and religious freedom against other rights, especially judicially created modern liberties that have traditionally been seen as immoral or sinful by world religions such as Christianity and Islam.[75] In law the European Court of Human Rights in Strasbourg, under the aegis of the Council of Europe, and in politics the European Union are pursuing an increasingly secular agenda.

For example, the Council of Europe has declared that "states must require religious leaders to take an unambiguous stand in favour of the precedence of human rights over any religious principle." This assertion contradicts, and undermines, any sound conception of religious liberty. First, the declaration constitutes a state instruction to religious communities on what their theological principles—as reflected in the stances of their religious leaders—must not be. This approach represents de facto the imposition of the French model on all European nations, a model in which religion may be controlled and manipulated by the state.

Second, asserting the "precedence of human rights" over religious principle is highly ambiguous and potentially problematic unless the precise content of the human rights being claimed is clear. For example, an emerging issue in Western societies is the putative right of persons to engage in homosexual or bisexual acts and to live publicly in accord with the preferences that accompany a same-sex attraction. In some countries this right includes, or may soon include, the entitlement of persons of the same sex to the legal, social, and moral benefits of marriage. In some the right is articulated to encompass transgendered persons.

The rights claims of LGBT persons already constitute an emotional and contentious debate in law and public policy. What is striking for our purposes is the way the debate has cast aside any notion of fundamental rights, especially the right of religious freedom, that might stand in the way of the implementation of new rights. Courts have on occasion simply asserted a right to perform homosexual acts or to marry a person of the same sex. Some judges have inferred these rights from existing constitutional guarantees such as privacy, liberty interests, or equality under the law. In some Western societies these kinds of judicial findings are resisted by traditional religious communities. In the United States, for example, the involvement of such communities in the democratic political process has led to laws and policies rejecting a special status for LGBT rights. The threat to religious freedom arises not because of the outcome per se—that religious preferences about LGBT rights are rejected—but because of the *process* by which they are rejected by the courts. When religiously informed moral qualms reflected in local or state laws are swept aside by judges asserting their own policy preferences, religious freedom is in jeopardy.[76]

In sum, it seems a reasonable inference that the decline in a robust conception of religious freedom among Western societies, some of it due to a decline in religious observance, helps to explain why religious freedom has no exceptional place in the foreign policies of these nations. If this inference is correct, it indicates a distinctly negative development in international affairs. The achievement of religious freedom in nations outside the West will not simply serve to empower the voices of those who defend traditional sexual morality—although it may well have that effect. As history and contemporary scholarship strongly suggest, religious freedom can become the very engine of stable, liberal, and humane democratic polities. To the extent that Western nations, including the United States, are losing the capacity to understand the value of religious freedom and to advance it effectively within their respective foreign policies, the goals of stable democracy and all it portends, universal human dignity, and international peace will be all the harder to achieve.

Notes

1. Mary Ann Glendon, *A World Made New: Eleanor Roosevelt and the Universal Declaration of Human Rights* (New York: Random House, 2001), 70.
2. For a discussion of this document and its meaning, see Thomas Farr, "Dignitatis Humanae and Religious Freedom in American Foreign Policy: A Practitioner's Perspective," in *After Forty Years: Vatican II's Diverse Legacy*, ed. Kenneth D. Whitehead (South Bend, Ind.: St. Augustine's Press, 2006).
3. The Pew Forum on Religion and Public Life, *Global Restrictions on Religion: Full Report*, December 2009, http://pewforum.org/newassets/images/reports/restrictions/restrictions-fullreport.pdf, 8.
4. Glendon, *A World Made New*, 168.
5. See the Pakistan chapter of the State Department's *Annual Report on International Religious Freedom*, http://www.state.gov/g/drl/irf/rpt/index.htm.
6. Ibid. Also see Pew Forum on Religion and Public Life, *Global Restrictions on Religion-Full Report*, 28.
7. Pew Forum on Religion and Public Life, *Global Restrictions*, 1.
8. See, for example, Roger Trigg, *Free to Believe?* (London: Theos, 2010).
9. See Farr, *World of Faith and Freedom*, 20–25, 177–78.
10. Brian J. Grim, "Religious Freedom and Social Well Being: A Critical Appraisal," *International Journal for Religious Freedom* 2, no. 1 (2009): 3.
11. Farr, *World of Faith and Freedom*, 265–72; also see Thomas Farr and Dennis R. Hoover, *The Future of U.S. International Religious Freedom Policy: Recommendations for the Obama Administration*, 2009, https://www.globalengage.org/attachments/829_IRFpolicyreport_final_lowres.pdf.
12. Giles Kepel, *The Revenge of God: The Resurgence of Islam, Christianity, and Judaism in the Modern World* (University Park: Pennsylvania State University Press, 1994). Also see Monica Duffy Toft, Daniel Philpott, and Timothy Samuel Shah, *God's Century: Resurgent Religion and Global Politics* (New York: Norton, 2011), especially chapters 1 and 8.
13. See, for example, the August 2009 Gallup poll that tests for religious devotion in a survey of 114 countries, http://www.gallup.com/poll/142727/religiosity-highest-world-poorest-nations.aspx. The poll found that the global median proportion of adults who say religion is an important part of their daily lives is 84 percent.
14. Peter Berger, ed., *The Desecularization of the World: Resurgent Religion and World Politics* (Washington D.C.: Ethics and Public Policy Center, 1999), 10–11.
15. Baha'i International Committee, *The Baha'i Question: Cultural Cleansing in Iran* (New York: Baha'i International Community, 2005), 9.
16. John P. Clark, "On Taoism and Politics," *Journal of Chinese Philosophy* 10 (March 1982): 65–87.
17. See, for example, remarks about Jewish views on proselytism by Professor Randi Rashkover, *Report of the Georgetown Symposium on Proselytism & Religious Freedom in the 21st Century*, March 3, 2010, 4–5.
18. José Casanova, *Public Religions in the Modern World* (Chicago: University of Chicago Press, 1994).
19. "Analyst Insights: Religiosity around the World," *Gallup World Report*, February 18, 2009, http://www.gallup.com/video/114694/Analyst-Insights-Religiosity-Around-World.aspx. Also see Todd M. Johnson and David B. Barrett, "Quantifying Alternate Futures of Religion and Religions," *Futures* 36 (2004): 947–60.
20. See, for example, Robert D. Woodberry and Timothy S. Shah, "The Pioneering Protestants," *Journal of Democracy* 15, no. 2 (2004): 47–61.
21. The Pew Forum on Religion and Public Life, *Muslim Networks and Movements in Western Europe*, September 16, 2010, http://pewresearch.org/pubs/1731/muslim-networks-movements-western-europe.
22. See Christopher M. Blanchard, "The Islamic Traditions of Wahhabism and Salafiyya," *CRS Report for Congress*, January 24, 2008, http://www.fas.org/sgp/crs/misc/RS21695.pdf.

See also Hamid Algar, *Wahhabism: A Critical Essay* (Oneonta, N.Y.: Islamic Publications International, 2002). For a different interpretation, see David Commins, *The Wahhabi Mission and Saudi Arabia* (London: I. B. Tauris, 2006).

23. See a report by the U.S. Commission on International Religious Freedom, *Saudi Arabia Policy Brief*, Fall 2007, 12–15, http://uscirf.gov/reports-and-briefs/policy-focus.html.

24. Greg Bruno, *Iran's Nuclear Program* (New York: Council on Foreign Relations, March 10, 2010), http://www.cfr.org/publication/16811/irans_nuclear_program.html. Also see Vali Nasr, *The Shia Revival: How Conflicts within Islam Will Shape the Future* (New York: Norton, 2006).

25. Farr, *World of Faith and Freedom*, 80–91.

26. Ibid., 90–91. Also see Lawrence E. Harrison, *The Central Liberal Truth: How Politics Can Change a Culture and Save It from Itself* (New York: Oxford University Press, 2006), 35–56.

27. Samuel P. Huntington, *The Third Wave: Democratization in the Late Twentieth Century* (Norman: University of Oklahoma Press, 1993), 77–78, 83; George Weigel, "Catholicism and Democracy: Parsing the Other Twentieth Century Revolution," in *Soul of the World: Notes on the Future of Public Catholicism* (Washington, D.C.: Ethics and Public Policy Center, 1996), 99–124.

28. See, for example, Ayaan Hirsi Ali, "How to Win the Clash of Civilizations," *Wall Street Journal*, August 18, 2010.

29. See Paul A. Marshall, *Religious Freedom in the World: A Global Report on Freedom and Persecution* (Lanham, Md.: Rowman & Littlefield, 2008), 201, 400.

30. Johnston and Barrett, "Quantifying Alternate Futures of Religion and Religions," 947–60.

31. Alfred Stepan, "Religion, Democracy, and the 'Twin Tolerations,'" *Journal of Democracy*, October 2000, 37.

32. Ibid., 39.

33. Ibid., 39–40.

34. Ibid., 45.

35. Daniel Philpott, "Explaining the Political Ambivalence of Religion," *American Political Science Review* 101, no. 3 (2007): 505–25.

36. Daniel Philpott, remarks, in *Report of the Georgetown Symposium on Religion, Democracy, and Foreign Policy of the Obama Administration*. November 3, 2009.

37. Brian J. Grim and Roger Finke, "Religious Persecution in Cross-National Context: Clashing Civilizations or Regulated Religious Economies?," *American Sociological Review* 72, no. 654 (2007).

38. Grim, "Religious Freedom and Social Well Being," 39–40.

39. Ibid., 41.

40. For example, democratic peace theory holds that democracies rarely fight each other. See Michael E. Brown et al., eds., *Debating the Democratic Peace* (Cambridge, Mass.: MIT Press, 1996).

41. Farr, "Dignitatis Humanae," 237–50.

42. Ibid.

43. Huntington, *The Third Wave*, 77–78, 83.

44. Daniel Philpott, "Christianity and Democracy: The Catholic Wave," *Journal of Democracy* 15, no. 2 (2004): 32–46.

45. See Allen D. Hertzke, *Freeing God's Children: The Unlikely Alliance for Global Human Rights* (Lanham, Md.: Rowman and Littlefield, 2004), 183–236. Also see Farr, *World of Faith and Freedom*, 111–33.

46. Farr, *World of Faith and Freedom*, 111.

47. International Religious Freedom Act of 1998, Pub. L. 105–292 [United States of America], October 27, 1998, http://www.unhcr.org/refworld/docid/3ae6b54b0.html.

48. U.S. Department of State, *Annual Report on International Religious Freedom for 1999*, September 9, 1999, http://www.state.gov/www/global/human_rights/drl_religion.html.

49. Farr, *World of Faith and Freedom*, 135–160; Also see Madeline Albright, *The Mighty and the Almighty: Reflections on America, God, and World Affairs* (New York: Pan, 2007), 68–70, 75–76.

50. Farr, *World of Faith and Freedom*, 203–5.

51. Pew Forum on Religion and Public Life, *Global Restrictions*; Marshall, *Religious Freedom in the World*, 8–11; Farr, *World of Faith and Freedom*, 151–52, 182–85, 203–4, 79–86.

52. Farr, *World of Faith and Freedom*, 17; Marshall, *Religious Freedom in the World*, 11.

53. George Weigel, *The Final Revolution: The Resistance Church and the Collapse of Communism* (New York: Oxford University Press, 1992), 26–33.

54. Farr, *World of Faith and Freedom*, 53–77.

55. See Thomas Farr, "Obama Administration Sidelines Religious Freedom Policy," *Washington Post*, June 25, 2010, http://www.washingtonpost.com/wp-dyn/content/article/2010/06/24/AR2010062405069.html.

56. Farr, *World of Faith and Freedom*, 66–77.

57. See, for example, the discussion of China's designation as a country guilty of particularly severe violations, in ibid., 150–54.

58. Ibid., 1–26.

59. Ibid.

60. Barack Obama, "Call to Renewal Keynote Address," Call to Renewal's Building a Covenant for a New America conference, Washington, D.C., June 28, 2006, http://www.barackobama.com/2006/06/28/call_to_renewal_keynote_address.php.

61. Barack Obama, "Remarks by the President on a New Beginning," Cairo University, June 4, 2009, http://www.whitehouse.gov/the_press_office/Remarks-by-the-President-at-Cairo-University-6-04-09/.

62. Farr, "Obama Administration Sidelines Religious Freedom Policy"; Chicago Council on Global Affairs, "Engaging Religious Communities Abroad: A New Imperative for U.S. Foreign Policy," February 23, 2010,http://www.thechicagocouncil.org/Files/Studies_Publications/TaskForcesandStudies/Religion_2010.aspx; U.S. Commission on International Religious Freedom, "Annual Report of the United States Commission on International Religious Freedom," May 2010, http://www.uscirf.gov/images/annual%20report%202010.pdf.

63. White House, "National Security Strategy," May 2010, http://www.whitehouse.gov/sites/default/files/rss_viewer/national_security_strategy.pdf.

64. Ibid.

65. See chapter 2 of Farr, *World of Faith and Freedom*, "The Intellectual Sources of Diplomacy's Religion Deficit," 53–77.

66. In late 2011 the new Canadian government formed by Stephen Harper announced that he would establish an office of religious freedom in the Canadian Foreign Ministry.

67. See comments by German Chancellor Angela Merkel in June 2010 that protection of religious freedom is an important part of German foreign policy. U.S. Commission on International Religious Freedom, "Germany: A New Partnership for Religious Freedom," press release, August 17, 2010, www.uscirf.gov. This press release is revealing of how unusual it is for a Western European leader to make such remarks.

68. Farr, *World of Faith and Freedom*, 171.

69. Ibid., 127.

70. See David Little, "Does the Human Right to Freedom of Conscience, Religion and Belief Have Special Status?," *Brigham Young University Law Review*, January 2001.

71. John Finnis, "Why Religious Liberty Is a Special, Important and Limited Right," Notre Dame Law School, Legal Studies Research Paper No. 09–11, October 30, 2008, http://ssrn.com/abstract=1392278, 2.

72. Michael Novak, *On Two Wings: Humble Faith and Common Sense at the American Founding* (San Francisco: Encounter Books, 2001), 77–85; Gerard Bradley, *Religious Liberty in the American Republic* (Washington, D.C.: Heritage Foundation, 2008), 10–11.

73. Peter Gay, *The Enlightenment: The Rise of Modern Paganism* (London: Norton, 1995).

74. Pew Research Center, "Secular Europe and Religious America: Implications for Transatlantic Relations," April 21, 2005, http://pewforum.org/Politics-and-Elections/Secular-Europe-and-Religious-America-Implications-for-Transatlantic-Relations.aspx.

75. Trigg, *Free to Believe?*, 38.

76. See, for example, *Perry et al. v. Schwarzenegger et al.*, 2010 U.S. Dist. 3:09-cv-02292-VRW, https://ecf.cand.uscourts.gov/cand/09cv2292/. Also see *Roemer v. Evans*, 517 U.S. 620 (1996), http://caselaw.lp.findlaw.com/scripts/getcase.pl?court=US&vol=000&invol=U10179.

INDEX